Segregation and Assimilation in York, Western Australia

A mid-twentieth century truth-telling case study

Roland See

The production of this book was supported with a grant from:

WESTERN AUSTRALIAN HISTORY FOUNDATION

Cover Design by Brittany Wilson | Brittwilsonart.com from an original concept by the author

Cover Images:
1. Photograph of George Kickett Snr, Scott Blurton and Walter Kickett sitting in front a camp on the
York Reserve, ca. 1940s (courtesy Marion Kickett).
2. Western Australia, Government Photographer, "Avon Terrace, York looking south, 1947",
slwa_b2046652_3, call no. 007964D (SLWA).
3. Map of York: Department of Native Welfare, Reserve for Natives – York, series 2030, consignment
993, item 1933/0341, (SROWA).

Recommended citation: See, R 2025. Segregation and Assimilation in York, Western Australia - A mid-
twentieth century truth-telling case study. The Book Reality Experience, Leschenault, Western
Australia.

NATIONAL
LIBRARY
OF AUSTRALIA

**A catalogue record for this
book is available from the
National Library of Australia**

Table of Contents

Table of Figures

Acknowledgements

This book is dedicated to all the Aboriginal families who lived in Balardong, York, for long or short periods between 1923 and 1974. The below list is not exhaustive, and some family names may have been unwittingly omitted if they were not mentioned in the records available to this author (in reverse alphabetical order):

Yarran, Winmar, Walley, Ugle, Stack, Pickett, Parfitt, Ninyette, Nebro, Narrier, Narkle, Mourish, Mimel, McGuire, Lawson, Lawrence, Kickett, Jones, Jacobs, Jackson, Indich, Humphrey, Holmes, Hill, Hart, Harris, Garlett, Ford, Fitzgerald, Egan, Dodd, Dickie, Dabb, Cowan/Cohen, Bropho, Blurton, Bolton, Bateman, Bandry/Boundry …

This book is developed from a short local history student paper about the York Reserve, written by this author in 2019 while studying history at Curtin University. George Kickett provided the initial inspiration for writing about the York Reserve. George had shared childhood stories about his upbringing on the reserve prior to the assignment being tasked. When this author conceived the idea to write about the York Reserve, George kindly agreed to take part in an oral history interview, which formed the basis of the student paper. Without George's initial willingness to share his memories, this book would not have come into existence.

Special thanks go to Dr Marion Kickett for reading the manuscript, providing highly valuable feedback and insights, sharing personal stories and making available family records and photographs from her personal collection, which have been included in this book.

Many thanks are also directed towards the following persons, professional services and institutions providing advice, support, research material and ideas, and engaging in information exchange: Dr Lenore Layman (for providing valuable feedback and support) and the Western Australian History Foundation; Bella Bropho; Geraldine Metcalf, Breanna Jackson-Reid; Audrey Nettle-Narkle; Jane Osborne; Cher Burgmann and Landgate; Dr Denise Cooke; Dr Anna Haebich; Dr Bri McKenzie, Dr Tod Jones and Dr Shaphan Cox of Curtin University; the staff at the State Records Office of WA; staff at Aboriginal History WA; the third-floor staff at the State Library of WA; Mark Chambers for sharing space at the microfilm work stations; Jackie Phillips of the York Society; the Parliamentary Counsel's Office WA; Elite Editing; the team at Book Reality; and Ruth See.

When researching for the student paper in 2019, the following persons kindly provided advice to my queries: staff at the York Regency Museum, at the York Court House and at the York Society; Sheena Hesse of the Uniting Church Archives WA; and Kevin Trent of Uniting Church York.

This book was written on Whadjuk Noongar Boodjar and the author acknowledges the Whadjuk Noongar people as the original custodians of the land.

Introduction

York was the first inland town in Western Australia to be settled by Europeans—a process that commenced in 1831.[1] It is located on the custodial land of the Balardong Noongar people who had populated and managed the area for millennia before the onset of the settler-colonial invasion.[2] From 1831 onwards, the settler-colonial *land-grab* spread increasingly in all directions, ever reducing Aboriginal access to their ancestral lands. However, by the turn of the century (1900), across the South West Land Division, which stretches from just north of Northampton down to Esperance in the south, many Aboriginal people were still able to live in the bush and partially survived off the land by hunting and trapping in combination with farm work. Many families also lived on settler farms or moved between farms and the bush, as Aboriginal people were generally not welcome in towns. Then, a new agricultural program that aimed at the maximisation of land use transformed the South West landscape within a decade between 1903 and 1914, and left the majority of the Aboriginal population poverty stricken and homeless by the onset of World War I. Large swathes of land were cleared for wheat growing and, as a result, many Aboriginal people started moving towards towns as there was nowhere else to go.[3]

Anna Haebich's book *For Their Own Good* discusses in detail the situation in the South West Land Division from 1900 until 1940 and, to some degree, this present book builds on the seminal work laid out by Haebich. Following a Royal Commission concerning the treatment and condition of Aboriginal peoples, new legislation was effectively introduced in Western Australia in 1906 with the *Aborigines Act 1905* and its subsequent amendments. This legislation took away from Aboriginal people the basic rights that were enjoyed by white settler-Australians who were, at the time, primarily of Anglo-European stock.

It euphemistically aimed at 'protecting' Aboriginal people through the attempted total control of their lives in a most invasive, restrictive and repressive way based on biological- and cultural-racist assumptions inferred from social Darwinist principles.4 Some sections of the 1905 Act were provisions that enabled strictly enforceable segregation, but these often required a local settler-Australian demand for their implementation. This book places great emphasis on such local demands. Although state legislation enabled segregation and persecution of Aboriginal people, the local position was often the deciding factor in the implementation of such provisions and inhumane injustices. From Federation in 1901 until 1967, the Australian Constitution dictated that Aboriginal matters were to be dealt with by the federal states, which all had their own oppressive laws concerning Aboriginal and Torres Strait Islander peoples. Therefore, most legislation referred to in this book only applied to Western Australia.[5]

While this book is concerned with a local history in principle, it may be regarded as a case study for mid-twentieth-century Aboriginal history relevant to country areas in most parts of the South West Land Division. Under the banner of the ongoing truth-telling process, the book's main aim is to be of educational value. To this end, an effort has been made for this book to be intelligible as a stand-alone work for any reader who may be unfamiliar with the topic under discussion. While some events presented here might have been relatively unique to York, many other incidents and developments occurred in a similar way in other towns in the South West Land Division, and were not unlikely across the rest of the country either. Local situations, processes, events and idiosyncrasies will be discussed, often in reference to state-wide policies and trends. We will frequently be considering the triangular relationship between state government agencies on one side, local non-Aboriginal community members and local authorities on the other side, and Aboriginal people often caught in between. As the title suggests, the overarching themes are segregation and assimilation. The period under review aligns with the official existence of York's town reserve because this reserve symbolises the very essence of segregation. It was a place that was allocated for Aboriginal people to stay, located outside of the townsite. The very existence of the reserve was inhibitive against social inclusion, yet its absence does not mean that social inclusion was automatically achieved when the reserve was closed down. By 1950, the Western Australian State Government was officially attempting to integrate Aboriginal people into settler-Australian society under the policy buzz word 'assimilation'. However, as we will see, social inclusion into settler-Australian spaces was always conditional. In this book, 'assimilation' will be only referred to in relation to policy; otherwise, 'integration' appears to be a more appropriate term to discuss actual historical accounts, as the latter term emphasises physical integration over the former term's ideologically charged connotations.

During large parts of the period under review, Australia defined itself as a 'white' nation and anyone who did not fit the criterion of being 'white' had to prove themselves, over and over again, to be worthy of being tolerated within white Australian spaces.[6] Keeping this notion in mind, a recurring observation will be that tolerating Aboriginal people within 'white spaces' was closely aligned with their perceived worth in terms of labour and spending capacity. The majority of events discussed here occurred during the 1940s and 1950s, with an additional focus on the 1960s. The emphasis on certain periods is dictated by the source material that was available to this author. This, by itself, is to a large degree reflective of the response that the Aboriginal presence in York had evoked during various periods. The main sources drawn on are state records and newspaper articles, as well as various other sources. From 1923 until the late 1940s, we will witness intensifying demands by some vocal sections of York's settler-Australian population for the segregation of Aboriginal people with the ultimate outcome having been the near total social exclusion from the municipal area of York. From the late 1940s until 1974, we will witness local responses to more inclusive state-sanctioned policies. These local responses were first expressed in resistance to the social inclusion of Aboriginal people, particularly in the early years. Later, we will discuss some well-meaning efforts emanating from the settler-Australian community and developments that took place on the reserve. Housing, living arrangements and movement within settler-Australian spaces form a central part of this book. Further emphasis is placed on the policing and enforcement of the racist state legislation, as well as *modes of exemption* from this legislation.

A few notes about settler-Australian York in 1923 may assist in setting the scene: At the time, the York District had a population of approximately 3,000 people. The town is located 98 kilometres from the Perth Central Business District by road, being situated at the western end of the Western Australian Wheatbelt region. York's economy in 1923 was predominantly based on agriculture. For the first three-quarters of the twentieth century, York was also connected to an extensive railway network spreading from Perth through the Wheatbelt and southern regions, which was still expanding in 1923.[7] From 1871, there were two local authorities in the district. The York Municipal Council was responsible for the geographic area of the York townsite, while the York Road Board was responsible for the remaining rural areas of the York District. The municipal council was made up of a number of councillors representing four 'wards' (east, west, north, south) headed by the mayor, and official communication was usually facilitated through the town clerk. The road board's equivalent to a council mayor was the chairman, heading a number of road board members, and official communication was usually facilitated through the secretary. All non-administrative council and board positions were appointed annually via democratic elections. As the reserve-to-be was located outside of town, it was within the jurisdiction of the road board. Both local authorities had their own health inspectors, who we will also come across in this book several times. The Aborigines Department was centrally administered from Perth with very few staff and little finances at its disposal. In York, and in most other towns, a local police officer, generally the sergeant in charge, was commonly appointed *local protector of Aborigines* and took on extra duties on behalf of the Aborigines Department, implementing welfare and population control measures. The police in York serviced both local authority areas.[8]

Legislation will be frequently referred to in this book, for example, the *Aborigines Act 1905*. The year indicates the version of the legislation that was current at the point in time under discussion. In the example of the *Aborigines Act*, 1905 was the original or 'principal' Act. It was amended in 1911, 1931, 1936, 1940, 1941, 1947, 1954, and 1960, and then completely overhauled in 1963. In 1936, its name was changed to the *Native Administration Act* and, in 1954, it became the *Native Welfare Act*, while still being based on the original law text of 1905. The amendment Acts often only took effect in the following year. Therefore, in relation to the *Aborigines Act 1905*, an event that took place in 1924 will be discussed by referring to the *Aborigines Act 1911*. Making these distinctions is important as some clauses changed significantly over time, for better or worse, while other clauses were deleted altogether or new clauses were added. All referenced state legislation is freely available on the website of Western Australia's Parliamentary Counsel's Office.[9]

Spelling and grammar errors in quotations have not been marked with '[sic]' as they are too numerous at times. It is acknowledged that there are various spelling variations for certain names as 'Noongar' and 'Balardong'. The author does not claim that one spelling is more accurate than the other; however, in the case of 'Balardong' this spelling variety has been selected for this text as it is consistent with quotes and references within this book.

The reader should be warned that many quotations contain derogative and offensive language. Some language was deemed acceptable by white Australian standards at the time and some was also deemed offensive then. Rather than paraphrasing, these quotations have been placed intentionally in an attempt to convey the prejudice and racism of the period under review, to make it somewhat emotionally accessible to the reader. The term *native* is frequently used in this book in quotations, legislation and various dated terminology relating to Aboriginal people. In twenty-first century Australia, the term *native* is widely considered inappropriate and offensive and should not be used to describe an Aboriginal person or people. The same applies to terms referring to biological degrees of Aboriginal ancestry, for example, *half-caste* or *full-blood*.

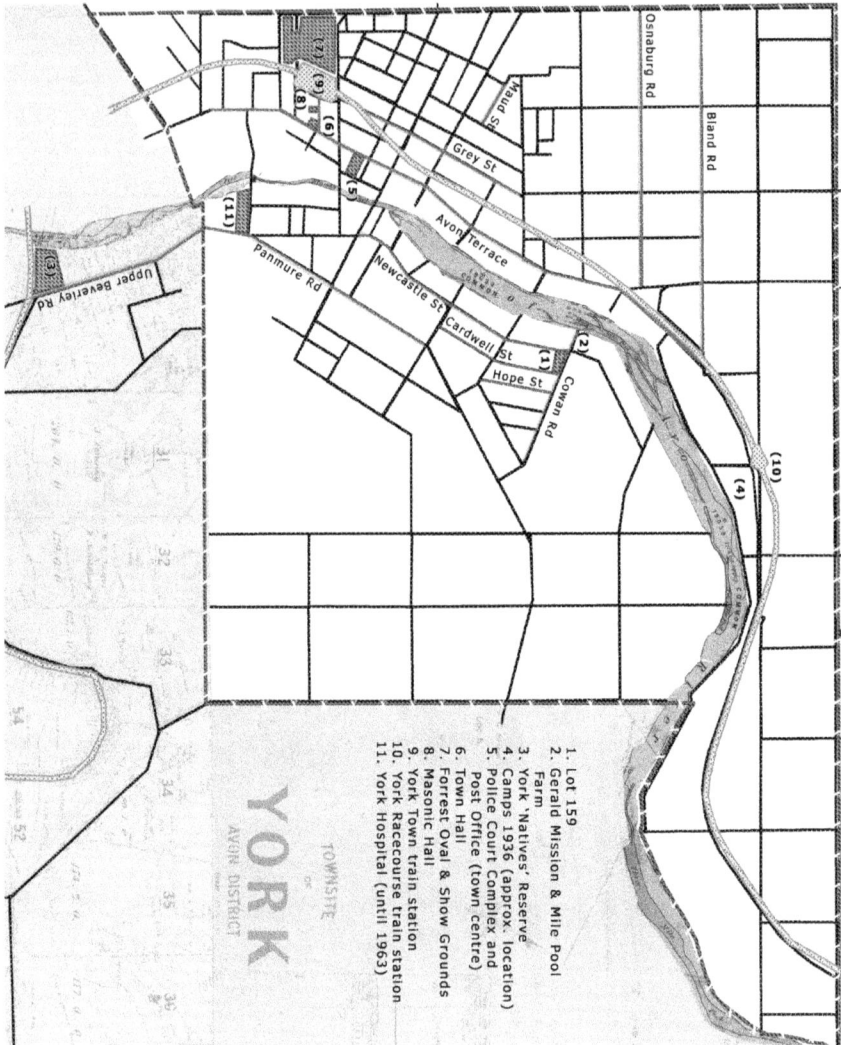

Figure 1: Map of York townsite

Chapter 1. 1920s

1.01 Early years—from Mile Pool to Cold Harbour

In December 1923, York-born settler resident William Thomas Craig wrote to the Aborigines Department, inquiring about a block of land across the road from his own land at Mile Pool, located within York's municipality, where he had been living for thirty-six years.[1] Craig voiced the belief that it was 'marked out' for Aboriginal people to camp on, which they would often do, asserting that 'every Christmas there has been a gathering there'.[2] He advised that it had come to his attention that this block had been 'thrown open' for sale as part of a larger area of land. Craig stated that he was advocating on behalf of the Aboriginal people in anticipation that they may retain this block for camping purposes, noting that it was 'well out from the centre of the town' and generally a suitable location. Craig notably also commented that he employed Aboriginal people and that he was 'aware how they appreciate the fact that they have a place to camp on without any interference'.[3]

Indeed, there is evidence of ongoing Aboriginal use on and close to this section of land, at least since 1852, when the later Mile Pool property was cleared and commenced serving as a *Native Institution*. This Native Institution was initially run by the Wesleyan Methodists, Mr and Mrs Smithies, under the name Gerald Mission.[4] After only two years, the Native Institution was returned to government ownership and managed by Mr and Mrs Pope; however, the institution was eventually shut by the end of 1855 as it was deemed non-viable.[5] A map from 1851 indicates that the later Mile Pool farm estate and a much larger section of land opposite the estate were reserved as Native Institution. The block

1

of land mentioned by Craig is located just across Cowan Road in its immediate vicinity.[6]

The future father-in-law of Edith Cowan, Walkinshaw Cowan, purchased the farm some years later; however, he sold it by 1867.[7] He was 'Guardian' and 'Protector of Natives' for the York District from September 1848 until he was appointed resident magistrate of York in 1863—and with this appointment, the 'Protector' position was abolished until it was reintroduced more than twenty years later.[8] As Cowan had reportedly developed positive relationships with some Aboriginal people, it may be assumed that he tolerated Aboriginal people camping opposite his farm.[9] In March 1884, it was reported that corroborees were being held nightly at Mile Pool and that Aboriginal people 'have come so far as the Victoria Plains and Dandaragan'.[10] In 1888, when William Craig bought the property from Richard Gallop Jnr, the *Western Mail* wrote that, although ownership had changed several times since the Mission days, 'its vicinity is the chief rendezvous of the natives whenever they visit the township in any number'.[11] Reportedly, land at Mile Pool on the western side of the Avon River has also been of cultural significance for Aboriginal people for a long time.[12] In conclusion, it can be said that there is evidence that Aboriginal people had been camping at the same spot for at least seventy years when Craig sent his letter to the Aborigines Department.

In settler-Australian terms, the block of land in question was York Town Lot 159, which was reserved as 'Public Utility', located at the corner of Newcastle Street and Cowan Road.[13] A town plan dated 1855 showed this block to be part of reserve 673A, which encompassed Lots 151 to 159.[14] In 1893, the Municipal Council of York sought to have the area gazetted as a reserve for recreational purposes and it became reserve 2342, excluding Lot 159, as it was anticipated that this may be used in future for a 'school or institute'.[15] Lot 159 was separately gazetted as reserve 2359. The proposed school or institute were never built, but as Lot 159 remained crown land and was not administered by the municipality, it enabled Aboriginal people to continue camping in this locality.[16] However, in October 1923, the municipal council applied to have the area converted into municipal endowment land, which would allow council to lease out the land and simultaneously provide it with municipal oversight and ownership.[17]

On receipt of Craig's letter, the Aborigines Department approached the Department of Lands and Surveys to have Lot 159 declared a 'reserve for Aborigines'. This occurred after the Commissioner of Police had voiced his support in the matter when writing that there was no Aboriginal reserve in York, that Aboriginal people had used this block for years and that his local officer was not aware of any other suitable block for an Aboriginal reserve in York.[18] The Department of Lands and Surveys approached the municipal council who strongly objected to the proposition that Lot 159 be declared an Aboriginal reserve. Council claimed that this block was seldom used by Aboriginal people and suggested a more suitable block on Beverley Road at Cold Harbour Estate, which was apparently 'mostly used' by Aboriginal people.[19]

Whether the council's claim regarding the frequency of land use was true at the time seems to be almost impossible to ascertain but it is more than likely that different families used different camping grounds. Nevertheless, the presence of Aboriginal people did not accord with the council's economic and developmental aspirations. The rationale behind the conversion to municipal endowment lands was that the council would then be able to lease out land, for example, to farmers for livestock grazing, and those farmers would be obliged to erect fences and clear bush areas on the blocks. The erected fences would then become the municipality's property after an anticipated ten-year term of lease and, as such, save costs to the municipality. As per council's wish, Lots 151 to 159 were eventually turned into municipal endowment land in August 1924.[20]

The newly proposed block on Beverley Road also happened to be located just outside the municipality—a feature that would have appealed to many settler-Australian residents of York. Police Inspector T. Houlahan reported in April 1924 that it is:

> about 1 ¼ miles from York Post Office, and contains about 10 acres with a frontage to Avon River. There is plenty of shelter and firewood on this block, and I think it is suitable for a

camping ground for abo. Natives, and owing to the size of the block, I think it is better for the purpose than the block referred to in Mr W. Craig's letter.[21]

Houlahan went on to say that he spoke to Craig, who was apparently happy with the suggested block on Beverley Road and that he 'said all he wanted was to see that a camping ground was available for the natives'.[22]

The Deputy Chief Protector of Aborigines was satisfied with the proposal. On 25 July 1924, this block of ten acres, one rood (Reserve 8567, Lot 25, Cold Harbour Estate), which was originally gazetted as a public reserve for access to water in 1903, now had its purpose changed to 'Camping Ground (Aboriginals)'.[23] The water reserve had been originally established when the state government bought Cold Harbour from the estate of the deceased settler Joseph Hardy and then sub-divided the land to throw it open for sale. During this process, the Surveyor General approached long-term York settler resident W.M. Parker, inquiring about the Aboriginal name for Cold Harbour with a view to renaming the estate. Parker advised that he had obtained the name of Mount Brown, which was apparently 'Noorgellin', from an Aboriginal person, and he suggested it would be appropriate to rename Cold Harbour as the 'property takes a large slice of this range at the south side' of Mount Brown.[24] However, in the end, the Department of Lands and Surveys decided to stick with Cold Harbour.[25]

The gazettal of the York Reserve in 1924 as a camping ground for Aboriginal people was notably carried out under the *Land Act 1898* and not under the *Aborigines Act 1911*.[26] The gazettal under the *Land Act* merely prescribed the purpose of land use, whereas a declaration under the *Aborigines Act* would have provided the Aborigines Department with a whole range of enforceable control measures concerning Aboriginal people and their interaction with non-Aboriginal people on the reserve.[27] It is not clear whether this occurred intentionally or was the result of an accidental oversight. Generally, the department endeavoured to exert maximum possible control over Aboriginal people.[28] The Chief Protector of Aborigines, Auber Octavius Neville, who served from 1915 until 1940, was only in charge of the northern part of Western Australia between 1920 and 1926. Meanwhile, the southern part was administered by the Deputy Chief Protector Frederick Aldrich, who had no experience with Aboriginal matters (just like Neville when he commenced) and was chiefly concerned with his other area of responsibility at the Department of Fisheries.[29] During his term, the majority of town reserves in the south were declared under the *Land Act*.[30] If this was not the result of oversight but indeed intentional, Aldrich may have weighed up the loss of direct control over Aboriginal people against having fewer mandated responsibilities, and considered the latter favourably.

Over the next few years, it appears that the *native reserve* was not used as a permanent place of abode and Aboriginal people seemingly did not frequent York in any large numbers at the same time. On the Aborigines Department's file for the reserve, there are no entries between 1924 and 1935, and very few newspaper articles mention Aboriginal people in York over the next few years. This indicates that Aboriginal people, when staying in York, kept largely inconspicuous public profiles and would only have been present in small numbers at any time. The local press in country towns was quick to report on anything concerning Aboriginal people if their presence upset the imagined ideal landscape of *white Australia*. In 1927, the municipal council carried a motion to have police remove a group of Aboriginal people to 'their own camping ground'.[31] The group had camped at the Mount Brown nature reserve and their presence apparently spoilt settler-Australians' use of the recreational area as the campers allegedly showed 'no regard for the sanitation or decency'.[32] The department's annual report for 1928 indicates that only seven Aboriginal people were known to reside in the whole York District and none in the following year. While the department's population statistics should not be seen as a complete reflection of reality, such statistics are generally able to suggest a trend.[33]

Chapter 2. 1930s

2.01 Returning to York

In 1932, during the Great Depression, the York Road Board opposed a petition signed by 330 residents to have a ration station established in York and it was argued by the board's chairman W.G. Burges that 'York had for many years been practically free from natives and he did not see why they should be encouraged back now. The camp they now occupied was filthy and undoubtedly the proper place for their camp was out in the country.'[1] While York was a town where food rations had been issued in the past to Aboriginal people, by the 1920s, this practice had ceased. Chief Protector Neville had intended to save costs, and simultaneously push Aboriginal people towards moving *voluntarily* to the two existing *native settlements* at Carrolup and Moore River, by closing a substantial number of rationing depots in the South West Land Division between 1917 and 1920.[2] When Aldrich was in charge in the south, he halted the push towards settlements and established several town reserves as he considered them to be more cost effective; however, he did not simultaneously reintroduce the ration depots that were earlier abolished by Neville.[3]

The petition was organised by the then mayor of York, Charles Alfred Foreman, who claimed that there were forty starving Aboriginal people in York at the time. In the lead up to the petition, Police Sergeant Donahue reported that he had approached Councillor Thorn who advised him that he had been in York for many years and had never seen any Aboriginal people camping there. According to Donahue, Thorn 'added confidentially that the Mayor has a personal interest in trying to get a native station. He is a skin buyer and he is very partial to buying some cheap skins' from Aboriginal people.[4] Neville then went to York and reported afterwards that the alleged starving Aboriginal people did not 'belong' to York but to Quairading and Northam, where ordinarily they should receive rations. He discovered that the number of Aboriginal people currently staying in York were twelve adults and twenty-two children, and he ascertained that the men were working for various farmers and were able to earn sufficiently to provide for their families. Neville 'also learned that most of the natives, particularly those from Quairading, were really at York to enable them to send their sick children to the local hospital and he found, too, that Mr Foreman had encouraged them to stay at York, apparently in his own business interests'.[5] Neville further reported that 'it was openly hinted in York that Mr. Foreman desires the services of natives for his own purposes'.[6]

It is difficult to ascertain Foreman's true intentions. As Neville had been possibly still preoccupied with his desire that Aboriginal people would be moving voluntarily to settlements, this petition might have seemed counterintuitive to the department's efforts and, as such, Foreman's petition was prone to be readily dismissed by Neville even if there was some evidence of hardship. Nevertheless, some statements and later actions by Foreman do suggest that his intentions were not necessarily aimed only for the benefit of Aboriginal people. Neville interviewed Foreman, who reportedly:

> could give no coherent reason for his action in organising the petition. However, he pointed out that York was an early settlement and it would be nice to have some natives about the place. Then he though the expenditure of some £30 or £40 weekly in the town would be a good thing.[7]

While expenditure by Aboriginal people will be a recurring theme in this book, Foreman's claim, as quoted by Neville, that it would be 'nice' to have some Aboriginal people in York seems rather ridiculous given the overall racist and segregationist attitudes present at the time. Simultaneously, the claims made by Road Board Chairman Burges and Councillor Thorn that Aboriginal people had not really been present in York for quite some time may have been made with the intention to deny

Aboriginal people their right to stay in York based on the premise that they were *not belonging*, as Neville had commented. Following this logic, Aboriginal people would have forfeited their right to 'belong' to this locality because of their alleged prolonged absence.

While Foreman's intentions appear to have been self-serving, it would be a fallacy to accept Neville's and the police's conclusion that he was completely responsible for Aboriginal people moving into York at the time by luring them into town. First, Neville's comment that Aboriginal people who came to York in 1932 did not 'belong' to York needs to be challenged as it is based on a purely settler-Australian belief system that denies Aboriginal traditional ownership and sense of belonging to country that is not based on one locality. Traditionally, Aboriginal people have been moving along family districts, which Noongar people call a 'run'. Since the onset of settlement, moving along runs also increasingly became a necessity to navigate the ongoing displacement through the ever-expanding forceful European *land-grab*. According to Marion Kickett, her family's run stretched from 'Beverley, York, Quairading, the lakes and Sawyers Valley right down to Mundaring'.[8] Marion Kickett's branch of the larger Kickett family relocated permanently to York in 1932, as per her own account:

> My grandfather, Thomas Kickett Junior, moved between certain towns and the bush (his run) to prevent his children from being removed to a mission. However, in 1932 he made the decision to stay permanently on the reserve in York. The land allocated for the purpose of a native reserve in York was in fact a traditional camping site of the Kickett family. My grandfather had a strong connection to this site, as he had stayed there on many occasions with his parents for most of his young life. My father informed me that there were many other camping sites throughout their run, however most of these traditional camping sites were no longer available to the Balardong people.[9]

Second, a growing Aboriginal population in Balardong Country, and the South West Land Division in general, may have also provided an incentive for Marion Kickett's family and other Aboriginal families and individuals to relocate to York permanently, or more long term than previously. According to the annual reports of the Aborigines Department, the Aboriginal population in the South West Land Division had increased from 1,603 in 1919 to 2,576 in 1932.[10] In 1928, Quairading District was estimated to have an Aboriginal population of 205 persons, which was the second largest after Pingelly with 240 persons (excluding Moora with 443 persons, as Moore River Settlement was included in that town's figure). In 1929, Quairading's Aboriginal population had increased to 326 persons, which included a very large proportion of children.[11] While these numbers were estimates, a trend signifying a population boom in this district is clearly recognisable (though this sudden increase was likely dominated by migration rather than natural increase) and with such growing population numbers, resources to make a living likely became increasingly scarce. Additionally, the 'hard times' of the Great Depression had set in by 1930, which saw many Aboriginal people lose their primary means of income in seasonal farm work.[12]

Many people seemed to have been rather desperate. For example, it was noted in 1930 that a rumour went around in Quairading that rations were being issued in York, which had the effect that many Aboriginal people left the district for York but returned once they realised that this rumour was not true.[13] In 1931, Neville commented on Aboriginal people in the Quairading District looking for work, inferring their desperation: 'I was struck by the way natives are trying to find work. They are roaming the country looking for work, and some of them getting a day here and there.'[14] For the financial year ending 30 June 1933, Quairading counted 115 Aboriginal people being issued rations due to hardship, which was the highest number for any rations station in the whole South West.[15]

Therefore, it does not appear unlikely that growing population numbers and economic considerations had provided an incentive for Thomas Kickett's family, as well as other Aboriginal people, to relocate to York at this point in time. The Kicketts, notably, would be the only family staying on the reserve for a continuous period of forty years thenceforth. Also, notwithstanding adverse opinions within York's settler-Australian community in regard to the new residents' status, if these supposed newcomers were Noongars of the Balardong language group, they certainly did not come from outside into a new territory but merely relocated within their own traditional territory. However, in line with the colonial legal assumption of *terra nullius*, which denied Aboriginal people any ownership of their country and which was only overturned in 1992 when the Australian High Court handed down the crucial Mabo Decision,[16] the process of settling Western Australia's Wheatbelt region held little regard for Aboriginal territorial concerns. In this tradition, from the late 1930s to the early 1950s, the authorities in York would repeatedly call for the removal or segregation of Aboriginal people in and around town.

For the best part of the 1930s, it appears that the presence of Aboriginal people in York was tolerated to some degree. As mentioned earlier, the Aborigines Department's 'native reserve' file does not contain any documents between 1924 and 1935, and then only administrative matters until 1938, while the local newspapers do not seem to have reported much on matters concerning local Aboriginal people in this period. The absence of negative news reporting may be indicative of a less contentious period, as local newspapers were usually quick to report on any real or perceived issues relating to Aboriginal people. This does not mean that Aboriginal people in York were not subjected to racism and otherwise unjust treatment during this period. One possible reason for the absence of outspoken opposition towards Aboriginal people at the time was that the Aboriginal population in the York District was growing only slowly throughout the 1930s. The Aborigines Department counted an Aboriginal population of six persons in 1933, none in 1934, nineteen in 1935, and between forty-eight and forty-three persons in the years 1936 to 1938. These figures should not be taken as definite population numbers because many families were seasonally transient or needed to temporarily relocate to evade authorities. The latter was a practice, for example, to protect children from being taken, as indicated by Marion Kickett further above. In the mid-1930s, Australia was still going through the Great Depression and the Aborigines Department noted that work was 'not plentiful' in York.[17] However, with the above-cited population figures, it still appears reasonable to conclude that the Aboriginal population in the York District was growing towards the second part of the 1930s.

2.02 Access to drinking water

In December 1935, settler-Australian resident of York Wilfred Henry Lawrance wrote to the York Municipal Council and suggested that a water tap be made available for Aboriginal people who were camping close to his property and had been drawing water from his tap. The council indicated it would consider the proposition as long as the Water Supply Department covered the costs.[18] Lawrance's property was located close to the race grounds at the northern end of town, where he leased Lots 16 and 17 on the municipal endowment lands reserve 121 (located between Third and Eighth Roads north of the Avon River).[19] The council contacted the Water Supply Department where it was internally noted by the Managing Clerk A.V. Holmes in an all-too-common contemporary racist choice of wording, that for 'some time, Lawrance … has complained of wastage of water by the blacks, who are camped on Crown Lands adjoining his property and causing his account to show excess consumption'.[20] The Water Supply Department approached the Aborigines Department and offered to lay water for an estimated cost of £3 and a minimum annual charge of £1. Chief Protector Neville rejected the offer as the Aboriginal people in question were not camping on the prescribed native reserve on Beverley Road and, with this decision, the York Municipal Council considered the inquiry closed as it was not prepared to carry the costs itself.[21] However, now Neville made inquiries with police as he wanted to know why these Aboriginal people were not using the reserve. Sergeant A.M. O'Connor reported in January 1936 that Aboriginal people had been previously using the 'native reserve' and would obtain water from private property without permission. When they were eventually prevented from obtaining water, they moved on to the crown lands adjoining the endowment lands at the race course. O'Connor suggested that if water was laid on the reserve 'the trouble could be overcome as the native reserve is as convenient as the Crown Lands they have been using recently'. O'Connor also noted that the 'natives have horses with them at times and this increases the consumption of water'.[22]

The lack of access to fresh water, as well as sanitary facilities, was a common feature of town reserves across the Wheatbelt region at the time, and Aboriginal people often depended on the good will of—or some form of arrangements with—neighbouring settler-Australians. In particular, in localities where Aboriginal population numbers were increasing, obtaining fresh water from sources without an agreement could no longer remain undetected.[23] In the case of York, this meant that Aboriginal people were unable to use the only land that was allocated to them and they were yet again displaced, this time due to an apparent attitude of indifference towards their basic needs for survival. Seemingly, as long as Aboriginal people were able to procure water by whatever means, the Aborigines Department did not ask how this water was obtained and whether Aboriginal people had to resort to *stealing* it, as defined by settler-Australian law, and as such, further confirm contemporary negative views about them. After all, the reserve in York had existed for eleven years when the water issue became apparent and it does not seem that providing access to drinking water on the reserve was ever given serious consideration by the Aborigines Department in these eleven years. In the South West Land Division, the Aborigines Department often had arrangements with the local police to cart water to the reserves; however, there is no evidence that this had occurred at any time in York since 1924.[24]

In March 1936, Chief Protector Neville visited the camps close to the race course. He noted that the site was generally suitable but that Lawrance's water was the only source available in the area. Neville then visited the 'native reserve' on Beverley Road. Neville commented that it was 'an excellent site, except that a lot of rubbish has been dumped there at some time or another, but not lately. There is a large pool in the river near-by, affording water for washing, etc., but presumably not fit for human consumption'.[25] Before his site inspection, Neville had inquired with the Department of Works and Labour about the costs for laying water to the reserve on Beverley Road. He was advised that the total costs would be £13 for laying approximately sixty metres of three-quarter inch pipe (roughly 7.6 cm in diameter) to a point forty metres within the reserve, and erecting a three-feet standpipe (roughly ninety cm in height). The annual charges for the supply of water would be £1 plus further costs for possible excess consumption.[26] Following his site visit, Neville commented that he understood the reasons for the supposedly high costs for laying water as a pipe would have to be conveyed under the road. Neville further commented that the 'site is not ideally situated because of the proximity of the main road, but it is fairly near the hospital ... and would not be occupied by any great extent. However, the question is, can we secure the water at a reasonable rate'.[27]

Neville attempted to obtain a good deal, trying to convince various state departments that it was customary to provide water free of charge to Aboriginal people. In his inquiries, he cited the lack of available funds as his chief argument for seeking free-of-charge provision of water; however, he was repeatedly denied his request.[28] In late June 1936, Lawrance wrote directly to the Aborigines Department, stating that he had promised those Aboriginal people who camped on the crown lands that he would be advocating on their behalf for water to be supplied to the reserve. He stated that they were still using water from a tank he had placed next to the tap. However, once this water was used up, Lawrance was unwilling to further supply water, commenting that 'for a few years or more I have allowed them free water—which I have had to pay for to Gov. Water Supply. For several reasons I have found it necessary to discontinue this privilege of freedom to my water tap ...'[29] Lawrance then voiced the belief that the reserve was inspected by Police Officer O'Connor and a local representative of the Department for Water Supply, when it was determined that laying water was too costly as it was apparently not acceptable for the water tap to be installed close to the road. Lawrance alleged that the apparent reasoning behind this logic was that a tap installed close to the road would encourage Aboriginal people to camp close to the road as well. By implication, this was not desirable as Aboriginal people were preferably kept out of sight. Lawrance argued that a tap could be installed close to the road to keep costs low but Aboriginal people could be simultaneously ordered to camp further inside the reserve.[30] As with many seemingly supportive settler-Australians in historic records, it is difficult to establish whether Lawrance was genuinely concerned for the well-being of the Aboriginal people he 'advocated' for or whether he only wished for them to relocate as soon as possible. Nevertheless, his letter may have provided a hint of urgency to Neville to take action.

By September 1936, Neville advised that the Aborigines Department would be able to finance the installation of the water pipe through its revenue estimate.[31] Neville may have been further encouraged to undertake this expenditure due to a series of newspaper articles in the *West Australian* in July of that year, which strongly criticised the deplorable situation of Aboriginal people in the southern half of the state.[32] This criticism also echoed sentiments expressed in the report of the Mosley Royal Commission on the situation of Aboriginal people in Western Australia, which was released early 1935 and that would influence the amendment of the Aborigines Act in late 1936.[33] Only a few days before Neville commissioned the installation of water on the reserve, Western Australia's state budget was announced, which had a small surplus and provided an increase of £5,959 to the Aborigines Department's allocated funds. While this increase was criticised in the press for being insufficient to ameliorate the situation of Aboriginal people in the whole of Western Australia, it would have enabled Neville, for example, to pay for necessary ad hoc expenditures, such as the installation of water on the reserve in York.[34] The tap was finally operating by late October 1936 and had cost the Aborigines Department £11 5s. To establish an idea of the value, these costs may be viewed in comparison with the Western Australian weekly basic wage of 1936, which was fixed at £3 11s 9d for male adults and £1 18s 9d for female adults in agricultural areas (read: one pound, eighteen shillings and nine pence).[35]

2.03 Proclamation, blood quantum, 1936 amendment

On completion of the installation of the water supply, Neville realised that the reserve in York had not been proclaimed under the *Aborigines Act* and he issued instructions that this 'must be done right away'.[36] Chief Secretary E.H. Gray signed the proclamation under section 10 of the *Aborigines Act 1911* on 27 November 1936, which became effective when published in the *Western Australian Government Gazette* on

11 December 1936.[37] As briefly discussed above, this proclamation changed the legal status of the reserve significantly. Under the *Aborigines Act 1911*, the department could move any Aboriginal person onto a reserve or remove any Aboriginal person from a reserve to another district as it saw fit. More importantly, the local government bodies did not have any jurisdiction over reserves proclaimed under this Act. Any issues concerning the native reserves, real or perceived, had to be addressed with the department.[38] Further, non-Aboriginal people were not allowed to enter reserves unless authorised by the department. Originally, this section was conceived to provide Aboriginal people with a certain degree of protection from ill-meaning settler-Australians; however, it was often used for the social control of the people it was supposed to protect.[39] The latter section remained under various amendments of the Act until 1972. Penalties for breaches against this section of the Act varied over time. In York, breaches of this section were prosecuted on three occasions in 1947, 1948 and 1952, each of which will be discussed further below.[40]

When Neville requested the proclamation, an amendment bill for the *Aborigines Act* was currently being debated in State Parliament and would be eventually proclaimed as the *Native Administration Act 1936* on 27 April 1937. This may explain the apparent urgency when Neville requested to have the reserve in York proclaimed under the Act as he was anticipating gaining even more control over the lives of Aboriginal people, in particular, in the South West Land Division. One important aspect of the amended legislation was its definition of who was to be legally deemed Aboriginal. During the 1800s, Australian settler society and its law makers had adopted the North American *blood quantum* theory to categorise Aboriginal people in degrees of mixed descent, or its absence, by using the blood analogy as a measurable quantity. The first legislation in Western Australia that categorised Aboriginal people in such a way was assented to in 1874. According to this logic, *full-bloods* were Aboriginal people with both parents of *pure* Aboriginal ancestry. The term *half-caste* was used in Australia, initially to describe a person with one Aboriginal parent and one non-Aboriginal parent; however, the term was later also applied to Aboriginal people with various degrees of mixed ancestry.[41]

It has been argued that the blood quantum categorisation of Aboriginal people in settler societies like Australia served the ultimate goal to statistically eliminate the Aboriginal presence. This would assist in diminishing any possible claims of Aboriginal people to landownership as original inhabitants and consequently soothe the settler-colonial consciousness, because it could be claimed that if there were no *real* Aboriginal people left, settler-Australians did not have to feel guilty for taking their land.[42] Since the onset of European occupation and settlement in Western Australia, there had been a slowly but steadily growing Aboriginal population of mixed descent, which made up over half of the Aboriginal population in the South West Land Division by the turn of the century (1900). The children of mixed descent resulted from parental unions entered into through relative free will, as well as from many non-consensual sexual contacts between male European settlers (and various other men who were non-Aboriginal but not necessarily of European origin, such as sealers, whalers, merchants or gold miners) and Aboriginal women.[43] Almost always, if one parent was of European ancestry, that parent was male and the mother was of any degree of Aboriginal ancestry and likely grew up in an Aboriginal social environment. This fact assists in explaining why light-skinned Aboriginal people considered themselves (and still do) Aboriginal rather than non-Aboriginal.

Anna Haebich noted that nineteenth-century colonists saw Aboriginal people of mixed descent:

> as being in a state of cultural and racial limbo. They were not considered to be "real" Aborigines: it was widely believed that they knew little about Aboriginal traditions and that Aborigines of full descent would have nothing to do with them.[44]

By the 1890s, across the Western world, biological racism turned increasingly into an ideology or a 'religion of whiteness' with the result that *miscegenation* (producing ethnically diverse offspring) was no longer deemed a tolerable option within Western Australian settler society, which imagined itself as purely *white*.[45] Thus, the blood quantum classification of Aboriginal people not only served to statistically eliminate *pure* Aboriginality, and with it settler-Australian moral responsibility, it also ensured that people of mixed descent were not readily accepted into the majority European population, if this was their desire, by insisting on degrees of non-whiteness. When the *Aborigines Act 1905* came into force, it covered the majority of Aboriginal people in Western Australia. Next to Aboriginal people of full descent (according to blood quantum theory), it covered *half-castes* who lived with an Aboriginal person of full descent as husband or wife, any *half-castes* who habitually lived or associated with Aboriginal people of full descent, and *half-caste* children until the age of sixteen. So-called *quadroons*, or *quarter-caste* Aboriginal people, who had one grandparent of full Aboriginal descent and three non-Aboriginal grandparents (or two grandparents of half-Aboriginal descent on either parental side and two non-Aboriginal grandparents, for example), were excluded from the provisions of the Act.[46]

Since the original proclamation of the *Aborigines Act 1905*, second and third generations of Aboriginal people of mixed descent were born, which apparently caused Western Australia's settler society great concern, as 'the half-caste problem' was commonly talked about. While Aboriginal people in the South West Land Division, regardless of degree of descent, remained living in the same circumstances on the fringes of settler society and were largely rejected by the white community, an increasing proportion no longer fell under the *Aborigines Act* and thus, could legally not be controlled by many of the draconian laws aimed at Aboriginal people. Further, in 1922, a magistrate reportedly set a precedent when he ruled 'that a child of two half-caste parents was not a half-caste, which has caused a tremendous amount of trouble for the Aborigines department'.[47] A.O. Neville himself grew to believe in the concept of *biological absorption* to successfully integrate the Aboriginal population of mixed descent into settler society within a few generations. He recognised that these Aboriginal people were subjected to undue racist attitudes and subsequent ill treatment, but instead of wishing to address these racist attitudes held by settler-Australians, he sought to appease them. Neville's belief system was based on the same racist assumptions; however, he did not use perceived biological inferiority to justify the abhorrent treatment of Aboriginal people. Rather he viewed his charges in a paternalistic way, as people he sought to protect. To do so, Neville literally aimed at *breeding out* the colour through social engineering, for which he required maximum possible control over Aboriginal people of all degrees of descent. The means to this end were mostly dictatorial and socially destructive, though Neville considered them necessary to *free* Aboriginal people from *their* misery.[48] It should be noted, however, that Neville's ideas did not necessarily resonate with wider settler-Australian beliefs and that the promotion of miscegenation continued to be largely frowned upon, in particular, within the then-popular pseudo-scientific field of eugenics, whose followers adhered to principles of blood and race purity and who considered miscegenation a deterioration of the European genetic pool.[49] This racialist belief system promoting white purity was widely present in settler-Australian mainstream discourse at the time, and would only slowly turn after the horrors of the Holocaust became widely publicised post-1945. As is well-established, the industrial mass murder of six million Jews and other minorities in Europe was based on the very same ideas of racial purity and eugenics.[50]

Nevertheless, by the *Native Administration Act 1936*, Neville was able to extend the reach of the department's control. The terms *Aborigine* and *half-caste* were replaced by the all-encompassing term *native*. Persons covered by the Act included now all Aboriginal people of varying degrees of descent, with some notable exceptions. *Quadroons* (a quarter Aboriginal descent) over twenty-one years of age were exempted, as well as quadroons under twenty-one years who did not associate with nor live in the manner of *natives*. Additionally, persons 'of less than quadroon blood'[51] born prior to 31 December 1936 were exempt from the Act unless they wished to be included. Sexual intercourse between a person deemed native ('native in-law') and a person not deemed native was now prohibited, whereas prior to the amendment, only co-habitation (living together) was an offence. The new Act also required any marriage of Aboriginal people to be approved by Neville, which was supposed to further assist him in his grand social engineering plans. Penalties for breaching any sections of the Act were harsh. For a first so-called offence, a person could be sentenced to a maximum of £20, three months of imprisonment or both. A second offence could attract up to £50, six months of imprisonment or both. The maximum penalties for third or subsequent offences were £100, twelve months of imprisonment or both. Neville's former title of Chief Protector of Aborigines was now changed to Commissioner of Native Affairs.[52]

2.04 First recorded agitation by York's local authorities against reserve dwellers 1938–1939

In the year after the proclamation of the *Native Administration Act 1936*, York's local authorities commenced a series of complaints about Aboriginal people and the reserve in York. Whether the authorities felt encouraged through the amended legislation is not known; however, the new Act was discussed in the Western Australian press and one commentator identified it as one of only two significant pieces of legislation that were produced during Western Australia's 1936 session of Parliament (the other relating to taxes).[53] As discussed above, according to statistics of the Department of Native Affairs (and its predecessors), the Aboriginal population numbers in York were rising and settler-Australian residents of York would have come to realise that the Aboriginal presence in York was now a permanent feature. On 17 November 1938, the town clerk, A.E. White, wrote four clinical and dispassionate lines to the Department of Native Affairs on behalf of the York Municipal Council:

> A reserve exists at York, about 1½ miles from the main part of town, and a considerable number of natives are now thereon.
>
> Sanitary conditions are very bad, and the town swimming pool is in danger of pollution.
>
> A number of natives appear to spend most of their time around the town.
>
> My council wishes these people removed to a more distant reserve.[54]

The idea to request the removal of the York Reserve was formalised at the monthly municipal council meeting when Councillor Clifton John Ashbolt had moved that 'the Aborigines Department be asked to have the natives moved from the reserve'.[55] The proposal was carried by all present councillors (Alfred John Lock, Albert Francis Noonan, Vernon Calcott Veryard, Charles Alfred Foreman, Joseph Hermann Prunster, Sylvester Joseph Marwick, Frederick Ashbolt and Percy Albert Reginald Ashworth) and the mayor, Albert Thorn. The news article that reported on the council meeting only stated that the request came about due 'to the absence of adequate sanitary conveniences'.[56] Working towards the provision of adequate sanitary conveniences seemingly did not occur to council as a solution to the issue, which suggests that the alleged public health issue was a welcome opportunity to dispose of unwelcome residents. In early December, Neville visited York and met with the town clerk and the local sergeant of police when it was decided not to take any action in relation to the request as most Aboriginal people had 'moved on elsewhere'[57] and there were only very few on the reserve. Neville commented that the 'Kickett family had a properly constructed latrine, but I gathered that visitors had been using the railway bridge, hence the complaints'.[58] While Neville's conjecture regarding such an inventive way of relieving oneself, which would have included multiple persons of all ages, may or may not have been correct, there was nothing further reported in the local weekly newspaper in regard to the alleged pollution of the river in the month preceding the meeting—although there were reports about the pool (within the Avon River) as the annual swimming season was to open on 13 November. If the opening of the swimming season was ever threatened to be 'stained' by human faeces, one would expect a public outcry in the local newspaper; however, this was not the case.[59]

When Neville visited the reserve, he also collected census data of everyone present. One family was visiting from Beverley at the time to attend the hospital in York, and Neville noted that this family's eighteen-year-old daughter was 'nearly white'.[60] He requested that 'respecting the colour' of this young woman, a copy of his report be placed on her father's personal file held at the Department of Native Affairs' head office in Perth, where, at the time, all records were kept.[61]

In the 1920s, Neville had introduced the keeping of personal dossier files on Aboriginal people, which served to increase the department's knowledge of and control over the lives of Western Australia's Aboriginal population.[62] The fate of this young woman from Beverley or her children, if she had any, is not known to this author; however, it is certain that Neville was taking notes to further his social engineering project with the ultimate aim to *breed out* colour. Neville or his next two successors may have later used this information to make a decision on a marriage application, which he might have denied if the groom-to-be had a darker complexion (measured by blood quantum) than the young woman, or, worse, to order the removal of the young woman's child or children if their skin colour was also deemed to be 'nearly white' or white.

The *Native Administration Act 1936* enabled Neville to decide whether children of lighter skin colour may grow up in an Aboriginal social environment with their families or instead be separated from family and culture, for example, at Sister Kate's Home for light-skinned *quadroons*, which was established in 1934 in the Perth suburb of Queens Park. Neville had issued instructions across the state for departmental officers and local protectors—the latter were usually police officers— to look out for light-skinned Aboriginal children with the intention of removing them from their families. Parents were also pressured into 'voluntarily' placing their children into an institution if they experienced hardship or thought the children would receive adequate education. Once signed over, parents often came to realise that they were unable to have their children returned if they so desired. That these forced removal practices occurred throughout Western Australia is a sad but undisputable fact, and the practice was upheld by Neville's next two successors, Bray and McBeath, until 1948, when the Crown Law Department ruled that *quadroons* could not be kept at an institution against their parents' will.[63] The practice of forceful removals of fair-skinned Aboriginal children did continue after the 1948 Crown Law ruling; however, this was done under the *Child Welfare Act* by declaring that parents had neglected their children. The result was often the same in that Aboriginal children were separated from their families and culture; however, the intention behind the removals had by then officially shifted from Neville's vision of the eventual biological absorption of Aboriginal people of mixed descent to misguided welfare concerns. It must be emphasised that it was not only so-called 'quarter-caste' children who were removed from their parents. All Aboriginal children were subject to potential removal, though children of mixed parentage were most affected during the first half of the twentieth century. Removal practices also preceded Neville's commencement at the department, when the common argument for removals was that children with white blood needed to be rescued from Aboriginal environments, before Neville added the social engineering aspect.[64]

Back in York, only five months after the municipal council requested the removal of Aboriginal people from the reserve, the York Road Board wrote to the Department of Native Affairs on 18 April 1939, voicing the opinion that the reserve should be closed as it was apparently too close to town. Board members present were Chairman Hon. G.B. Wood MLC (Member of the Legislative Council of Western Australia), W.G. Burges, N.P. Burges, T.W. Marwick, J.V. Fairhead, J.C. McLachlan and the secretary, J.E. Sparke. The road board's stated central reasoning was as follows: 'It would appear that the native children make themselves most objectionable to other children when passing by their camps, which are pitched very close to the road'.[65]

When Neville replied, the tone of his letter suggests that he was getting increasingly annoyed with York's local authorities. He advised that he knew the position quite well, had visited recently and was unable to appreciate how there should be any objections to the circumstances. According to Neville, only two families were permitted to permanently live on the reserve and others would sporadically visit when seeking medical attention at the hospital. He pointed out that the site had been suggested by the municipal council in 1924, that the department went to some expense to lay water on the reserve in 1936 and that the few Aboriginal people who had been living in York's municipal area were 'finally removed to this reserve'[66] in the same year. Neville continued by stating that before York's Aboriginal population was moved to the present reserve, 'objections were raised to their camping, here, there, and everywhere, and I had hoped that there would be no further complains of this sort'.[67]

Neville inquired with the local protector Police Sergeant Lewin Henry Clifford about the allegations of 'objectionable' behaviour displayed by the children living on the reserve and also questioned whose children would be actually subjected to the alleged bad behaviour as the reserve's location was not within a densely populated area. Clifford advised that he received one report of Aboriginal children chasing settler-Australian children, who would sometimes ride past the reserve calling out 'nigger niggers'[68], on their bicycles. Clifford was explicit in pointing out that the children living on the reserve were otherwise 'well behaved' and only reacted to the racist vilification to which they were subjected.[69] On 17 May, Neville wrote to the road board that there would be no trouble if it were not for 'the white children teasing'[70] the Aboriginal children. Neville ended the road board's inquiry by stating, with a somewhat salty tone, that he did 'not think the matter is one which need cause your Board any concern at the present time'.[71] In the local press, Neville's reply was briefly mentioned; however, no further comments by road board members were reported on this matter.[72]

A little over two weeks after Neville's reply to the road board, at the municipal council meeting, councillors C. Foreman and A.F. Noonan suggested approaching the Department of Native Affairs to see whether it was possible 'that sheds for the use of natives be erected in the reserve near the railway bridge'.[73] Crucially, it was argued that if 'this were done a stricter supervision could be kept on the natives camped there'.[74] While the local press emphasised the alleged necessity for stricter supervision of Aboriginal people, the letter that was sent by York's new town clerk, Charles B. Vincent, to the department emphasised humanitarian concerns and only briefly mentioned increased supervision towards the end of the letter, which has been quoted in full below:

> My Council desires to draw your earnest attention to the hardship which natives have to endure as a result of lack of accommodation adjacent to York. Quite recently there have been large numbers of natives camped on the banks of the Avon River without any covering or provision for sanitary

arrangements. Apart from the danger to the health of our people, it is very hard on the natives, as you will be ready to agree.

It is suggested that some shedding be provided and suitable sanitary conveniences. It should not be difficult for your agents to see that the camp is left in sanitary condition and that some supervision is exercised.[75]

Of course, it is quite possible that the humanitarian concerns were discussed in the council meeting; however, it appears unlikely that they were given primary attention, as the news reporting on these meetings usually detailed the essence of the discussion, which was, in this case, increased supervision of Aboriginal people. This seems of particular importance if one considers that only a few months earlier, the council had requested the complete removal of Aboriginal people from York without hesitation. Therefore, it appears more likely that the humanitarian concerns emphasised in the town clerk's letter were meant to manipulate the department into taking action that would result in the anticipated increase of departmental oversight.

Neville ascertained that there had been a 'gala day' recently at York, where an annual 'foot-running carnival' was being held. It was noted that this tradition commenced in the 1870s or 1880s and had been won by Aboriginal people on occasion. Therefore, a number of Aboriginal people visited York to witness or take part in the event; however, their usual place of abode was reportedly at Geeralying (located between the towns of Narrogin and Williams) and not on the York Reserve.[76] This would not be the last time that the local authorities entered into an apparent state of panic because a few more Aboriginal people than usual were seen about town. On 19 June, Neville attended a meeting in York with council members, Sergeant Clifford and a couple of other town officials. He reiterated that only two families were permanently camped at the York Reserve and that others came in occasionally. Neville claimed 'that those permanently there appeared to have fair accommodation so far as it went, and it was doubtful whether they could be induced to leave there to occupy lean-to sheds'.[77] However, he indicated that he was willing to supply up to half a ton of galvanised iron 'for erecting temporary habitations for visitors, and lavatory accommodation for them,' and that the town clerk and Sergeant Clifford were to inspect the reserve to ascertain the quantities required.[78]

Two months later, the town clerk, Vincent, sent plans for the 'Proposed Native Camps'. He suggested that these camps, which were basically two-roomed sheds, be pre-cut in Perth and that council would arrange for their installation. Vincent advised that the proposed accommodation would meet 'the minimum requirements of the local position'.[79] Neville replied that there must have been a misunderstanding, as his limited funds only allowed for the supply of galvanised iron as discussed during the meeting, and that he was still willing to supply these materials but was unable to finance the structures as proposed by council. On 21 September 1939, the acting town clerk, Miss E. Reynolds, advised that it was decided at the most recent council meeting that 'at the present moment no action be taken' without any further explanation.[80] As reported in the local newspaper, the mayor, A. Thorn, pointed out that the suggested improvements to the reserve, as initially discussed in June, would 'have to be arranged for'[81] and that it was not for council to pay for the works required. Councillor Prunster moved that no action should be taken. Then, Councillor Foreman reportedly voiced that:

> he had altered his opinion regarding natives. Many were not deserving much consideration. They would lie and steal to attain their ends and were ungrateful and lazy. They should not be encouraged about towns. He knew the control of natives was a difficult problem, but it should be attended to by Government.[82]

Foreman went on to suggest that little 'trouble would be encountered if the Government dealt with natives as was now being done at mission centres'. Council members reportedly agreed with Foreman.[83]

While it is not being disputed that some Aboriginal individuals may have adopted practices that were considered illegal to survive the harsh socioeconomic environment in a society where they were regarded as second-class humans, any public utterances by Foreman should be taken with a pinch of salt. Earlier in the same year, he was being investigated for supplying alcohol to Aboriginal people, which was considered a criminal offence in the South West Land Division until mid-1964, and even later in other parts of Western Australia.[84] As suggested further above, Foreman's actions seemed often to be more self-serving than anything else he may have claimed. In relation to the supply of alcohol, it appears unlikely that he risked criminal prosecution without gaining anything from it. Therefore, it also seems not unlikely that he had a business-based fallout with some Aboriginal individuals. Perhaps some people realised that they were given a bad deal, as was noted in 1933 (see discussion in chapter 2.01), and they confronted Foreman about it. When the council was advised that the Department of Native Affairs would not be able to fund improvements on the reserve, as had been requested, Foreman's comments suggest he was politically back-pedalling by declaring York's Aboriginal population undeserving, to absolve council of its decision not to further pursue the officially requested improvement of Aboriginal people's livelihoods. Further, Foreman's comments, to which the other councillors agreed, that Aboriginal people should be ideally institutionalised on missions, exemplifies a general attitude: York's Aboriginal population was not really considered a part of the local fabric but was more like an alien presence for which the state government department was solely responsible—fiscally and otherwise. With this episode, the 1930s drew to a close; however, the interactions between York's local authorities and the Department of Native Affairs over these last two years were only a harbinger of the events that would unfold in the 1940s.

Figure 2: York Reserve - Billy Kickett and Sam Winmar in front of a camp (courtesy Marion Kickett)

Figure 3: York Reserve: Woman and children in front of a camp— Back row: Vivienne Narkle, Judy Narkle, Merle Narkle, Pressie Narkle; front row: Audrey Narkle (courtesy Marion Kickett)

Chapter 3. 1940s

3.01 Unsettled whites and grand dreams of segregated settlements

At first, the new decade started in a similar manner to the way the former had concluded in relation to correspondence between York's local authorities and the Department of Native Affairs. Commissioner Neville effectively retired on 20 March 1940 and was replaced by his former deputy Francis Illingworth Bray. Otherwise, not much else had changed.[1] In July 1940, at the monthly road board meeting, N.P. Burges 'referred to the unsatisfactory manner in which natives were living in the district'[2] and it was decided to advise the Department of Native Affairs 'that the York Road Board views with alarm the manner in which natives are allowed to live in the district and hopes that steps will be taken by the department concerned to make them work for their livelihood and generally become more useful'.[3] The letter that was then sent to Native Affairs also claimed that an 'increased number of aborigines' were now living in the district.[4] Acting Commissioner Bray wrote to Sergeant Clifford seeking information on the situation in York. Bray pointed out to Clifford that there appeared to be some abled-bodied Aboriginal men receiving rations but, according to reports from farming districts, there was a shortage of labour 'owing to the enlistment of white citizens'[5] as World War II had broken out in September 1939. Bray continued that if farmers were in need of labour and Aboriginal people in York were to refuse working, then he might approach the Minister for Native Affairs 'for the issue of warrants for the removal of one or two of the worst families as a disciplinary action. However, the "lily may be over-painted", and the position may not be as bad as reported'.[6] Bray further commented that if the department had a 'settlement' in the

Eastern Districts, it would be able to handle situations such as this—implying he could have easily purged the district of Aboriginal people whom the department identified as undesirable.[7]

These so-called settlements for Aboriginal people were departmentally run institutions in the South West Land Division and could be described as the pinnacle of segregationist policies in the twentieth century in Western Australia. While Neville had initially hoped that Aboriginal families would voluntarily move to these settlements, this did not eventuate. Most children and adults who resided there did so largely involuntarily, and the settlements resembled a mix of run-down boarding schools and internment camps. Individuals and families who survived on rations were often targeted for removal, as well as children who were taken from their families for various reasons. Children were schooled to become servants and labourers for white employers, while many adults were just expected to *sit out* their existence in spatial confinement, often removed from their own Country.[8]

In mid-1940, there was one settlement operating, the Moore River Native Settlement, located in the Northern Wheatbelt region at Mogumber, 120 kilometres north of Perth. However, a second settlement at Carrolup, located 290 kilometres south of Perth, close to the Great Southern town of Katanning, was being prepared for re-opening and would once again serve as a settlement institution for segregationist purposes. The above suggested analogy to internment camps is not that farfetched if one considers that Neville had declared the area surrounding Moore River Native Settlement a *prohibited area* in August 1932 to limit abscondence. Under the *Aborigines Act 1911*, Aboriginal people without a permit were not allowed to enter a prohibited area and absconders from Moore River could thenceforth be sentenced to up to six months of imprisonment, if caught, as they had to cross through this area to escape. This prohibited area was only revoked in 1954, along with all other prohibited areas in the state.[9] Prohibited areas will be discussed in more detail further below (see chapter 3.12).

Neville had tried to secure suitable land for a farm settlement in the Eastern Wheatbelt since 1937 and his successors would pursue the matter until 1948 when the new Commissioner of Native Affairs,

Stanley Middleton, discontinued the idea. For the most part, the department was trying to secure suitable settlement land by considering abandoned farms that were available through the Agricultural Bank and it hoped to establish a farm settlement somewhere around Merredin or Bruce Rock. The whole idea was a complete failure as no abandoned farmland that was on offer had the quality of soil or other characteristics required for a self-sufficient farm settlement.[10] Had the department been successful, this would have likely resulted in even more forceful removal of Aboriginal families and individuals across the Wheatbelt. In York, during the 1940s, some families and individuals were earmarked a few times for potential removal to a settlement but avoided it in the end (at least while at York). As suggested by comments made by departmental staff and local protectors, those families who were not forcefully removed either managed to stay temporarily out of reach, or they were given ultimatums to cease certain behaviours, which they complied with to the department's (temporary) satisfaction—or both. However, had a settlement opened in the Eastern Wheatbelt, these families would have likely been deported as well. Across the state, from its inception until the 1950s, the department would have very likely destroyed many more families and interfered with many more lives— and more intensively than it already had—if it had not been for financial constraints. The records on hand make it very clear that it did not lack will.[11]

At the time of the road board's complaint in July 1940, the Eastern Wheatbelt *settlement solution* was at the forefront of departmental wishful thinking. It may have eventually saved some Aboriginal people from deportation, as it was hoped that the settlement would be opened in the not-so-distant future, and that Carrolup would re-open very soon, too. Therefore, the commissioner was perhaps more inclined to postpone taking action and instead issue warnings and ultimatums. Meanwhile, local protector Sergeant Clifford replied to Bray that there were actually very few Aboriginal people in the York District. He referred to his annual mid-year departmental census returns and advised that there were a few passing through York picking dead wool (wool picked from sheep carcasses), and the occasional one on 'holidays' ('holidays' may also be read as 'fulfilling cultural kinship obligations').

There were three families at Gwambygine and one on the reserve. The latter family had currently left York and Clifford expressed that he hoped it was for good. There were some other individuals who were, for example, living on settler-Australian farms. Clifford advised that he would issue rations when the need arose, including to people who were at York to attend the hospital, but he cited Neville's former instruction that York was not to become a ration station. Clifford went on to state that he could see no reason for the road board to be concerned about Aboriginal people in York. In relation to available employment, Clifford advised the 'farmers, by what I can see of them, have a little work at times, but do not agree with filling out the permit etc.'[12]

Since the *Aborigines Act 1905* had come into force, non-Aboriginal people who wished to employ Aboriginal people were legally obliged to obtain work permits. Following the amendment of the *Aborigines Act* in 1936, employers had to pay increased fees for their permits, which were to finance the newly established Natives' Medical Fund. Not only was this to serve as a source of revenue for the Department of Native Affairs (to alleviate expenditures for medical costs), it also further increased the control over Aboriginal people and their movements.[13] Given that the legislation was only introduced in 1937 and World War II had started in 1939, when a number of the settler-Australian rural labour force had started to enlist, farmers around York appeared to have been still generally reluctant to employ Aboriginal people on the new conditions. Thus, despite the road board requesting that Aboriginal people in York obtain work at once, such work was unlikely to be readily available to everyone. The records do suggest, at times, that some individuals were not keen on seeking employment to begin with; however, this appeared to be a minority among the Aboriginal population in the York District. Commissioner Bray advised the road board on 28 August 1940 that he was fully aware of what was going on in the York District and that no action needed to be taken at this juncture, as no Aboriginal people were residing in York. At this opportunity, Bray also advertised the idea of settlements rather enthusiastically.[14]

By mid-December, however, the York Road Board wrote yet again to the Department of Native Affairs about 'the very primitive sanitary arrangements at present in existence at the native reserve'.[15] Road board member C.M. Thorn had initiated the inquiry which was seconded by N.P. Burgess. Road Board Secretary J.E. Sparke advised that he had spoken to Sergeant Clifford who had agreed that immediate steps should be taken to improve the situation. He added that apparently eighty Aboriginal people were currently staying at the reserve, which would explain the prevailing unsatisfactory conditions.[16]

Commissioner Bray approached Clifford to ascertain the minimum requirements for sanitary conveniences as he was prepared to have some erected if his budget allowed it. He also asked why there were apparently so many Aboriginal people currently in York and if they were usually 'domiciled' in other districts, in which case, he suggested, they should be returned to their own places of residences forthwith. Clifford confirmed that recently about eighty persons had camped on the reserve; however, when he did another inspection on 5 January, he only counted twenty-seven persons, including children. Clifford reported that given only the Kickett family owned a private toilet, he had handed out a spade to other people present to dig a trench for their sanitary needs. Clifford recommended that two toilets be built, one for 'ladies' and one for 'gents', and he voiced the belief that if the reserve could be kept clean, then this would resolve a lot of the ongoing complaints. He further advised that sanitary removals would be carried out by a contractor, costing thirty shillings annually. Bray asked Clifford to obtain quotes for toilets to be erected and also to approach the road board to see whether they may be willing to attend to the ongoing removal of 'night soil' (human excreta in latrines) from the planned toilets. Bray remarked that it was actually customary for local authorities to carry out the removal of night soil and he only knew of three localities where this was not the case (Albany, Derby and Port Hedland). Clifford obtained quotes for the erection of toilets but by 7 February he was still waiting for a reply to his inquiry about the night soil removals.[17]

3.02 Medical treatment in York

Meanwhile, Sergeant Clifford had also reported that the majority of visiting Aboriginal people were from Beverley and Quairading and that he had been unable to send them back to 'their' respective districts as many of their children had suddenly become sick and had to be treated at the hospital in York. Clifford claimed that the illnesses the children suffered from were rather mild and would merely serve as an excuse, first, to have a valid reason to remain in York, and second, to be eligible to receive rations. Clifford ensured Bray that he would only issue rations once he had confirmed with the local health professional, Dr Ward, that the children of any particular family who requested rations had actually presented to the doctor and been found to be sick.[18] If Clifford's allegations were correct, this would be a fitting example of Aboriginal passive resistance to settler-colonial injustice. By navigating the settler-Australian system to their advantage, Aboriginal people were able, at least temporarily, to defy racist policy that would otherwise legally allow for their expulsion from the district on the whim of white authority.

However, there is also a flipside to the above example of passive resistance. Namely, Clifford was unable to order Aboriginal people out of the district as long as they underwent medical treatment at the hospital in York, because it was known that they experienced issues at hospitals in the districts where they commonly resided at the time. They often received inadequate treatment, or the department disagreed with the fees requested for treatment or in-house medical treatment of Aboriginal people was refused altogether. For example, in 1939, it was reported that the only accommodation for Aboriginal people at Quairading Hospital was on the veranda and, therefore, the Department of Native Affairs chose to continue transferring Aboriginal people to York for medical treatment. Additionally, there was a disagreement about the treatment fees.[19] A report on maternity accommodation in the South West Land Division, dated July 1936, stated that at Beverley Hospital accommodation was reserved only for 'whites' and that all maternity cases from Beverley and Quairading were sent to York where admission of Aboriginal women was never refused.[20] While the medical treatment was perhaps more adequate than in other localities, hospital beds for Aboriginal people in York were also not located inside the building. In February 1949, it was reported that the 'hospital has provision for 25 beds, two of which are located on the verandah downstairs for use of male natives and two on verandah upstairs for use of female natives'.[21]

One deciding difference between the York Hospital and hospitals in some surrounding districts where issues arose was that the hospital in York was a public one. Other hospitals, for example, in Quairading and Beverley, were run by local committees, and were consequently more independent and could refuse treatment to Aboriginal people or demand higher-than-usual treatment fees if they chose to do so.[22]

In February 1941, a month after Sergeant Clifford reported about visiting Aboriginal people allegedly trying to avoid a forced premature departure from York by seeking medical attention, the Department of Native Affairs imposed new rules in relation to the issuing of medication. Henceforth, the local protector would have to sign off on any medication to be issued by a chemist if the Department of Native Affairs was to pay the bill. The local protector, Sergeant Clifford at the time, had to confirm that the hospital was unable to supply required medications free of charge, that subscriptions had been ordered by a doctor and that the Aboriginal person concerned was unable to pay the bill and was not working under a permit.[23] An Aboriginal person working under a permit would have been eligible for paid medical treatment through the Native's Medical Fund, which was covered by the permit fees. Initially employers did not eagerly request these permits, as mentioned above (see chapter 3.01).[24]

In January 1942, Clifford reported that farmers in the York District generally did not want to employ Aboriginal people, aside from a few exceptions, even if there was a labour shortage. At the time, Commissioner Bray was considering removing some 'loitering' Aboriginal people from Guildford in Perth to York if there was a labour shortage owing to the ongoing war, but he had to scrap the idea due to Clifford's report.[25] While permanent work may not have been plentiful, during the 1942–1943 financial year, there was a total of twenty-seven single and casual permits issued for twenty-two individual Aboriginal persons in the York District. In many cases, employment was not consistent throughout the year and payments into the Native's Medical Fund were accordingly inconsistent but, somehow, a local police officer was expected to make a fair and reasonable judgement on a person's eligibility for subsidised medication based on their economic standing.[26]

The pharmacist in York, E.B. Stacy, ensured the department in March 1941 that his business had 'endeavoured to supply only those natives who are indigent. There are quite a number who pay for their medicines ...'[27] Being labelled 'indigent' (destitute) was a requirement to receive free medication and also to receive regular rations but, at the time, it was also a possible ticket for removal to a *native settlement*.[28] These new measures in relation to the control of issuing medication would last until 1948 when Stanley Middleton became commissioner and brought in a somewhat more progressive attitude towards the administration of his department. Simultaneously, in the same year, the Department of Health assumed most health-related responsibilities concerning the state's Aboriginal population that were, until then, controlled by the Department of Native Affairs.[29]

FORM No. 2.

THE NATIVE ADMINISTRATION ACT, 1905-1936

Application for Permit for Employment on Land.

To the Police Officer in charge of the Police Station at—

York

* Insert names in full and address.

I, * *Gerald John Lightly* of *York*

hereby apply for a Permit to employ within the *York*

† Insert name. Magisterial District on land † *Thomas Kickett*

a native.

Dated the *4th* day of *August* 19 *38*

(Signature) *G. Lightly*

REPORT OF POLICE OFFICER.

To *Commissioner of Native Affairs*

~~Protector of Natives~~

York.

I have to report that Gerald John Lightly is a farmer in York District. He is a suitable person to employ a native and I have granted him a permit, but he states that it is only temporary employment, for Kickett

York 5·8·38

H. Fawcett Sergt 1123

final ... 679 attached 5/1/38

Figure 4: Example application for permit to employ an Aboriginal person - Department of Native Affairs, item 1934/0016 (courtesy Marion Kickett)

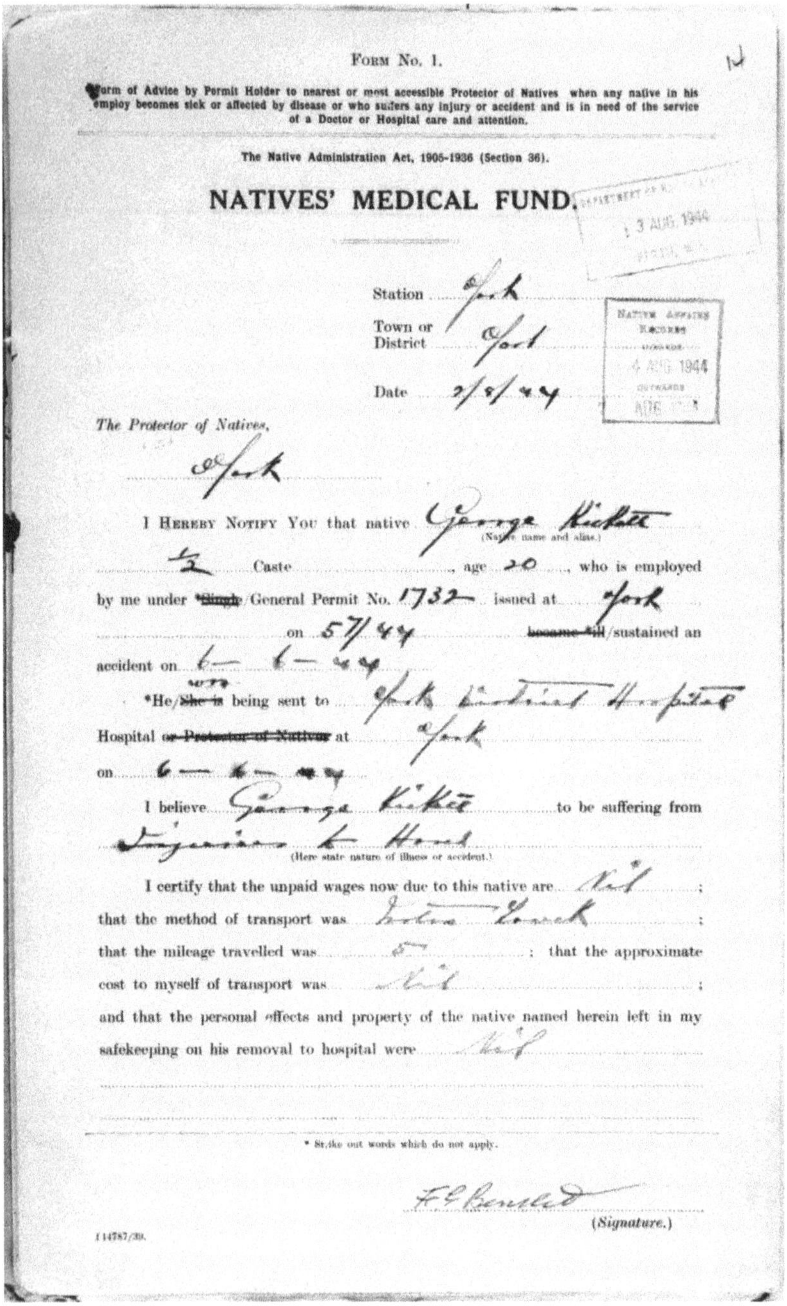

FORM No. 1.

Form of Advice by Permit Holder to nearest or most accessible Protector of Natives when any native in his employ becomes sick or affected by disease or who suffers any injury or accident and is in need of the service of a Doctor or Hospital care and attention.

The Native Administration Act, 1905-1936 (Section 36).

NATIVES' MEDICAL FUND.

Station York

Town or District York

Date 2/8/44

The Protector of Natives,

York

I HEREBY NOTIFY YOU that native George Kickett (Native name and alias.)

½ Caste, age 20, who is employed by me under ~~Single~~/General Permit No. 1732 issued at York on 5/7/44 ~~became ill~~/sustained an accident on 6-6-44

*He/~~She is~~ was being sent to York District Hospital

Hospital ~~or Protector of Natives~~ at York

on 6-6-44

I believe George Kickett to be suffering from

Injuries to Hand (Here state nature of illness or accident.)

I certify that the unpaid wages now due to this native are Nil;

that the method of transport was Motor Truck;

that the mileage travelled was 5; that the approximate cost to myself of transport was Nil;

and that the personal effects and property of the native named herein left in my safekeeping on his removal to hospital were Nil

* Strike out words which do not apply.

F G Bendel (Signature.)

14787/39.

Figure 5: Example medical fund form for Aboriginal employees - Department of Native Affairs, item 1938/1265 (courtesy Marion Kickett)

3.03 Continued agitation against the reserve

We are now returning from our medical treatment-related digression to early February 1941, when Sergeant Clifford was still waiting for a reply to his inquiry with the road board about the removal of night soil. York's municipal health inspector, J.A. Wyss, had visited the reserve and tabled a report to the municipal council meeting on 4 February, wherein he recommended that 'a strong protest be forwarded to the Commissioner for Native Affairs regarding the conditions under which these natives are living'.[30] He stated that seventy to eighty men, women and children lived on the reserve and noted also that sanitary arrangements were wanting, the area was littered with rubbish and 'a number of inmates are suffering from various complaints'.[31] The town clerk, C.B. Vincent, forwarded the report to Commissioner Bray and indicated that the York Municipal Council was of the 'opinion that the Natives should be removed entirely from the locality, and hopes that your department will take steps to have the reserve closed'.[32]

Interestingly, only one of the two local newspapers mentioned the health inspector's report and none stated that council had decided to request that the reserve be closed. The *York Leader and Quairading and Dangin Herald* reported that the health inspector considered that 'some drastic action should be taken', while the *York Chronicle*'s report about the council meeting did not mention the reserve at all, and such an omission was unusual for this publication.[33] This could mean that Vincent had requested the closure of the reserve without the council's decision on the matter, given that it was common practice to report in the local press which councillor or councillors moved certain agendas. Vincent also approached the York Road Board, seeking to combine efforts to have the reserve closed. The road board agreed and decided then to seek cooperation from the council in arranging a deputation to the Department of Native Affairs 'if the desired results were not obtained by correspondence'.[34] The road board's secretary, J.E. Sparke, wrote to Commissioner Bray, citing inflated population numbers and more or less demanding that the reserve be closed. However, he acknowledged that the sanitary arrangements were being attended to and revealed that these were not the real cause of concern for the road board;

rather, it was the very presence of 'coloured people' in increased numbers:

> Quite apart from the sanitary arrangements, which are being given attention to by your department, the position is one that needs investigation.
>
> Recently from 80 to 90 coloured people have been camped on this site, so it needs no stretch of imagination to picture the conditions existing.
>
> I am not certain as to whether this reserve is gazetted as a camping ground for aborigines, and I shall be pleased to have your advice in this direction.
>
> In the event of such being the case, I understand that steps will be taken in the direction of having it cancelled as such, as under existing conditions it is an absolute menace to the town of York.[35]

Later in February, Commissioner Bray replied to both the municipal council and the road board in two separate but similar letters and made it clear that the reserve would not be closed. He advised that two additional conveniences would be installed on the reserve and that the local protector would withhold rations until all rubbish had been burned and the camps been tidied up. Bray explained that the current higher-than-usual population numbers were caused by people receiving medical treatment from Dr Ward and a water shortage in the Quairading district, and he suggested that with the first rains, the visiting Aboriginal people would be returning to 'their' districts.[36] Indeed, in the summer of 1940–1941, Quairading experienced a severe draught, along with some other Wheatbelt towns, and by mid-February there was only one months' worth of water left in the local water reserve supplying Quairading and Dangin.[37] While Bray did not act on the local authorities' request to close the reserve, he voiced his sympathy for both their situation and requested the same in return:

The natives must camp somewhere, but of course they should do so under satisfactory sanitary conditions ... I regret it is not possible to remove all natives from York. They belong to the Eastern Districts and would be unhappy elsewhere. A Settlement is contemplated for the Eastern Districts, but funds are unavailable at the moment owing to the War, and no action can be taken for some time.[38]

With this reply, the matter was put to rest for the time being. The municipal council returned thanks for the advice received, while it appears that the road board did not bother replying. A combined deputation did not occur. However, the erection of two conveniences took some time. Bray was seemingly keen to have the toilets built as soon as possible as he pressed on with the matter in April and urged in an internal memorandum to 'keep faith with the York authorities'.[39] Eventually, by late July, the toilets had been erected by contractor George Turvey for £11 5s; however, arrangements for emptying the night soil pans were still to be made. Bray asked Clifford to approach the council for free-of charge removals and noted that if no arrangements could be made, from time to time, Clifford would have to supervise Aboriginal people disposing of the nightsoil themselves.[40] The council replied that it was unable to assist in the matter as the reserve was located outside of the municipal area within the road board's jurisdiction, where it was not permissible to spend ratepayers' money. Therefore, pans were bought and installed by Clifford, while the Kickett family was made responsible for sanitary removals. The department was obviously not willing to pay for sanitary removals at this point in time and, therefore, Clifford imposed this responsibility on a person whose presence on the reserve was permanent. His foresight was confirmed when he reported in early November 1941 that sanitary removals were carried out while the Kicketts were currently the only family on the reserve.[41] As discussed earlier (see chapter 2.01), seasonal fluctuations in Aboriginal population numbers were the norm, not only in York but across the entire South West Land Division. However, there may have been another reason why there were no 'visitors' currently present at the reserve. In early October, a visiting Aboriginal man from

Geraldton was diagnosed with cerebral meningitis and the whole reserve was placed into a ten-day 'lock-down'—or, more precisely, reserve dwellers were barred from entering town. Anyone at the reserve who did not live in York permanently would have likely left the district to avoid these restrictions.[42]

Sometime earlier, and seemingly not associated with the issues at the reserve, in March 1941, former mayor and councillor Charles A. Foreman once again voiced his concerns about Aboriginal people. This time, he directly approached the Department of Native Affairs. Initially, Foreman had called on Bray in support of an Aboriginal man who was currently in York requesting that he be issued rations as his family was experiencing hardship, having been unable to earn an income by picking dead wool. However, during ongoing correspondence, Foreman started to talk about 'good and bad' Aboriginal people in York and he singled out three males as 'evil doers' who had allegedly 'been thieving, begging, obtaining goods and money under false pretences and making themselves a nuisance'.[43] He claimed that the council and road board had been agitating for the removal of these three individuals for some time. Then, Foreman alleged that he had had several business agreements in the past, supplying certain men and their families with food stuffs so they would be able to go out among farms, gathering dead wool, collecting manna gum and shooting foxes. It was agreed that on their return, on a fixed day, Foreman would collect what they had brought and pay them a balance. However, Foreman claimed that he had been tricked several times, as in 'many cases before leaving they arrange for a Jew or some buyer to go out before you are due and they sell to him. In other cases, they get assistance and clear out or refuse to go.'[44]

Over the course of three letters, Foreman's wrath turned from personal issues with three individuals to more or less all Aboriginal people residing in York, who he agitated against and demanded that swift action be taken. Bray intimated to Sergeant Clifford that he doubted that the situation was as bad as Foreman made out but requested a report, nevertheless. On 9 May, Clifford delivered a report on the three alleged 'evil doers', that portraited the three men in a more positive than negative way. Clifford also noted that all three were dead wool pickers and that business transactions between them and Foremen had been evidently in the former's favour. Clifford further reported that the only current complaints in York had been voiced by Foreman, who:

> was convicted on 23 July 1940 of supplying Liquor to Natives and fined £20.0.0 and costs, and at the time was a member of York Municipal Council and he was later defected and I feel sure he has no time for the local Police, ever since he was before the Court and his grievances are indirectly hitting at me.[45]

Bray advised Foreman that he did not think that his criticism was justified. Foreman was obviously not happy and replied for a final time, writing:

> you say my Statements have not been Confirmed, which is in substance designating me as a liar. I throw the Insinuation in your teeth and if you are inclined, come up and say it to my face. If your department have made up your minds to continue your bungling methods (and everybody knows they are) and not prepared to be helped by friendly facts that is your business. I regret very much you have adopted the attitude you have …[46]

One should keep in mind that Foreman was not just an isolated individual with a personal grievance but, as a former member of the municipal council, counting, in total, some thirty-one years' involvement with York's civic matters, including five terms as elected mayor, he appeared to have wielded influence on the public discourse in York.[47] Therefore, it seems not unlikely that his strong opinions and alleged experiences with Aboriginal people in York shaped public opinion, at least to some extent. His influence was also evident in the example discussed above (see chapter 2.01), when Foreman was campaigning for York to become a rationing station and was able to obtain 330 signatures in 1932 for his petition. This was, at the time, ten per cent of the entire district's population and twenty per cent of the population within the municipality.[48]

3.04 Curfew

Most towns in the South West Land Division had, at some stage, an effective curfew whereby Aboriginal people had to be out of town by 'sunset' or sometimes, more precisely, by 6 pm or 7 pm.[49] Legally, under section 41 of the *Native Administration Act 1941*, any police officer or justice of the peace was able to order Aboriginal people out of a town or municipal district if they were deemed to be 'loitering'. This section of the legislation was in force from 1906 until 1955, and it was readily applied to anyone in town after working hours when it suited police or local authorities.[50] However, enforcement of such curfews under these sections of the Act also depended on the local police's eagerness to do so. While it is quite possible that curfews were imposed in York during the 1920s and 1930s, there is no evidence to this effect in the records available to this author. If curfews had been imposed in York during the two preceding decades, these were likely not permanently enforced, because in March 1942, an Aboriginal woman wrote a letter to the police complaining that a curfew had been recently imposed. This woman had originally come from Narrogin and moved to York when marrying a local man; therefore, she may not have been aware of earlier curfews imposed:

> I am writing you this letter to ask you whether you gave the York Police permission to send the native out at six o'clock and to call them black bastard. Constable Page the one was using the word. We can't get no store when we come from work and we can't walk down the street without. Please do something about it.[51]

Constable W.J. Page and his senior officer, Sergeant Clifford, were questioned in relation to the allegations. Constable Page stated that he had 'been ordering the natives out of the York Township after 6 pm unless they were going to the Pictures and then they have been allowed to remain near the Picture Hall'[52]—which was done under the instruction of Clifford. Unsurprisingly, on public record, Page vehemently denied having called any Aboriginal persons black bastards. Clifford confirmed that he had given orders for the enforcement of a curfew, adding that they had 'had a lot of troubles with natives getting liquor and several natives complained to me about not being able to get their stores by 6 pm'.[53] Clifford continued, alleging that the complaints about not getting stores were due to two individuals who had been in town on a particular day for the whole afternoon, and had only placed their orders at 5 pm. Apparently, this was unreasonably late and, therefore, Clifford argued, it was their fault if they could not collect their stores on time before being ordered out of town. Further, Clifford ensured that he had never heard any complaints about Constable Page's conduct. Commissioner Bray approved of the action being taken and this was the end of the matter.[54]

3.05 A new presence in town—Aboriginal town dwellers

Mid-twentieth century Western Australian law did not outright prevent Aboriginal people from living in a rental house or purchasing their own house or farm; however, as it was often the case, legislation was also in this regard conditional. Under the *Native Administration Act 1941*, any Aboriginal person who was not deemed 'full blood' and did not live in the manner of 'traditional full blood inhabitants or their full blood descendants' could legally rent any home without applying for a permit through the Department of Native Affairs or its local representative.[55] Various records with census data suggest that from the mid-1930s, the majority of Aboriginal people counted in York were deemed to be of mixed descent and, therefore, were legally able to rent houses without seeking departmental approval.[56] While legally entitled to do so, Aboriginal people in the South West Land Division during the early 1940s did not often rent (and even less so buy) a conventional house. Even if they wished to live within towns, the financial situation of many Aboriginal people, on one hand, and the general unwillingness of settler-Australian home owners to lease their property to Aboriginal people on the other, provided for limited opportunities. Further, under the *Land Act 1933*, Aboriginal people of any descent were legally able to purchase crown land not exceeding 200 acres; but, yet again, this was not often a feasible option in the early 1940s due to financially and socially inhibitive factors.[57]

Until this point in time, during the period under review in this book, any families of Aboriginal descent that may have lived in town had most likely done so without constituting an Aboriginal presence. They would have kept to themselves or were perhaps not affected by the *Native Administration Act* due to their degree of ancestry. Single Aboriginal women may have also lived in town throughout the period, working as 'domestics' in private households, but these, too, would not have been perceived as an alien presence as they were kept under tight white control. Nevertheless, by February 1943, it had come to the attention of York's municipal council that two houses in town, which were located on Newcastle Street and Panmure Road, had been occupied by Aboriginal families. Councillor Albert F. Noonan brought up the matter and claimed that 'several complaints had been made with regard to their behaviour in houses which they occupied and which were definitely overcrowded', and he demanded that 'necessary drastic action be taken'.[58]

Councillors J.H. Prunster and Fred Ashbolt suggested that the health inspector should undertake an inspection of the homes. The local health inspector, J.A. Wyss, accompanied by a police officer, went to the two houses twice within a week to check on the number of persons sleeping at the homes and to survey the state of the houses. On the second occasion, they attended in the middle of the night at 1am. Such overzealous effort, outside ordinary working hours, strongly suggests that the aim of this inspection was to find something that would have breached local by-laws or other legislation such as the *Native Administration Act*. By attending at night time, the inspector could be sure they would meet everyone who was currently staying at the house, some of whom may have been absent during a daytime inspection. The two homes were deemed overcrowded on both occasions and it was decided that the occupants would 'be written to stating that overcrowding will not be permitted and regular inspection of the premises will be made'.[59]

Other than overcrowding, the newspaper had nothing to report on the 'behaviour' of the occupants. It appears that the council chose to persecute Aboriginal people who dared to move into town and it did so through the local by-laws in relation to overcrowding, as there were seemingly no other means to take 'drastic action' as requested by Noonan. Of course, overcrowding is certainly not desirable from health and social perspectives. Overcrowded homes are also likely noisier than homes with fewer occupants, and may cause friction in any neighbourhood where this is the case. Overcrowding was often the result of seasonal transience or the general lack of a permanent place of abode, which affected many Aboriginal people who would move from place to place, staying with extended family members, *here and there*, to survive. Perhaps some of the visitors showed little consideration for the neighbourhood; however, this would have been at least partially a reflection of the century-long Aboriginal experience with the racist attitudes and policies of settler-Australians.

Around the time of the inspection of the two houses, Councillor Christina Foreman (Charles A. Foreman's wife, herself one of the first female municipal councillors in Western Australia, elected once in 1935 for one term and then again elected councillor from 1940 to 1951[60]) moved during the municipal council meeting on 16 March 1943 that the Country Municipal Council Association be approached to ask the state government to 'provide decent housing accommodation for all natives on native reserves adjacent to the towns, where they congregate and remain for any length of time, and that strict supervision be exercised by local governing authorities to prevent overcrowding'.[61] Given that this request was voiced at the same time as when the two houses occupied by Aboriginal people were publicly identified as problematic, it does not appear unlikely that Christina Foreman asked for improved housing on the reserve with a view to having all Aboriginal people who were not deemed to be the main occupants at the two houses in town shifted to the reserve. In this way, they would be segregated and controlled.

The public eye would continue to check on Aboriginal residences in town. In February 1944, the council discussed an apparent increase of the Aboriginal population in the York District as Aboriginal people were seemingly 'coming from miles around to take up residence in York'. Councillor J.H. Prunster 'felt strongly on the question and said that it appeared to him that they were allowed to camp anywhere without any thought of sanitary conveniences and were a menace to the health of

47

town'.[62] On this occasion, Councillor James Francis Harman criticised settler-Australians who rented homes to Aboriginal people and made particular reference to the house on Newcastle Street, as reported in the *York Chronicle*:

> The position was steadily getting worse and he condemned the practice of house-owners renting houses to them. Just recently a family of them had taken up residence in a house owned by Mrs. Rich, which was in need of repair, and he thought that the person responsible for the renting of this house was deserving of severe censor.[63]

There is no clear evidence as to why the owner of the property seemingly had no issues renting their house to an Aboriginal family, while the local representatives of York voiced their objections in no uncertain terms. However, Mrs Pearl Rich and her late husband Samuel had been, among other professions, skin, wool and mallee-bark dealers since at least 1906. As mentioned above, in 1941, Charles Foreman had complained about a competing buyer whom he referred to as a 'Jew'. As the Rich family happened to be of Jewish background, it is not unlikely that they were the alleged competing buyer referred to by Foreman. Therefore, it appears reasonable to conclude that Mrs and Mr Rich would have had, over the years, frequent contact with Aboriginal people, buying from them skins and dead wool, as well as mallee bark in the earlier decades. Consequently, it does not seem farfetched that the Richs may have developed somewhat friendly relationships with certain Aboriginal people in town, which may have resulted in Mrs Rich not being part of the strictly segregationist faction of town folk.[64]

It should also be noted, however, that Mrs Rich left York in July 1941, moving to South Perth after the passing of her husband. She must have been keen to rent out the property on Newcastle Street, which was the former family home, as it was in need of repair and attracted costs through being unoccupied. In March 1942, Mrs Rich had requested to have her rates reduced, given that the residence was vacant at the time; however, her request was rejected and it can only be assumed that she was not too impressed with this decision.[65] This suggests that Mrs

Rich's motivation to rent out her former family home to an Aboriginal family may have been multi-faceted, given that she most certainly knew that it would likely upset quite a number of settler-Australians in York. Considering the opposition by the local authority, following a departmental patrol inspection in February 1944, acting Inspector Donegan reported that several houses in York were occupied by Aboriginal people and that he found these houses to be mostly tidy and clean.[66]

While the council was legally unable to prevent Aboriginal people from renting houses in town, the situation was different for people who lived in camps. In August 1944, it was reported that an Aboriginal family had 'camped in a double tent opposite Lee Ackman's garden, with water laid on and hessian conveniences' and it was 'decided that they be allowed to remain there temporarily'.[67] Lee Ackman was the trading name of the Chinese market gardeners and brothers, Ah Lee and Ah Quon, who had their property on Bland Road in the north-western part of town.[68]

As a general rule, across Australia, Chinese residents were not afforded the same regard as white Australians at the time and, similar to Aboriginal people, they had to prove their worthiness to be tolerated, if not accepted. As these Chinese brothers had been in trouble with the law several times, their social status was not well advanced. This may have influenced the decision to allow this particular Aboriginal family to remain opposite the Chinese market gardens, because even if Ah Lee and Ah Quon had had objections, their opinions would likely not have counted much anyway. Further, this Aboriginal family lived in a tent, which was seemingly better regarded by the local authority than a camp made of corrugated iron and hessian bags. A month later, the York Chronicle reported that Aboriginal people 'had erected three camps on land owned by Miss Kindelan and that they proposed buying the land'.[69] The article stated that they 'were advised that Council would not permit camps being erected in the municipality and they have decided not to purchase and proceed to the reserve'.[70] The property in question was likely part of suburban town Lot 261, on the corner of Cowan and Hope Roads, opposite the municipal endowment block Lot 159, which had been a traditional camping ground, as discussed in the beginning of this book (see chapter 1.01). Rose Alvina Kindelan of Pool Street, who had lived in York for over eighty years, formally sold this block later, in August 1951, to an Aboriginal family.[71] However, it appears that an informal purchase had occurred earlier, as a patrol report by a Native Affairs officer in January 1950 stated that the same family lived in a camp on their own block at the very same location. The records do not indicate whether this was the same family as the one who wanted to purchase the block in 1944 and who were told they would not be permitted to erect camps.[72]

In early October 1944, the *York Chronicle* reported that a 'complaint had been received about the condition of the native camp at the Mile Pool' and that it was decided 'that the necessary action be taken to have them removed'.[73] While not stated explicitly, it seems very likely that this article was about the same family who had initially endeavoured to purchase the land they camped on, as Mile Pool was located in close proximity. In March 1945, Councillor Harman raised in the council meeting that 'a number of natives were camped near Monger's Bridge over the weekend' and it was decided 'that the police be asked to take action to have them removed'.[74] Later in the same year, W.J. Randell of Cowan Road was granted a request for 'permission to erect a fence around the small reserve adjoining his block to keep natives from his dwelling'.[75] These few examples suggest that council was quick to have any Aboriginal people removed who dared to put up camps in town, and prevented Aboriginal people from setting up camps in the first place within the municipal boundaries during this period. The situation would only slowly start to change during the 1950s; however, not without vocal opposition.

In June 1947, the rented residence in Newcastle Street was yet again discussed at the council meeting when Councillor Christina Foreman requested an inspection by the health inspector as she was of the understanding that 'between 40 and 50 natives congregated' at the house.[76] At the time, the town of York had just been declared a *prohibited area*, a designation that will be discussed in more detail below (see chapter 3.12). However, this was likely the reason for a heightened public interest in the presence of Aboriginal people within municipal boundaries. The health inspector reported no real concerns:

These premises were visited at 7 p.m. on Saturday, June 21 by myself and the local Protector of Natives. Six adults and three children were found in the house, which comprises three bedrooms and sleep-out, kitchen and dining room. A subsequent inspection was made in daylight on June 30. The house, although somewhat unsightly externally, appears to be quite dry and is kept reasonably clean. Instructions were given to provide a regulation refuse bin and it was ascertained that a bi-weekly pan service is being paid for. It was stated by the occupier that, although a number of friends and their children often visited them, they did not sleep there and the Sergeant of Police stated that he has had no complaints regarding them for some time.[77]

The above quote exemplifies that the council's hysteria appeared to be once again unwarranted. It may well have been the case that there were occasionally larger numbers of visitors who stayed for a few nights, which caused Councillor Foreman's source to raise the concern. However, it cannot be stressed enough that overcrowding was largely a reflection of draconian settler-Australian-imposed laws and socioeconomic exclusion. Even if there were settler-Australians willing to rent their homes to Aboriginal people, the seasonal nature of income fostered transience. Aboriginal people could not just erect camps in town. The only freely available place was the reserve outside of town, but if one had extended family living in a house, it would appear logical to go there as the first port of call. Further, being Aboriginal did not mean that one would automatically have good relations with every other Aboriginal person, which may have been a further consideration for some Aboriginal families and individuals who chose not to stay at the reserve if there was another option. Three months later, the home on Newcastle Street was once again visited by the health inspector who 'ordered to carry out a number of improvements' but otherwise did not note any concerns.[78]

3.06 Banned from the cinema

We are returning to early 1944, when the ability of Aboriginal people to take part in the public and social life of York was to be further curtailed. At first, this episode started similarly to 1942. On 3 March 1944, an Aboriginal woman residing in York wrote to Commissioner Bray, complaining that two weeks earlier, all Aboriginal people had been banned from attending the cinema. She asked for the commissioner's help to have the prohibition lifted and questioned the difference between 'white man and coloured' people, given that all paid taxes, and most were working under a union ticket; also, when going to the movies, people would not 'go hanging around looking for drink'.[79] Two weeks earlier, the council had decided to impose a 7 pm curfew. At the municipal council meeting, it was determined that York's Aboriginal population was growing, which was identified as problematic, and following a 'disturbance' on the previous weekend, it was agreed that certain control measures should be implemented.[80] The call for these measures implied that the 1942 curfew, discussed earlier (see chapter 3.04), had not been continuously enforced.

This apparent 'disturbance' resulted in an Aboriginal man being gaoled for offences that would not have applied to a non-Aboriginal person. The man was charged under the *Native Administration Act 1941* for 'receiving intoxicating liquor' and 'loitering' on Avon Terrace on Saturday 12 February. He seemingly did not agree with the application of the law specifically targeting Aboriginal people and was subsequently also convicted under the *Police Act 1892* for resisting Sergeant Clifford and Constable Vinicombe in the execution of their duty. How this act of 'resistance' took shape is not known but, given that there were no associated assault charges, it appears likely that there was no violence committed by the accused. He pleaded guilty to the first two charges but maintained a plea of not guilty in relation to the third charge. He was sentenced to fines totalling £12, which were immediately defaulted to thirty-six days of imprisonment in the York Gaol, as he was either unable or refused to pay. This Aboriginal man was in the company of an Aboriginal co-accused, who was not deemed Aboriginal 'in-law'. The co-accused was fined under the *Police Act*

1892 for being 'drunk' and was charged with the same 'resisting execution of duty' charge as the legally Aboriginal man; however, the Aboriginal man who was deemed non-Aboriginal in-law received fines totalling only £3, which he paid within a week. It appears likely that the legally non-Aboriginal man was only arrested due to his association with the legally Aboriginal person. Whether or not the men had caused a scene in front of the town hall, which may have attracted police attendance, or whether they were picked on by overzealous police officers is not indicated in the court records. What is a fact, though, is that the legally Aboriginal man spent over a month in a small cell, basically for being Aboriginal. Both men were sentenced by Justice of the Peace and Councillor A.F. Noonan only. The *Native Administration Act 1941* generally required either a magistrate or two justices of the peace for making legal decisions because justices of the peace did not necessarily have to have a legal background (Noonan worked with cars; he owned 'Noonan's Garage') but a legal provision allowed for a single justice of the peace under certain circumstances.[81] Notwithstanding that the alleged disturbers had already been punished on a personal level, York's municipal council cried for more preventative summary action to be taken against the collective Aboriginal 'other'.

The *York Chronicle* reported that Councillor (and Justice of the Peace) Noonan 'considered that the Government was not making adequate provision for the control of the natives and it was a problem that, sooner or later, would have to be tackled. Other adjacent towns were imposing restrictions upon them and York would have to do likewise'.[82] Councillors Henry Gordon Wake, H.J. Prunster and F. Ashbolt agreed that some action should be taken and Councillor Harman proposed a 6 pm curfew. Mayor A. Thorn weighed in that 'there were some respectable and very capable families of natives living here and he felt that some consideration should be shown to them'.[83] Councillor Christina Foreman also voiced concerns that a 6 pm curfew would be too harsh as some Aboriginal people 'were unable to procure their stores until last thing'.[84] Eventually, a 7 pm curfew was agreed to, and that the local protector would be able to issue permits where he considered warranted.[85] In the following week, acting Inspector Donegan of the Department of Native Affairs visited York on a Tuesday and the local newspaper reported a few days later that it had become apparent that the curfew could not be enforced until such time it was gazetted a by-law.[86]

Coincidentally, on the same day of the inspector's visit, the cinema proprietor of the local picture shows banned Aboriginal people from attending the pictures.[87] It seemed that if the curfew could not be enforced instantly, at least the picture show proprietor, Mr Clarence 'Paddy' Baker, was able to ensure that incentives for Aboriginal people to stay late in town were severely diminished. Mr Baker did not live locally but used to travel across the South West Land Division, showing pictures in various country towns. Between 1931 and 1956, he travelled to York twice a week to show 'Baker's Talkies', and after a break of a couple of years, he continued to show pictures at York at least until mid-1959.[88] It is not known to this author whether he conspired with those townspeople who wished to have a curfew imposed or whether he made the decision to ban Aboriginal people coincidentally, of his own volition, once council had formed the belief that a curfew could not be imposed for the time being. Nevertheless, Baker and some council members would surely have had some deep discussions about the affairs in town that also affected Baker. What is known is that he had discussed the matter with the local police.

The council was aiming for a permanent solution that would not depend on a police officer's eagerness to enforce a quasi-curfew: having to verbally order individuals out of town, which could be simply enforced through section 41 of the *Native Administration Act 1941*. A month after the newspaper reported the apparent by-law hurdle delaying the implementation of a curfew, local protector Sargeant Clifford reported to the Commissioner of Native Affairs that he did usually enforce a curfew: 'Natives are not permitted to be about streets of York after dark unless going to pictures, which I have never objected to'.[89] The records reveal that Clifford was seemingly also the person who instigated banning Aboriginal people from the pictures in the first place, albeit temporarily and not permanently. He had suggested to Baker that the measure be put in place for a few weeks to summarily punish alleged bad behaviour. On the other hand, Clifford commented that the disturbance discussed in the news article was nothing out of the ordinary for a country town and he had not personally received any 'inquiries' in relation to this matter. In later communication, Clifford admitted that the cinema management had received several complaints about the alleged poor hygiene of Aboriginal patrons and that this was the actual reason for banning Aboriginal people from the pictures. Clifford further noted that until putting the ban in place, York had remained the only country town in the wider region where Aboriginal people were allowed to attend the pictures, which had apparently caused an increase of the Aboriginal population in York, through people both moving there and visiting on the weekends.[90]

Commissioner Bray replied to the Aboriginal woman's letter after he had commented to Clifford that she would likely have been banned from the pictures due to her own 'unsatisfactory behaviour'. He insinuated the same in his reply to the woman in a most condescending tone but promised he would investigate the matter.[91] Then, on 27 March, Bray wrote a further letter in reply:

Dear Madam,

Further to my letter of the 15th inst. [this month], I have since made inquiries about the attendance of natives at the Picture Shows and have ascertained that the Management decided to exclude natives because of complaints about the lack of cleanliness on the part of some natives. It also appears that natives were congregating at York, especially for the purpose of attending the Picture Shows, and since some of them obtained drink and misbehaved themselves, it became necessary for the local Protector to stop them from entering York in the hours of darkness.

This is regrettable, but there have been various complaints about the large numbers of natives at York, and as the Hon. Minister personally saw numerous natives at the local camp over one weekend and directed me that they were to be dispersed to employment, I agree with the action taken at York to control the situation.

However, I am discussing the matter further with the local Protector and quite possibly some arrangements will be reached for those natives who were clean and well behaved to attend the Picture Shows.[92]

From a twenty-first century perspective, it appears incomprehensible how Commissioner Bray could have possibly thought that his letter constituted a satisfying answer. The way it is written suggests that Bray sought the recipient's understanding for the present situation, aiming at an unspoken 'fair enough' response. To have reserve dwellers 'dispersed to employment' is a comment that had elevated significance during the war years, when certain measures were put in place pertaining to Aboriginal rural labour, which we will discuss further below (see chapter 3.08). Bray and Sergeant Clifford then arranged for a pass system to come into effect which would allow 'deserving' Aboriginal individuals to enter York in the evenings and thus enable them to attend the pictures. For this to occur, Bray had thirty blank passes sent to York. However, as reported by Clifford, the cinema proprietor, Mr Baker, did not agree with the proposal and wished to keep the total ban in place. The Aboriginal woman wrote a further letter to Bray after Clifford had told her the news that the pass system would not work. Within this letter, she questioned:

> Why should we be punished for the bad one. We live a clean and respectable life and are capable of living as any white person so what's the difference about pictures. You can come up and see for yourself. As for Sergeant Clifford, I think he is only one side affair.[93]

The 'difference' was clearly a matter of race. As for Clifford, it is difficult to gauge his intentions and how much he may have weighed in on Baker's decision to implement an outright ban, as Baker's own intentions were only indirectly communicated through Clifford. There is no direct correspondence with Baker in any of the records available. Whatever Clifford's stance was, his successor, Sergeant W.G. McGuigan, would later report Baker to have held the same sentiments.

In late March 1946, an Aboriginal woman living on the reserve wrote to Deputy Commissioner Charles Lewis McBeath, seeking permission to attend the picture shows, questioning why all Aboriginal people in York were punished 'on account of a couple of foolish natives around here'.[94] McBeath, who was not familiar with the situation, therefore contacted McGuigan and advised that he would have no objections if Aboriginal people were admitted to the pictures one night a week. McGuigan was now local protector in York and he replied in April 1946:

> Approximately 12 months ago a disturbance took place amongst a large number of natives attending the picture gardens adjoining the York Town Hall. As a result of which, several natives were arrested & convicted for disorderly behaviour. This occurrence really provided the management with an excuse to refuse admission to any of the natives, as patrons had been complaining over a period of years regarding the filthy habits, and general bad behaviour of natives attending the show – especially the children. ... Mr. Baker is the proprietor, with whom I have had many interviews concerning this subject, and he has always expressed himself averse to admitting natives; more particularly at the present time, as the hall is usually filled to capacity without the natives.[95]

It appears that McGuigan's information was not entirely correct in some points and inflated in others. The disturbance he referred to would have been the incident of February 1944, two years earlier, as discussed above (within this chapter), and there were only two Aboriginal persons convicted. There were no other incidents recorded in the York police charge books for this period that would match McGuigan's claim.[96] Even more intriguing is the comment about the hall being at capacity now in 1946. Seemingly, Baker was more inclined to tolerate Aboriginal people, whom he reportedly did not want, at times when they provided a probably much-needed cash infusion. In 1944, World War II was still raging and settler-Australians from the York District were serving in the war effort in some way or another, some of whom would have otherwise been attending the picture shows. By 1946, many had returned home and were seemingly also attending the pictures, which meant that Baker no longer needed Aboriginal customers' money to survive.

At a municipal council meeting on 3 June 1947, Councillor Christina Foreman argued that Aboriginal people should be allowed to attend pictures on Tuesdays 'and that a special section should be set aside for them'.[97] During a visit of the Minister for Native Affairs to York in October 1947, Foreman reiterated her position by voicing the 'opinion that the natives should be permitted to attend the pictures provided they were kept in a separate section of the hall. This would be part of their education. If given the chance, the natives would become good citizens in the year to come'.[98] The records available do not reveal when the ban on Aboriginal people attending the picture show was exactly lifted but this was likely at some point during the 1950s. However, the spatial segregation in cinemas, as suggested by Foreman, occurred later, informally, and remained an unwritten 'given' well into the 1960s, as reported by anecdotal evidence: Aboriginal people would stay at the back.[99] From May 1948 until 1960, approximately forty-eight Aboriginal individuals obtained conditional citizenship when living in the York District, which would have made it increasingly difficult for the cinema proprietor to justify his outright ban.[100] Saul Yarran, who grew up in the York District, explained in the book *Us Fellas* that his parents obtained conditional citizenship to be able to attend the pictures, among other 'privileges' otherwise not accessible for Aboriginal people. Saul Yarran's father obtained conditional citizenship in 1951.[101] Conditional citizenship for Aboriginal people and 'exemptions' from the *Native Administration Act* will be discussed in more depth further below (see chapter 5).

It is not unlikely that the personal hygiene of some individuals may indeed have been relatively poor, which could have been unpleasant in a closed room ('Baker's Talkies' were held both in the town hall and in the adjacent picture gardens[102]). Given that, for example, those people who lived on the reserve had, at the time, no access to ablutions or laundry facilities, it would have been quite difficult to keep up with settler-Australian expectations of hygiene. That the alleged ongoing bad behaviour prior to the ban was mentioned for the first time two years after the ban had been implemented poses the question as to why it was not raised earlier, and whether, with time, memories had become somewhat distorted and inflated. Nevertheless, the outright ban of all Aboriginal people, and the lack of willingness to admit those individuals who were identified as conforming with settler-Australian standards and expectations of cleanliness and behaviour, strongly suggests that it was about more than these trivialities. The banning of all Aboriginal people from the picture show was very likely based on a racist belief system that justified the summary exclusion of an entire population group. Officially, council members did not request the pictures embargo as a way to have the intended curfew enforced, once they had formed the belief that a change of by-laws was required for the enforcement of the curfew (amending the by-laws was not brought up again, which suggests that Inspector Donegan had erred in relation to by-laws). However, there is also no indication that anyone openly objected to the exclusion of Aboriginal people from the picture show at the time when the ban was introduced by Mr Baker.

3.07 Segregated public toilets

The council's segregationist attitudes are also evident in a separate matter that commenced simultaneously in 1944. On 31 March, York's Health Committee—consisting of councillors Fred Ashbolt, Christina Foreman (who had actually left the impression on Inspector Donegan that she was more in sympathy with Aboriginal people than other people he had spoken with in town and that she appeared not to be 'bothered' by the local Aboriginal presence[103]) and H.G. Wake—produced a report about some much-desired public toilets in York's town centre. The committee tabled a building proposal to council, which was adopted by the same and included separate toilets for Aboriginal people. The council approved the proposal unanimously.[104] Fortunately, these segregated 'public conveniences' were never built as originally intended. York would have had segregated public toilets with three single standing blocks for 'Ladies', 'Gents' and 'Natives', had they been built in 1944 as planned. However, the public toilet proposal took until 1951 to be realised and, by that time, segregated toilets were not mentioned anymore. The delay in building the toilets was caused by ongoing administrative and fiscal issues and was not related to the segregationist nature of the original plan. In August 1947, Councillor Foreman was still arguing that segregated toilets would be necessary but this was unsurprising as York had just been declared a 'prohibited area' for Aboriginal people, which will be explored in further detail below (see chapter 3.11-14).

In March 1949, the town clerk, Leslie George Baker, approached the Department of Native Affairs asking whether it would be prepared to provide financial assistance for the erection of separate conveniences for Aboriginal people as part of the proposed public toilets project. A few days later, the town clerk wrote another letter, advising that the erection of public toilets would be further delayed and the department was asked to consider erecting purpose-built conveniences for Aboriginal people in the townsite. Following a discussion in April with Town Clerk Baker and his health inspector, the departmental Acting Inspector Hawke reported that council was hoping that the department could erect a sanitary convenience for Aboriginal people at Avon Park 'as the one already provided there had been taken over by the natives to the exclusion of the white community'.[105] It is not clear what Baker meant exactly by 'taken over' but it is worth mentioning that the council decided in September 1945 to have the then apparently not working conveniences at Avon Park repaired so Aboriginal people could use them and be simultaneously prohibited from using the toilets in the town hall.[106] Returning to 1949, while the department had seemingly no problem with the idea of segregated toilets, it rejected the request to contribute financially by providing a somewhat paradoxical reason for its decision. It was reported that:

> Mr. Baker was informed that the department considered this more a responsibility of the Council, by reason of the fact that the natives were part of the community. Some were rate payers and all contributed towards trade in the area ... The department would look upon it as a commendable effort, were the Council to provide facilities for the Natives in the town area, similar to that now in existence in Quairading.[107]

This was the end of the conversation and when the final plans of the public conveniences were agreed on in December 1949, segregated toilets were no longer included. This was apparently a result of monetary considerations combined with the fact that Aboriginal people's movements within the municipality were severely restricted at that point in time.[108]

3.08 Under constant scrutiny: World War II forced labour scheme and punishment by deportation

Leaving the issues with attending the pictures and segregated toilets aside, we continue in 1945, when the usual inspections and complaints by local authorities would, by mid-year, culminate in the deportation of some Aboriginal people to Carrolup Settlement. Returning from holidays, Sergeant Clifford inspected the reserve in mid-February and reported on its alleged current dirty state from a sanitary point of view. The weekly removal of night soil pans had been attended to since April 1944 by contractor Joseph O. Close for five shillings per week. However, reserve residents were still required to change the pans and leave full pans outside the toilets for the contractor to collect. Apparently, this did not occur regularly and the contractor also complained about the general dirty state of the pans. Sergeant Clifford's ad hoc solution for the unsatisfactory sanitary situation was an old-fashioned dispersal tactic, as per his own account: 'I have hunted a lot away from reserve leaving at present about five families'.[109]

Less than a month later, the York Road Board was exercising its complaint muscles. First, the road board approached parliamentarian Charles Collier Perkins, who was Member of Western Australia's Legislative Assembly (MLA) for the York electoral district from 1942 to 1950 (after 1950, York fell under the newly created electoral district of Avon Valley).[110] Perkins wrote to the Department of Native Affairs on 10 March 1945, suggesting that a departmental inspector visit the Aboriginal reserve at York due to numerous complaints that had allegedly been received, and he added that 'they are living under most primitive conditions & fouling the roads and also the river bed'.[111] Perkins further commented that he thought 'there must be a few bad natives there too' and he referred to a recent incident where an Aboriginal man allegedly attacked a farmer with an axe. Perkins wrote that this man 'living in Mrs. Swanson's property recently attacked the owner of the adjacent paddock. The gin was swinging an axe & I believe the situation was ugly for a while'.[112] 'Gin' is a derogative term that was usually used to refer to Aboriginal women. So, Perkins either confused his derogative terminology or he wanted to state that there was also an Aboriginal woman, swinging an axe.[113]

Either way, Perkins' hearsay story occurred somewhat differently. The *York Leader and Quairading and Dangin Herald* reported the incident, which occurred on 22 February, as it had been dealt with in the York Police Court on 9 March. An Aboriginal man and his wife were convicted of assaulting settler-Australian farmer Aloysius Joseph Taylor. The couple's son, who was initially charged with hitting Taylor with the back of an axe and who admitted to having used an axe handle, had his case dismissed. The accused's stories were markedly different to that of Taylor and his witness, James Fairhead. There was apparently either a dispute concerning Taylor's fence or killed livestock owned by Taylor. What actually happened will probably never be known, and there were allegations on both sides, but it is interesting to note that the newspaper sanitised the court proceedings, which were also recorded in the magistrate's evidence book. The news piece omitted that Taylor allegedly said to the Aboriginal man: 'I will screw your neck you black nigger' and also 'you black niggers I will shoot you' or 'you black bastards I will shoot you'[114] (depending on different witness statements).

Taylor claimed that the Aboriginal man allegedly called him a 'German bastard' without further explanation, which may have been just a generic insult without a deeper, personal meaning as World War II was still waging at the time. Alternatively, the insult may have inferred that Taylor was being racist, as news of German genocidal atrocities had already made their way to Western Australia by late 1944. Taylor's alleged insults were obviously more than just generic swear words as they conferred a much heavier and value-laden verbal assault on the status of Aboriginal people within white Australia. It was noted that any use of swearing was denied by all people concerned. Whatever occurred, there was no 'axe-swinging' Aboriginal person aiming at a settler-Australian farmer, as suggested by Perkins' letter. Hitting someone with an axe head or handle is not the same as aiming at someone with the sharp blade of an axe, ready to slaughter. Furthermore, the person who admitted to using the axe to aid his father had his charge dismissed and the two convictions concerning his parents only resulted in fines, which suggests that the judiciary did not consider this incident particularly serious. Additionally, in the period between being charged and being sentenced no accused persons were held in custody.[115]

Perkins himself lived in Bruce Rock at the time, which is just under 150 kilometres away from York and, therefore, he would have mainly relied on secondary accounts from road board members. He suggested to the Commissioner of Native Affairs that an inspector be sent to the reserve at York, citing experience from other places in his electorate where a visit by a departmental officer would usually be able to pacify disgruntled local authorities when paying a visit.[116] The road board also undertook to write the Department of Native Affairs directly, following the conviction of the Aboriginal couple, in relation to 'the unpleasant conditions existing at the native reserve on the upper Beverley road … and other matters connected with natives which required suitable action'.[117]

As per Perkins' indirect request, Commissioner Bray swiftly sent departmental Inspector J.H. Bisley to York, but he was only able to make it by April, the following month, due to staffing issues. After Bisley's visit, he reported that the reserve was fairly clean, except for a few rubbish heaps that needed to be buried. He found the conveniences to be in a 'filthy condition', organised a clean-up and warned all Aboriginal people present 'what would happen if they were found in this condition again'.[118] He also arranged for the stand pipe to be repaired, which was inflating costs due to a leak. Bisley further reported the alleged unsatisfactory conduct of the family that was involved in the above-mentioned incident (within this chapter) with farmer Taylor, and cited complaints by the townspeople and the road board. He strongly recommended that this family be removed to Carrolup, along with another family, a separate couple and an individual person.[119] One of the arguments for Bisley to recommend removal was that those families or individuals whom he identified for deportation were, at the time, apparently not working, despite there being no shortage of work according to the market gardeners and farmers with whom Bisley had spoken. These potential employers complained that they were unable to keep Aboriginal people longer than a few days. Bisley reported that he tried to explain to Aboriginal people on the reserve that it was important to display good and continuous work ethics, as work would be less easy to obtain once the war was over and employers would likely only employ those individuals who had proven themselves during the war years. Bisley was told that at the market gardens, one could earn between twelve and fifteen shillings per day.[120] Only a few months earlier, the weekly basic wage for a rural male worker in the South West Land Division was set to £5 0s 9d.[121] If we assume a six-day working week and multiply the maximum amount per day quoted by Bisley, which is fifteen shillings, then the weekly wage would have been £4 10s. This indicates underpayment, even with the highest rate quoted.

However, if employment was indeed not taken up eagerly as claimed by Bisley, the reasons for this would have likely been many-fold and not easily understood or accepted from a contemporary, often righteous, settler-Australian perspective. One should never forget the draconian laws that Aboriginal people were subjected to. Consequently, some families may have moved around in order not to be torn apart by the department. Some employers were probably also not treating Aboriginal people in a respectful manner, which may have led to some individuals choosing to engage in as little work as necessary, on a casual basis, sacrificing a higher income for more freedom from insulting conditions. In relation to weekly expenditures, the upside of living on reserves was that it did not require payments for rent. Additionally, as discussed above (see chapter 3.02), families would come to York from other districts for medical treatment or for a 'holiday', and some people may have only required a few days' work to get by, before returning to their main place of abode or moving on if they were transient. Aboriginal people would also likely have remembered that only a few years earlier, during the Great Depression and early war years, work was difficult to come by at all, and only now that there was a labour shortage due to the war were settler-Australians more inclined to employ Aboriginal people. This two-faced sudden demand for their labour would not have escaped Aboriginal people's attention, which may have resulted in some individuals' cynicism limiting their enthusiasm to engage in employment on a regular basis. After all, for many Aboriginal people at the time, there was also no future to work towards; there was only today.

By late 1941, a serious shortage in rural labour became increasingly evident, and in response, the Department of Native Affairs openly voiced its intention to take a hard-line approach on Aboriginal people who it identified as not being regularly employed, regardless of individual circumstances. A new policy to this effect was rolled out by early 1942. When Commissioner Bray briefed his minister on the new policy in March 1942, he explained that the department had secured cooperation from the police to implement a system of forced labour, which entailed the deportation of all unemployed *detribalised* Aboriginal people to a settlement for 'disciplinary treatment'. These removals under ministerial warrant were already underway in March, and after completion of this 'treatment', these Aboriginal persons would be placed into rural employment under supervision. If their conduct was deemed unsatisfactory or they walked off their job, they would be immediately returned to a settlement for further 'disciplinary treatment'. Drawing an awkward but revealing comparison on the methods of the enemy in tones of admiration, Bray spoke with a sense of pride in relation to his own scheme:

> Elsewhere, except in Germany, I doubt whether methods such as these have been adopted in dealing with the forced labour of natives, and I am pleased to say that our instructions have already had a good effect in that our workable natives are now mostly employed.[122]

When circulars with instructions about this scheme were sent out to all local protectors, Sergeant Clifford at York reported in early April that all Aboriginal people were engaged in some sort of work but he ensured continuous observation of the situation.[123] The following year, Sergeant Clifford reported that Aboriginal people in York remained employed but many were engaged in the charcoal industry. During the progressing war years, Aboriginal people were only permitted to work in farming or pastoral jobs with very few exceptions. Being aware of this requirement, Clifford sought permission that local Aboriginal people be allowed to continue with employment in the charcoal industry. The request was granted, as Bray considered that burning charcoal was in the interest of the national war effort because it ensured an ongoing supply of fuel to the commercial transport system.[124]

The main objective of this forced labour scheme was certainly to ensure the ongoing supply of labour for the rural industries. However, this form of population control also served another purpose. In May 1942, the Kojonup District Road Board expressed concerns in relation to Aboriginal people's behaviour towards settler-Australians in the event of a Japanese invasion and the board suggested that Aboriginal people should either frequently report to police stations or be enrolled in some form of national service, such as the Voluntary Defence Corps or Labour Corps, to exert an increased degree of control. Bray pointed out that this was a matter for the military forces but his reply did suggest that he took the concerns seriously, stating that he thought that a 'round-up of natives in the district' was a good idea, and he advised that he would make some inquiries.[125]

Mandated enrolment into some form of national service did not eventuate; however, Bray's inquiries appear to have set in motion considerations at the Perth headquarters of the Australian Military Forces that resulted in imposing severe restrictions on the movements of Aboriginal people from Northampton, north of Geraldton, up to just north of Perth, along the coast and between fifty and 100 miles inland. These restrictions affected all Aboriginal people within this area who looked at least somewhat 'coloured', regardless of whether they fell under Western Australia's *Native Administration Act 1942*. York was seemingly not affected by this particular policy; however, Aboriginal people living in York who had relations in the affected area, for example, at the Moore River Native Settlement or the New Norcia Mission, were unable to visit them and vice versa. The most severe restrictions were lifted in August 1943 but in the case of enemy landfall, all Aboriginal people in this area (then extended to just south of Perth) were to be rounded up and deported some 800 kilometres north-east of Perth to the small town of Malcolm in the Goldfields region.[126]

Initially, it appears that Bray regretted having made his inquiry and he indicated in an internal memorandum that he thought the military went too far:

> I do not think the half-caste would let us down, but possibly he would be more enthusiastic to our cause if we treated him as a human being. Treat a man as a dog and he might act as a dog. Allegedly there have been mutterings of discontent against the restrictions, but the half-caste has nothing in common with the Japanese, and in my opinion they are not likely to help them.[127]

Bray further expressed that he thought it was unfair on most Aboriginal people affected, especially if they were already engaged in regular employment, and he also expressed the fear that these measures might have the long-term reverse effect of causing unrest and driving Aboriginal people, who would have otherwise been loyal to white Australia, to support the enemy. Farmers in the affected areas were reportedly rather in favour of these harsh restrictions, as they ensured that Aboriginal employees were unable to walk off their place of employment without being 'hunted down' by military forces, which guaranteed the farmers a reliable supply of labour for that period. The potential unrest that Bray had warned about did not eventuate.[128]

The initial request by the Kojonup District Road Board and the way it resonated with military personnel, who were largely locals, does reveal the extent of anxiety among parts of the settler population, which was likely representative of many settler-Australians in the South West Land Division, if not the whole of the state. That the Aboriginal population in general was deemed a potential enemy collaborator is indicative of settler-Australian awareness of the ongoing injustices it had been imposing on Aboriginal people in Western Australia—at the time, for over 100 years. Social and physical exclusion, unwarranted incarceration, racial vilification, sexual abuse, murder and displacement tended to be omitted from the collective memory of the state's settler history—though, unsurprisingly, a proportion of the settler-Australian conscience appeared to have become suddenly painfully aware of these previously 'forgotten' memories in the face of a potential enemy landfall. This was evident to Bray himself and he discussed it with his minister, though his arguments were based only on economic exclusion and exploitation.[129]

For departmental staff, these severe Commonwealth-imposed measures may have assisted in normalising the marginally less severe departmental policy of its forced labour scheme and the subsequent removal in case of non-compliance with the same. That an Aboriginal uprising against the Commonwealth military orders did not occur would have also encouraged the department, as this suggested that the Department of Native Affairs would be able to implement its own similar policy without great difficulties. This 'normalisation' effect meant that what were first considered extraordinary measures during war times turned into justifiable practices during times of peace, which was also evident in York.

In York, the war-related forced labour scheme was only implemented from 1945, owing to the previous relatively positive reports about Aboriginal employment in the district. However, due to the aforementioned complaint (within this chapter) to Perkins in the same year, and Bisley's subsequent patrol report, the forced labour and deportation scheme was to be executed now, somewhat belatedly. Nevertheless, as we will see, the assessment criteria identifying liability for 'disciplinary treatment' were altered to justify the use of this scheme in a post-war society. As World War II was seemingly drawing to a close, Commissioner Bray's focus for using coercive means appeared to have shifted from war-related labour concerns to behaviour-corrective population control. For example, on 13 July, it was reported in the local newspaper that the Country Municipal Councils Association had circulated a letter from Commissioner Bray who advised that 'if natives were indolent, cheeky, insolent, and a source of annoyance to residents he would make enquiries and take suitable action'.[130] It is not difficult to see how this letter would have encouraged holders of negative sentiments towards Aboriginal people to report alleged unsatisfactory conduct in town. However, in reply to a letter by the District War Agricultural Committee, who suggested that efforts be made so that

Aboriginal people could be better employed in Northam, York and surrounding districts, Commissioner Bray advised he would work closely with police but also cautioned that an Aboriginal presence in towns did not necessarily indicate unemployment.[131] On 4 July, Bray then wrote to the Commissioner of Police, acknowledging that there may be some instances of unemployment and loitering in those districts but he also remarked that:

> the presence of natives about towns is not always a sure indication of their employment. Quite a number of natives congregate about towns for the long weekends in social community with their friends, and often, too, they come into towns for the purpose of doing business and purchasing stores. Sometimes, too, they enjoy a few days' respite on the same lines as white people who often take holidays; therefore, the presence of natives about towns should not be taken invariably as proof that they are unemployed.[132]

Beside employment and general conduct, the new, though interlinked, reason to recommend people for removal to a settlement was now the alleged misuse of social benefits payments for children.[133] In 1941, the federal government introduced *child endowment*, which was the first nation-wide and non-means-tested social security payment for parents and institutions with children in their care. Aboriginal families were entitled to such payments under the provision that 'they were living under conditions comparable to those of normal people in Australia, and where the habits of the person maintaining the children are not nomadic'.[134] While it was generally commented that since introducing these payments, the situation of Aboriginal children had immensely improved, observers (qualified and otherwise) also noted that some Aboriginal families were not spending the endowments for the benefit of their children. In 1942, Bray already stated that the misspending of child endowment money was not peculiar to Aboriginal people but he voiced the belief that about seventy per cent of Aboriginal parents misspent their endowment monies and should be supervised.[135] By late 1945, a system was introduced that enabled the Department of Native

Affairs to control the release of the entitlements through a trust fund when the department believed that a 'mother' was misusing the benefits. If this was deemed to be the case, cash payments were replaced by orders on local store keepers, who had a list of prohibited items they were not allowed to hand out, which included 'face powder, ice cream, adult clothing and various luxury items'.[136]

Such was the focus on child endowments during 1944–1945 that Bisley reported separately on every family's handling of these payments during his inspection and made recommendations on each.[137] While there was also public critique of some settler-Australians' use of child endowment monies, Aboriginal Australians were seemingly in the firing line of public scrutiny due to their fragile existence at the real and imagined fringes of white Australian society.[138] This public outcry went to such extremes as those expressed by Narrogin's branch of the Country Women's Association, who suggested in September 1944 that all child endowment monies for Aboriginal people should be withheld to finance segregated schools and hospital wards.[139] Just a month earlier, the editor of the *Narrogin Observer* alleged in a nasty reply to a letter to the editor by Isabel McBeath (who had criticised white Australia's regard of Aboriginal people) that Aboriginal people engaged in promiscuous breeding schemes to secure child endowment monies.[140] At the time of Bisley's investigation, national child endowment had just been increased from five shillings per child per week to seven shillings and six pence per week per child.[141] For example, a family with five children eligible for child endowments would have received £1 15s 30d (decimalised: £1.77) per week. This kind of payment would have been a nice bonus but would not necessarily have been able to make up for all expenditures required for the family. It took a few years, to the beginning of the next decade, for departmental officers to catch up on this fact.[142]

It may well have been the case that some Aboriginal parents in York and elsewhere spent their children's endowment payments in ways for which they were not intended; and if this was the case, this would have been for various reasons. Whether justifiable or not, they do not need to be scrutinised here, particularly because although some settler-Australian parents misspent their endowments, there was no government department that monitored all white Australian families by default to ensure that child endowment payments were spent appropriately. What should indeed be scrutinised is the Department of Native Affairs' conclusion on how to address the alleged misuse. On 15 June 1945, in relation to York, Deputy Commissioner McBeath wrote to Inspector Bisley at Carrolup that:

> In most cases your recommendations have been adopted and natives either warned regarding their unsatisfactory conduct or warrants taken out for removal to a Departmental Institution for disciplinary detention.[143]

Disciplinary detention was now the department's way of addressing the alleged misuse of child endowment payments, irrespective of parents' budgeting skills and abilities. It seems that this harsh punishment aimed at Aboriginal people was not so much imposed because they did not spend the money on their children but for *misusing* a privilege that was only to be had by *deserving* Aboriginal people who lived like 'normal' Australians, as hinted at in the above-cited eligibility criteria. Arguably, the Department of Native Affairs would not have been able to justify such drastic measures in relation to child endowment payments had it not been for the World War II forced labour scheme that opened up such opportunity.

In early July 1945, the local protector, Sergeant McGuigan, acknowledged receipt of twelve warrants that had been issued for deportation to Carrolup. However, McGuigan was unable to execute the warrants by himself as he was not able to transport all these people by train. A plan was conceived that involved a former military truck that was yet to be commissioned to the Department of Native Affairs. The truck would be transporting stores from Perth to Carrolup and, on the way, it would collect Aboriginal people from York, as per the warrants, as well as 'any indigent natives that may be found at Beverley'.[144] It took until October for this to occur and, given that McGuigan advised that he was unable to accommodate these people in the York Gaol, at least one person escaped this destiny temporarily by simply moving on. It is not known whether this person was aware of the warrant, which was likely executed at some point in time somewhere in Western Australia. Generally, any kind of arrest warrants were distributed throughout the state to all police stations via the Western Australian *Police Gazette*. Subsequently, in the York Gaol, persons from other districts frequently 'did time' in relation to 'warrants of commitment' that had been issued in other districts. As the reasons for their incarceration usually did not relate to local matters and did not involve local court appearances, unless they were caught due to re-offending in York, the local newspapers did not tend to report their arrests and they did not feature in local crime statistics.[145]

On 15 October 1945, an Aboriginal woman living in town wrote to the commissioner complaining about the removals that had taken place. She questioned the rationale of taking women and their families away from their homes just to be sent 'to the Settlement just to live like Cattle and to live there in filth and dirt and scabys and lice that is not very nice after living a clean live'.[146] She also referred to the accusations of living in overcrowded houses and pointed out that Carrolup was just as overcrowded.[147] While overcrowding certainly occurred at Carrolup as well, the difference was that it was not located within a settler-Australian community, and therefore, there was no white public to take offence and demand that action be taken to ameliorate the situation. Out of white sight, out of white mind.

Commissioner Bray replied to the woman's letter by claiming that he had been reluctant to issue those warrants but he noted that it had been necessary, explaining that 'there is no doubt in my mind that the recent removal of certain natives from the district was justified because of their insanitary living conditions and because of the improper expenditure of Child Endowment moneys'.[148] He continued by indirectly threatening the author of the complaint letter when stating that there were 'still some families to be dealt with, and unless they improve their living conditions and spend their Child Endowment moneys for the welfare of their children, there will be no alternative but to consider the advisability of having them removed to the Carrolup Native Settlement'.[149] This threat was perhaps not necessarily directed at the author of the letter but Bray might have anticipated that word would go around. Bray did not mention unemployment or underemployment at all now in his reply letter, and neither in more recent communication concerning warrants for deportation, which may be an indicator that Inspector Bisley's assessment of the situation in April was not quite correct. However, Bisley noted in a separate report in early November that most Aboriginal men in the district were by then working on shearing (as mentioned briefly further above, labouring jobs available in the country were often seasonal with fluctuations of busy and idle periods throughout the year – see chapters 2.01 and 3.05). Bisley also noted that the sanitary conveniences on the reserve were 'exceptionally clean' when he visited.[150]

Having found the sanitary conveniences in an 'exceptionally clean' state must have confirmed the Department of Native Affairs' apparent conviction that all it took was a certain degree of coercion to enforce discipline and induce behavioural change. This is a prime example of this archaic way of thinking that, in a similar vein, tends to confuse respect with fear by trying to gain the former through coercion and discipline, but only gains the latter while fostering contempt in return. Grown contempt was clearly evident in a reserve dwellers' alleged verbal abuse when police attended the reserve in August 1948, looking for a young Aboriginal woman for whom they had an arrest warrant due to some broken windows in town. Referring to the settler-Australian obsession with the state of the sanitary conveniences on the reserve, the mother of the young woman for whom the police were looking reportedly greeted the officers by suggesting that Seargent Meyer should check the toilets, and she reportedly also expressed the hope that he may fall into those toilets. This woman was charged with being disorderly on the native reserve due to an alleged fifteen-to-twenty minutes' verbal abuse towards the police—an allegation that she vehemently denied in court. If the mother was indeed in a heightened emotional state, it would not have been surprising, given that police were looking for her daughter combined with the fact that police and departmental staff generally inspected the reserve at liberty to execute their repressive agendas, laden with self-righteous attitudes. According to the Aboriginal mother and another family member, police entered the reserve calling the inhabitants a 'bloody lot of bastards' or 'bloody bastards'.[151]

All three police witnesses (Seargent George E. Meyer, Constable George Royston Mitchell and Constable Arthur Percy Cole) denied any improper conduct by police and the police witnesses conveniently outnumbered the Aboriginal witnesses by three to two. The woman was found guilty and sentenced to a fine.[152] The sentencing *magistrates in lieu* were justices of the peace Albert Francis Noonan and Philip Maurice Aldworth Glass—the reader may wish to remember this duo for later. The young Aboriginal woman for whom the police were looking on the reserve (and who remained living in York) was never charged with any offences in the York Police Court over the next three decades.[153]

This is one of the few examples that suggest the attitude of police officers in their approach towards Aboriginal people. Usually, the records tend to provide certain causes of action taken by police or departmental staff in a rather clinical manner and we can only assume or imagine how personal interactions occurred. Similar to the axe incident, this case is able to shine some light on such interpersonal interactions in the context of the antecedents. Therefore, this example may further enhance appreciation for why some Aboriginal people, as stated by a Noongar personality, 'produced deep-seated resentment of authority' and turned 'aggressively antisocial or, if not that, apathetic'.[154] Observing from a different vantage point and claiming that he had gained an appreciation for the situation of Aboriginal people by studying personal files for several years since being in office, then Commissioner Middleton tentatively concluded in 1955 that if 'a trained psychiatrist were to check through the official sheaves of paper recording the lives of these unfortunate people it would be surprising if he did not marvel that so much injustice could result in so little violent reaction'.[155]

3.09 Going to school

In April 1946, the headmaster of York's public school, J.E. Deacon, wrote to the Department of Native Affairs reporting that there appeared to be a large number of Aboriginal children in York who were not attending school and he had received complaints about the 'mischief allegedly caused by them'.[156] While Commissioner Bray advised Deacon that action would be taken, he learned from departmental Inspector Bisley that there were currently a number of Aboriginal families visiting York to attend a funeral and some were also looking for employment; thus, Bray does not seem to have requested that further action be taken at this point.[157] Four months later, Deacon, speaking at the annual conference of the Western Australian State School Teacher's Union, was paraphrased in the *West Australian*. Although seemingly arguing from a rather inclusive point of view, Deacon criticised the poor attendance rate of Aboriginal children at the York school in alarmist terms, exaggerating population proportions and using words like 'swarms', feeding into the well-trodden siege narrative:

> He said that at York there were no more than six coloured children attending the school. Yet if one were to visit the town on a Saturday afternoon, the impression would be gathered that there were as many natives in the town as whites. Swarms of coloured youngsters were running round the streets and were not receiving any education at all. He considered that a more forthright educational policy should be adopted with the coloured children. The half-caste population appeared to be growing, and if the children were permitted to continue roaming the streets as they did now, then there would be serious trouble in a few years.[158]

As a matter of fact, that as many as six Aboriginal children were attending a public school in York was due to a relatively recent development. Up until the early 1940s, there was no clear policy or effort made by the Education Department that focussed on Aboriginal children. Mission schools and the two governmental institutions, Carrolup and Moore River, had been providing education outside the white Australian mainstream. The Education Department recorded 'coloured' children separately if they attended state schools but there was nothing in place to include Aboriginal children in mandated education. Simultaneously, some towns staged outright protests if the number of Aboriginal children attending school exceeded the carrying capacity of their white Australian imagination. The common critique was based on the claims that Aboriginal children were a bad influence on settler-Australian children and that they suffered of poor hygiene. The only obvious solution to those vocal sections of settler-Australians was either segregated teaching within schools or the total exclusion from state schools.[159] The *Education Act 1928* and preceding legislation did not discriminate in relation to Aboriginal children; however, a new clause in the Education Department's 'regulations' was introduced in April 1920 that allowed for Aboriginal children to be excluded from school if objections to their presence were raised by settler-Australian parents. The regulations stipulated that Aboriginal children 'may' be excluded, subject to approval by the Minister for Education. However, during a white public outcry at Wagin in 1933, it became clear that the Education Department was interpreting the discretionary clause as legally binding, until Premier Collier intervened and clarified the position. For the record, the local police officer and the headmaster in Wagin reported that some of the Aboriginal children who were to be excluded or segregated due to alleged habitual uncleanliness were cleaner than some white children.[160]

Nevertheless, some Aboriginal children did go to state schools at the time. In 1937, the Education Department recorded 409 'coloured' children attending state schools in Western Australia, less than one per cent of the average weekly enrolment rate of the state, which had 57,674 students. Out of this number of 'coloured' children, 380 children were listed as Aboriginal, nineteen as Chinese, one as Tongan, two as Indian, one as Japanese, one as 'Negro,' one as Eurasian and four as Māori. There were none recorded for the York District, none for Northam and Quairading or Beverley. A little further south along the train line, nine Aboriginal children attended school in Brookton and twelve in Pingelly. Simultaneously, it was estimated that approximately 1,000 Aboriginal children between Perth and Albany did not receive any education.[161]

However, basic education was provided in some places. According to anecdotal evidence, in York, during the 1920s and into the 1930s, basic schooling was provided in a tin shed at the Craigs' Mile Pool farm. The Craigs had allowed or even encouraged a Methodist teacher to conduct teaching lessons for a few hours three days per week. This arrangement had come about due to the Craigs employing Aboriginal people, some of whom lived on their property, after Lot 159 had been converted to municipal endowment land, as discussed at the beginning of this book (see chapter 1.01). During this period, there would have been no more than a 'handful' of children taught at any time, as suggested by the small Aboriginal population on official record. Further, the employment-related transience of most families frequenting York until the early 1930s meant that many children would not have had continuous education either. Reportedly, boys went to grade three, while girls had to leave after grade two and the education received was limited to learning the ABC and how to write and read their names. The owner of the Mile Pool farm, W.T. Craig, passed away in 1929 but his much younger wife, Louisa, continued to run the farm and employ Aboriginal people for up to thirty years thereafter. Therefore, it does not appear unlikely that Louisa Craig was the driving force behind this basic schooling arrangement during the 1920s and early 1930s.[162]

By 1940, the Departments of Education and Native Affairs were considering providing education to all Aboriginal children in the South West Land Division. A survey was conducted with information gathered by local protectors, which indicated that in the York District, only three children attended state school at Gwambygine, and that there were apparently no other school-aged children in the district requiring education. A family with children from the York Reserve was believed to have relocated to Beverley and another family staying in York with three school-aged children was believed to be only temporarily in the area. Both assumptions proved to be incorrect.[163]

By the end of 1941, compulsory school attendance for Aboriginal children was slowly being rolled out and, unsurprisingly, it was met with localised protests that were also supported by some members of Parliament. At least in relation to attending school, such public protests demanding exclusion or segregation did not appear to have occurred in York, which was likely a result of relatively low enrolments during the initial period; however, some individuals did express their personal dissatisfaction.[164] By late 1942, 500 Aboriginal children were attending state schools and, in the following year, the figure had risen to 700 children. Commissioner Bray observed that many parents appeared to believe that child endowment payments were tied to school attendance. This was not the case at the time but he had no intention of telling parents otherwise. However, if parents did not voluntarily send their children to school, non-compliance was added to the criteria for deportation to a settlement, as discussed further above (see chapter 3.08):

> If they live in camps on reserves near towns, and should their camps be unsatisfactory, or should they be poorly clad, or should their children fail to attend school, they are removed to settlements.[165]

On the other hand, the Education Department was still able to reject Aboriginal children if they were deemed 'habitually unclean or infected with disease'.[166] The above discussed Education Department regulations were amended in 1944 and now made specific reference to health and hygiene in relation to Aboriginal children. Non-Aboriginal children could be excluded from school for these reasons as well, but their exclusion could only be enforced temporarily, while Aboriginal children could be permanently excluded from school.[167] In a perverse twist, those Aboriginal families who sent their children to school but whose children were excluded under the regulations, were now also liable for deportation to a settlement, according to the Department of Native Affairs' policy of the 1940s.

By the end of the 1940s, public outcries about Aboriginal children attending state schools had largely ceased and the department turned its focus to the enforcement of school attendance, as absenteeism was very common. At this time, the department was ceasing the practice of removing whole families to settlements and reoccurring absenteeism was punished through the cancellation of child endowment payments once parents were taken to the Children's Court, which Commissioner Middleton found to be a 'very potent weapon'.[168] At a meeting in September 1949, which was attended by staff from both the Department of Native Affairs and the Education Department, absenteeism was discussed and it was agreed that better housing conditions would likely lead to better attendance rates, as better housing would provide for a more conducive learning environment. Another aspect came to light, which was arguably even more important. Many Aboriginal children reportedly left school early at eleven or twelve years of age, and the reason for doing so was identified to be the same as for general absenteeism: The majority of Aboriginal children did not see a future in which they could make use of their education and generally lacked education-based goals to strive for due to the 'wall of prejudice'[169] they faced. The headmaster of York's school, William Pirrett, was also present at this meeting and he discussed an Aboriginal girl from York, whom he had been trying to convince to carry on with her studies; he conceded that the only reason that she had not left school yet was her interest in sports. The Department of Native Welfare was seemingly aware that absenteeism could largely be explained by factors that needed to be addressed within settler-Australian society. Nevertheless, by the early 1950s, it collaborated with the Education Department, who took the lead in instigating the removal of children to institutions due to chronic non-attendance. It was still widely believed that force and coercion were justified means to an end to 'lift up' Aboriginal people despite their often-alleged *natural* disadvantage. Instead of educating settler-Australians on universal human rights, Aboriginal families were punished, torn apart and had trauma inflicted on them largely due to settler-Australian intolerance and ignorance.[170]

We now return to York in October 1946, two months after then Headmaster Deacon had spoken about 'swarms' of Aboriginal youngsters roaming the streets. When departmental Inspector Bisley called on the headmaster, he advised that the six Aboriginal children who were attending state school all attended clean and were improving their attendance. He did not add anything further to his earlier concerns, except for acknowledging that he would receive the Aboriginal students from the Gwambygine 'bush school' by the end of the year ahead of the school's upcoming closure. An interesting note about these small bush schools is that Aboriginal children were reportedly often rather welcome and did not face the same resistance from white parents. This was because such small schools often relied on the attending Aboriginal students to justify their ongoing viability.[171] While we have been discussing state schools so far, it should be noted that there was also a

79

Catholic convent school in York. Bisley called on Father O'Mahoney, who reported that all Aboriginal children attended neat and tidy but were not regular in their attendance; however, O'Mahoney requested that the department did not intervene as he was making weekly visits to the parents of his enrolled students. As to Headmaster Deacon and the question of why he had no further complaints to discuss, one possible reason may be that, recently, a new police sergeant, George Meyer, had taken over duties in York. Meyer may have acted in a stricter fashion towards Aboriginal people than his predecessor McGuigan; Bisley's report hints at this possibility.[172] Bisley also visited the reserve and ascertained that the one family with school-aged children did not send their children to school as they were receiving home schooling 'correspondence', which the family had commenced some time ago when camping several miles out from York, and the head of the family indicated that he had no desire to change this practice. Bisley was shown some specimens of the children's work, which he though were reasonably good, but he commented that, without supervision, he failed to see how these children would be able to advance 'a great deal'.[173] In summary, he opined that eventually, the whole family would have to be removed to a departmental institution. Fortunately, this did not eventuate.[174]

Thenceforth, school enrolments increased in York. In 1947, Sergeant Meyer reported that ten Aboriginal children were attending York's state school and twenty-two were attending the convent school. This ratio was more than reversed by 1951, with twenty-nine Aboriginal attendees at the town's state school and only four at the convent school. The enrolment rate had also increased because, in 1947, there were 146 Aboriginal residents recorded for York—a number that had decreased to ninety-five by 1951, and thus increased the total residents–student ratio.[175] There are no similar complaints of the nature voiced by Deacon in later records. This might be due to personality or change of circumstances. Deacon's complaints certainly accorded with the broader dissatisfaction voiced by white Australians in York at this particular point in time, as we shall see in the following section.

3.10 Increasing anti-Aboriginal sentiments in York—antecedents for near total social exclusion

In addition to the complaints about Aboriginal children 'roaming the streets' of the town, in 1946, renewed segregationist sentiments were expressed in York, which would culminate in the municipality of York being declared a 'prohibited area' for Aboriginal people by mid-1947. In May 1946, a curfew for Aboriginal people was once again on council's agenda. At the municipal council meeting on 21 May, Councillor H.G. Wake voiced the intention to have a 6 pm curfew declared, which was reportedly supported by other councillors present who 'gave instances of natives camping near the bridges and of offensive behaviour'. However, the news article reporting on the council meeting did not define 'offensive behaviour'.[176] The next day, Town Clerk C. Vincent promptly wrote a letter to the Department of Native Affairs, which is worth quoting in full due to the voiced segregationist fantasies that were not reported in the newspaper, in particular, the second paragraph:

> I am directed to bring under your notice a complaint regarding the ever-increasing number of natives in this district. They camp in the town in the daytime and create nuisance everywhere they go: They are not ordered out of town in the evening as is the practice elsewhere and most of them are unclean and apparently not working and living a generally hopeless existence. This, of course, is no fault of theirs.
>
> My Council appreciates that proper colonies should be provided where these natives can eventually gain citizenship and asks that proper housing be provided, pending the initiation of a colony scheme.
>
> This Council also asks that you issue instructions for these natives to be out of the Municipal area by 6pm daily.[177]

While the main message is clear, there are some interesting nuances in the letter that could be interpreted in different ways. Vincent wrote that living a generally hopeless existence was 'of course, no fault of theirs'. Did Vincent express sympathy for Aboriginal people subjected to the whims of white Australian society? Or did he perhaps infer racist inferiority? Or was this statement meant in a sarcastic way, implying that it was indeed the fault of individual behaviour? The comment about gaining citizenship is equally interesting. Vincent may have genuinely held the paradoxical belief that Aboriginal people should gain citizenship over time by proving themselves worthy to live among settler-Australians while living in a segregated community, and thus earning the assumed privilege of citizenship. However, Vincent may have also continued in a sarcastic way, while actually disapproving of the issuance of conditional citizenship for Aboriginal people in Western Australia. This special citizenship legislation had only begun to be implemented at the beginning of 1946, and news of it had entered settler-Australian discourse via the print media.[178] Thus, his comment could have implied that if Aboriginal people were given citizenship, this should occur in a segregated setting, which, in turn, would make this citizenship meaningless and mean that settler-Australians would not have to have contact with Aboriginal people. While there is room for various interpretations of the town clerk's subtleties, the bottom line was clear: The council had asked for a strict curfew to be implemented. The additional request for proper housing may appear laudable on first reading. However, the stated preference was that Aboriginal people should be moved to a 'colony', as they were not considered members of settler-Australian society, and the requested provision of proper housing was only seen as a temporary arrangement pending the implementation of the *final solution*.

The Department of Native Affairs promised it would look into the matter and Inspector Bisley was instructed to visit York as soon as possible. Deputy Commissioner McBeath commented that he could not understand complaints about Aboriginal people camping in town during the day and being around town in the evenings as these were 'all matters adjustable by the local Protector'.[179] Bisley was further instructed to check on unemployment and to warn all Aboriginal people not in employment to leave the district to secure work elsewhere, otherwise they would be marked for deportation to a native settlement.[180]

Simultaneously, local protector and Police Seargent McGuigan furnished a report to his senior at the police department, voicing the belief that the Aboriginal population in York had been growing over the previous three months, which he attributed to the gradually decreasing demand for Aboriginal labour in the region, on account of the return of ex-servicemen and the reluctance of many farmers and primary producers to employ Aboriginal people due to alleged unsatisfactory work performances during the war period. He also reported that police in York were devoting a considerable amount of their time to preventing Aboriginal people from 'loitering unnecessarily'.[181]

On the other hand, Sergeant McGuigan wished to point out how most local settler-Australians in York were seemingly prejudiced against Aboriginal people. He referred to a sports competition held in York on 3 June to exemplify that a lot of generalised prejudice was unwarranted. Of the more than 2,000 visitors in attendance, McGuigan reported that approximately 460 spectators were Aboriginal people who had come from districts stretching from Toodyay to Albany (450 km across), and that the general conduct of most Aboriginal attendees had been good. However, McGuigan noted that a few persons had obtained alcohol, and that the behaviour of the few reflected a negative light unfairly on the whole Aboriginal crowd.[182] In the end, only one person was charged and convicted—for being drunk at the railway station.[183] This suggests that other than potential offences against the racist *Native Administration Act*, there would not have been real disturbances.

The *York Leader and Quairading and Dangin Herald* reported in an unusual, almost neutral tone about Aboriginal attendees, writing that there 'was an exceptionally large attendance of "the dusky" population of the State and as usual the York Sports became the place for reunions of many of the native sections from all parts of the State.'[184] The news article did not comment on any of the alleged conduct issues to which McGuigan referred. The absence of the usual 'Aboriginal menace' narrative may be, in part, explainable by the rather good sporting outcomes of Aboriginal competitors on this day throughout various disciplines, which was also noted in the paper. Particularly, in the discipline of 'jumping', the best four ranks were achieved by Aboriginal athletes.[185] The other local newspaper that reported the sports competition, the *York Chronicle*, did not mention Aboriginal people at all.[186]

While it should be noted that the former publication's articles tended to be more comprehensive than the latter's—regardless of the topic reported on—it also must be noted that the 'jumping' results with an all-Aboriginal top four were completely omitted from the *York Chronicle*'s news piece, which listed all other results. There is no evidence that it was omitted deliberately, but it makes one wonder whether the *York Chronicle* actively denied Aboriginal people space in its publication if the news was not of a negative, sensationalist nature.

Back in June, when McGuigan reported to his senior officer, he made also reference to the claim that Aboriginal people were camping in town and he pointed out that when this occurred, it was usually people awaiting the 'convenience of transport' as Aboriginal mobility had increased significantly.[187] For example, Aboriginal families of the district that were located at places like Gwambygine and Gilgering had to come regularly to town to collect child endowment moneys. When acting Commissioner McBeath visited York in late June, McGuigan ensured him that Aboriginal people were not allowed in York during the hours of darkness. However, occasionally, some Aboriginal people arrived by train after sunset and they would be briefly in town to purchase food stuffs, which must have been upsetting to some settler-Australian residents making complaints. While McGuigan acknowledged that the Aboriginal population in York had increased, he voiced the belief that the situation remained the same and had not worsened, as some other people had suggested.[188]

Around the same time, shop owner and councillor-to-be Albert 'Bert' W. Bungate wrote an angry open letter to the York Municipal Council, requesting that immediate action be taken in relation to Aboriginal people hanging around in front of his shop at the corner of Avon Terrace and South Street, opposite the Royal Hotel. Bungate claimed that when he was serving in World War II, his shopfront had turned into a meeting place for Aboriginal people and, on his return, this had not changed. He wrote that in his absence, the shopfront 'was allowed to become a filthy and dirty place, created by these natives'.[189] He went on, theatrically, that food stuffs, peelings, and skins of fruit were dropped 'with no regard nor justice to anyone'.[190] Bungate continued that Aboriginal people congregating in front of his shop would 'stand in stork fashion with their backs to window, and have one foot on the window frame'[191], and thus, cause damage to the paint of the building. In his rage, Bungate racialised a type of behaviour that cannot be ascribed to any racial or ethnic group. It may have been more typical for members of the working class to hang out at street corners; however, even this is debatable depending on the locality. In fact, on several occasions over the next few years, York police charged small groups of non-Aboriginal people for obstructing footpaths and throughfares in town. Bungate requested swift action by council to have these people, who met at his shopfront, removed, and he threatened to contact higher authorities if no action was taken within five days. True to his word, he contacted the local press after seven days.[192]

The *York Leader and Quairading and Dangin Herald* reported on the next municipal council meeting, in which Bungate's letter was discussed. However, the news article cited more information than was contained in the actual letter: 'at times it was almost impossible to enter his shop owing to number of natives around the doorway'.[193] The newspaper must have mixed up its facts. It appears likely that Bungate had voiced the latter complaints in person during the municipal council meeting or outside in private conversation, given that he was just about to be elected a councillor himself.[194] Further, councillors H.G. Wake and C.J. Ashbolt also happened to be the publishers of said newspaper and, therefore, may have confused some written and verbally transmitted 'facts'. If anything, this shines a light on the local press' potential biases, as Councillor Wake, in particular, had been openly outspoken against Aboriginal people for a longer period. As to Bungate's public opposition towards Aboriginal people, it should be noted that he had an 'electrics and radio shop'. Most Aboriginal people in and around York at the time would have been unlikely to have ever entered his shop due to the absence of electricity in their private lives—for example, the reserve at York was only connected to electricity by 1967.[195] Therefore, Bungate received no apparent benefit from dealing with Aboriginal people, as opposed to some other settler-Australian townspeople, who benefitted monetarily from the Aboriginal presence in York and were likely more moderate in their opposition, if not demonstrably favourable towards them.

The monetary value that Aboriginal people presented to some townsfolk did not escape McBeath's attention when he visited York in late June, and he reported as follows:

> Whilst sitting in the tea rooms I took particular notice of every customer that entered this business, and during the fifteen minutes to twenty minutes that I was there having a cup of tea, I noticed that only three white people came in to make purchases whilst there were at least six or seven natives. The latter made purchases of foodstuffs and I would say that in this period the business took at least three or four times as much from the natives than the white customers. It appeared to me that the person serving behind the counter realised fully their value as customers because the natives appeared to me to receive equal, if not slightly better attention than the white customers.[196]

McBeath did not mention whether the person who served at the counter knew who he was, as this could certainly have influenced that person's behaviour. However, during this visit to York, McBeath also had the impression that the municipal council was not overly anxious to have York declared a prohibited area for Aboriginal people because there were a number of local business people who were members of the council. A prohibited area declaration was believed to be detrimental to some peoples' businesses, but this did not mean that these people wished for Aboriginal people to socialise in town—in particular, after close of business, when there was no monetary benefit to be gained by their presence. Meeting with the town clerk, Mr Vincent, McBeath referred to the recent sports event and pointed out that each of the Aboriginal visitors—men, women and children—could be estimated as having spent at least £2 per head, 'and this being so, they put in the pocket of the local business people from at least £800 to £1,000'.[197] This was a rather substantial amount at the time. Following the discussion with the town clerk, McBeath formed the belief that the recent formal complaint by the council was the outcome of a circular letter distributed by the Murchison Road Board Association and forwarded to all road boards, which aimed to solicit support for a certain number of their ideas in regard to segregation and housing for Aboriginal people on reserves. The York Road Board had then kindly forwarded this circular to the council.[198]

While the circular letter may have fuelled discussions, it did not result in the formal complaint (as McBeath had suggested it did) because the circular was received by council after the complaint had been written. With the benefit of historical hindsight, we know that Aboriginal people being discussed as a problem topic had been part of public discourse in York for quite some time by then, and therefore, racist sentiments would not have been caused by a circular letter alone. However, when this circular letter was received, it prompted Councillor Wake to refer to 'his previous proposition' for York to be declared a prohibited area, 'the same as Northam', which had been declared one in April 1940.[199] Councillor Frederick Ashbolt voiced opposition to the proposal, which was somewhat unsurprising as he owned a grocery store on Avon Terrace and would have perceived the declaration of a prohibited area as potentially detrimental to his business. Ashbolt may also have objected on humanitarian grounds; however, his business considerations would have likely played a major part in his opinion. Mayor Thorn also objected and commented that Aboriginal people 'were more sinned against than sinning'. Councillor Christina Foreman agreed with the objections of Ashbolt and Thorn and it was decided to approach the Commissioner of Native Affairs during the investigation process that was assumed to have been triggered by the circular letter.[200]

The anticipated 'investigation' did not occur but a couple of months later, on 6 August, Acting Commissioner McBeath attended the municipal council meeting in York to discuss 'native matters'. The council voiced its unhappiness with the Department of Native Affairs' past actions and the official primary point of critique was the lack of housing. It was observed that there was virtually no shelter on the reserve and that there was a house in town with four rooms, occupied by precisely thirty-four Aboriginal individuals. It was further stated that

Aboriginal people had become 'house conscious' and, if housing was provided, there would be no 'menace'. Mayor Thorn said:

> it was not within the council's power to do any work outside the municipality. The natives were trying to keep clean. They sent their children to school, where they were expected to compete with children who had good homes. They were good sportsmen and would be an asset to Australia if they were properly controlled.[201]

Thorn's observations about Aboriginal children and their inequitable living conditions in relation to learning outcomes probably had some merit. However, he was quick to point out that council was unable to help in this regard at all, as the reserve was outside the municipality. This convenient excuse for inaction had become a standard phrase for members of the municipal council. While it is correct that the reserve was located within the jurisdiction of the York Road Board, the actual land was purely administered by the Department of Native Affairs and it appears unlikely that the road board would have objected had council desired to erect some sheds for humanitarian reasons. Thorn voiced the belief that the erection of sheds would suffice when McBeath stated that the department had no money for housing, and that if the department provided housing in York, other districts would request the same. It would not have been impossible to erect a few sheds if the council had been seriously concerned about living conditions on the reserve and truly believed that such sheds would improve the situation for Aboriginal people and, by extension, the situation for settler-Australians.

Time and again, a somewhat sympathetic person recognised an issue but when it came to taking action themselves, concerns were quickly muted as the conscience was apparently soothed by pointing responsibility towards another administrative entity. It does make sense that the Department of Native Affairs was identified as responsible for the betterment of Aboriginal people's lives, given that the department otherwise attempted to inject itself in all possible ways into the lives of Aboriginal people. However, people who are genuinely concerned about any population group's livelihoods and truly believe that some sort of assistance is required for the betterment of the group, while faced with government inaction, would arguably try to organise some sort of well-intended 'grassroots' support. Clearly, this did not occur, and it seems that merely pointing out that 'something needs to be done' was hoped to be sufficient. Thorn's last sentence is also telling, when he voiced the believe that Aboriginal people would be an asset to Australia if properly controlled. The notions of 'control' and 'menace' were slipped into the conversation under the guise of humanitarian concerns. Equally petty, McBeath raised in reply that he had the option of declaring York a prohibited area but thought that the business people would object, citing, once again, the recent sports meeting and the estimated spending of Aboriginal people.[202] While McBeath, in a way, reasoned against the declaration of a prohibited area, he also kept 'planting the seed' for the consideration of such an area.

Only a few days after McBeath's attendance at the York Municipal Council meeting, Garnet Barrington Wood, who was then the MLC for East Province and simultaneously a member of the York Road Board, spoke in Parliament about child endowment payments for Aboriginal people in general and also commented about Aboriginal people in York. Wood echoed the sentiments of the *Narrogin Observer*, discussed above (see chapter 3.08), alleging increased 'breeding' among the Aboriginal population to live off child endowment payments, along with an increasing unwillingness to work. Notwithstanding that Wood's comments read as though he was discussing rabbits instead of humans, one should not forget that child endowment was only introduced five years earlier. It seems difficult to fathom how anyone could observe and conclude over such a short period that Aboriginal people were intentionally having more children than before to obtain government payments. There was no denying that the Aboriginal population in the South West Land Division was growing, and that many Noongar families were rather large; however, A.O. Neville had already publicly written about this fact fifteen years earlier when the introduction of child endowment was still years away. Woods, holding such hysterically distorted prejudices, reported that at the June sports meeting, forty Aboriginal people were playing 'two-up'. Two-up was, at the time, an illegal coin tossing gambling activity that was also common among soldiers during World War I and has since been enshrined in Anzac folklore. Now Wood voiced the believe that half of the money being betted was derived from child endowments. L.B. Bolton, MLC, interjected that two-up was Aboriginal peoples' 'national game', likely inferring that Aboriginal people playing two-up should be left alone. Without replying to Bolton, Wood continued that someone had called the police, and when the sergeant approached an old Aboriginal woman, requesting that she cease gambling, she reportedly replied: 'You won't let us gamble, so we will drink instead'.[203] One should not forget that Aboriginal people in York and elsewhere were severely deprived of entertainment options that were available to settler-Australians, and playing two-up was just one way of enjoying some form of group entertainment, in spite of white Australian oppression. Wood did not elaborate on how he came to the conclusion that half of the gambled money was derived from child endowments but he railed about how child endowments should not be issued directly to Aboriginal people, but should instead be administered by government agencies. He also referred to the alleged appalling housing conditions on the York Reserve and suggested that the state government take hold of child endowment payments to provide better housing on country reserves.[204]

Following Wood's address, in reply, Acting Commissioner McBeath was requested to provide some commentary on the allegations. McBeath advised that the situation in York was well under the control of the Department of Native Affairs. Except for three families who received their child endowments via orders for 'food stuffs', there was no reason to believe that any other Aboriginal families would misappropriate these payments. He advised that two departmental officers were closely supervising the state-wide payment of child endowments through the services of the local protectors. This mechanism of control over individual child endowment payments would only be discontinued in mid-1951. McBeath stated that the 'majority of detribalised parents are spending their Child Endowment moneys in a sensible manner for the welfare of their children, and it is somewhat a pity that criticism is offered against the payment of Child Endowment to native parents'.[205] McBeath then addressed housing and claimed that the earnings of

Aboriginal people in the York District were equal to 'white rates' and that, judging by Wood's comments, Aboriginal people in York were 'too lazy to provide themselves with good camps'.[206] He continued to insist that Aboriginal people were handling substantial moneys at the time and were therefore undeserving of housing on reserves, which would cost the tax payer £90,000 for its provision across the whole South West Land Division. This claim was, once again, generalisation, not least because he cited as an example a family who was not really a representative case, having lived in a locality eleven kilometres outside of York. The acting commissioner was happy to defend Aboriginal people's eligibility for the Commonwealth-funded Child Endowment Scheme; however, when it came to housing that would have to be paid for by departmental funds he did not have, McBeath denied the need for such provisions and deflected, claiming that Aboriginal people could provide better housing for themselves if they chose to do so. McBeath also left a note for acting Inspector J.H. Bisley, which unveiled the political sensitivity of Wood's complaint: 'I wish you to pay some attention to the York people. They are causing a lot of criticism'.[207]

Bisley ventured to York on 17 October 1946, where he first met with Mr Haley and Mr Fairhead of the York Road Board. They made the usual complaints about the type of camps on the reserve and the number of Aboriginal people 'congregating' at York at different periods of the year. Bisley pointed out that local races and shows were 'gala days' for Aboriginal people, 'and provided they behaved themselves nothing could be done to prevent them from attending these functions'.[208] Bisley also stated 'that the reserve was intended as a camping ground for Aboriginal people when they came to town on business, and not as permanent place of Abode'.[209] This latter point would be memorised by the board members and brought up again at a later time when attempting to have the permanent reserve residents removed. According to his own account, Bisley then outlined the department's policy that employers of Aboriginal people should provide housing for their employees and families and, claimed that if this was carried out, there would be fewer people on the reserve. Additionally, Aboriginal children could travel to school in York on the bus provided by the Education Department. Bisley seemingly hit a brick wall with this suggestion, as Mr Fairhead informed him 'that the bus was overcrowded at present and would probably be more so in the New Year'[210], in anticipation that the bush state school at Gwambygine was going to be closed down.

There is no indication that Fairhead considered that Aboriginal children could take the bus. The very idea seemed to be inconceivable and he produced a justification that sought to emphasise the needs of settler-Australian children as above those of Aboriginal children. As discussed earlier, the school at Gwambygine was also attended by Aboriginal children who would have required the school bus service as well, as they were expected to attend the school in York the next year, joining the six Aboriginal children that were already attending the state school at the time.[211]

Despite this apparent obstacle from the road board, it requested to be more involved. The board seemingly felt left out, as the Department of Native Affairs had recently been communicating more with the municipal council than the road board about matters in York. In particular, council had discussed the provision of shelters with McBeath, which resulted in some light public bickering between the two local authorities. After all, both the municipal council and the road board aspired to use different means for the same ends. Both local authorities disapproved of Aboriginal people living in their respective jurisdictions. The council could be therefore appeased with the thought that Aboriginal people lived in good shelters on the reserve outside of the municipality. However, the road board was less willing to accept the Aboriginal presence in their jurisdiction this close to town, which provided relatively easy access for visitors. The road board may have grudgingly tolerated the reality of having the reserve in its jurisdiction but it felt entitled about having a say in anything concerning the reserve, while it still hoped for the establishment of a settlement further away— ideally, in another district.[212]

Bisley also visited the widow of W.T. Craig at Mile Pool, Mrs Louisa Craig, who was employing Aboriginal people, as previously mentioned (see chapter 3.09). At the time, she had one permanent employee who lived in a 'mud bat' (mud brick) cottage on site with his family, and two casual hands. However, it was ascertained that she had failed to obtain work permits for these workers under the *Native Administration Act*

1941. Mrs Craig was warned that she would be fined for not taking out permits and was reminded that she had been prosecuted in the past for the same omission.[213] There may have been different reasons for not applying for a work permit for Aboriginal people. Most employers would not have appreciated the Department of Native Affairs interfering with their businesses, and would not have been happy with paying additional fees. Some employers may have been sympathetic to Aboriginal people and, therefore, may have disliked the department for the oppressive control it exerted over Western Australia's Aboriginal population. These hypothetical sympathetic settler-Australian employers may have simply refused to cooperate with the rules imposed by the *Native Administration Act* out of sheer principle. Mrs Craig's attitude towards the *Native Administration Act* is not known to this author, but she and her late husband had reportedly always had a good relationship with Aboriginal people. Alternatively, she may simply have forgotten to take out or renew permits—although, one Aboriginal employee who lived on Mrs Craig's property had been working for her since at least 1942 as the records indicate that she took out a permit in that year.[214]

Whatever her attitude towards this system, not taking out permits deprived her employees and their dependants of eligibility for the payment of medical costs through the statutory Natives Medical Fund, in place between 1939 and 1955 (having come into operation in 1937, the medical fund was initially run on a voluntary basis for the first two years).[215] Mrs Craig continued to have Aboriginal employees living on her property, but in 1949, she was once again prompted to take out a permit and it was reported that she was generally reluctant do so. Aboriginal people kept working and living at Mile Pool until at least 1951, as evidenced in departmental patrol reports. Aboriginal people may have even worked at Mile Pool until Mrs Craig's death in 1959, after which her properties were sold. While racist motives cannot necessarily be inferred from the failure to take out permits, this surely indicates a certain degree of indifference on the part of the employer towards their employees' well-being when it comes to saving costs.[216]

Bisley found only a couple of families to be residing at the reserve at the time of his visit and noted that there were generally not large numbers of Aboriginal people in York; however, he anticipated an influx around Christmas because in previous years, the majority of Aboriginal people from Quairading and Badjaling had made their way to York around the same period.[217] In McBeath's late-November reply to Bisley's report, he referred to some 'family brawls and arguments' that needed to cease immediately or McBeath would see that these families were removed from York.[218] In the same letter, he claimed that Aboriginal people were now in a better position to provide improved camps for themselves, and Bisley was required to advise reserve residents that they were compelled to do so. McBeath further instructed Bisley to look for a more suitable site for a reserve.[219] Sergeant Meyer also suggested to look for another location that was further away from town and off the main roads and requested a lithograph showing available crown lands in the York District. Meyer pondered whether, if finding a new location failed, all employers of Aboriginal people would need to be forced to house their employees. Meyer was either a bit overzealous in his ambitions or there was no suitable crownland available for this purpose, as his request does not appear to have been further considered in any realistic way.[220]

Four months later, in March 1947, Sergeant Meyer issued final warnings to the same families that were warned in November. Records suggest that a main point of contention, as far as the department was concerned, was that members of both families kept contacting the Department of Native Affairs about issues with each other and the department was not interested and demanded that this practice must cease or there would be drastic consequences. Simultaneously, during a court hearing for alcohol-related 'offences' under the *Native Administration Act 1941*, the only justice of the peace who sentenced the accused persons voiced a 'strong and final warning' to all Aboriginal people that were present 'as to the manner in which any future disturbances, particularly at the local reserve would be dealt with'.[221]

Although a provision in the *Justices Act 1936* enabled the practice of having only one justice of the peace to hand down sentences if only one was available within ten miles, this practice undermined the intention of the legislation because two justices of the peace were required under the Act. The reason, as briefly discussed above (see chapter 3.06), was that justices of the peace were often laypersons in relation to law matters.[222] In most cases, justices of the peace were business persons with hardly any background in law, while mayors of towns and chairmen of road boards automatically became justices of the peace by virtue of their offices.[223] In theory, a potential ignorance of legal practice was meant to be mitigated by two persons making decisions together. The single justice of the peace on this occasion was Albert Francis Noonan, who would succeed Thorn as the next mayor of York by mid-year. Noonan was a defender of white Australian principles and he strongly promoted the immigration of members of the 'true British race'[224], which he believed to be essential for Australia's advancement. With his warning voiced in court, he provided an indication of how Aboriginal matters would be handled in York henceforth.

3.11 York to be declared a prohibited area

At the time when Noonan issued his warning, the municipal council had recommenced debate about a prohibited area and curfew, and had corresponded with the Department of Native Affairs regarding this for slightly more than two months. The *York Leader* reported that on Christmas Eve, 1946, the council discussed a letter received from the town clerk in Northam regarding the 'control of natives'. It was agreed that a 6 pm curfew for Aboriginal people should be requested and that the local protector should be able to issue discretionary permits for select Aboriginal individuals who may be permitted in town during curfew hours.[225] While the council decided the matter on 24 December, the acting town clerk, Leslie George Baker, had actually written to the Department of Native Affairs already on 18 December, claiming that he was conveying the council's wishes when requesting that York be declared a prohibited area, as had Northam some years ago. Baker may have had a discussion with one or several counsellors beforehand and presumed, or was led to believe, that this course of action would be decided; however, the report in the newspaper indicates that not all councillors thought the same, and that he did not act on the council's behalf when sending the letter.[226]

Acting Commissioner McBeath contacted Sergeant Meyer seeking his comments on the council's proposal before he would consider the request. When the council met on 21 January 1947, it was advised that the Department of Native Affairs was considering the proclamation of a prohibited area, as requested. It was subsequently reported that the council merely discussed the request for a curfew and wished that the department be advised accordingly. The news report of this discussion at the council meeting is very brief and does not reveal whether council was aware that Town Clerk Baker had overshot his appointed responsibilities.[227] However, Baker then advised the department that 'Council's requirements regarding natives in this District have been misinterpreted,' and that the council only wished for a daily 6 pm curfew to be put in place. While Baker was on holidays, the person acting in his position, Mr P.T. Peddie, reiterated the 6 pm-curfew request and apologised for the misunderstanding.[228] According to the *York Leader and Quairading and Dangin Herald*, the department replied in February that the council had definitely requested a prohibited area and, as the council was 'now asking that natives should not be allowed in the town after 6 pm it was evident proof that they were of benefit to the local business houses'.[229] Most likely in reference to the public conveniences debate, it was suggested that the council provide some 'facilities' for Aboriginal people in acknowledgement of their economic value.[230] Interestingly, the copy of this letter has been removed from the corresponding departmental file, as evidenced by a missing folio number. As it was up to local police officers to enforce curfews, the only decision that McBeath had to make was whether to have York declared a prohibited area. It is true that the enforcement of prohibited areas also depended on local police officers; however, the declaration of a prohibited area, in contrast to the 'loitering' clause, left less room for interpretation.

Had Baker admitted that he requested the prohibited area of his own volition, McBeath might have ceased considering the request, but given that Baker apparently did not wish to admit that he overstepped his decision-making abilities, McBeath's conclusion as to the reason for the council's alleged change of mind seems logical. On 4 March, Sergeant Meyer submitted a report that would arguably have swayed McBeath to initiate the declaration of a prohibited area. Sergeant Meyer claimed that, initially, he had been against the idea of York being declared a prohibited area. However, he reported that he had spoken with local residents, business people and farmers and was unable to gain much support for his opinion. According to Meyer, following these discussions, he also formed the belief that it was necessary that York be declared a prohibited area from 6 pm until daylight the following morning. Meyer appeared not to be aware that 'prohibited area' meant a prohibition applying twenty-four hours a day, seven days a week, unless an Aboriginal person was in legal employment at the time of being in that area. Giving further reasons for his change of mind, Sergeant Meyer mentioned recent alcohol-related convictions and that one white man had entered the reserve without permission. Apparently, this man had been allowed to 'dance' with an Aboriginal woman on the reserve, and if this was not a euphemism for sexual relations, then Meyer's comment just shows how inconceivable the idea was to him that Aboriginal and settler-Australians could socialise together. In any event, a prohibited area would not have made a difference to a settler-Australian person entering the reserve, who would regardless be liable for prosecution for doing so under the *Native Administration Act 1941*. Notwithstanding Meyer's supposed changed attitude, he pointed out that only a small proportion of Aboriginal people in York displayed unsatisfactory behaviour and he urged that the utmost discretion be used in executing the law. If this was possible, he wrote, he would support the proposition that York be declared a prohibited area.[231]

On 1 April 1947, McBeath wrote to the Minister for Native Affairs, Robert 'Ross' McDonald (it was McDonald's first day in office), and recommended that he have York declared a prohibited area. He cited that, for some time, the local council and some residents had been 'pressing for this action to be taken because of the unsatisfactory behaviour of natives after the hours of sunset. The misconduct on the part of the natives is mostly in relation to liquor, and I am supporting this proposal now because the situation has not improved'.[232] McBeath explained that arrangements could be made if Aboriginal people had to enter the townsite to access medical attention or visit the town 'to conduct legitimate business'.[233] Apart from shopping for food stuffs, attending church services was also deemed 'legitimate' business. While the declaration was still being considered by Minister McDonald, a certain Mr R. Mitchell of the United Aborigines Mission at Kellerberrin requested to commence fortnightly church services from mid-April, and offered to collect all Aboriginal persons who wished to attend, saying he would return them after the conclusion of the service. In anticipation that the prohibited area would be declared, Mitchell was allowed to proceed with his proposal under the provision that, should the services result in 'any undue congregation of natives', McBeath would have Mitchell's permit withdrawn.[234] Before agreeing to the declaration, McDonald sought the consent of Charles Perkins, Member of Parliament for the York District, who became involved in York matters concerning Aboriginal people in 1945, as discussed earlier (see chapter 3.08). Perkins did not raise any objections, and thus, McDonald went ahead. On 29 May 1947, the townsite of York was declared 'to be an area in which it shall be unlawful for natives not in lawful employment to be or remain'.[235]

3.12 Prohibited areas

At this point we shall discuss prohibited areas in more detail. Under the *Aborigines Act* and its various amendments between 1906 and 1955, the Governor of Western Australia could declare virtually any place in Western Australia a prohibited area 'whenever in the interest of the natives'.[236] The quoted cynical clause would hardly have been able to fool anyone at the time that it was anything other than 'doublespeak' for 'whenever is in the interest of white Australians'. This kind of cynicism also did not escape new departmental staff in 1949, who possessed a more progressive attitude when discussing the prohibited area in Carnarvon.[237] However, to soothe their own consciences, this clause would have enabled those settler-Australians who considered themselves highly virtuous to claim that this form of segregation was protecting Aboriginal people's interests. A declared prohibited area also took responsibility from the local police, who could claim that they were merely executing the governor's order when enforcing section 42 of the Act, which reads as follows:

The Governor may, by proclamation, whenever in the interest of the natives he thinks fit, declare any municipal district or town or any other place to be an area in which it shall be unlawful for natives, not in lawful employment, to be or remain; and every such native who, after warning, enters or is found within such area without permission, in writing, of a protector or police officer, shall be guilty of an offence against this Act.[238]

The most conspicuous prohibited area in Western Australia was declared for the City of Perth in 1927. The then Chief Protector of Aborigines, A.O. Neville, had played with the idea for some time but when he received increasing reports of Aboriginal people working and hanging out at a working-class amusement park, to which he was opposed, Neville pressed for Perth City to be declared a prohibited area. The amusement park was called 'White City' and was located at the Perth Esplanade within the City of Perth's municipal boundaries (Perth's inner city). Following the declaration, written correspondence between Neville and the police suggests that police were initially resistant to taking action against these Aboriginal people, whom they considered were behaving appropriately at White City. The amusement park closed after 1929; however, the prohibited area remained in place until 2 June 1954.[239]

In 1940, Commissioner Bray noted in an internal memorandum that, to his knowledge, the prohibited areas in Broome and Perth were frequented by Aboriginal people and generally no action was taken, while in places like Northam, Wyndham, Hall's Creek, Kalgoorlie and Boulder, the prohibitions were rigorously enforced. However, during the course of the 1940s, there was an increase of Aboriginal people coming from the country to Perth, and the department ordered 'camp-natives' removed from the city. As a consequence, breaches against the prohibited-area section of the *Native Administration Act 1941* were frequently dealt with in the Perth Court during the course of the 1940s, and convictions resulted in fines and terms of imprisonment. In 1947, the department wished to decrease the size of Perth's prohibited area, chiefly to exclude East Perth from the prohibition because this locality had become an area where Aboriginal people were able to rent cheap housing. At this point, it was realised that the *Native Administration Act 1941* did not allow for the amendment or cancellation of prohibited areas, and because of that, the *Native Administration Act* was subsequently amended by December of that year to allow for the decrease of Perth's prohibited area to occur.[240]

The majority of prohibited areas were in country towns in the Goldfields, Murchison, Gascoyne, Pilbara and Kimberley regions. For example, Northampton was declared a prohibited area as early as August 1906 and would remain so until 1954. Thus, this town attained the record of having been the longest lasting prohibited area in Western Australia. Whether Northampton's prohibited area was enforced for the entire period is not known to this author. In the South West Land Division, except for Perth, there existed five prohibited areas. These were Gnowangerup and Northam from 1940—the latter with a slight amendment in 1947, which was actually unlawful at the time of proclamation in March of that year, as the *Native Administration Act 1941* did not yet allow for amendments and cancellations. Then, there was York from 1947, as well as the area surrounding the Moore River Settlement from 1932, as discussed earlier (see chapter 3.01). York was the last country town to be declared a prohibited area and only one more declaration followed in 1950, which brought the total number of prohibited areas in Western Australia to thirty-seven. The last declaration occurred in the Perth suburb of Mt Lawley, where Alvan House was located, which was a boarding school for Aboriginal girls.[241] The prohibition was gazetted in December 1950, prior to the opening of Alvan House in early 1951. As the proposition of opening Alvan House had attracted a community and public backlash, Commissioner Middleton wanted to ensure that no Aboriginal people would be able to 'loiter' close to the home. Simultaneously, he also wanted to prevent the girls from being distracted, while mitigating negative community and press responses. Aboriginal people who worked in the zone were reportedly not affected by the prohibition, and parents of the girls were also allowed to visit with prior approval from the department.[242]

All prohibited areas were cancelled in 1954 before the *Native Welfare Act 1954* was assented, and went into effect the following year, which saw the section about prohibited areas removed. The department had for some time tried to amend the *Native Administration Act* but amendment bills failed several times in the State Parliament's Legislative Council. Therefore, all prohibited areas were revoked in 1954 to affect a quasi-amendment in relation to this section of the legislation.[243]

Sentences under the *Native Administration Act 1941* could be harsh, as already discussed (see chapter 2.03), ranging from fines to up to two years of imprisonment for repeat 'offenders'. In any event, it was up to the judiciary to decide what penalty they deemed appropriate. The reported convictions in newspapers suggest that often fines were issued for breaching the legislation in Perth, but terms of imprisonment were also issued at the lower order. In many cases, persons charged under this legislation would have also spent at least one night in police custody. Still, the very threat of breaching the law would have served as a deterrent against many Aboriginal people entering the town. This would have been particularly true for those who tried to keep a low profile and understandably were not keen on police questioning them about their whereabouts. After all, recorded convictions for being in a prohibited area only show us the few who dared to ignore the racist law; they do not tell us how many people were actively deterred from entering a prohibited area by complying with the law. As briefly discussed above, in police courts, in the absence of a magistrate, sentences for offences against the *Aborigines Act 1941*, as well as a variety of criminal, traffic and civil matters, could be handed down by two justices of the peace. Justices of the peace would often hold strong, locally biased views about Aboriginal people in their jurisdiction. In particular, during the 1940s, York's police court records indicate that, frequently, only one justice of the peace was available to hand down sentences and that this was not only a one-time occurrence in February 1947 in the lead up to the declaration.[244]

On 4 June 1947, the Department of Native Affairs advised Sergeant Meyer of York about the proclamation and issued instructions outlining the implementation of the new policy that affected Aboriginal people in York:

It will now be unlawful for natives, not in lawful employment, to be, or to remain, in the prohibited area except with a written permit issued by your good self as the Local Protector of Natives in accordance with Section 42 of the Native Administration Act 1905–41.

No doubt occasion may arise when it will be necessary for you to issue permits for natives to reside within the Prohibited Area, subject of course, to good behaviour.

When such permits are issued, it is within your power to set forth where the native or natives shall live within the area. Every care should be exercised in the issue of permits for the employment of natives within the Prohibited Area.

Would you kindly take action to advise all natives of the proclamation that has been issued, also advise them that they must be in possession of the necessary permit to visit the townsite …[245]

Apparently having been unaware that the proclamation had already occurred, Councillor Christina Foreman started a discussion at the municipal council meeting on 3 June, opposing the imposition of a prohibited area. She reasoned that the situation with Aboriginal people in York had improved over recent years. Town Clerk Baker advised that only a curfew had been requested, and was being considered. However, newly elected Mayor, A.F. Noonan, countered that Northam had been declared a prohibited area where Aboriginal people 'enjoyed certain liberties' and he continued that a 'prohibited area declaration would give the police more power to deal with any emergency should it arise'.[246] Councillors Fred Ashbolt and Foreman moved that no curfew or prohibition be proclaimed. This was amended by councillors Gordon H. Wake and Sylvester J. Prunster, who disagreed and wished to seek an exact interpretation of the curfew and prohibited area. The amendment of the motion was carried by all other councillors present and a letter was sent to the department.[247] On 17 June, the Department of Native Affairs replied with an explanation similar to the instructions issued to

Sergeant Meyer. The letter did not state that the prohibited area had already been declared—and, therefore, it is unclear at what point council learned of this fact. Nevertheless, McBeath had requested that Meyer advise the town clerk in due course.[248]

3.13 Discussions at the York and District Progress Association

Mayor Noonan and councillors Foreman and Wake were all speakers at a meeting of the York and District Progress Association held on Monday 12 May 1947, with three departmental officers in attendance, when McBeath openly stated that York would be shortly gazetted a prohibited area. This would have caused Foreman to bring up the matter at the council meeting in June, as discussed above.[249] The meeting is interesting as opinions were exchanged outside the usual correspondence between local and state government authorities, although some members of the association were also councillors and road board members. Departmental staff had been invited to the association's meeting to have a discussion with the welfare of Aboriginal people in mind; however, during the meeting, it became once again clear that the focus, at least for some more vocal attendees, was on Aboriginal people being perceived as a problem for settler-Australians, which they sought to address for their own benefit. In an internal report about the meeting, McBeath commented that, except for one person, no other speakers could actually claim to have had anything to do with Aboriginal people in their daily lives.[250] The *York Chronicle* reported that all speakers stressed that something should be done to:

> endeavour to uplift the native but it would be necessary to introduce full education facilities for the children. It was considered that it was next to impossible to do anything with the adults. It was also considered that the matter of doing something for the betterment of the native was a matter which the Government should take up more earnestly.[251]

While critique of the state government was surely warranted, the speakers of the association suggested segregated schools as solution for the children's *uplifting*, whereby their own children would not have to have any contact with Aboriginal children. They also insisted that Aboriginal adults were incapable of personal development or socioeconomic advancement, while refusing to acknowledge that the current situation of many Aboriginal people was the result of the daily racism they had to face. It is telling that McBeath used exactly the same argument in a letter to Minister Ross McDonald in 1948, when advocating for the provision of housing on Aboriginal reserves to provide better chances for the children who did not receive a supposedly advantageous education at institutions. McBeath's letter further suggested that he would consider removing all Aboriginal children to institutions if it were not for public opinion that would not permit such a step being taken.[252] However, at the meeting of the York and District Progress Association, he seemingly attempted to free everyone concerned of any responsibility by voicing the belief that it would be a very long time until Aboriginal people could be educated to the standard whereby they could take their place in the community—estimating this to be 'somewhere in the vicinity of 150 years'. McBeath also talked about conditional citizenship, which he generally opposed, as he believed that most Aboriginal people were not ready yet, as they merely 'acquired the whites' vices and eventually ended up further back' than where they started.[253] At the time of the meeting there were no individuals in York that had yet been granted conditional citizenship; however, people certainly took notice of the comments by McBeath, as settler-Australians would openly oppose the granting of conditional citizenship to Aboriginal people from York sometime later.[254]

It was reported that almost 'every speaker was obviously very concerned with the miserable and disgraceful conditions under which natives were existing on the York Reserve'.[255] McBeath claimed that these conditions had not arisen before 'white farm labourers became scarce, and before child endowment payments were instituted. Before this, natives did not live permanently on the reserve.'[256] Obviously, McBeath did not establish his facts correctly in this instance, as it was noted earlier that one-to-two families had lived permanently on the reserve for several years before the introduction of child endowment. While he acknowledged the change in labour demands during World War II, McBeath attributed the supposedly higher wages to be earned in the York area, and child endowments, to an increase of more permanent residents on the York Reserve. However, he completely disregarded that the Aboriginal population was generally growing across the region. For example, census data collected by the local protector indicates a growth from fifty-nine individuals in June 1944 to 146 persons in June 1947, while the adult-to-children ratio only increased marginally.[257] Statistically, this suggests that per capita employment opportunities for Aboriginal people in the York District would have simultaneously decreased.

Attendees complained that they were required to pay Aboriginal people the same wages as settler-Australians, while insisting that their performance was not equally satisfactory. McBeath advised that under clause 13 of 'the award', Aboriginal people could be paid less following consultation with the local protector.[258] McBeath alluded to the Farm Workers Award of 19 December 1946, which covered, for the first time, Aboriginal farm employees in the South West Land Division. However, it also included a provision enabling employers to pay Aboriginal workers less if their work performance was deemed to be 'less efficient'. There was also a similar provision for non-Aboriginal workers, who could be paid less if unable to perform to standard expectations, but the provision relating to Aboriginal people handed power on decision-making to the Department of Native Affairs and its auxiliaries. The lower wages were to be agreed to by a local protector and the Aboriginal employee, while the commissioner had a right to disallow agreements for less pay, either on request of 'the Union' (the Australian Workers' Union) or of his own volition under the *Native Administration Act 1941*. The Department had pushed for this clause to be included. This provision remained in force until 27 November 1964, when this racist clause was dropped from the award. Whether local farmers in York made use of clause 13 is not apparent in the records available to this author.[259] However, referring to the request for better housing on reserves, McBeath invoked racist rhetoric to justify inaction by reminding all attendees 'of the serious problems the housing shortage had created for whites and' that he 'was sure the meeting would not agree with preferential treatment in the procuring of houses for the natives before the whites'.[260]

McBeath then advised the association that the department 'did not entirely agree that segregation was the solution, as isolation produced an inferiority complex, and therefore in time a minority class of poor whites'.[261] As contradictory as this statement sounds at first, it illuminates that McBeath and the Department of Native Affairs were still following A.O. Neville's belief in biological absorption—namely, that the Aboriginal population of mixed descent in the South West Land Division would eventually become 'white'. Thus, McBeath warned that segregation would lead to the creation of a 'minority class of poor whites'. He then advocated for the proposed settlement scheme to upskill Aboriginal people in a segregated environment, and advised that York would be declared a prohibited area soon, as mentioned earlier. The mission of the departmental officers in attendance appears to have been one of appeasement. Any comments of understanding or sympathy for the Aboriginal people's situation were followed by condemning judgements on the state of their assumed collective abilities, capabilities, inferiority and degree of motivation, based on racialised stereotypes of the time. Unsurprisingly, on conclusion of the meeting, the officers received a 'hearty vote of appreciation'.[262] When reporting the meeting to the Minister for Native Affairs, Ross McDonald, McBeath reiterated his idea from the previous year to find a more 'suitable' location for the reserve, further away from the main road. Probably because McDonald had only been in office since April 1947, he seemingly agreed with the proposal without making further inquiries.[263] With this proposal, McBeath not only endorsed continuous segregation but also increased isolation from the settler-Australian community.

3.14 Following the declaration of the prohibited area and its enforcement

Following the declaration of the prohibited area, for the reminder of the year, public opinion expressed through the council was largely focussed on Aboriginal people living in houses in town, which has been discussed in detail further above (see chapter 3.05). However, there were two exceptions worth mentioning. The first was Minister Ross McDonald's visit to York in October 1947, when stopping by on his way to Badjaling Mission. He was accompanied by Charles Perkins, MLA for York, James Isaac Mann, MLA for Beverley, and McBeath, who met with local representatives. The only original idea voiced by McDonald was about additional finances he was apparently trying to secure from the Commonwealth. Everything else he was quoted as saying was a reproduction of McBeath's opinions voiced to the Progress Association in May and, therefore, unlikely penned by McDonald himself. McBeath, on this occasion, publicly stated that a better site for the reserve would be sought, while Sergeant Meyer openly disproved of segregation and suggested that more farmers should take on Aboriginal people in permanent positions. Somewhat surprisingly, Road Board Secretary Haley stated that Aboriginal employees were an asset in the district and that the Aboriginal population was entitled to some consideration. When not speaking to members of the State Parliament, Haley was usually rather dismissive or ignorant of Aboriginal people's needs within the road board's district. The entire meeting appeared to be a meaningless, self-serving publicity stunt for McDonald and his entourage.[264] Another matter that was brought up during a council meeting in late 1947 that did not relate to Aboriginal housing in town, was a request by a café located on Avon Terrace. The proprietors, 'Malig, Jhafer & Ado' of the Bright Spot Café, asked for permission to open a separate eating room for Aboriginal people. The request was 'held over', as approval was reportedly subject to a report from the health inspector; however, this matter was apparently not brought up again during the following council meetings.[265]

It is not known to this author how many permits were issued to Aboriginal individuals to be in the prohibited area for 'legitimate reasons', as this kind of information is only retained on personal files (if at all), which are only available to be viewed by direct descendants.[266] Between the proclamation in 1947 and its revocation in 1954, eighteen convictions occurred in York for being in a prohibited area without permission. These concerned fourteen individual persons on nine occasions. Seventeen of these supposed *offences* occurred between 1 November 1948 and 28 January 1950, while one last offence was recorded for 24 February 1951. However, the absence of convictions prior and after these dates does not tell whether the law was utilised successfully to threaten Aboriginal people into compliance with the imposed spatial prohibition within York's public sphere. To the author's knowledge, almost all of the convicted persons resided outside the municipal boundaries. At least one person was known to be working regularly and would have likely held a permit to be in town during business hours. On two occasions, the enforcement of the prohibited area resulted in imprisonment. In January 1949, a man from Beverley was asked to leave the prohibited area. When he refused, police tried to arrest him and he assaulted the police officer. He received a fine for being in a prohibited area but was sentenced to six months' imprisonment with hard labour for the assault, which would not have occurred in the first place had police not told him to leave town for being Aboriginal. The following year, another man was sentenced to one months' imprisonment for being in a prohibited area and two months' cumulative incarceration for receiving alcohol. Therefore, this man was entirely penalised for being Aboriginal under the *Native Administration Act 1947*, without having done anything that one would regard as remotely criminal. A non-Aboriginal person could not have been persecuted by the law in such a way. In both cases, York's Mayor A.F. Noonan was one of the two sentencing justices of the peace. The second justice of the peace was P.M.A. Glass, in 1949, and undertaker Stephen Phillip Harvey, in 1950. Mayor Noonan was certainly more outspoken against Aboriginal people than his predecessor Mayor Thorn, which would have affected his sentencing. However, the police officer laying charges and prosecuting the accused was also a critical variable in the equation of racist law enforcement.[267]

From September 1948, the sergeant of police in York was Louis Samuel Dowsett, whose personal way of policing likely correlated with the harsh sentences imposed. A couple of months after commencing his position in York, he also took on duties as the local protector for Aboriginal people. Some years earlier, he was stationed in Northam, and there, he had already been prosecuting breaches for being in a prohibited area.[268] Dowsett was the first police officer in York to charge an Aboriginal person with being in a prohibited area and it appears likely that he laid the majority of such charges (in some instances the court records do not list the police officer's name). The first two persons in York who were convicted for being in a prohibited area were also sentenced under the *Native Administration Act 1947* for receiving alcohol, and this type of charge had apparently been deemed sufficient by the previous sergeant of police, Meyer, when occasions arose.[269] However, with Dowsett in charge of the York Police, policing appeared to change from targeting Aboriginal people who were engaged in very specific disapproved behaviours (for example, the consumption of alcohol) to the attempt to enforce nearly complete social exclusion as it was made possible under the law.

On 24 January 1949, Sergeant Dowsett contacted the department by telephone and complained about the situation in York as he saw it. His telephone call was seemingly triggered by the assault on his person when trying to arrest the Aboriginal man from Beverley for being in a prohibited area, as discussed above. Tellingly, Dowsett advised that the man was 'slightly under the influence of drink but not to any extent'[270], which suggests that Dowsett did not need to intercept this man for reasons of public safety. Dowsett claimed that he had been so severely assaulted that he had to excuse himself from duty for a period of two weeks.[271]

Dowsett may have exaggerated, but even if he did not, it would not be surprising if someone reacted in a violent manner when suddenly confronted with yet another layer of oppressive sanctions against oneself and one's people for the unspoken but obvious *offence* of not having the same skin colour as the occupying force in one's own traditional country. As discussed earlier, the public records tend to be silent about the way that police, departmental officers and members of the local authorities interacted with Aboriginal people on an interpersonal level; however, the handwritten annotations and various other comments left on public records suggest that interactions would frequently have occurred in a belligerent or otherwise derogative manner. It was noted that during the telephone conversation, 'Sergeant Dowsett seemed very upset and indicated that the natives were making his position untenable. He has only a Police Constable as a subordinate officer'.[272] Dowsett may have been subject to certain expectations in relation to the way he was to enforce the law as it was at the time, and his predecessors also persecuted Aboriginal people, as did his successors; nevertheless, personal biases and attitudes displayed in interpersonal interactions should never be disregarded in such an analysis.

Since Dowsett complained about his allegedly 'untenable' position, we should have a closer look at the local court statistics. These will surely not be able to 'paint the whole picture' of the dynamics in York at the time, but an analysis of the crude statistics does provide some insights into how convictions had the potential to inflate negative settler-Australian community biases.

Between May 1947, when the prohibited area was enacted, and late January 1949, Aboriginal individuals were convicted of sixty offences in the York Police Court. However, only twenty-one out of these sixty offences could be regarded as criminal. They related to nine incidents involving thirteen individuals and consisted of assaults, thefts, damaging property and burglaries; thirteen out of these twenty-one offences were committed by juveniles. The remaining thirty-nine convictions mainly consisted of offences that specifically targeted Aboriginal people and constituted breaches of compliance with racist population control measures. Only two of the criminal offences were linked to circumstances surrounding the enforcement of the population control measures and, therefore, nearly two-thirds of these sixty convictions can be identified as purely repressive in nature. On a larger timeline, and with reference to the assault on Sergeant Dowsett, between January 1941 and December 1962, there were only a handful of convictions of Aboriginal individuals for assaulting police officers recorded in York. All of the recorded assaults against police officers occurred in combination with the law enforcement of racist legislation targeting Aboriginal people, which was mainly related to obtaining, supplying and consuming alcohol and various other segregationist and oppressive impositions.[273] These statistics suggest that the interpersonal conduct of certain police officers would have contributed to the few instances of physical reactions by Aboriginal individuals when being persecuted by white Australian law. Concerning the telephone call on 24 January 1949, it was further noted that:

> Sergeant Dowsett suspects that the supply of liquor to natives
> is committed through the medium of Certificates of Citizenship
> holders, although he cannot obtain the evidence. He is of the
> opinion the liquor is procured at Spencer's Brook and is being
> brought there by natives coming to York.[274]

Spencer's Brook is a small locality that is located approximately 27 kilometres north of York on the way to Northam, which had, at the time, a licensed hotel. However, on the record, it was not further elaborated as to from where, specifically, Dowsett thought the alcohol was being obtained. Given that Dowsett voiced the suspicion that alcohol was procured 'through the medium of Certificates of Citizenship', it is not unlikely that alcohol was legally purchased at a hotel outside of York, which was under Northam's jurisdiction, in which case, the scheme (if there was one at all) was less likely to be detected by York's police. Certificates of (conditional) citizenship will be discussed in more detail shortly (see chapter 5). For now, it will suffice to note that, at the time of Dowsett's complaint, there was only one Aboriginal person in York who had obtained a certificate of citizenship (in May 1948) and there were approximately seven persons in Northam.[275] Thus, it is not unlikely that certain Aboriginal people with citizenship rights in York, Northam or from elsewhere obtained alcohol to supply it to those in York who wished to enjoy a drink but who were barred from obtaining alcohol through the *Native Administration Act 1947* and various other legislation.

Dowsett, the local justices of the peace and others appeared to hold the contemporary common belief that Aboriginal people should not consume alcohol, as they allegedly 'couldn't hold their liquor'. This belief served to justify the existence and application of the racialised prohibition in law, and such people likely saw conditional citizenship as a threat to the imagined peace they aimed to defend.[276] Such people would have perceived their righteous actions as a moral necessity, and they would have been irritated by the increasing options for Aboriginal people to consume alcohol—Aboriginal people who might also, at times, have told 'white Australia' what they really thought of their outcast position vis-à-vis settler-Australian society once the effects of alcohol had lowered the bar of self-constraint.

It is interesting to note that the last conviction for being in a prohibited area in York occurred in January 1951, even though the prohibited area remained in force for another three years. Soon after this final conviction, it must have become local practice to no longer enforce the prohibited area, given that a departmental patrol officer observed in March 1953 that there were no restrictions imposed on Aboriginal people in York.[277] It may have been that police had developed an awareness that the emerging state-based policy of Aboriginal 'assimilation' (to be discussed in more detail later—see chapter 5.02) was at odds with the enforcement of the prohibited area, notwithstanding officers' personal opinions that were not necessarily in absolute favour of Aboriginal integration into the settler-Australian community.[278] As briefly mentioned earlier within this chapter, all prohibited areas in Western Australia were cancelled in 1954, when the department experienced continuous difficulties introducing new legislation that was to abolish prohibited areas altogether. These parliamentary struggles would eventually result in the *Native Welfare Act 1954* which came into force in mid-1955.[279]

In August 1948, Stanley Guise Middleton was appointed Commissioner of Native Affairs, and was principally against the outright segregationist sections of the legislation. Following his own appointment, he also brought in new staff who appeared to share similarly progressive views. Middleton noted in his annual report for 1951 (published in 1953), that there had been no further convictions in relation to the prohibited area in the Perth metropolitan area since departmental officers had started to contest charges in court.[280] After some time, this change in the departmental attitude emanating from the city may have influenced local police and justices of the peace not to further persecute Aboriginal people under section 42 of the Act. Departmental attempts to discourage the enforcement of prohibited areas in the country are evident in the case of the Great Southern town Gnowangerup, where the department approached the local road board asking for consent to the cancellation of the town's prohibited area (the request was declined).[281] Another, perhaps concurrent, possible reason is that the convictions that had occurred forced Aboriginal people in York largely into compliance with these severely oppressive measures. After all, the last one-off conviction for being in a prohibited area in 1951 targeted an Aboriginal man who did not usually reside in York and may not have been fully aware of the proclamation. He incurred no other charge on this occasion and only appeared in York Police Court on one other occasion in 1956 for receiving alcohol. Therefore, the only two times that this man appeared in the York Police Court between 1941 and 1962 were for being Aboriginal.[282]

Seventeen out of these eighteen convictions for being in a prohibited area occurred over a relatively short time span of fifteen months, which would have left a strong psychological effect on York's Aboriginal population with the ultimate aim of enforcing compliance with the prohibition. Also noteworthy is that, except for one instance, all other charges were laid on Saturdays. One Saturday coincided with New Year's Day, 1949, when seven persons were charged simultaneously. Two of the seven were also charged with receiving alcohol, but that was all; there were no other charges suggesting poor conduct. The *York Chronicle* also reported only about the sentences imposed, without commenting further about any potential incident leading to the charges. Sergeant Dowsett reported to the department that two people were charged with 'drunkenness'. It is not known whether the two individuals convicted of receiving alcohol merely had a couple of sips or were outright intoxicated in public. If intoxicated in public, settler-Australians could also have been charged under the Police Act. The York police charge books indicate that this occurred more or less frequently at the time, but the same individuals were often convicted repeatedly, which suggests that police targeted certain settler-Australian individuals they considered problematic or undesirable. Nevertheless, the case on New Year's Day was clearly an act of summary punishment aimed at all Aboriginal persons present for no other reason than being Aboriginal in an imagined *white space* outside of business and working hours. It is not surprising that the majority of cases occurred on weekends when Aboriginal people had no economic value to settler-Australians. They were barred from pubs and from the cinema. Perhaps Mayor Noonan anticipated these occasions to be the kind of 'emergency' situations he was referring to at the council meeting in June 1947. While sixteen of the eighteen charges resulted in fines, this does not mean that individuals did not also spend a night or two in custody as indicated in the York Police charge books.[283]

Enforcing this prohibited area was the final attempt at banning a population group of undesirables from the public sphere in York during leisure time. Pointedly, 'undesirable' was not defined by individual character but by the questionable concept of 'race', expressed through equally spurious measures of blood quantum. While the majority of convictions for being in a prohibited area resulted in monetary penalties, it is perhaps not so much the convictions that occurred that matter but rather those that did not. The force of fear of prosecution resulted in an unquantifiable silence in public records, while ensuring compliance with the law by all but a few Aboriginal people in York most of the time. Anecdotal evidence suggests that the legacy of the prohibited area declaration outlived its legal existence in York. Many Aboriginal people, in particular, reserve residents, had behaviours relating to the prohibited area and curfews:

> so ingrained in them, that they got their business done really quick—as quick as they could—and then got home. Because, even though, it was maybe two o'clock in the afternoon, they didn't want to be in town; did not want to come across the police and being questioned—they got home.[284]

In the case of York, the prohibited area was arguably one of the worst manifestations of Western Australian segregationist legislation in the twentieth century because, by default, it applied to all Aboriginal people who fell under the *Native Administration Act*. This type of oppressive population control would only be trumped by the absurd punitive action taken against those Aboriginal individuals who were thought to abuse their newly gained rights and privileges, which they had acquired through modes of exemption from being deemed 'native in law'.

Municipality of York.

P.O. Box 22.
Telephone No. 72.

24 MAY 1946
PERTH, W.A.

Town Hall,

York, Western Australia.

22nd May, 1946.

The Chief Protector of Aborigines,
Aborigines Department,
Murray Street,
PERTH.........W.A..

Dear Sir,

I am directed to bring under your notice a complaint regarding the ever-increasing number of natives in this district. They camp in the town in the daytime and create nuisances everywhere they go: They are not ordered out of the town in the evening as is the practice elsewhere and most of them are unclean and apparently not working and living a generally hopeless existence. This, of course, is no fault of theirs.

My Council appreciates that proper colonies should be provided where these natives can eventually gain citizenship and asks that proper housing be provided, pending the initiation of a colony scheme.

This Council also asks that you issue instructions for these natives to be out of the Municipal area by 6 p.m. daily.

Yours faithfully,

TOWN CLERK.

Figure 6: Complaint letter from the York Municipal Council – Department of Native Affairs, item 1938-1037, SROWA

NATIVE ADMINISTRATION ACT, 1905-41.

PROHIBITED   AREA.

PROCLAMATION.

WESTERN AUSTRALIA
To Wit

LIEUTENANT-GOVERNOR.

By His Excellency Sir James Mitchell, K.C.M.G.,
Lieutenant-Governor in and over the State of
Western Australia and its Dependencies in the
Commonwealth of Australia.

W H E R E A S by Section 42 of the Native Administration Act, 1905-41, the Governor may by Proclamation,
whenever in the interests of the natives he thinks fit, declare
any municipal district or town or any other place to be an area
in which it shall be unlawful for natives not in lawful employment to be or remain : NOW, THEREFORE, I, the said Lieutenant-
Governor, by and with the advice of the Executive Council, do
hereby declare the townsite of York to be an area in which it
shall be unlawful for natives not in lawful employment to be
or remain.

GIVEN under my hand and the Public Seal of the said
State, at P E R T H, this ...29th..... day of
....May....... 1947.

By His Excellency's Command,

MINISTER FOR NATIVE AFFAIRS.

GOD   SAVE   THE   KING ! ! !

Figure 7: Proclamation of York municipality as 'Prohibited Area' - Department of Native Affairs, item 1947/0270, SROWA

Chapter 4. Jan 1949 to June 1950

4.01 Departmental patrols—at the dawn of assimilation policy

Moving on from the explicit discussion of the prohibited area, we will now be returning closer to timeline-based events, continuing in 1949. This year saw the inauguration of a more efficient form of Aboriginal population control. When Stanley Guise Middleton became Commissioner of Native Affairs in August 1948, he started restructuring and decentralising the Department of Native Affairs. Queensland-born Middleton had worked in Papua New Guinea's colonial administration in various roles for twenty-two years and prided himself having gained great experience in dealing with 'natives'.[1] He also introduced more frequent patrols throughout the South West Land Division, conducted by new departmental staff, and it was anticipated that the practice of using police officers as local protectors would slowly be phased out. During these patrols, officers attempted to meet as many Aboriginal families and individuals as possible in any given district to address current policy agendas, for taking census information to stay up to date with Aboriginal people's movements and to meet with local protectors, authorities and other civic agencies. The dynamics within the often-strained triangular relationship between a district's Aboriginal population, local authorities and the Department of Native Affairs (later Native Welfare) was usually commented on in reports furnished by the patrol officers. Middleton was strongly welfare oriented, critical of the draconian legal liabilities he had inherited, and his ultimate aim was to lift Western Australia's Aboriginal population to a reasonably equal standard of living within settler-Australian society. Although increased welfare ambitions were aimed at the whole Aboriginal population of Western Australia, the anticipated state of equality was conditional.

Aboriginal individuals and families were expected to prove their 'worthiness' as 'deserving' of equal living standards on par with settler-Australian society, if they so desired. Many parliamentarian, departmental and community-based commentators voiced the belief that the present generation of Aboriginal adults was unable to achieve this state of reasonable equality and focus was laid on the next generations through the means of education and improved living conditions. This attitude is clearly evident in the patrol reports available.[2]

The first patrol under Middleton was conducted in February 1949, when departmental officers went to Badjaling, Quairading, York, Beverley, Brookton and Pingelly. Interestingly, the visit to Quairading confirmed the department's newly attained attitude towards prohibited areas. The Quairading Road Board was discouraged from applying to have the town declared a prohibited area when it inquired about such declaration. The visiting patrol officer, W.A. Gordon, reasoned that next to the administrative 'inconvenience' to the local police officer, the prohibited area would have placed restrictions on Aboriginal people in relation to obtaining stores, and would have created an 'inconvenience' to Aboriginal domestic workers in town. Gordon stipulated, as a further counter argument, 'the desire for the natives to become accustomed to the mode and ways of living of the white community'.[3] Thus, Quairading was never declared a prohibited area—a situation that could have ended differently had the road board made the request only one year earlier, when McBeath was still acting commissioner.

A further 'inconvenience' that Gordon did not mention was that departmental officers like himself had to attend court hearings if an Aboriginal person was charged for any offences. Their role was comparable to that of a free-of-charge duty lawyer, who was heavily biased against the defendant. Appearing in court on behalf of Aboriginal people was actually one of the duties of the local protectors in Western Australia but as these protectors were usually the local police sergeants who often prosecuted (or persecuted) the charges, departmental officers had to attend in lieu of the local protectors when this occurred, if attending was practicable. Other arrangements were also possible. For example, a month earlier when Sergeant Dowsett was apparently assaulted, as discussed above (see chapter 3.14), Dowsett was requested to arrange the local Methodist minister to appear on behalf of the Aboriginal defendant. The court records indicate that the Methodist minister did not appear, though it is not known whether Dowsett approached him. When speaking to the Quairading Road Board during the patrol, departmental Officer Gordon was well aware that he had to attend the next day at the York Police Court for a 'prohibited area' charge, as the local protector of York, Sergeant Dowsett, was prosecuting the matter. Given that the officers already had a tight schedule, attending court would have certainly counted as a further 'inconvenience' to Gordon.[4]

Having arrived in York and finished with court, the officers went only to four homes on this occasion, due to time constraints. The observations and comments in the patrol report perhaps enable the reader to visualise the homes of some families, to some extent. However, one should always acknowledge the biases within the qualitative descriptions and comments of these patrol officers. One home was a 'camp constructed of corrugated iron and in poor condition' situated on council property, on the eastern side of the Avon River. On the reserve was also only one building at the time, which was described as a 'two roomed shack built of corrugated iron, with a lean-to shed attached'. Two men lived in a house 'of European style' at Mrs Craig's Mile Pool farm (this building was possibly a remnant of the 1850s mission). Another house was occupied by an elderly couple and was noted to be owned by a family member. It was described as 'brick construction consisting of two bedrooms, lounge and kitchen, all furnished on European standard. This house was found to be clean and tidy and a credit to the occupier.' Regarding this fourth house, this was the first time, in records available to this author, that a house was noted to be owned by an Aboriginal person in York.[5] In July, Dowsett reported of an empty house owned by an Aboriginal woman of York and he suggested that a family of eight who were living in a 'leanto in conditions far from satisfactory' might be able to move into this house. Within the same year, this was the second house reportedly owned by an Aboriginal person in York which was previously unheard of in this town judging by the records available to this author.[6]

While the departmental stance was now generally anti-segregationist, condescending paternalism remained a strong feature in these reports under Middleton's administration and would remain so throughout the 1950s. Under the subheading 'Behaviour of Natives', it was noted that 'Sergeant Dowsett advised that apart from intermittent outbursts, the natives generally are kept in control'.[7] Notwithstanding that Dowsett had complained only three weeks earlier that the situation was 'untenable' (see chapter 3.14), his white masculinity appears to have got the better of him when he met the departmental officers, and he could claim that the potentially problematic (in settler-Australian view) Aboriginal population of York was being kept under control—by implication, under control through Sergeant of Police Louis Dowsett. He provided some further general information. For example, he advised that the majority of Aboriginal people were employed as farmhands and engaged in rabbit trapping. He claimed that the average wage that was being paid ranged between £6 and £7 per week. In comparison, the basic wage for men working in the South West Land Division was set at £6 4s 4d by 9 February 1949, while women's basic wage was set at £3 7s 2d. Dowsett's local census records held at the police station showed that forty-one adults and seventy-eight children were believed to reside in the greater York District.[8]

4.02 The first Aboriginal country housing program that was not to be

During this first patrol, the local health inspector of the municipality, W. Hooton, was interviewed as the council had intimated that it would have two 'native houses' condemned that were situated on council property. This meant they would be declared unfit for human habitation under the *Health Act 1948* and the municipal council had the power to evict anyone living in a condemned structure. The Department of Native Affairs requested that action be delayed pending the implementation of a certain housing program. Middleton then wrote to the municipal council on 23 February. He advised that the department 'has recently drawn up a Building project to include Native Reserves, the implementation of which will be put into effect when the building position allows'. Town Clerk L.G. Baker replied on 11 March 1949, advising that the council had decided to defer taking any action to demolish the two houses in anticipation of the department's housing program.[9] This 'housing program' was the first of its kind for Aboriginal people in Western Australia, outside of government institutions and missions—but as we will see, it was unable to fulfil any expectations that Middleton may have had for the improvement of the living conditions of town and reserve dwellers in York.

In the second part of 1948, the provision of improved housing on reserves, and potentially within towns, was deemed desirable and initial discussions about a potential scheme were had between the ministers of Health and Native Affairs. By November, Middleton was obtaining quotes from a Mr O.A. Doran of Victoria Park in Perth for twenty prefabricated 'improved camps' to be erected in selected localities in the Wheatbelt and Great Southern regions. In December, State Cabinet approved of a reduced number of ten 'camps or small houses' under the condition that they were not built by Mr Doran's company. Doran had a contract for 100 houses under the (post-World War II) War Services Settlement Scheme and the state government was anxious that nothing would delay the completion of this program. Doran had offered to build one improved camp for every ten War Services homes, and to obtain the building materials from a different source, so that the Aboriginal housing scheme would not interfere with the War Services Settlement Scheme contract. However, any further involvement of his company, other than providing building plans, was subsequently denied. As Doran was the only contractor in the Perth metropolitan area to build prefabricated homes, the department had to find a different way. In May 1949, Middleton formally applied to the State Housing Commission to build the homes; however, in July, he was advised that the application was deferred, 'owing to the current shortage of building materials'.[10] Because of this deferral, Middleton initiated the creation of departmental 'mobile works units', each consisting of a 'white tradesman' and two Aboriginal 'carpenter's labourers'. These mobile works units were anticipated to travel from reserve to reserve to undertake improvements, and it was also proposed that they may build pisé houses. 'Pisé de terre' is the French term for rammed earth, and was often referred to simply as 'pisé'. By November 1949, two mobile works units were operating in Western Australia (one in the southern half and one in the northern), which were hardly sufficient to make any immediate impact across the state. Simultaneously, for reasons of political expediency, the resources for ten improved camps were reallocated to the Perth metropolitan area, while it became policy to encourage Aboriginal people in the country to purchase their own blocks in towns where the (one) mobile works unit was anticipated to potentially assist with erecting basic homes.[11]

4.03 Patrols II

Departmental officers were back in York in June to formally object to the conditional citizenship application of a man from Yoting, which was held in the York Police Court. The application was subsequently denied. They also inspected the reserve. On 6 June, there was a 'sports meeting' at York, which Aboriginal people from other areas attended, and some stayed on the reserve for up to a couple of weeks afterwards. Once again, the state of the latrines was complained about and Sergeant Dowsett claimed that the removal service may cease in the near future as the contractor was 'objecting to the work on account of the dirty state the latrines were sometimes in'.[12] Officers ordered those people present to maintain the latrines in a fit state and, at the next patrol, a month later, it was reported that the latrines were found to be 'very clean'.[13] The ongoing complaints about the state of the sanitary conveniences over the past ten years serve as prime example of the racist logic that underpinned how settler-Australians conceived of the Aboriginal 'other' as a uniform entity. The reader may remember how the Kickett family was made responsible for the maintenance of the latrines that were erected by the department in the early 1940s, despite the fact that this family had their own toilet. The few families that called the York Reserve their home on a permanent basis during different periods were held accountable for the sanitary conduct of any number of visitors to the reserve.

Until the 1950s, the reserve was the only place to go for most Aboriginal people if they wished to visit York without getting harassed by the local authorities. The permanent residents had, in theory, no say whatsoever in who could stay and who could not. Nevertheless, it seems quite reasonable to assume that the families who called the reserve their home also developed a sense of territorial ownership. This does not mean, though, that they would have, nor should have, felt responsible for the conduct of people that may have been visiting, largely uninvited. However, the dominant settler-Australian view hardly acknowledged individuals within reserve settings and the dynamics within these forced temporary communities. Therefore, the view was that it was a singular body—*the natives*—who left the latrines in a dirty state, and now, in 1949, the same uniform 'natives' were ordered to maintain cleanliness or face certain consequences. The principle of individuals being 'guilty by association' was twisted so that a whole population group was 'guilty by descent'. In the end, the contractor, Mr Cherrington, did not refuse to undertake the night soil removals at the reserve per se, as Dowsett had suggested he would. However, Cherrington simply kept dumping the night soil from the emptied pans on open ground close to the lavatories, before eventually breaking his contract at York in late June, as he was unhappy with his pay and the council was unwilling to pay more. The council took over night soil removals for the next few years and continued servicing the reserve by charging doubled fees, which it justified due to the distance from town.[14]

There are no further complaints by contractors on record in relation to night soil removals at the York Reserve. In January 1950, it was reported that an Aboriginal family was living on the council's rubbish dump on Ninth Road and the bread winner worked for the council in sanitary disposals. Perhaps this was one of the reasons that no further complaints came from sanitary removalists. If this Aboriginal council employee took part in the sanitary removals on the reserve, he would likely have done the job without a default antipathy towards attending the reserve. He may have been given the dirtier tasks, too, so white employees would have had no reason to complain.[15]

During the next patrol, in July 1949, two applications to marry were discussed and Sergeant Dowsett questioned departmental officers as to whether it was advisable that one of the couples who worked at Mr Dall's farm should marry. Given that they were already living together, it was recommended that it was better for the couple to marry 'under such circumstances'.[16] Under the original *Aborigines Act 1905*, a female Aboriginal person was required to seek permission if she wanted to marry anyone but an Aboriginal man. However, this section was amended in 1936. Thenceforth, until 1955, any person deemed legally 'native' had to seek permission from the Commissioner of Native Affairs if they wished to marry. A form had to be filled out that required the applicants to declare their own 'nationality or caste' and the 'name and caste of parents'[17], as well as the names of all children of both applicants. In this case, local protector Sergeant Dowsett agreed with the application and sent it off to head office, but he could just as well have objected to the marriage. This section of the Act was conceived by A.O. Neville to serve his grand social engineering scheme with the aim of *breeding out* the colour, as discussed above (see chapter 2.03).[18]

When Middleton became commissioner, these applications were increasingly less scrutinised in racialist terms. Records suggest that, at least in the South West Land Division, in many cases, the applications were likely regarded as a mere remnant formality that had to be completed rather than considered seriously. However, local protectors and the department still had the legal power to decide a couple's future, and some marriages were denied because of social-welfare concerns. Whether these paternalistic concerns had merit on some occasions is beside the point, as there was no such provision for couples of non-Aboriginal ancestries. This practice infantilised Aboriginal people until this section of legislation was abolished. Further, as long as they existed, these application forms provided valuable demographic information for the department.[19]

Likewise, in July 1949, the newly appointed health inspector of the York Road Board, Herbert William Noel Haley, who we have already come across as the secretary of the same local authority (see chapters 3.10 and 3.14), became involved by conducting his own inspection on the reserve. He identified the dumping of night soil issue discussed earlier in this section. He counted eleven unlicensed dogs, 'most of them within the living quarters of the natives',[20] and he advised Aboriginal people present that the number had to be 'reduced' and that Dowsett was to follow up. He found a considerable amount of rubbish to be scattered around and offered that the road board would collect it if residents were to gather it up. He made suggestions to the department on how to flyproof the lavatories' pans and he pointed out that the latrines lacked disinfectants. Haley insisted that disinfectants must be provided and that local health supervision would ensure regular use by reserve dwellers. Haley pointed out that while water was laid on the reserve, there were no provisions for bathing or laundry facilities, which led him to conclude that this was the reason that reserve dwellers would not 'interest themselves to any extend in personal hygiene'.[21] In relation to concerns about hygiene, Haley then made a revealing comment:

> As some of the children attend local schools, action might be
> taken to provide an ablution shed for individual bathing and the
> provision of wash troughs under cover might encourage more
> regular cleansing of clothing and bedding.[22]

This quote suggests that Haley's main concern in relation to hygiene was how it may have affected the settler-Australian population in York. After all, York was still a declared prohibited area and the time that reserve residents spent in town, except for children attending school and some women engaged in domestic work, would have been accordingly very limited. There must have been complaints from parents regarding the hygiene of Aboriginal children attending school. Therefore, it is likely that Haley suggested that amenities be installed not for the well-being of the reserve's children, but ultimately for the sake of non-Aboriginal townspeople. Even if Haley was somewhat sympathetic to the reserve children and did not wish for them to be subjected to conflict at school because of differences in personal hygiene, the idea of improving the children's living conditions seems to have emanated only from Aboriginal children's moving within contested 'white spaces'. However, as was often the case, the claims about the children's state of personal hygiene may also have been exaggerated and universalised.

Two weeks later, a further layer of population control was instigated when Haley advised the department that he was going to implement weekly inspections on the reserve accompanied by Sergeant Dowsett. Head Office ordered a four-gallon drum of phenyl disinfectant to be sent to York, which was to be bottled by Dowsett and distributed when required. It is not difficult to imagine that Dowsett resented the additional duty. Haley also had ideas for housing improvements on the reserve and advised that there were disused schools in the district at Doodenanning, Mount Hardy and Green Hills, all of which had sheds or houses attached. He suggested that these buildings could potentially be transported to the reserve; however, this never eventuated. Lastly, Haley requested that when departmental officers were to visit the reserve, the local health authority (which was Haley himself) should always be contacted to keep the health aspect to a reasonable standard in a co-ordinated effort.[23]

In the following month, the road board discussed complaints that had been made about unlicensed dogs from the reserve 'becoming a menace at places' and it was decided that an inspection should be made 'in an endeavour to rectify the position'.[24] It seems that 'inspection' was the new go-to remedy for the road board, as it grew increasingly comfortable with the idea of imposing itself on Aboriginal affairs in its jurisdiction, as opposed to earlier years, when it merely cried for the Department of Native Affairs or a higher authority to take some form of action when it was displeased with certain states of affairs on the reserve. Concerning canines, under the *Dog Act 1948*, any adult male Aboriginal person could register one dog free of charge. Any number of dogs exceeding the number of Aboriginal adults 'in such party' were liable to be destroyed by any police officer.[25] Thus, if there were ten adults on the reserve, one might think that they could own ten dogs among the group or 'party'. However, the legislation was not clear as to whether Aboriginal women counted, as they were not eligible to register a dog free of charge. Also, the identifier 'party' left room for interpretation. This section was introduced before town reserves became the predominant camping ground for Aboriginal people in the South West Land Division. Did it mean dogs owned within the family unit or was the total number defined by the generalised social group of reserve residents? There was certainly room for Aboriginal people to navigate the system by distributing dogs among reserve dwellers but there was also room for police to interpret the law as they saw fit. Dogs owned by Aboriginal people in York had been targeted already two years earlier.

In 1947, local member of Parliament G.B. Wood complained to the department on behalf of farmers whose live stock had apparently been interfered with by dogs from the reserve and McBeath ordered that all unlicensed dogs were to be destroyed. It might have been the case that dogs from the reserve were a nuisance to farmers and their owners may not have cared as much as those farmers would have appreciated—in particular, if dogs from the reserve had killed sheep, as had been alleged. However, if this was the case, the hypothetically nonchalant attitude of dog owners regarding the supervision of their canines would have been hardly surprising, given that Aboriginal people had to live in such an antagonistic environment. While the relationship between people and animals in the country may not be comparable to the relationship that many city dwellers might have with their pet dogs, that the majority of dogs reportedly lived in the reserve residents' 'quarters' suggests that they were, to some extent, considered companions. Therefore, when police attended the reserve and killed 'excess dogs', this would have likely added further emotionally laden resentment towards white Australia.[26]

As the 1940s drew to a close, it must have dawned on many settler-Australians in York that Aboriginal people were going to be part of the community eventually. It was reported in December 1949 that there were four families in York who lived in 'shacks' on their own blocks. Night soil was apparently buried in the backyards, which raised further health concerns.[27] At the same time, Road Board Health Inspector Haley kept true to his word and conducted regular inspections. In November, he commended the reserve residents for keeping the place clean but railway workers at the nearby railway bridge reportedly did not maintain 'proper sanitary facilities' which negatively affected reserve dwellers, according to Haley's own observations.[28] This was a rare positive public comment on the reserve. With the dawn of the new decade, the reserve was increasingly considered the lesser 'evil', as Aboriginal people started purchasing their own blocks and moved into the sphere previously reserved for white Australians. Next to the physical presence of Aboriginal people in town, a gradual uptake of conditional citizenship throughout the 1950s would further assert the Aboriginal presence within the realms of settler-Australian civic life.

4.04 Patrols III—the new decade

Following his first patrol in the Central and Eastern Wheatbelt in January 1950, departmental Patrol Officer Bruce Alan McLarty succinctly summarised the sentiments of local authorities and the non-Aboriginal public within this region:

> Most local governing bodies are prepared to admit that they are good spenders and constitute a necessary source of labour; but their living conditions present a problem to the health authorities and racial prejudice militates against their absorption into the community life. They take the view that the department should immediately solve these and other problems. In other words they wish to reap any benefit that might accrue to the community through the natives' presence without being in any way concerned with the disadvantages. This has resulted in hostility to the department and this hostility is being transferred to the natives.[29]

McLarty had worked with Middleton in Papua New Guinea's colonial administration and he also had a background in journalism, which may explain his progressive attitude and analytical skills, unlike some previously employed field staff.[30] When speaking with Town Clerk Baker about hygiene-related matters at Aboriginal camps, McLarty advised him of the department's policy encouraging Aboriginal people to buy their own blocks and improve their living conditions by first erecting tents and later building better houses once material became available. Baker agreed, in a way, by stating that, from the town's perspective, it would not be good for all Aboriginal people to be 'collected' on the reserve, and that provided Aboriginal people complied with health regulations, they would probably be given some latitude in the matter of their housing. Then Baker intimated that he personally considered Aboriginal people a financial asset to the town and would not like to see them moved. However, he was unable to speak on behalf of the council—in particular, due to a news article in the current issue of the *York Chronicle*, which reported on a deputation to the Minister for Native Affairs, Hubert Parker, in relation to complaints about conditional citizenship rights. Baker also cited the general 'public feeling' in the district to be adverse. He went on that the article and public resentments had probably affected the attitude of the council members at the subsequent meeting. There is no evidence that Baker was intentionally trying to impress McLarty by portraying himself as understanding and being a potential ally of the department when facing McLarty directly and making these statements about his own opinions but the reported statements did come across a bit like that.[31]

When prepping the Minister for Native Affairs, Hubert Stanley Wyborn Parker, in March, for a proposed tour through the districts, Commissioner Middleton noted a tendency of antagonistic or 'tongue in cheek' reactions of the local authorities and the lethargic and oft-time hostile attitudes of local protectors. However, Middleton then surmised that police and local authorities would probably adopt a different attitude in the minister's presence.[32] Only a month later, Parker of the Liberal Party was replaced by Victor Doney of the Country Party, and all advice given by Middleton had likely evaporated, figuratively speaking.[33] But so, too, would have evaporated the potential impact of the deputation concerning conditional citizenship, which had been organised by the Beverley Road Board. In York's local press, the deputation was only reported as a cut-and-paste news piece with a brief comment voicing regret that York's municipal council and the road board had not been invited to join. One aspect of which the local authorities would have taken notice was that Minister Parker advised the deputation that local authorities were entitled to be informed about any conditional citizenship applications. However, Parker's advice did not have any legislative backing and was likely based on his own beliefs as to what should have been a common curtesy towards local authorities.[34]

4.05 The second Aboriginal country housing program that was not to be

During three patrols in 1950, departmental officers kept surveying the housing situation in York as they had done the previous year. By May, a new housing scheme had been conceived. As previously, Aboriginal people were encouraged to buy their own blocks, but under the new scheme, they would start saving money by paying small amounts into a savings fund for the construction of a house built of rammed earth (pisé). The anticipated price was initially between £80 and £100 but, by October, required funds in the vicinity of £200 were already being talked about. The work was again to be conducted by that one mobile works unit and it was acknowledged that it may take a while until the program was completed. In May and June 1950, departmental officers attempted to approach all Aboriginal families in York to gauge potential interest in the scheme and it was noted that most Aboriginal people 'appeared to be rather sceptical, and in some instances it was hard to convince them that action was definitely going to be taken'.[35] Nevertheless, in July, some families agreed to open up their own savings accounts and made initial payments. However, in many cases, payments did not progress much after a short while and departmental officers acknowledged that a major factor in ceasing payments was the uncertainty around the whole housing scheme, as there were no definite answers available in regard to costs and building time frames. Even departmental officers commented that it was hardly surprising if York's Aboriginal population had no faith in the government to provide these homes in the near future. The sceptics were not wrong, as this second housing scheme also never eventuated.[36]

Consequently, for the time being, many Aboriginal people living in the York District remained living in camps—also known as 'humpies'—with a few notable exceptions. Judgemental comments were rife when certain individuals did not immediately jump at the first opportunity to build much improved camps or cottages, when it was believed they were financially capable of doing so. For those who purchased their own blocks, it would have likely taken a while to become accustomed to the idea of 'owning' land as per the meaning within settler-Australian capitalist society, which denied Aboriginal ownership of Country as the original custodians, and promoted individualistic forms of ownership. From the onset of European invasion up until the point in time under discussion, the majority of Aboriginal people living within settled areas had camped at the mercy of local government authorities and white farmers, or the Aborigines Department and its successors, on reserves declared under the Act

(1905–1947). This, in combination with the necessity to move around the country due to seasonal employment opportunities, meant that Aboriginal people usually lacked any certainty as to how long a camp-style home could remain in any given place. Therefore, structures were often transportable rather than permanent. Putting significant effort and time into a likely ephemeral structure seems counterintuitive. Some homes in York in the early 1950s were described as follows:

- A 'rambling tin building on the reserve'.
- An 'iron and hessian house' near Northam Road on land owned by a member of the wider family.
- An 'iron and hession house containing two bedrooms, kitchen, a double and two single beds, table and dresser, on their own block at the corner of Cowan Road and Hope Street'.
- A 'good brick house on Hope Street' owned by a family member who also owned the above-mentioned block near Northam Road.
- One family 'camped on private property in a well kept native-type camp'.
- Another family was 'living in the old school house at Gwambagine. The building is in a bad state of repair'.
- An elderly single man lived 'in a small camp made of flattened oil drums lined with wheat bags'.
- In 1951, one family was 'living on their block of approximately 4 acres in Spicer Road off Main Street. ... It is of substantial construction being whitened mudbrick and corrugated iron roof'. However, this home had been previously condemned in May 1950 and the family had camped outside of town at Burgess Siding for a while, until being able to return.
- Also in 1951, several camps were grouped together at Gilgering. One was described as 'consisting of a few super bags and petrol drum tops over a rickety framework'.

- A 'bag and tin humpy 15' x 20", housing a family of eleven, located on the rubbish dump. This was then replaced with the next home mentioned below, after the family was talked into purchasing their own block of land.

- One home situated on a block on Hope Street owned by the family was described as 'most dilapidated one-room tin shanty. There is only one bed, no fireplace' ... 'On the day of the visit the wind was howling through open spaces and holes in the wall and it was no surprise to note that the children were suffering from colds.' Nine months later, it was reported that this 'one roomed, scrap iron shanty remains unimproved'.[37]

In particular, in relation to the last example, it should be noted that the family had signed up for the savings fund and was waiting for a pisé house to be built by the department, which was never going to eventuate.[38] While varying degrees of condescension and paternalism were always present in the patrol reports, the description of Aboriginal homes in the York District at the beginning of the 1950s arguably had to have a somewhat negative tone by necessity to advance the need for a housing scheme. This was unless the homes were considered of European standard—then, these homes and the families who occupied them could serve as positive examples for the department to argue that Aboriginal people were in principle able to live in advanced home environments on par with settler-Australians. The belief that most Aboriginal people lacked this ability was a common prejudice of the time, of which departmental staff were well aware.[39]

4.06 Adverse news reporting and local protector wanted

In April and May 1950, feelings started to run high in both local government jurisdictions of York. With the appearance of a handful of camps within the municipality of York, apparently public discontent also grew, as suggested in the *West Australian* in early April 1950:

Complaints have been received by the York Municipal Council about the conditions under which certain natives are living within the municipality. Ratepayers in the locality consider that they are justified in asking that the humpies which have been erected be removed.[40]

On 13 April, Town Clerk Baker wrote to the Commissioner of Native Affairs advising that the municipality's health inspector had conducted an inspection in the north-eastern side of York and found the sanitary conditions at 'the camps' most unsatisfactory. He requested, on behalf of the council, that immediate action be taken, 'preferably by causing the occupants to be removed' to the reserve as soon as possible.[41] Interestingly, there was no corresponding news article in the local newspaper. In March, it was reported that complaints were made 'regarding the unsanitary conditions prevailing at a residence in Newcastle Street where natives were in the habit of congregating'. The same residence was discussed the next month by the municipality's Health Committee and it was decided that the owner would be given three months to take out certain repairs and improvements, including the provision of new toilets.[42] However, this residence was a rental property, not a camp, and was not even mentioned in the current patrol reports. Someone within the council's sphere in York would have had good relations with staff at the *West Australian* newspaper, feeding sensationalist news to Perth, while the *York Chronicle*'s editor seemingly chose to be a bit more discreet on this occasion.

Departmental officer B.A. McLarty replied to council's request and advised that, given the concerns voiced were a local health matter, it was for the council to take action if required and, if necessary, to prosecute those Aboriginal persons concerned. He referred in particular to one camp in the east ward of town. McLarty further wrote that it was not the desire of the department to shield Aboriginal people from their civic responsibilities, and their removal to a native reserve, even if this were possible, was not considered a solution to the problem. Furthermore, he reasoned that the department did not wish Aboriginal people to receive any special treatment in these matters and he recommended that the council took whatever action necessary as it would 'in the case were they white persons'.[43] In an awkward way, McLarty promoted equality but completely ignored issues of inequity, namely, that Aboriginal

133

people had, in most cases, a much more disadvantaged starting point than settler-Australians.

At the council meeting prior to the one when the council discussed McLarty's answer, it received an invitation to a conference on 'native matters' at Katanning, to which representatives of local governments were invited. When discussing the invitation, Councillor Phillip M. Glass was reportedly ranting about 'armchair administrators',[44] whom he accused of condoning the alleged appalling conditions in which Aboriginal people lived in a certain area in York. The way that Glass was paraphrased suggests that he was concerned rather about the 'conditions' with which settler-Australians had to live in their neighbourhoods, and not so much the conditions that Aboriginal people had to endure. The municipal council decided to send Mayor Noonan and Councillor Glass to the conference.[45] At the next meeting, council was seemingly up in arms about McLarty's reply. Glass lamented that the reply did not come from the commissioner but from McLarty, who was lower in the departmental hierarchy. Glass was also unhappy that he had been publicly criticised by Native Affairs Minister Doney for his 'armchair administrators' remarks and complained that the council still did not know what patrol officers were doing when they visited York. Referring to McLarty's advice that the council could condemn camps, if necessary, Glass noted that affected people would then have to move to the reserve, where they were apparently not wanted by the department, and that Aboriginal people were 'definitely not wanted in the town unless they conformed to the health and building by-laws laid down by the council and observed by other citizens'.[46]

That the majority of Aboriginal people concerned were not considered citizens at the time did not seem to have occurred to Glass; however, at the Katanning conference a month later, he would be vocal about conditional citizenship for Aboriginal people, among other topics. At the council meeting, Mayor Noonan asserted that it was a matter for the department to provide better housing 'but apparently the department expected them to be accepted just as they were'.[47] In the end, it was resolved that a condemnation notice be issued for one camp, that departmental patrol officers should always call at the council and that a reply from low-ranking McLarty was not acceptable. The foregoing episode once more exemplifies how Aboriginal people were considered a foreign body—a problem—within settler-Australian spaces. It was grudgingly beginning to be accepted that Aboriginal people may live among white Australians within town but if they failed to live up to the expectations of settler-Australians, then the assumption was that they reverted to being a problem managed by the Department of Native Affairs, rather than a community problem. Diplomatically, Town Clerk Baker toned down the sentiments voiced by Glass and Noonan in his next letter to the commissioner on 9 May, when advising of the council's resolutions.[48]

Following the two-month period of vocal opposition to Aboriginal housing in the municipality of York, the road board's health inspector, Mr Haley, contacted the department on 16 May to advise that the road board was taking action in relation to one home in their district to have it condemned but requested that a departmental officer inspect the conditions before taking any action. Sprinkling antagonism between the lines, Haley asked whether any action had been taken in relation to his report from the previous year. He further wished to confirm whether the reserve was set aside as a permanent residence, or was solely for the use of itinerant Aboriginal people. In internal departmental correspondence, it became apparent that the communication skills of departmental Officer Francis William George Andersen, who was dealing with the matter, were somewhat wanting as he had failed to reply to Haley's report. However, Andersen had not completely ignored the report, and he wrote to Commissioner Middleton that he had requested that disinfectant be sent to York. In relation to the building of ablution blocks and improving the toilets, Andersen advised that this was to be completed by the mobile works unit but he claimed that, 'owing to the hostility of the Board and Council', he was unable to estimate when the unit would be able to work in York as he had 'first [to] discover what obstacles and conditions we have to face there'.[49] This comment is somewhat surprising, as the one thing that both local government authorities repeatedly expressed was that they wanted improvements in Aboriginal sanitary and living conditions without having to contribute to them. In relation to housing, both the council and road board insisted that local building by-laws be adhered to, but regarding the erection of ablution blocks and toilets, it seems unlikely that either local authority would have opposed the construction of any kind of sanitary infrastructure, as long as they did not have to attend to it.

Andersen also pointed out to Middleton that the reserve was indeed for the use of transient Aboriginal people, but that this was purely a departmental matter. He concluded that the 'reserve is for native purposes and outside bodies have no control over its use'.[50] This correspondence was seemingly not further discussed at the next road board meeting, as Andersen, once again, may have forgotten to reply to the query. However, the road board was vocal about Aboriginal matters, as reported, again, by the *West Australian* on 23 May. In reply to a Health Bulletin article written by Middleton, who condemned the fact that there were no policies by local authorities to encourage Aboriginal people to settle in 'good quarters'[51], the newspaper wrote about the road board's attitude towards Aboriginal people:

> Board members said that it was not possible to mix native and white populations. People who wrote about assimilating natives into white communities, members said, should first make a practical test. It was easy for city people to suggest matters that would not affect them.[52]

The second sentence of the above quotation very much mirrors Glass's comments but, according to the *West Australian*, the board expressed a more damning view by openly defending ongoing segregation as a matter of principle. By and large, the road board usually echoed the council's sentiments but would often allow the council to step into the foreground when taking action in relation to mutual interests concerning Aboriginal people in the district.

Interestingly, as had occurred when reporting the recent council meetings, the *York Chronicle*'s article about the road board's meeting was a little less radical in tone. Reporting about the same board meeting, the *York Chronicle* noted that it was debated whether the board should send a representative to the upcoming conference in Katanning (York Road Board delegates did not attend the Katanning conference but they attended a preliminary meeting at Beverley where delegation was seemingly handed over to council members). The paper also reported that board members voiced the common prejudices that it was useless to try changing adult Aboriginal people, that focus should be placed on the youth and that child endowments should be paid in goods and not cash, 'as some of them, more often than not, spend it on gambling'.[53] If these sentiments sound familiar, it is probably because G.B. Wood, MLC, was still a member of the road board and had, in 1946, brought up the same allegations in Parliament, as discussed above (see chapter 3.10). However, in the *York Chronicle*, there was no direct quote promoting the idea that mixing Aboriginal and white Australians was impossible.[54] It is not suggested here that the *West Australian* inflated facts, but rather, that the *York Chronicle*, at this point in time, seemingly sanitised its reports. There is strong evidence that members of the road board held on to a segregationist ideology. In October 1950, departmental Officer McLarty attended a local carnival in York, off-duty, where he was subject to the road board's chairman, William Henry Robinson's, strong opinions about Aboriginal people living among settler-Australians. McLarty reported that he talked with the chairman about Aboriginal matters but, when he used the term 'assimilation', Robinson apparently became 'violently and personally abusive, uttering derogatory personal remarks,' and McLarty declined to continue the conversation.[55]

In the same week as the two different newspaper articles were published, in late May 1950, departmental officers visited York again. On arrival in town, Sergeant Dowsett announced that he would relinquish his appointment as local protector (which he eventually did, some months later). He had been threatening to do so for a while and had commented earlier that he 'had too much work to do without worrying about natives'.[56] From this point onwards, the department was looking for a local protector who was not a police officer. The school master, Mr Moore, was approached, as he showed seemingly genuine interest in Aboriginal children. Councillor and grocery store owner Frederick Ashbolt was also approached after some Aboriginal people who were interviewed stated that he was the only person in town who did not hate Aboriginal people and might be willing to take on the local protector role. Simultaneously, departmental Officer Andersen commented that Ashbolt was the only person in the council he knew of 'who has opposed the Council in any of their attacks against the department and against natives'.[57] As already discussed above (see chapter 3.10), Ashbolt's open show of sympathy with the plight of Aboriginal people in an otherwise largely hostile social environment would have been, at least partially, based on his own business considerations. Both Ashbolt and Moore declined after considering the proposal. Some months later, the department also asked a Salvation Army officer, as well as a pastor (Reverend Warwick Shaw Bastian) and a solicitor (Roland Iddison). All three men declined. To approach solicitors was Middleton's brainchild, as he thought that solicitors were ideal candidates because they would also be able to represent Aboriginal people in court on an honorary basis. Iddison was said to be sympathetic to Aboriginal people; however, he eventually declined the offer, claiming that his lawyer's practice was not well established yet and he feared loss of business arising from negative sentiments within the settler-Australian community if he were to accept the local protector position.[58]

For the other persons who were approached, this fear of community sentiment was perhaps also the deciding factor in declining the offer. Commissioner Middleton was trying to shift the role of local protector from auxiliary policing to purely welfare-dedicated duties. The proposed candidates were advised of this shift in an attempt to make the role more attractive, which proved to be unsuccessful. The proposed candidates may have sensed that there would be a marked difference between theory and practice, as suggested by the following example. Five years later, it was internally discussed that local protectors were becoming increasingly less important and that formal appointment to the position was no longer strictly necessary as they only fulfilled a minimum of administrative duties by occasionally issuing ration orders and train fares. However, Central District Officer McLarty suggested that the numbers should not be reduced as relationships with these protectors were '*harmonious*' and, more importantly, they were 'useful as intelligence agents'.[59] The double-sided reality of a local protector's duties, which were made up of welfare on one side and policing and control on the other, would not have escaped potential welfare-minded supporters of Aboriginal people. Therefore, another possible reason for declining the appointment as local protector was that the persons approached may not have wished to be part of the state government machinery with its aspired-to omnipotence. Further, being sympathetic towards a certain cause does not mean that one automatically has the motivation and time to invest in it. Ashbolt, for example, had his grocery store and municipal council work to attend to, which he cited as the main reason for declining the local protector position.[60]

During the patrol in late May, officers attended a road board meeting. Board members reportedly remained generally hostile towards Aboriginal people in the district, except for Secretary Haley, who still seemed approachable. The same old complaints and sentiments were brought up during the visit. However, at a meeting with members of the municipal council, attendees appeared to be slightly more positively inclined. Those present were Mayor Noonan, Councillor Glass, Town Clerk Baker and Health Inspector O'Leary. Council was seemingly fixated on housing. Health Inspector O'Leary had even assisted an Aboriginal family, who owned a block on Hope Street, to design a corrugated iron house for them that satisfied York's by-laws. The building permit had been approved by council the previous week under condition of strict supervision by O'Leary.[61] Departmental officer Andersen explained the current housing scheme and that change would not occur overnight. Apparently, Mayor Noonan and Councillor Glass expressed appreciation of the department's endeavours. Noonan also suggested that land be set aside for a 'native village'—in other words, a segregated community. However, he reportedly backtracked when it was explained that such a situation was undesirable. At the time, the department still believed that the pisé housing scheme would eventuate and promoted it accordingly, showing council a rough sketch of the homes to be built. Andersen went on reporting that council members had instantly agreed to the plan and informed him that they would not place any restrictions on the department's plans since they preferred some improvement to be made to the existing conditions. Andersen then commented that this was the reverse of what Sergeant Dowsett had told him some months ago. Apparently, Dowsett had informed Andersen that the council would refuse permission to erect anything but the normal type of home. The health inspector then denied that this had ever been suggested by the council.[62] It may never be known what the true story was. Both the local authorities and Sergeant Dowsett were known to act friendly and to be somewhat submissive during personal interactions with departmental officers or the minister, but when among themselves (as reported in the local press), their discussions would often devolve into defensive siege narratives.

Sergeant Dowsett presents a prime example of how important personality-driven choices and actions can be within a system of oppression. Dowsett appears to have been an archetype of the 'authoritarian personality'. Such an authoritarian personality 'attaches itself to figures of strength and disdains those it deems weak. It tends toward conventionalism, rigidity, and stereotypical thinking; it insists on a stark contrast between in-group and out-group, and it jealously patrols the boundaries between them'.[63] He would not have been the only police officer or local government representative in York displaying such traits; however, he was certainly the most reported on, as evidenced by departmental records. As we have learned (see chapter 3.14), he was the first police officer in York to charge Aboriginal people for being in the prohibited area, even though the law had already been in force for over a year prior to his arrival in York. Dowsett combined forces with the council to attend a meeting in preparation for the Katanning conference, where policy 'solutions' were conceived with a view to increasing control over Aboriginal people and gaining greater influence over mandated powers concerning Aboriginal rights. He was the only police officer to attend this meeting, among representatives of four road boards and one municipal council, which indicates that he was more invested in righteous population control matters than the average police sergeant. While Dowsett's recorded behaviour towards Aboriginal people suggests that he held largely little regard for individual needs, in the presence of departmental officers he would sometimes boast that he was going to take certain actions in support of Aboriginal individuals; departmental officers severely doubted Dowsett's sincerity.[64]

Furthermore, it was noted in several departmental patrol reports that Sergeant Dowsett had aggravated certain situations, and in at least a few instances, departmental officers had reversed the seemingly unreasonable directions Dowsett had issued to Aboriginal people in his role as local protector. For example, Dowsett had ordered several individuals to relocate away from the reserve—a directive that was then nullified by a patrol officer of the department after the individuals complained.[65]

Dowsett's apparent righteousness and lack of consideration for the plight of Aboriginal people in York also came to light during the patrol in May 1950, when all Aboriginal people interviewed were quite outspoken concerning the 'attitude of Sergeant Dowsett whom they openly stated they hated'.[66] Health Inspector O'Leary also commented on Dowsett's attitude. He stated that Dowsett had introduced him to Aboriginal people and, at first, he thought the way that Dowsett treated Aboriginal people was appropriate and warranted. However, after he had witnessed departmental Officer Anderson's more positive approach, he apparently gained an understanding of why Aboriginal people in York despised Dowsett. Soon after Dowsett had relinquished his role as protector, it was noted that the relationship with the local authorities appeared to be improving since Dowsett was no longer the local representative for the Department of Native Affairs. After Dowsett's retirement from the police force in 1953, Patrol Officer B.A. McLarty interviewed an Aboriginal man at York who reportedly did not make a secret of his 'deep rooted antipathy to the department', having been 'led to believe' that the department prevented him from buying a disused school building south of York. Insisting that the department had nothing to do with the affair, McLarty explained that this Aboriginal man commented repeatedly, 'Sergeant knows all about it', and McLarty continued that this case provided another example of the harm that Dowsett had done to the department's relations with Aboriginal people in the York District.[67]

The Dowsett example carries one important lesson: that the strength of systems of oppressions depends on their agents and the willingness of those agents to perform their duties with zeal. In this case, the system's policy makers were actually trying to lessen the oppressiveness of the system to some degree, while its agents, such as Sergeant Dowsett and various members of York's local authorities, were trying to uphold it. This becomes more evident in the following discussion about modes of exemption from the oppressive laws in combination with the policy of 'assimilation'.

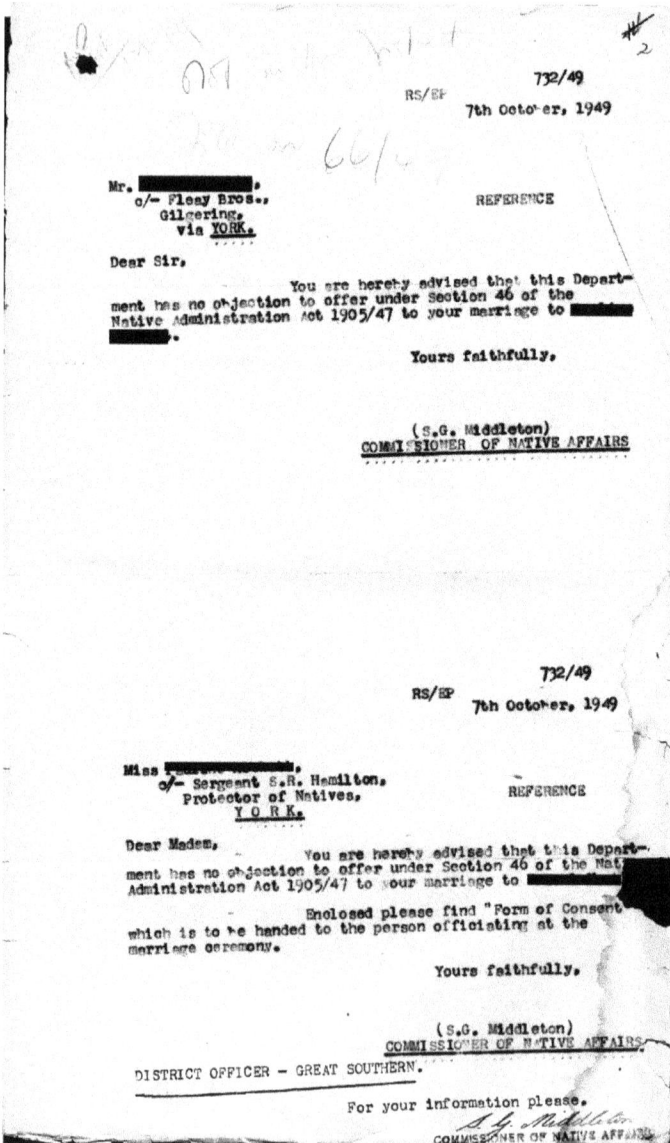

Figure 8: Example marriage application approval - Department of Native Affairs, item 1949/0066, SROWA

Chapter 5. Modes of exemption

Although conditional citizenship has already been mentioned several times, this form of legal exemption from the oppressive state laws regulating Aboriginal lives will now be discussed in more detail, along with another mode of exemption. Further reference will also be made to the concept and reality of 'assimilation'. As with most other laws concerning Aboriginal people that have been discussed so far, the following legislative provisions were also state-based, which means that they were only applicable to Western Australia.

5.01 Exemption certificates

From 1906 until 1964, the *Aborigines Act* and its subsequent amendments provided for the issuing of exemption certificates, whose holders were basically freed from the provisions of the Act—almost. Exempted persons remained under supervision and could have their exemptions revoked.[1] Such exemption only applied to the *Aborigines/Native Administration/Native Welfare Acts* and not to any other legislation. For example, under the *Licensing Act 1911*, the sell and supply of alcohol to Aboriginal people was forbidden and Aboriginal people were not allowed to be on licensed premises unless they worked there. Hence, while all alcohol-related punitive provisions under the *Aborigines/Native Administration/Native Welfare Acts* were nullified when an exemption certificate was granted, exempted Aboriginal people were still technically not allowed to enter a hotel and hotel proprietors could be prosecuted if they served alcohol to an exempted person. Despite this legal shortcoming of the exemption certificate, Commissioner Bray commented in 1943 that exemption certificate holders were generally able to make purchases of alcohol 'because the Police authorities view the Certificate holders in a benign way under the Licensing Act'.[2] In 1942, Bray himself encouraged the Commissioner of Police to retain this practice (which had been in place since the first exemptions were issued) when a local protector pointed out the discrepancy within the law. However, this attitude within the police department changed by 1947. The change of practice was not something that was openly publicised, and, still in 1950, a person at York with an exemption complained that he was not served alcohol and was told by a departmental officer that this refusal was within the law. While attitudes differed from locality to locality, the trend towards a stricter interpretation of the law was caused by increasing numbers of exemptions being issued and the introduction of conditional citizenship, accompanied by increased police and community awareness in relation to exclusionary legislation. Only by mid-1964, after exemption certificates had been phased out, was the alcohol prohibition on Aboriginal people in the South West Land Division lifted, yet it was upheld in other regions of Western Australia. The prohibition was completely removed by 1972.[3]

Further legislation that had specific exclusionary clauses applying to Aboriginal people included the *Land Act 1933*, the *Electoral Act 1907–1940*, the *Dog Act 1903–1948* and the *Shearer's Accommodation Act 1912*, as well as the *Education Act*'s regulations from 1920, discussed earlier (see chapter 3.09).[4] While exempted Aboriginal people could not be considered legally Aboriginal under the *Aborigines/Native Administration/Native Welfare Acts*, neither could they be considered non-Aboriginal under the same Act, as it was argued that they still had Aboriginal blood. In practice, this meant that exempted Aboriginal individuals were able to enter reserves or have sexual intercourse with non-exempted Aboriginal persons without being punished for doing so. The latter point particularly bothered the commissioner and the absence of convictions for such acts was not for lack of trying by police and the department.[5]

The Minister for Native Affairs/Welfare had the authority to approve such exemptions, which were issued through a local protector or departmental staff. Although the minister made the ultimate decision on an application, the chief protector and later commissioner of the department prepared a case for or against the granting of an exemption and, consequently, had the ability to exert significant power over the final decision. Until 1940, only some 200 exemptions had been granted since the *Aborigines Act 1905* had come into effect.[6] A.O. Neville was determined not to have any exemptions granted to Aboriginal individuals whom he suspected might supply alcohol to non-exempted individuals, and he introduced a rigid application process. During the mid-1920s, when F. Aldrich was in charge of the Aborigines Department in the southern part of Western Australia, he was generally opposed to issuing exemptions out of principle, arguing that exemption certificates would put their holders under immense peer pressure to obtain alcohol, regardless of individual circumstances. Consequently, very few exemptions were granted in the South West Land Division during Aldrich's tenure.[7]

The issuing of exemption certificates (as well as later conditional citizenship certificates) was rigorously publicised. This occurred only in the *Western Australian Police Gazette* until 1942, and thenceforth, was publicised in the more accessible *Western Australian Government Gazette* from 1942 onwards. In the period under review, it appears that, in York, only four exemption certificates were issued—between 1948 and 1956. However, at least three more exemption certificate holders moved to York after having received exemptions in other localities across the Wheatbelt region, and these later gained conditional citizenship. When the practice of issuing exemption certificates ceased after October 1960, approximately 2,000 exemption certificates had been issued to individual applicants since 1906 across the whole of Western Australia. Exemptions would often additionally cover a man's wife and their children under fourteen years of age.[8] On 23 August 1961, all exemptions were cancelled as they were deemed to no longer serve any useful purpose.[9] The *Native Welfare Act 1963* dropped the provision of exemptions, which came into being in mid-1964.[10]

5.02 Conditional citizenship and assimilation

In late 1944, a further mode of exemption was introduced with the *Natives (Citizenship Rights) Act 1944*, which would remain in force until 1 July 1972. With a citizenship certificate, an Aboriginal person was completely freed of any legal 'disabilities' otherwise affecting Aboriginal people in Western Australia who were legally deemed 'native' under the legislation. Such citizenship is here referred to as *conditional citizenship* because the granting of citizenship certificates under this legislation was always conditional. In a perverse role twist, holders of conditional citizenship were liable for prosecution under those sections of the *Native Administration Act 1941* that applied to non-Aboriginal people because a conditional citizenship holder was now 'deemed to be no longer a native or aborigine'.[11] While exemption certificates were approved and issued by the Department of Native Affairs, conditional citizenship was considered and approved (or rejected) by a magistrate in court.[12]

Conditional citizenship was introduced only a few years before the social and cultural *assimilation* of Australia's Aboriginal peoples entered the discourse of interstate politics. The eligibility criteria for conditional citizenship quoted on the next two pages coincidentally aligned very much with the idea of assimilation. By the late 1940s, it had become accepted knowledge that Aboriginal people would not simply *die out*, as it had been widely assumed well into the twentieth century that they would, and a permanent solution for the betterment of Aboriginal livelihoods across the country was anticipated. Aboriginal activists at the time had sought social inclusion but they were largely greeted with settler-Australian expectations that Aboriginal people would have to forfeit their Aboriginality to be accepted and absorbed into an imagined homogenous *white Australian* culture.[13]

Western Australia had adopted a policy of assimilation, in particular, for the Aboriginal population in the southern part of the state, based on recommendations of the 1948 *Bateman Report*, which was the result of a state-wide inquiry into Aboriginal affairs, similar to the Royal Commission from the 1930s. While national conferences had been discussing assimilation since 1948, a national policy of assimilation was only agreed on much later in 1961.[14] Through the 1950s and 1960s, assimilation was interpreted in many different ways by various governments and their agencies, social movements and associated groups, local communities and individuals. Interpretations ranged from the strict model of social and cultural absorption, which sought to eradicate Aboriginal identities, to models of integration that sought social inclusion without the destruction of Aboriginal identities. The latter model of 'integration' was officially adopted in Western Australia by 1970. In public discourse, some people started using 'integration' interchangeably with 'assimilation' by the mid-1960s.[15] At the dawn of the 1950s, assimilation was becoming a buzz word in departmental patrol reports of the Central District that included York. The situation of Aboriginal persons who had been visited and were subsequently discussed in such reports was often measured against stages of advancement towards assimilation. A person's status in relation to conditional citizenship was usually integral to the assessment of the patrol officers.[16]

As stated above, the enactment of conditional citizenship preceded the advent of an official assimilation policy. Western Australian Aboriginal individuals who served in Australia's armed forces during World War II provided the major impetus for the introduction of the Natives (Citizenship Rights) Bill in recognition of their service. However, the department also aspired for an improved version of the exemption system under the *Native Administration Act 1941*.[17] Applicants had to sign a statutory declaration to the effect that they had dissolved tribal and Aboriginal associations for two years prior to making this application (except for lineal and first-degree relatives, which excluded, for example, siblings, uncles, aunts and cousins), and that they had served in the Naval, Military or Air Force of the Commonwealth of Australia and were honourably discharged. If the applicant had not served in the forces, they had to declare that they were otherwise a 'fit and proper person to obtain a Certificate of Citizenship'.[18] The magistrate making the decision had to be satisfied that the applicant fulfilled the following criteria:

(a) for the two years immediately prior the applicant has adopted the manner and habits of civilised life

(b) the full rights of citizenship are desirable for and likely to be conducive to the welfare of the applicant

(c) the applicant is able to speak and understand the English language

(d) the applicant is not suffering from active leprosy, syphilis, granuloma or yaws

(e) the applicant is of industrious habits and is of good behaviour and reputation

(f) the applicant is reasonably capable of managing his own affairs.[19]

While the bill was assented to on 23 December 1944, it took over a year, until 7 January 1946, for the first conditional citizenship certificate to be granted, which occurred in Geraldton. By 1971, approximately 2,470 persons in Western Australia had been granted conditional citizenship on application. When the *Native Welfare Act 1954* came into force in 1955, any Western Australian Aboriginal person who had served at least six months overseas in Australian Forces, and had been honourably discharged, was automatically considered a 'citizen' and did not require a conditional citizenship certificate.[20]

In 1948, the Crown Law Department ruled that children of a parent with conditional citizenship were not covered by the certificate. As blood quantum classifications of Aboriginality still dominated departmental thinking, it became apparent that if children were not covered by their parent's certificate, this would lead to awkward legal outcomes. For example, one officer noted that 'a child of full blood parents, one only of whom holds Citizenship, would be according to our policy a half caste in law', and would have to be recorded as such on departmental records.[21] This absurd legal logic was seemingly not followed through with in relation to record keeping but perhaps the officer's comment serves as a good example for how fragile this artificial system of blood-quantum classification could be. The *Natives (Citizenship Rights) Act* was amended in 1950 so the children of a conditional citizenship rights holder were also covered and could be listed on the certificate thenceforth. According to Government Gazettes, of all the conditional citizenship rights holders in York, only one had their children listed on a (replacement) certificate issued in 1962. This suggests that in York, there may have been no practical need for most certificate holders to have their children listed on paper. Children listed on certificates are not included in the aforementioned number of persons granted conditional citizenship; however, in the whole state, approximately 540 certificates (including some replacement certificates) did have children listed. Initially, these children lost their conditional citizenship status when turning twenty-one years of age. An amendment of the Act in 1958 sought to ameliorate this situation; however, regulations that were introduced after a change in government nullified this attempt until the following amendment of conditional citizenship legislation.

Eventually, from 1 July 1966, these children received automatically conditional citizenship certificates upon turning twenty-one years of age. Due to this change in legislation, approximately 140 certificates were issued automatically in the South West Land Division.[22] This was rather ironic, as these certificates had had literally no use at all in the South West since mid-1964 because, under the policy of assimilation, oppressive legislation had been gradually scaled back. In 1960, all legal restrictions in relation to Commonwealth payments had been lifted. In 1962, Aboriginal people were given the vote in federal and Western Australian State elections, and as of 1 July 1964, the alcohol ban on Aboriginal people in the South West Land Division was abolished as well. Thus, (unless an Aboriginal person from the South West Land Division wished to travel to another region and buy alcohol while being there) the last remaining incentives to obtain conditional citizenship in this region had faded away. In the South West Land Division, the last conditional citizenship certificate was granted on 21 July 1964 to a resident of Goomalling. Thereafter, no person in this region seemingly bothered going through the process of being scrutinised for their 'worthiness' to be issued a certificate that stated what every Aboriginal person knew anyway—that they were born a citizen of Australia. This strongly suggests that most Aboriginal people did not obtain conditional citizenship because of any aspirational pride in the status that it would confer on them but solely for pragmatic reasons: to escape the oppressive mechanisms enabled through state legislation.[23] Thus, it would have come as a surprise to these children of certificate holders when they received these useless certificates upon turning twenty-one years of age.

5.03 Conditional citizenship, alcohol and settler-Australian opposition in York

Since the early days of granting conditional citizenship, criticism had been voiced by the Department of Native Affairs, local authorities and the public, alleging that many Aboriginal people who were granted conditional citizenship were not yet ready or were unworthy. This criticism was often based on allegations that certificate holders would use their newly gained rights to supply alcohol to Aboriginal people who did not possess conditional citizenship or that their own alcohol consumption would negatively affect their livelihoods. However, the decision to grant conditional citizenship was made solely by a magistrate in the applicant's district. Acting Commissioner McBeath complained that, despite the department regularly voicing objections to the granting of citizenship certificates to certain individuals, these objections were often ignored.[24] By December 1949, the local press in York started to report strong objections to the alleged 'indiscriminate' issuing of citizenship certificates and bemoaned the apparent consequences for the community. Once again, alcohol was at the forefront of this criticism.[25]

Let us try putting these complaints in perspective: In May 1948, for the first time, an Aboriginal resident of York received conditional citizenship and a further six certificates were issued by June 1950. In addition, one or two citizenship rights holders from Northam appear to have relocated to York at this time. In this period, four of these roughly nine persons with conditional citizenship were charged and convicted of seven offences in the York Police Court—six for being drunk and one for being at an Aboriginal camp (as a legally non-Aboriginal person). There were no offences for supplying alcohol, no actual criminal offences and no violent or nuisance-type offences recorded for any of these citizenship rights holders in this period. If there were suspicions, there was clearly no evidence, and it appears not unlikely that prejudice often formed the basis of presumed 'truths'. One of these nine persons was later, in 1953, twice convicted for supplying alcohol and had to serve four months' imprisonment with hard labour on one of these occasions.[26] Notwithstanding that the racist prohibition placed on Aboriginal people was never ethically defendable, this one person may have been regularly supplying others with alcohol already in the earlier years. If conditional citizenship certificate holders were supplying others with alcohol, this should also be interpreted as an act of passive resistance in navigating oppressive laws.

In this period between May 1948 and June 1950, three settler-Australians were convicted for supplying alcohol to Aboriginal people in York. For the same period, a total of twenty-two persons deemed legally Aboriginal were convicted of fifty-five offences. These offences included twenty instances of 'receiving alcohol', as well as the majority of breaches for being in a prohibited area, which we have discussed further above. However, for this entire period, there were only two incidents when offences in relation to alcohol and nuisance behaviour seemed to correlate. Namely, one person was convicted in April 1949 for receiving alcohol and behaving in a violent manner on a train, and there was a brawl involving seven persons on South Street in November 1949. Given that police appeared to charge Aboriginal people rigorously if they were obviously under the influence of alcohol while being in town, it may be inferred that these convictions covered the majority of instances that could have led to complaints about antisocial behaviour in combination with conditional citizenship rights. Consequently, it appears that, once again, a judgement based on opinion and not necessarily on facts was summarily handed down to the Aboriginal population of York by vocal sections of the settler-Australian community when they were complaining about the 'indiscriminate' issuing of citizenship rights.[27] Discussing the statistics hereunder is merely an attempt to point out that the public outcry regarding citizenship and alcohol appears to have been emotional and inflated. That alcohol may have been abused by some individuals is not being disputed here; however, the status of settler-Australians' citizenship was never questioned due to alcohol abuse. The emotional aspect of the complaints made was arguably based on the righteous settler-Australian assumption, confirmed through the law, that Aboriginal people did not have the birthright to consume alcohol. According to this logic, conditional citizenship certificate holders were thus seen to be abusing the good will of white Australian society to tolerate Aboriginal people within *their* white spaces.

5.04 The Katanning conference: Local authorities want a say in the granting of conditional citizenship

There is a reason for selecting this specific period prior to June 1950 in relation to the convictions just discussed. On 31 May 1950, York's mayor, Alfred F. Noonan, and Councillor Phillip M.A. Glass attended the conference on 'Native Affairs' held at Katanning, which was briefly mentioned previously (see chapter 4.06). Delegates were sent from seventeen road boards and three municipal councils stretching from York to Merredin and south to Albany. Reportedly, Noonan and Glass were the most vocal delegates regarding conditional citizenship rights, claiming that ninety percent of all alcohol supplied to Aboriginal people came from those with citizenship rights and they reiterated the belief that certificates were handed out indiscriminately to the detriment of the non-Aboriginal community. They put forward a motion that was largely adopted by the attendees of the conference. The points of this motion had been conceived and agreed on at the aforementioned meeting at Beverley (see chapter 4.06) two weeks prior to the conference, which was attended by Noonan and Glass, Sergeant Dowsett, and road board representatives from Beverley, York, Pingelly and Brookton. The motion demanded an immediate stop to the alleged indiscriminate issuing of conditional citizenship, it stipulated that applicants would have to reside for two years in the same district before they were eligible to apply, and it requested a five-year probationary period if conditional citizenship was granted. However, the following part of the motion would prove most influential: 'no Citizenship Rights to be granted to natives without the approval of the district local governing authority'.[28]

Commissioner Middleton, who was also in attendance, advised that he was indeed working on an amendment to the current *Natives (Citizenship Rights) Act 1944*. Up to this point, Middleton had been working towards taking the power for granting conditional citizenship from magistrates to hand it entirely to the Minister for Native Affairs, who would make decisions based on recommendations by the commissioner: Middleton himself. The Department of Native Affairs had been frustrated, as it was claimed that magistrates would often not listen to the department's opinions in relation to citizenship applications, handing out more than the department thought appropriate. Middleton argued that no one knew the applicants' background better than the department and, therefore, it could make the best judgement as to the applicants' readiness to attain conditional citizenship rights. Internal records suggest that Middleton and other departmental staff felt strongly about this aspired-to amendment.[29]

However, during the drafting process of the amendment bill, between July and October 1950, the proposed wielder of the power to grant conditional citizenship rights changed several times. The first draft allocated this power to a 'Court of Native Affairs' but this was changed a month later, introducing so-called Natives (Citizenship Rights) Boards, which would consist of one magistrate and one person nominated by the Minister for Native Affairs. However, the latter proposal would have required an amendment to the *Native Administration Act 1905–1947* and was consequently abandoned. The third draft of October 1950 became the bill that was presented to the Legislative Assembly. It introduced boards similar to those in draft two. A Natives (Citizenship Rights) Board would be created for each local government district, with the notable difference to the previous draft that each board was to consist of one magistrate and the mayor of the municipality or chairman of the local road board. Crucially, the boards' decisions were supposed to be unanimous and if one board member disagreed with the application, the application was dismissed without a right to appeal. The same principle also applied to complaints against a conditional citizenship rights holder. If the board could not agree, an application to suspend or cancel conditional citizenship had to be dismissed.[30]

This bill was very much in line with Noonan's and Glass' motion from the Katanning conference and it appears very likely that said motion provided the impetus for the introduction of these significant changes. The bill was introduced to the Western Australian State Parliament a year later in November 1951, having been delayed by the separate amendment in late 1950 in relation to the inclusion of children on certificates. The new bill caused heated discussions in both houses of Parliament. In both houses, repeatedly, the question was raised as to who had initiated these amendments. The Minister for Native Affairs, Victor Doney, refused to provide a satisfying answer but stated that it was neither the department nor a political party. Several speakers in Parliament commented that the bill would have been initiated by local authorities while Member of the Legislative Council for the Labor Party, Gilbert Fraser, pointedly surmised that it would have likely emanated from the Road Boards Association—the very body that organised the Katanning conference in 1950. Further, Labor Member of the Legislative Council Edmund Harry Gray argued that he thought it was very unlikely that the bill was the brainchild of Commissioner Middleton as he claimed to be familiar with his work and could not 'imagine his taking such a drastic and retrograde step'.[31] Gray's reasoning is very much congruent with statements made by Middleton himself years after he retired.[32] Minister Doney, who had been a longstanding member of the Country Party and who was Member of the Legislative Council for Narrogin, was afforded his ministerial position in April 1950, shortly before the conference in Katanning. As a defender of country interests, he may have put pressure on Middleton to incorporate the resolution based on Noonan's and Glass's motion. This would explain the relatively sudden switch from proposing that the Minister for Native Affairs should grant certificates, to creating 'Native Courts', then to the establishing of 'boards' with a ministerial nominee and, eventually, of boards with members of a local authority to preside over citizenship applications.[33]

The bill that was introduced to Parliament in November 1951 contained the provision that every applicant had to have held an exemption certificate under the *Native Administration Act 1947* for a duration of two years prior to their application for conditional citizenship. This section would have ensured that the department was still able to pre-select potential conditional citizenship applicants to allow only the most suitable candidates, as determined by the department, to apply. This section was voted out by Western Australia's Legislative Assembly as it was argued that it gave too much power to the department on decisions in relation to conditional citizenship.[34]

5.05 Unique dualism of Western Australian modes of exemption

Several states in Australia had some form of exemption policies in relation to their respective Aboriginal populations; however, Western Australian conditional citizenship with its own purpose-made legislation was a unique mode of exemption in Australia.[35] Simultaneously unique was the dualism that existed for nearly twenty years when both the exemptions from the *Native Administration/Native Welfare Acts* and conditional citizenship co-existed. This dualism began in 1945 when the *Natives (Citizenship Rights) Act* came into force and lasted until 1964, when exemption certificates were formally abolished following a complete overhaul of the *Native Welfare Act 1905–1963*. Commissioner Bray, who in 1944 initiated the inception of conditional citizenship, had actually anticipated the repeal of exemptions at the earliest opportunity, as he considered this provision superfluous once conditional citizenship had been enacted. However, once Bray had left office, this idea was dropped for the time being.[36] In October 1944, during the parliamentary debate in the Legislative Assembly regarding conditional citizenship, a two-year exemption period prior to application was also briefly discussed. South African born Hugh Allan Leslie of Wyalkatchem, Member of the Legislative Assembly for Mount Marshall, introduced an amendment that proposed a two-year exemption period prior to becoming eligible to apply for conditional citizenship. Leslie's argument put forward the following, arguably very distorted, underlying assumptions about how successful applicants would perceive themselves:

> The intention of the Bill is to cause a definite segregation of the native from his relatives and friends. Holding an exemption certificate, a native is watched until he gets full citizen rights and says 'I am now a white man, and I cut myself off from all my old relationships'.[37]

Leslie's motion for an amendment of the original bill was not carried; however, his proposal appears to have resonated with several departmental staff other than Bray. Between 1944 and 1950, various voices within the department advocated that applicants of conditional citizenship should be subject to a one-to-two-year probationary period due to the assumption that this would foster aspirations to achieve conditional citizenship through making long-lasting and positive (as defined by the Department of Native Affairs) lifestyle changes. By the turn of the decade, these lifestyle changes were increasingly identified as requirements to achieve assimilation into 'white society'.[38]

As discussed above (see chapter 5.04), Middleton's attempt in 1951 to make exemptions a legal requisite for the granting of conditional citizenship, which was likely influenced by Noonan and Glass speaking at the Katanning conference the previous year, had failed. Nevertheless, statistics compiled with data obtained from Western Australian Government Gazettes suggest that the aspired trial period by way of exemptions was frequently put in place informally. However, the department was only able to encourage Aboriginal people to apply for an exemption before applying for conditional citizenship (or rather, discourage them to apply without an exemption) because, as mentioned above, the hopeful applicant had to lodge their application for conditional citizenship directly at their local court and did not need to apply through the department. Though the department was still able to influence the decision by submitting a brief character report, the outcome depended on the magistrate's inclination to heed departmental recommendations or indirect inferences. Middleton instructed departmental staff who attended court hearings for such applications to remain as neutral as possible if questioned and only to openly object to an application when evidence regarding a person's alleged unsuitability for citizenship was available; for example, court records in relation to alcohol-related convictions. Departmental records suggest that, at times, magistrates were not interested in inferred hints submitted by the department, which irritated Middleton and his staff to no small degree; hence the initial push to have conditional citizenship issued by the Minister for Native Affairs.[39]

Expressed in numbers, it is evident that a significant proportion of conditional citizenship holders were subject to this dualism, though not the majority of citizenship rights holders during this period. Of all 533 persons who were granted citizenship certificates by July 1952 (when the amended citizenship legislation became effective), 209 (or thirty-nine per cent) were holders of exemption certificates prior to being granted conditional citizenship. More than half of these exemptions were issued before 1945.[40] By November 1951, when the amendment bill was being debated, 178 applications for conditional citizenship had been denied since the introduction of the *Natives (Citizenship Rights) Act 1944*.[41] It is notable that between January 1945 and July 1952, at least 199 persons applied for and were granted exemptions who did not, at any later time, receive conditional citizenship. It seems possible that a number of these 199 exempted individuals applied for conditional citizenship but were unsuccessful (thus making up a proportion of the 178 denied applications).

Over the period that this dualism was in place, at least 1,321 persons were granted exemptions who did not, at any later time, receive conditional citizenship. In the same period, 500 primary holders of conditional citizenship had been holders of exemption certificates beforehand (not counting children and replacements). In January 1960, for the last time, an exemption certificate was issued to a person who would later obtain conditional citizenship. However, only six more exemption certificates were issued thereafter to persons who did not obtain conditional citizenship before the issuing of exemptions ceased by the end of 1960.[42] The practice of issuing exemptions ceased in 1960 because of an amendment of the Commonwealth Social Services Consolidation Act that removed discriminatory references to Aboriginality that had excluded a large proportion of Aboriginal people from receiving aged-, invalid-, and widows-pensions (the latter included social benefits for women who had been deserted by their partners). Since the mid-1950s, the majority of exemptions were issued to Aboriginal people who required any of such pensions. Thus, the function of exemptions within this dualism had changed from a dominantly behaviour-based quasi-prerequisite for receiving conditional citizenship aimed at persons deemed semi-suitable to a purely welfare-based measure for individuals who were deemed unlikely to receive conditional citizenship—a measure that suddenly became obsolete four years before it was formally abolished.[43]

5.06 Conditional citizenship in York, cancellations and citizenship rights boards

In York, at least forty-eight persons were granted conditional citizenship. The first certificate was issued in 1947 and the last was issued in 1960 (not counting replacement certificates that had to be applied for in court). Of these forty-eight individuals, eight persons held exemption certificates prior to being issued conditional citizenship. The first person granted conditional citizenship in York, who incidentally also held an exemption certificate, was actually from Quairading. However, his story in relation to conditional citizenship is worth mentioning here due to its sheer absurdity. This Quairading man was granted an exemption certificate in July 1946 and then, 14 months later, in September 1947, he was granted conditional citizenship by Resident Magistrate K.H. Parker in the York Police Court. In 1951, the man's conditional citizenship certificate was cancelled 'because further investigation of the status of this person reveals that he possesses 3/16th native blood, and is not a native according to law'.[44] According to blood-quantum logic, this man was one-sixteenth less than a *quadroon* or *quarter-caste*. Among several possible constellations, he may have had one-*quarter-caste* parent and one *octaroon* (eighth) parent, which resulted in their offspring being considered *three-sixteenth-caste* and, therefore, not subject to legislation targeting Aboriginal people.[45]

These degrees of blood quantum logic are already difficult to comprehend and totally absurd in their own right, but matters became even more ridiculous some years later. In 1957, this man from Quairading, whose wife had passed away by then, approached the department asking that his children, who were 'legally natives by caste'[46] had this classification removed. While the man was not considered 'Aboriginal in law', his deceased wife and mother of their children would have classified as such. Therefore, their children were at least considered *quarter-caste*. Given that the man's children were under twenty-one years of age, the man's only option was to apply to the Minister for Native Welfare to have himself legally classified as a *native*, to apply for conditional citizenship and, with approval of the same, to have his children listed on his certificate. It is not known to this author whether the man considered it, but he did not choose this pathway. The idiocy of these kind of trappings did not escape departmental staff at the time and the officer who reported on this case commented that it 'illustrates the farcical legal tangle in which State legislation has become involved concerning the status of coloured people'.[47]

Until October 1959, conditional citizenship could be suspended or cancelled by a magistrate (or a citizenship board, from 1952) if the department or any civic person lodged a complaint regarding the alleged unsatisfying behaviour of a conditional citizenship certificate holder. Potential reasons for a cancellation or suspension were that a citizenship holder had not adopted a 'civilised' life or that they had been twice convicted under the *Native Administration* and later *Native Welfare Acts*. The latter included the supply of alcohol to 'natives in law' or entering a reserve, as well as sexual intercourse with an Aboriginal person legally deemed as such. Two convictions of habitual drunkenness also justified a complaint (three convictions for drunkenness in a twelve-month period caused a declaration of habitual drunkenness), as well as contracting a disease listed in the exclusionary conditions (leprosy, syphilis, granuloma, yaws). In York, no such cancellation or suspension occurred (certificates of residents in York were only cancelled due to death or when replaced with a new certificate); however, conditional citizenship holders would have been well aware that their civic status was revocable. Research suggests that between 1946 and 1959, in the whole state, only a dozen or so cancellations and suspensions occurred due to alleged unsatisfactory behaviour.[48]

As a matter of fact, in August 1953, the State Cabinet of Labor's Albert Hawke administration, which had been elected earlier that year, voiced the opinion that conditional citizenship should not be subject to cancellations for whatever reasons. While legally entitled to lodge complaints, the department followed Middleton's policy, confirmed by

Cabinet, not to intervene in conditional citizenship once certificates had been approved (very few complaints were lodged thereafter; however, these were most likely not initiated by the department). Whether conditional citizenship holders were aware that Cabinet had decided that certificates should no longer be cancelled is a different story. It may well have been the case that some local departmental staff or police officers continued using the threat of revocation to induce behavioural changes and compliance with the law of the day. Afterall, police officers were still able to lodge complaints in court despite Cabinet's decision. Across departmental records, a trend is evident that local officers did not always share the relatively more progressive views and policies conceived in head office. From 28 October 1959, the provision to cancel conditional citizenship was repealed from the *Natives (Citizenship Rights) Act 1958*. Thenceforth, the status of conditional citizenship was as had been originally recommended by State Crown Solicitor E.A. Dunphy in 1944, whose recommendation had been ignored. At the time, Dunphy had argued that the status of conditional citizenship should be acquired irrevocably 'for better or worse', and he voiced the belief that the virtue of the cancellation clause was purely political. Political it was indeed.[49]

The court statistics from York that we discussed above for the period from May 1948 to June 1950 should have illuminated that these claims made by York's local authorities and the press, about the alleged increasingly unbearable situation caused by conditional citizenship, appear to have been much inflated for political ends. Any instances of alleged misconduct or misuse of privileges resulted in public questioning as to Aboriginal people's ability to mix with settler-Australians. As to Mayor Noonan and Councillor Glass, their combined political power in the early 1950s should not be underappreciated. Not only were they members of the municipal council, they were also both justices of the peace who handed down most of the sentences discussed in the above statistics. And yet, these arguably highly biased local actors apparently managed to significantly influence the 1951 amendment of legislation affecting the entire Aboriginal population of Western Australia. This is not to say that all Aboriginal people would have wanted to gain conditional citizenship. In fact, many did not wish to go down this avenue or were outright opposed to the very idea of it because it was conditional and racist.[50] However, the influence wielded by Noonan and Glass translated to an attempt of blocking possibilities for Aboriginal people and resisting the presence of Aboriginal people within settler-Australian spaces if they did not conform completely to settler-Australian lifestyle and behavioural expectations.

In September 1952, Noonan was appointed the municipality's member for York's Natives (Citizenship Rights) Board, and, for the next five years, there was arguably no other person in the district who exerted more power over Aboriginal people's lives than he. Notably, in 1952 and 1953, there was not a single certificate of citizenship granted in York, and only two certificates were issued in 1954. Then, suddenly, 1955 and 1956 presented over fifty per cent of all conditional citizenship certificates granted in York.[51] One cannot but think that Noonan may have had an influence on this two-year gap. Perhaps he insisted on an informal probationary period before granting conditional citizenship but there is no evidence to support this proposition. A potential factor that may have played into the sudden granting of applications will be discussed at a later stage (see chapter 6.10) in relation to 'Coolbaroo' dances held at York and the amendment of the *Native Administration Act* in late 1954.

One notable aspect about Noonan is that he had virtually nothing to gain economically from Aboriginal people. Noonan was the proprietor of a motor vehicle mechanics service and dealership, 'Noonan's Garage', which he owned from the early 1930s until he sold the business in 1952. During the period when Noonan was active in local politics, Aboriginal people in York were unlikely customers of Noonan's services due to their economic standing and, therefore, he did not have to conceal his personal misgivings towards Aboriginal people in response to economic considerations.[52] In 1956, Councillor Frederick Ashbolt was nominated local member on York's 'citizenship board' while Mayor Noonan went on leave for an extended period. Ashbolt remained in the position until it became quasi-defunct after 1962, having only issued replacement certificates from 1960 onwards. Initially, Councillor Glass was approached to take up the board position in lieu of Noonan but he declined. Glass cited that due being a permanent member on the 'Bench' of the York Police Court, he thought it would not be appropriate as he had his 'own opinion in the matter of citizenship rights and he could be biased one way or the other'.[53] Noonan had seemingly not found this obvious conflict of interest to be an issue. Whether Glass declined out of truly ethical concerns arising from potential bias or because he could not be bothered with the task will probably remain unanswered. The acting mayor, Clifton John Ashbolt, who should have been considered first, was not even approached, which may be regarded as a silent declaration of bias. The court records for the Frederick Ashbolt period of York's citizenship board have survived and reveal that during this later period, not a single application was rejected.[54]

In September 1952, William Henry Robinson, chairman of the York Road Board, was nominated as the 'citizenship board' member for the York Roads District. Robinson's enthusiasm was limited but every local authority had to nominate one representative for its citizenship board. Before accepting membership, the road board questioned the logic of having two citizenship boards in the York District, each of which would have the same magistrate aligned. In January 1957, Robinson resigned from this position, complaining that he was often only given a few hours' notice to attend citizenship hearings. Robinson seemingly could not be bothered with the task. While the claim of having to attend at short notice cannot be rebuked, if this did occur, it would not have happened that often. Between 1952 and January 1957, there were fourteen successful conditional citizenship application hearings for twenty-eight persons (one to five applicants at a time) in the York magistrate's district. Thirteen of these hearings occurred in 1955 and 1956, of which approximately half were for applicants residing within the area administered by the road board.[55] If we consider that there were perhaps also few hearings that did not result in conditional citizenship being granted on that day, this would mean that Robinson was inconvenienced by this duty roughly once every three months in a two-year period. Robinson requested support from the municipal council to press for a review of the process of issuing conditional citizenship 'so that some of the legal responsibilities be taken off societies conducting public functions'.[56] Thus, Robinson suggested abolishing what Noonan and Glass had commenced in 1950. Ironically, the municipal council, including Noonan and Glass, decided to fully support the road board in this matter. Citizenship boards remained until the entire legislation was abolished in 1972. By June 1957, Frederick Ashbolt also accepted the role for the road board's membership of the citizenship board. At the time, the amalgamation of York's municipality and road board jurisdictions were heatedly discussed in the local press. Therefore, shifting any responsibilities from the road board to the council would likely have served a political purpose to ensure the council's dominance within the amalgamation process. From a humanitarian and ethical perspective, the conditional nature of this type of citizenship was never acceptable. However, one should appreciate that Aboriginal people living within the segregationist system of the 1950s had to balance principles against gaining improved livelihoods. That conditional citizenship could mean more than access to alcohol did not seem to move Robinson who was seemingly occupied with the apparent inconvenience of being a member on the citizenship board.[57]

A substantial proportion of Aboriginal people who lived within the road board's jurisdiction were reserve dwellers who were automatically excluded from consideration of conditional citizenship. Only legally classified Aboriginal persons were allowed to live on reserves and, therefore, no reserve dweller could claim that they had dissociated from other Aboriginal people 'in law'. This exemplifies the logic of conditional citizenship, which was an attempt to instil the desire in Aboriginal people to 'voluntarily' assimilate or integrate within white settler-Australian society through the application of push and pull factors. As per federal law, until 1960, any person who was deemed more than 'half Aboriginal' or 'nomadic' and not exempt from disabling state laws (in other words, not holding an exemption or citizenship certificate) was denied any form of pension or maternity allowance (not to be confused with child endowment payments. The former was stricter aligned with legal definitions of Aboriginality while the latter was conditional on modes of lifestyle being 'non-nomadic'[58]). For example, in 1950, a mother at York who was believed to be '9/16-caste' was told that she was ineligible to receive a maternity allowance as she was identified to have one-sixteenth more Aboriginal blood than a legal 'half-caste', and thus was deemed to have a 'preponderance' of

Aboriginal blood, which disqualified her from the payment. When the mother complained that she had received the bonus for her previous children, a departmental officer was quick to point out that this was a decision of Commonwealth Social Services Department and that the Department of Native Affairs merely provided advice to the Commonwealth department about this mother's degree of descent, as noted on existing records.[59] In fact, in 1942, the *Maternity Allowance Act 1912* was amended, giving the commissioner of the federal Social Services Department discretionary powers to grant the allowance to Aboriginal persons or the state government departments overseeing them if he thought this to be desirable. This provision was explicitly extended to reserve dwellers in 1944, although it remained discretionary.[60] Seemingly, the commissioner of the Social Services Department did not think payment was desirable in this case.

As reported by departmental officers, living on a reserve automatically disqualified people from several federal payments, regardless of degree of descent. There was one particular example that illuminates the rigidity of the Commonwealth Social Services Department and its 'customary prohibition' on reserve residents. In 1957, a departmental patrol officer assisted with a disability pension application for a reserve resident in York. The applicant was, at the time, believed unfit to live on her own and, even if she had wanted to, this person would have been unlikely able to move into town or elsewhere without assistance from her family. However, the application was subsequently rejected by the Commonwealth department because the applicant was living permanently on a reserve. The Department of Native Welfare then decided to issue rations in lieu of the denied pension.[61]

5.07 Conditional citizenship: Punishment for non-compliance

While Commonwealth and Western Australian state policies attempted to bully Aboriginal people into social and cultural assimilation through their 'carrot and stick' approaches, local authorities and law enforcement appeared to prefer using the proverbial stick without the carrot. The alleged misuse of newly gained civic rights in relation to

164

alcohol and its supply to Aboriginal individuals without any forms of exemption remained the primary point of criticism regarding conditional citizenship rights, which extended to the underlying idea of assimilation. Consequently, judicial action taken against Aboriginal individuals who had gained conditional citizenship was often swift and harsh when it was believed they misused their rights and thus disturbed the peace of the settler-Australian community. As discussed above, in the first two years of conditional citizenship being granted in York, holders of certificates were not convicted of offences in relation to the supply of alcohol, despite the local authorities' insistence that this occurred frequently. Most offences by conditional citizenship holders involved being 'drunk' under the *Police Act*. Given that conditional citizenship rights holders were claimed to be frequently offending against the *Native Administration Act 1947*—though seemingly without any proof—police and the local justices of the peace would have been frustrated that they were not able to bring the offenders to 'justice'.

Thus, the local lay-judiciary responded emphatically to the first opportunity they were provided with for enforcing 'justice' as they saw it. On 5 December 1952, an Aboriginal man, who had been granted conditional citizenship at Collie in April of the same year, was sentenced to three months' imprisonment for being 'unlawfully' on the York Reserve. The *York Chronicle* reported that he was living on the reserve and found to be in the possession of wine but there was no alcohol-related additional charge and no other reserve dwellers were charged with receiving alcohol.[62] The justices of the peace who handed down the sentence were none other than Mayor Noonan and Councillor Glass. Noonan may have felt empowered by his appointment to the citizenship board earlier in the year and may have wished to send a strong signal to those who did not intend to abide by the draconian rules imposed by white Australian assimilationists. This was the only time in the York District that a conditional citizenship holder was punished with imprisonment for being on the reserve. Only two similar offences have been recorded since the declaration of the reserve. One conditional citizenship holder from Northam received a fine in 1948 for such an 'offence' and a non-Aboriginal man also received a fine in 1947 for being on the reserve and 'dancing', as discussed previously (see chapter 3.11).[63]

However, the 1952 sentence would have left an intentionally long-lasting impression on the local Aboriginal population with the aim of ensuring compliance—although, only a few years later, it appears that this type of 'offending' against the *Native Welfare Act 1954* was no longer prosecuted. For example, an Aboriginal pensioner had gained conditional citizenship in June 1955 but was reported to be living on the York Reserve in June of the following year, and the departmental officer did not voice any objections. However, this man reportedly had a positive reputation among the settler-Australian population and, perhaps because of that, police chose not to act on this breach. By February 1957, this pensioner was boarding in town with another Aboriginal family. He may have been told to move off the reserve due to his citizenship but it also is not unlikely that the pensioner moved from the reserve more or less voluntarily, out of necessity, because he was not eligible to receive an old-age pension as a reserve dweller, despite having obtained conditional citizenship.[64] Anecdotal evidence suggests that Aboriginal people with conditional citizenship, out of fear of being persecuted, stayed away from the reserve or only approached it most carefully, via back roads, so as not to be detected. Reportedly, such visits only occurred if they were deemed highly necessary, for example, to pass on messages in relation to important family matters.[65]

The 1952 incident was followed over the next ten years by ongoing cases of York's police and justices of the peace persecuting conditional citizenship holders for alcohol-related offences. The following examples are only those that attracted terms of imprisonment; however, it should be noted that inability to pay a fine usually had a fixed term of imprisonment attached for defaulting. In April 1953, as briefly discussed above, a York-based conditional citizenship rights holder was sentenced to four months' imprisonment with hard labour for supplying alcohol. In January 1955, an Aboriginal woman with conditional citizenship rights was sentenced to six months' imprisonment with hard labour for supplying alcohol to six Aboriginal persons, who all received fines. This was the highest term of imprisonment imposed on an Aboriginal person in York for an alcohol-related offences, and one of the sentencing justices of the peace was, once again, Mayor Noonan. On several occasions, non-Aboriginal individuals were also sentenced to six months' incarceration for supplying alcohol to Aboriginal persons.[66] That 'white' suppliers of alcohol should also receive harsh sentences was unanimously agreed on at the 1950 Katanning conference, where local authority attendees were often also bench members in local courts.[67] In July 1955, a further Aboriginal man, who had gained conditional citizenship two weeks earlier, was sentenced to three months' imprisonment with hard labour by justices of the peace Councillor Glass and undertaker Stephen Phillip Harvey for supplying alcohol to relatives who were fined for receiving it. One year later, the same person was again sentenced to three months' imprisonment with hard labour for supplying alcohol to two Aboriginal men. One of these men was sentenced to three months in gaol for escaping legal custody and a concurrent one-month term for receiving alcohol. As he did not face any other charges, he was placed under police custody for the sole reason of having received alcohol—in other words, for being Aboriginal. A non-Aboriginal person would not have had any troubles with the law in this case. In total, between 1946 and 1962, at least thirty-nine sentences of imprisonment were handed down by justices of the peace in York's police court for alcohol-related offences targeting Aboriginal people. Eighteen sentences affected conditional citizenship holders and twenty-one sentences affected Aboriginal persons 'in law'.[68]

After 1956, there were no further terms of imprisonment imposed for supplying alcohol; however, behaviours regarding the personal consumption of alcohol were still targeted and punished. For example, one person with conditional citizenship was sentenced to eleven terms of imprisonment between 1957 and 1962, with sentences ranging from three days to two months and fourteen days. During this period, Noonan appeared less frequently in the York Police Court—but he was present when this man was sentenced to two months' imprisonment. Two days after this Aboriginal man was granted conditional citizenship in 1955, he incurred his first conviction in York, which was for supplying alcohol. By the end of 1962, he had accumulated a track record of thirty convictions, solely for alcohol-related offences—the majority for being drunk. This particular Aboriginal person may have had a problematic relationship with alcohol but these frequent prosecutions were unlikely to be intended for his benefit. This case indicates how Aboriginal persons were punished for adopting white society's vices, as well as its virtues.[69]

The above examples indicate the inventiveness in interpreting legislation at the local level. The *Native Administration/Welfare Acts*, as originally intended, were already inhumane and based on racist principles, albeit disguised as a protectionist agenda. However, the interpretation of this Act in relation to the *Natives (Citizenship Rights) Act* resulted in unforeseen outcomes that were not intended when either law was drafted. White Australia was still the assumed status quo when assimilation was conceived and the legal doctrine of *terra nullius* was still to be upheld for another forty-odd years. This helps to explain why Aboriginal people were expected to mimic settler-Australians in every way but the colour of their skin to successfully assimilate into white Australian culture and to formally cease to be Aboriginal when granted conditional citizenship, in particular, during the early years. By the beginning of the 1950s, a marked change became noticeable, with a shift from notions of biological absorption to cultural assimilation. The 1951 amendment of the *Natives (Citizenship Rights) Act* deleted the wording that stated that a conditional citizenship certificate holder 'shall no longer be a native or aborigine' and Commissioner Middleton commented in a circular memorandum to officers, missions and institutions that this 'offensive section has been deleted and pride of race can be maintained even under Citizenship'.[70] In reality, this meant that the department had no issue if individuals openly identified as being Aboriginal as long as they were able to fit within settler-Australian society and cut ties with former associations. Therefore, it was expected that Aboriginality would be regarded solely as an ancestral trait relating to the past, and not as a form of cultural identity in the present time.

Western Australia.
Natives (Citizenship Rights) Act, 1944, Regulations.
Form 1.
APPLICATION FOR CERTIFICATE OF CITIZENSHIP.

I (full name)..........................of (address)............................
HEREBY APPLY for a Certificate of Citizenship under the Natives (Citizenship Rights) Act, 1944.

Dated at   this   day of   19

....
(Signature of Applicant.)

To the Clerk of Courts
at............................

Received this   day of   19 , with fee of
Five Shillings.

....
Clerk of Courts.

N.B.—This application must be accompanied by a statutory declaration (Form 2), two references as to the good character and industrious habits of the applicant, and a photographic likeness of the applicant, in duplicate, unmounted, size 2½in. x 2in., showing head and shoulders.

_____

Western Australia.
Natives (Citizenship Rights) Act, 1944, Regulations.
Form 2.
STATUTORY DECLARATION.

I (full name)..........................of (address)............................
(occupation)............................ DO SOLEMNLY AND SINCERELY DECLARE as follows:—

1. I am a native within the meaning of the Native Administration Act, 1905-1941, and am of the full age of twenty-one years or over.

2. I wish to become a citizen of the State of Western Australia in accordance with the provisions of the Natives (Citizenship Rights) Act, 1944.

3. For the two years prior to the date hereof I have dissolved tribal and native association except with respect to lineal descendants or native relations of the first degree.

4. *(a) I have served in the Naval, or Military or Air Force of the Commonwealth of Australia (particulars relating to my enlistment being as follows: Unit..........No..........Rank..........) and have received (or am entitled to receive) an honourable discharge; or

*(b) being of good character and industrious habits I am a fit and proper person to obtain a Certificate of Citizenship.

And I make this solemn declaration by virtue of section 106 of the Evidence Act, 1906.

Declared at
this   day of
19 .
Before me:—
* Delete whichever is not applicable.

(This declaration may be made before a Justice of the Peace, commissioner for declarations, town clerk, road board secretary, electoral registrar, postmaster, classified officer in the State or Commonwealth public service, classified State school teacher, or member of the Police Force.)

Figure 9: Application form template for conditional citizenship - WA Government Gazette (1945), no. 42

5.08 York Police Court convictions statistics 1941 to 1962

The following four images show graphs demonstrating convictions in the York Police Court of Aboriginal people in the period from 1941 to 1962 (x-axis depicts number of convictions, y-axis depicts years when convictions occurred).

The first image (fig. 10) titled 'Convictions under the Criminal Code'

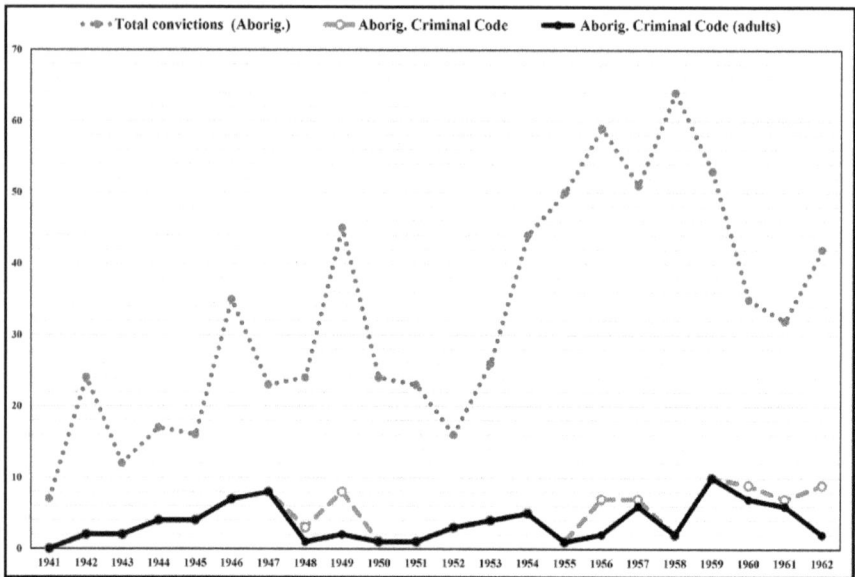

Figure 10: Convictions under the Criminal Code

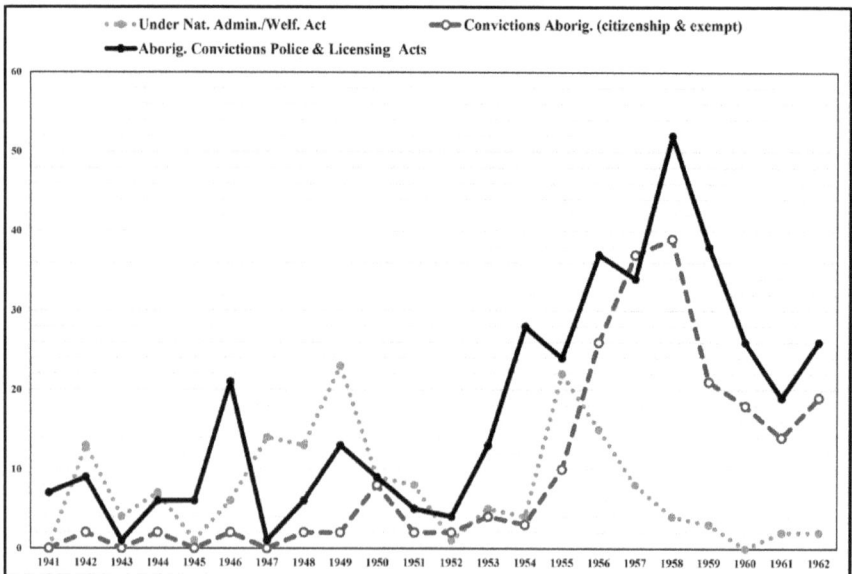

Figure 11: Convictions of offences specifically targeting Aboriginal people

170

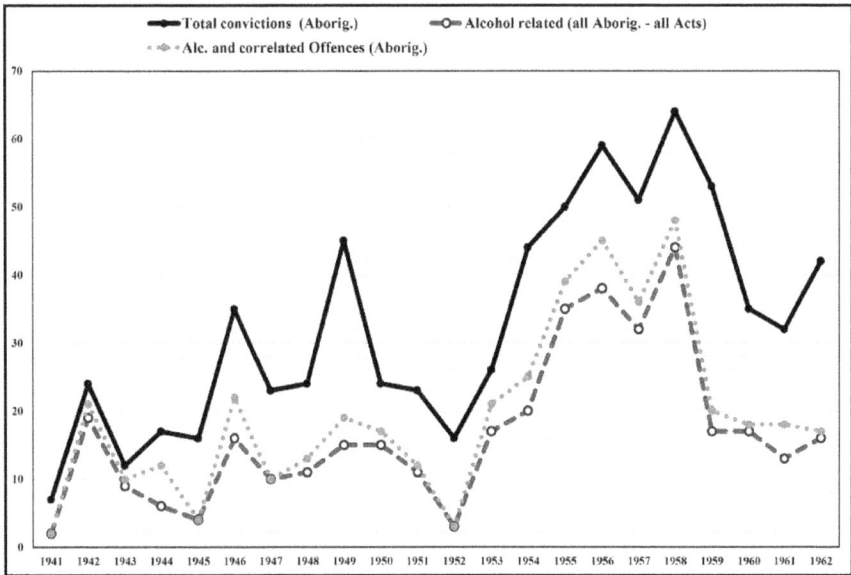

Figure 12: Alcohol related convictions

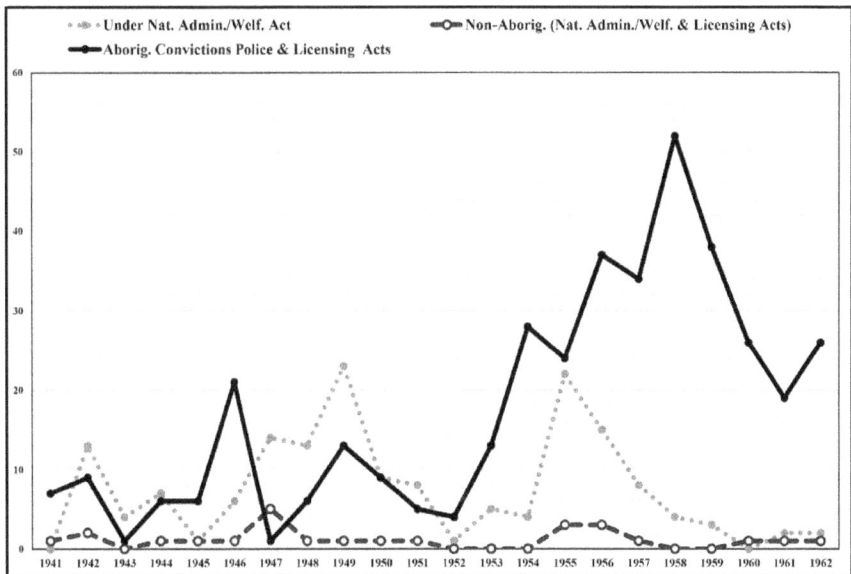

Figure 13: Convictions non-Aboriginal in relation to Aboriginal people

shows the stark difference between all convictions of Aboriginal people in the York Police Court and offences considered 'criminal' under the Criminal Code. Such criminal offences include assaults that resulted from the enforcement of racist legislation.

The image titled 'Convictions of offences specifically targeting Aboriginal people' (fig. 11) contains three graphs that show convictions of any Aboriginal persons prosecuted under the Native Administration and Native Welfare Acts, any convictions of Aboriginal people who were exempted from being classed as 'native' under the law, and all convictions of Aboriginal people under the Police and Licensing Acts (for example for 'drunkenness'). From 1955, there is a drop of convictions under the Native Administration and Native Welfare Acts which appears to be immediately offset by an increase of convictions under the Police and Licensing Acts.

The image titled 'Alcohol related convictions' (fig. 12) shows how closely related convictions of Aboriginal people and alcohol related offences were in York during the period 1941 to 1962. The dotted graph shows alcohol related convictions and associated, concurrent convictions, for example, disorderly behaviour and assaults.

The image 'Convictions non-Aboriginal in relation to Aboriginal people' (fig. 13) shows two graphs for convictions of Aboriginal people in York under the Native Administration/Native Welfare Acts, Police and Licensing Acts in comparison to one graph showing convictions of non-Aboriginal people for offences relating to interaction with Aboriginal people under the same laws (in relation to alcohol or entering a camp or reserve).

These statistics may serve as evidence for how 'white man's law' created an artificial Aboriginal offender image through the continuous enforcement of repressive measures. (data derived from: York Clerk of Courts Charge Books and WA Government Gazettes).

We now conclude the discussion about modes of exemption and assimilation and will be returning to June 1950, just after the Katanning conference had taken place.

Chapter 6. 1950s

6.01 Mid-1950 after the Katanning conference (I–V)

The Katanning conference appears to have empowered York's local authorities, who acted with increased assertiveness for a while afterwards. More departmental oversight was requested, as well as the prompt realisation of Aboriginal housing provision and other matters concerning Aboriginal people in York. When not satisfied with departmental responses and alleged inaction, higher instances were promptly approached. The first half of the 1950s was a period of changing times that witnessed the struggle between the state government attempting to impose 'assimilation' or integration of Aboriginal people into settler-Australian society and local communities and authorities showing resistance to these exogenous changes with Aboriginal people being caught in the middle. The changes that occurred were also not gradual but sometimes contradictory while assistance rendered for better living conditions and improved livelihoods remained conditional. Notably, mid-1950 formed the starting point for the following five sequences of events, numbered I to V.

6.02 I: At the games

We start with a very brief note on a sporting event. On request of the York Municipal Council and the York Road Board, immediately after the conference, a departmental officer attended a 'sports meeting' at York on 6 June as, allegedly, 'considerable misbehaviour had been experienced' in the past at such meetings.[1] The only newsworthy incident that the two local authorities may have referred to occurred two years earlier during a football match in May 1948 when York played against Merredin on York's home ground, at Forrest Oval. During this game, a violent brawl broke out between mainly female Aboriginal supporters of both clubs who reportedly clashed over 'the closeness of the scores'.[2] In time-worn racial-determinist fashion, the *York Chronicle* wrote that the closeness of the scores and resulting brawl was a consequence of 'the unleashing of their primeval instincts'.[3] It was noted that both teams had Aboriginal players. It would have almost been impossible for Aboriginal players to compete on that day, because in March 1948, the York Football Club had decided that Aboriginal players were no longer allowed to play for York. This decision was rescinded a month later without further explanation.[4] No similar occurrences were recorded on departmental files before or after this game, though the reader may recall G.B. Wood's, MLC, allegations in 1946 about Aboriginal people engaging in illegal gambling at sporting events (see chapter 3.10).

Cadet Patrol Officer D.F. Mercer attended the meeting, which was once again visited by Aboriginal people coming from a wide area ranging from Perth in the west, as far as Yalgoo in the north, Merredin in the east and Mount Barker in the south. Mercer estimated that approximately sixty per cent of the spectators were Aboriginal. He reported general positive conduct throughout the event and afterwards concluded that the Aboriginal proportion of spectators could in no way be considered a nuisance. After the sports meeting, Mercer went to the train station, where a large number of Aboriginal people were waiting for their trains home. There, Mercer found that 'segregation was evident, but the general conduct of the natives was excellent, in fact, better than many whites when boarding a train'.[5] The only somewhat negative observations he made were that three conditional citizenship holders were removed to the lock up for drunkenness and Mercer reported one further person under the influence of alcohol who was not exempt from the provisions of the *Native Administration Act 1947*. Overall, Mercer's verdict was that 'there was no room for complaint from any section of the white community'.[6]

Mercer's comment about the worse behaviour of some settler-Australians entering the train is valuable, as such comparisons were not often made on the record or in news articles. Dr Linley Henzell, the Commissioner of Public Health, who had also attended the Katanning conference, pointed out the hypocrisy of white prejudice with which Aboriginal people were constantly faced. Henzell commented during a discussion at the conference that too much emphasis was placed on the consumption of alcohol by Aboriginal people 'when the white could not attend an afternoon football match without demanding alcohol'.[7] When a road board delegate suggested that hotel licensees should be encouraged to refuse the sale of alcohol to conditional citizenship rights holders when there was a reasonable suspicion that this alcohol may be given to an Aboriginal person without any kind of exemption, Henzell 'quietly suggested that, as a nation which had the highest consumption of liquor in the world, it would be best to first put our own house in order'.[8] As laudable as Henzell's comment may sound at first, he seemingly did not consider Aboriginal people as part of the Australian nation when juxtaposing 'our own house' with Aboriginal people.

Except for the report on the sports meeting, there was no further discussion between the department and York's local authorities, or in the press, about the alleged poor behaviour of Aboriginal people at sporting events. Seemingly, until June 1950, the very presence of a large number of Aboriginal visitors to York caused certain sections of the settler-Australian community to panic. That there were no further recorded complaints was likely correlated with the slowly evolving process of assimilation and changing community attitudes. The settler-Australian community had to realised that calls for summary segregation and unreasonable population control measures, as they were implemented until recently, were generally no longer heeded to.

6.03 II: Reserve camps

In early July 1950, the York Municipal Council requested an official visit by Premier Ross McLarty, who obliged and visited York on 13 July.[9] The purpose of the visit was to address issues relating to infrastructure and various other matters, as well as to showcase York. McLarty also attended the York Reserve, together with the chairman of the road board, W.H. Robinson, and other board representatives, which would provide for headlines in York's local newspaper and in Perth. The *West Australian* article was titled, 'Native Dwellings Shock Premier', while the *York Chronicle*'s article was more moderately titled, 'First Hand Information—Native Reserve Visited'. Both papers quoted McLarty stating the following after his visit to the reserve: 'This is a shocking and deplorable state of affairs. Human beings should not be allowed to live under such conditions'.[10] The *York Chronicle* more or less copied the *West Australian*'s article, with a couple of added nuances:

> One of the shacks occupied by a native family is a rough wooden frame covered with a conglomeration of pieces of galvanised iron and bags which was far from waterproof. This family has been in residence in it for thirteen years. Other shacks on the site were of similar structure. The Board's health inspector Mr. H. N. Haley informed the Premier that suggestions made by this board to the Native Affairs department for the improvement of the buildings had been turned down on the grounds that the reserve was only a site on which travelling natives could camp.[11]

The board's representatives further expressed that they felt the department was shifting responsibility onto country local authorities. A suggestion was made that the department should provide selected Aboriginal families with tents similar to those issued to displaced persons at the time, and the road board offered to carry out the erection of such tents on the reserve. McLarty reportedly stated that he would take up the matter immediately with Commissioner Middleton.[12]

Premier McLarty wrote to the department six days later in relation to the complaints made by the road board and council. In particular, the local authorities alleged that they were ignored at Katanning, that Haley's report from the previous year had also been ignored and that local authorities were expected to provide amenities on reserves.[13] McLarty mentioned all points, as quoted in the news articles, and voiced the belief that a longstanding resident family should be able to afford rent, as they would earn collectively £22 a week during the chaff-cutting season (which runs for a few weeks per year).[14]

The department refuted all claims made by the local authorities. It also pointed out that while the current policy provided that, in future, reserves should only be used by transient Aboriginal people, this was currently not enforced and, in any event, the long-term resident family on the reserve was apparently not really interested in obtaining a house in town. The question of providing tents had been discussed after the Katanning conference and it was decided that tents would be a retrogressive step in the 'uplift' of Aboriginal people, so the idea was therefore dismissed. District Officer Andersen was asked to comment on the premier's letter and Andersen stated that he had always considered the York Reserve one of the best in the Central District as it had a water tab and two conveniences that were serviced. Andersen continued that, throughout the state, far worse conditions for Aboriginal people existed and he felt that improvements should be made on a broad basis across the state once funds and equipment were available. In other words, he recommended inaction in the case of York.[15]

Premier McLarty was provided with these recorded views by departmental officers and met with Commissioner Middleton on 27 September 1950 to discuss the position. Middleton promoted his strategy of 'wait and see' until a solution for the housing of Aboriginal people had been achieved by the Minister for Native Affairs and funding had been granted. However, Premier McLarty insisted that Middleton arrive at an instant solution. This discussion completed the premier's involvement, while Middleton was forced to conceive of an instant remedy for the reserve issue. The band-aid solution he discussed with departmental officers Andersen and McLarty (not the premier[16]) in late September was, without question, more retrogressive than the erection of tents and it was on par with the policies of his predecessors; the records do not indicate whether Middleton had discussed the following procedure with the premier. The road board was to be advised that its local health authority (Mr Haley) would need to issue warnings to reserve residents if their homes did not conform with local by-laws and health regulations (Middleton knew that they did not). If no action was taken by the reserve residents to have their homes comply with local by-laws and health regulations, Middleton instructed that these homes should be condemned through the local health authority and the occupiers evicted. If these reserve residents were then unable to provide better accommodation for themselves and their families, they would be declared 'indigent' and could 'be transferred to Moore River Native Settlement where adequate accommodation and keep would be provided by the department'.[17]

During a patrol, four days after the premier's visit to York, a young adult reserve resident of the Kickett family was interviewed who appeared not to be overly keen on obtaining a house in town, but indicated that he may start saving if he changed his mind. The heads of the family were away at the time of the patrol; however, from the comment by this one family member, it was inferred that the entire Kickett family was not interested in improving their living conditions according to white standards.[18] Reading between the lines, the family was thus accused of resisting integration into settler-Australian society. Given that Middleton was well aware of the reported attitudes of Aboriginal individuals and families towards the departmental housing policy, his September strategy appears to have been proposed with several intents: to appease the premier's request, to create an incentive to improve living conditions and also to punish the alleged refusal to embrace the state governmental policy of assimilation, if living conditions were not promptly improved.

It may have indeed been the case that, in 1950, the majority of the Kickett family was content to live on the reserve, shielded from white prejudice and day-to-day racism that, without a doubt, many Aboriginal residents in town had to endure. Life-long negative and traumatic experiences with white communities and state and local authorities may also have fostered reluctance to move into town—if not outright conscious resistance—particularly by the older generations. The reserve was also of considerably larger size (ten acres) than small town blocks, and it was located on the river, which provided a private swimming opportunity in summer. Further, obtaining a home through the departmental housing scheme meant increased supervision and scrutiny from departmental officers. Therefore, it does not seem unlikely that some individuals and families would have chosen greater freedoms on the reserve, without any rental costs, over 'improved living conditions' in town. Anecdotal evidence of former reserve dwellers who grew up on the York Reserve suggests that, while living in poverty, their family was comparatively happy on the reserve until the late 1960s and early 1970s. 'Comparatively happy' needs to be interpreted vis-à-vis the widespread negative attitudes held by settler-Australians in town towards Aboriginal people.[19]

On 5 October, District Officer Andersen, whose insufficient communication skills have already been discussed (see chapter 4.06), wrote to the York Road Board. Evidently referring to the premier's instructions, Andersen stated that 'a complaint' had been received in relation to the unsatisfactory living conditions of a family on the reserve. He noted that the department's housing program was awaiting approval from the state government but that the family in question was not interested in town housing anyway. Andersen continued by stating that the Department of Native Affairs was unable to take any action on the family, who had been living under their present conditions for a number of years, which had apparently been accepted by the road board's health inspector. Andersen then requested that the health inspector investigate the current conditions and 'take whatever action is required regarding the eviction of these people and the demolition of the buildings if necessary'. While principally acting in line with Middleton's band-aid solution, Andersen skipped the step whereby the family was supposed to be warned to improve their housing to satisfy building by-laws and that failing to do so would require the structures to be condemned. Camps or humpies were generally unable to satisfy local building by-laws but this does not justify Andersen's assumption that this would be the case and subsequent failure to notify the family. Seemingly with the 'Moore River Native Settlement solution' on his mind, Andersen concluded by requesting that he be advised of the course of action being taken 'so that arrangements can be made for the care of these people, if necessary'.[20]

H.W.N. Haley, who held the offices of both secretary and health inspector on the York Road Board, perceived Andersen's letter as an undue attack on his person. He replied swiftly on 7 October by stating in no uncertain terms that he thought Andersen's letter was based on 'ignorance'[21]; Haley wished it to be known that he was only appointed health inspector in July 1949 and that the department had failed to take action on his report that suggested improvements to the reserve. Having pointed out some further 'presumptions' by Andersen that he did not agree with, Haley then stated that, to his knowledge, the reserve was vested in the Department of Native Affairs as a camping ground for itinerant Aboriginal people. Further, the long-term resident family that had been living there for so long was a reflection on the supervision of the department; the road board had 'no jurisdiction whatsoever over the land and can evict no person therefrom'.[22] After venting his displeasure, Haley suggested cooperation to achieve the object of Andersen's letter. Haley, being the local health authority, could order the demolition of the reserve dwellings but the department, as the owner of the land, would have to be responsible for the work being carried out. Haley then commented that the family would probably move out of sight and erect similar dwellings elsewhere. However, he warned that 'to overcome discrimination', it would also be necessary to take similar action against other families in the district who lived under similar conditions.[23] Unaware of the department's post-eviction plan, Haley continued:

> The eventual outcome will be families of nomad natives roaming the countryside to find seclusion. Has your department any plan to absorb these families as their camps are demolished? I do consider that public health demands immediate action but any premature move will prejudice the ultimate object.

Haley then suggested summoning the Minister for Health to visit York, as such a visit would accelerate the government's approval for the housing scheme.[24]

Continuing with the emotionally charged correspondence, Andersen replied to Haley on 12 October. Along with some further petty personal bickering, he pointed out that local health inspectors were permitted to enter any Aboriginal reserve while exercising their function under the *Health Act* as per the *Monthly Health Bulletin*, No. 12, March/April 1950. He claimed that the department had, to this point, not received any official complaints about this family and reiterated that the department could only take action after the road board's health authority had declared the homes unfit for human habitation—once the family had already become homeless, and after the health authority had ordered the demolition of their camps. Citing Haley, who claimed that public health demanded immediate action, Andersen further wrote that he failed to see why there should be any delay in taking action if the matter was so urgent. Nonetheless, Andersen wished to make it known that the family had erected the structures without the department's permission and that none of the materials contained therein were the property of the department. In relation to other families in the road board's jurisdiction who may also have been faced with homelessness as a result of their camps being condemned, Andersen commented that he trusted 'that your health inspector will deal as impartially with employers who fail to provide proper accommodation and facilities'.[25] With this last comment, Andersen indicated that if the road board chose not to look at these other families living in camps at other locations, then the department would continue to ignore the fact that some employers did not provide accommodation, although they should according to the law. Whether Aboriginal people chose to camp away from private properties to retain independence was not part of this politically charged argument.

Andersen would have intentionally tried to aggravate Haley when writing 'your health inspector', given that he would have known that this was Haley himself. This correspondence is a prime example of maximum passive aggressiveness in official communication. Andersen made it clear that poor housing conditions on the reserve were a road board issue, and the board could either keep ignoring it or cause eviction; the department would only come to take charge of the suddenly homeless families. On other occasions, this kind of strategy would likely have sought inaction, as the department generally steered away from removing whole families to institutions in the South West Land Division; however, in this instance, it was in the interest of the department to provoke Haley to such an extent that he would initiate the eviction of the long-term reserve family, given that the premier had insisted that human beings should not be 'allowed to live under such conditions', as quoted in the newspapers, or not be 'expected to live in such a way', as in the premier's letter to the Minister for Native Affairs.[26]

On receipt of Andersen's letter, Haley was obviously not happy with the suggested course of action that saw the road board being responsible for evictions, and he tried a different tactic. Haley wrote on 14 October to Commissioner Middleton and requested assurance that action would be taken by the Department of Native Affairs so that no families could be permitted to camp permanently on the reserve. After all, Haley insinuated, the reserve was originally set aside as a camping ground for itinerant Aboriginal people, as Middleton would surely be aware.[27] On the same day, Haley also wrote to the Commissioner of Public Health. He summarised the current issue and claimed that the Department of Native Affairs was now pressing for action by the road board's local health authority to have the reserve dwellings condemned. Andersen's charade was either too obvious or Haley did not want to carry the responsibility of making the reserve dwellers homeless by pointing out that the department was the driving force. Haley also complained about the department's alleged lax supervision given that the long-term reserve dwellers had been allowed to live there for approximately fifteen years, and he ensured that the road board would not object to camps on the reserve if they were of a temporary nature. Haley also wished to ascertain to whom he should address the condemnation order, noting that the 'current occupier' (singular, assumingly the male head of the family) was illiterate.[28]

Commissioner Middleton replied on 25 October, discussing the *Native Administration Act*, which does not specifically provide for definitions of temporary or permanent living arrangements on reserves. He concluded that no action could be taken by the department, which was charged with the 'welfare—not persecution' of Aboriginal people, to prevent them from camping on reserves. He further discussed the issues with the slow progress of the current housing policy and finally illuminated that alternative accommodation provided by the department following an eviction would mean 'transfer to Moore River Settlement'.[29]

Unsurprisingly, Haley was still not satisfied with Middleton's answer and replied directly upon receipt of his letter on 26 October.

Haley argued that Andersen had quoted the *Health Bulletin* incorrectly, wherein it was actually stated that Aboriginal people who committed breaches against the *Health Act* 'on any place other than upon a reserve'[30] could be dealt with only be the local health authority in charge. He also kept inquiring about the origins of town reserves and their supposed purpose for itinerant Aboriginal people. On 30 October, Middleton, once and for all, clarified that no 'statutory authority exists to prevent reserves being used for permanent residential purposes'.[31] On 1 November, Commissioner of Public Health Dr Linley Henzell replied to Haley's letter from two weeks earlier after consulting Middleton. Henzell suggested that unless alternative accommodation could be supplied for the long-term reserve family, 'it would not be equitable to condemn that camp and demolish it' as it would only shift the problem into another neighbourhood or area. He expressed sympathy with the efforts of the Department of Native Affairs and commented that housing should not only be provided to white Australians. Other than requesting a report about the reserve camp from the health inspector, Henzell had nothing else to suggest.[32]

As the road board now stopped agitating for the removal of permanent residents on the York Reserve, Commissioner Middleton and the Department of Native Affairs had gained the perfect outcome. Having been ambushed by Premier McLarty to do something about the living conditions on the reserve, the department managed to place the onus on the road board as the local authority that would be 'persecuting' Aboriginal people; hence, the department could have claimed to have acted with welfare in mind if removal to Moore River had occurred. Had it not been for contacting the Department of Health, whose commissioner recommended inaction, Haley may have insisted on the demolition of camps and the department's initial plan would have likely been executed. However, in his function as local health inspector, Haley reported to the Department of Health and it would have seemed inappropriate to act against its commissioner's recommendations. Had the premier inquired now about progress on the matter, the Department of Native Affairs could have conveniently pointed the finger at the York Road Board, who was given all options and decided not to take any action. The department, however, had fulfilled its obligations without having to resort to the forceful removal of the Aboriginal family.

Underlying this political battle of shady pretences remained the claim that the long-term reserve residents did not wish to obtain housing in town and thus improve their living conditions. Therefore, the moral responsibility could be returned to the Aboriginal family, who could be viewed as at fault for the way they *chose* to live. The department was thereby gifted with a win–win situation at the expense of the long-term reserve residents. Following these meetings, correspondences and colliding egos, the situation was still the same as it had been during the premier's visit in July. If no quick change was to occur in relation to the housing conditions, perhaps at least some amenities could be provided to show that something, rather than nothing, was being done.

Figure 14: George Kickett Snr and Merle Narkle on the York Reserve with a camp in the background (courtesy Marion Kickett)

6.04 III: Reserve amenities

A few days before commissioners Middleton and Henzell sent their final letters on the reserve housing issue, departmental Inspector B.A. McLarty attended York while conducting a patrol across the wider region. He reported that during discussions with Haley, primarily in his role as secretary of the York Road Board, arrangements had been made that the board would provide the following facilities on the reserve:

(a) two army-type 'thunderbox' latrines

(b) French drain at the existing standpipe

(c) one shower, suitably enclosed

(d) brushwood sun-shelter and laundry facilities.

McLarty's report did not suggest that he had great difficulties making this arrangement. The road board's primary concern appeared to be about the policy of assimilation and long-term reserve residents; however, the board seemed to have made peace with the idea that the reserve was there to stay for some time and, thus, agreed to assist with erecting and improving facilities.[33]

On 1 December 1950, Haley wrote to McLarty, confirming that the road board would be assisting with the erection of the proposed facilities by providing labour at cost to the department. The total costs were quoted as £48 4s 3d, of which £21 were quoted for labour. Haley pointed out that the road board would have difficulties obtaining building materials due to state-wide shortages and he wondered whether the department may be able to assist with providing building materials. He also suggested that donated wash troughs may be secured and could be transported from Perth. Haley then proposed enlisting reserve residents on a 'busy-bee' principle to assist with the erection of the facilities to reduce costs; failing to do so, he warned, would have negative consequences for future building projects:

To prove that they are prepared to assist in improving their living conditions would raise local prestige and I am certain that if the employees of this Board are engaged on these works while husky native males sit by and watch, my Board will not hesitate in refusing to carry out any future improvements.[34]

Middleton promptly replied to Haley, advising that he was happy for reserve residents to assist if they were paid and the total labour costs were covered by the estimate. Before the letter could be discussed at the periodical road board meeting, the *York Chronicle* commented on Middleton's letter, stating that it would appear that self-help was not encouraged where Aboriginal people were concerned.[35] These attitudes by the road board and the *York Chronicle* exemplify, once again, that Aboriginal people were not considered part of the general community entitled to public works expenditures. After all, road board employees did not offer to carry out the work on a voluntary basis because more than two-fifths of the total costs quoted were for labour expenses. Moreover, given that road board employees received a regular wage, by erecting the reserve facilities, the road board would have likely gained a monetary benefit by cashing in 'labour costs' for employees who were paid anyway through rate payers' contributions.

By 18 January 1951, finances had been approved for the erection of the proposed improvements as per Haley's quote, and Haley was promptly advised. Haley voiced strong disapproval that Aboriginal people from the reserve would not assist unless paid but otherwise did not object to carrying out the work. He disagreed that five-gallon drums cut lengthwise were suitable containers for tasks such as the washing of clothing and bedding, as proposed by the department, and he questioned why cement troughs that were apparently offered free of charge had been rejected. Most importantly, he advised that local merchants stated that delivery of corrugated iron was currently subject to a waiting period of no less than six months and he asked whether the department was able to secure the same. Middleton arranged for fourteen seven-foot sheets of corrugated iron to be railed from Moore River Native Settlement to the York Road Board on 2 March 1951.[36]

Five months later, on 1 August 1951, Patrol Officer McLarty met Secretary Haley at the road board's depot. McLarty was advised that the road board would proceed with the erection of the planned facilities on the reserve once wintry conditions had subsided. All the required materials had been obtained and were sighted by McLarty, who also reported that the thunder boxes had been completed and were awaiting installation.[37] The wintry conditions subsided but nothing was being done. In December 1951, the road board discussed a circular letter from the Gnowangerup Road Board, which advocated that facilities should be provided on reserves along similar lines to those adopted in South Australia. The current building project was not discussed and the road board decided to ignore the circular letter's appeal.[38] The wintry conditions subsided a second time with no further notable progress recorded.

In February 1953, Cadet Patrol Officer A.G. Down visited York and noticed that no improvements on the reserve had occurred. He noted in his journal that Secretary Haley was not an unsympathetic person; however, he was reportedly of the opinion that he had been 'slighted by the department over arrangements for amenities on the York Reserve and has therefore refused to take any interest in native matters'.[39] In May, Officer McLarty provided a summary report to Middleton about the agreed arrangements and noted that he himself had sighted all the required materials and completed thunder boxes back in August 1951. Referring to Down's patrol report, McLarty was unable to relate to Haley's comment about feeling 'slighted' by the department, given that little appeared to have been done to carry the work out. McLarty wrote to Haley on 15 May 1953, asking why no work had been carried out to date. There is no reply letter in the corresponding departmental file and McLarty's letter was apparently not discussed at any monthly road board meeting until the end of the year.[40]

Following a patrol in late September 1955, Officer McLarty noted that the only amenities on the reserve were a standpipe and latrines, and he commented that he was thankful now that the road board's 'dilatoriness' in relation to the building proposal had led to its withdrawal. He explained his misgivings in that the only occupants were the longstanding reserve family, their relations and 'a few transients now and then'[41] whom he did not consider worthy of any extra government expenditure. The family reportedly did not show any interest in following the department's principal policy of assimilation, which apparently made them unworthy of improved living conditions in McLarty's opinion. This does not mean that other Aboriginal families in York were enthusiastic about assimilation; however, the simple desire to live in a house and not on a proclaimed reserve made them, by default, more worthy in McLarty's eyes than the reserve dwellers who did not seem to wish to leave the reserve. McLarty commented to Commissioner Middleton that, at this stage, there was no need to cancel the reserve as it served this one family and transient Aboriginal people. However, should the reserve be made subject to any special pressure by the road board or cause any other administrative difficulties, McLarty continued, its retention was not warranted.[42]

In late 1957, the chairman of the York Road Board, W.H. Robinson, attended a road board conference in Goomalling, where the situation of Aboriginal people living in country areas was discussed. He cited Premier McLarty's visit to the reserve in 1950 and lamented that nothing had been done to provide facilities on the York Reserve despite the promises made. Robinson suggested that rather than living on town reserves, Aboriginal people should be given small rural properties to earn a living; however, these should not be in close proximity to towns as this would have a detrimental effect on Aboriginal people's willingness to work. Following a discussion, a motion was carried that the government be approached to make funds directly available to road boards for the purpose of setting up town reserves. Rather than channelling moneys through government departments, where valuable funds would be wasted in administrative costs, the conference attendees claimed that road boards would be better suited to effectively provide facilities. That this was not necessarily the case, Robinson's own York Road Board had proven only a few years earlier, and no change of leading representatives had taken place since.[43]

The conference would bear no fruit, however, as the Department of Native Welfare had just commenced a new policy in relation to the erection of reserve facilities. Earlier, in 1957, Middleton had advised the Minister for Native Welfare that the department was now erecting ablution blocks, shelter sheds and latrines on departmental reserves at a cost of £500 per ablution block and £1,000 per shelter shed. However, only by 1961 was further action on the York Reserve considered.[44] In November 1961, Member of the Legislative Council Charles Roy Abbey wrote to the then Minister for Native Welfare, Charles Collier Perkins (who had okayed the gazettal of the prohibited area in York in 1947 when he was the local Member of the Legislative Assembly). Abbey stated that he had been informed that no ablution facilities were available at the York Reserve and requested that Perkins investigate the matter with 'a view to possible improvement in the future'.[45]

By 1961, the Public Works Department carried out such building contracts in combination with local contractors. However, progress still moved at a tiringly slow pace. Health Inspector Haley (now of the Shire of York, as road boards were transformed into shires by 1 July 1961[46]) wrote to the department on 30 January 1962 and requested that the recommendations made by an officer of the Public Health Department following a recent inspection to the reserve be attended to. These recommendations covered the improvements agreed on in 1950 with some further additions, for example, the installation of a septic tank.[47] Funds were only available for the financial year 1962–1963 and, in October 1962, tenders were finally being called. By September 1963, it was reported that the toilet/ablution block was still under construction and the contractor, a certain Mr Kaljuste, appeared 'to only work on these buildings at spasmodic intervals'.[48] By November 1963, the works were complete. As mentioned previously (see chapter 6.03), in July 1950, Premier McLarty had requested that urgent action be taken to improve the living conditions on the reserve. The agreed facilities that were meant to be erected in 1951 would have only been rudimentary but would have surely been appreciated by the reserve residents, who had to wait thirteen years for any works to be completed.

The urgency to complete the building endeavour on the York Reserve was apparently not obvious to the decision makers, as the agreements and correspondences from 1950 to 1953 had likely been forgotten under a pile of paper work, shifting personnel and the department's primary focus: housing in town. Additionally, reserve dwellers were considered unworthy and, moreover, Premier Ross

McLarty completed his tenure in February 1953, which meant that political urgency to heed to the premier's instructions, if it was ever real, ceased with the change of office. This wilful negligence by the department, as well as the road board during the early 1950s, would have made a perfect Petri dish for growing cynicism among the Aboriginal reserve dwellers, who had been persecuted since the 1930s.

Public interest concerning the reserve as reported in the local newspaper largely ceased in 1951. The focus of York's settler-Australian public shifted simultaneously with that of the department towards Aboriginal housing and living in town. When not moving into town, Aboriginal families also moved to other places in the district. For example, in May 1952, it was reported that two families were living on the reserve, while six families were living in camps at Gilgering Siding, south of York, bordering the Beverley district.[49] All these developments would have shifted the York Reserve further into the periphery of the public and departmental minds. We will now return to events in town, starting again in mid-1950. When we return to the reserve at a later stage, the focus will be on a housing program in the context of the assimilation policy, which commenced in the early 1960s.

6.05 IV: Segregation at the York Hospital maternity ward

The following episode provides a prime example of community resistance during the mid-twentieth century transitional period that saw a shift from Aboriginal segregation towards integration into settler-Australian society in Western Australia's South West Land Division. White Australian York was increasingly coming to terms with the reality that Aboriginal people were moving into town. It was publicly known that some individuals had already received conditional citizenship on application, and it had been openly communicated during patrols, at the Katanning conference and in the press that 'assimilation' of Aboriginal people was official state government policy. However, the heated debate about Aboriginal women at the maternity ward in York's hospital during the second half of 1950 made it evident that tolerating Aboriginal people within white community spaces did not necessarily equate to inclusiveness and the absence of segregation per se.

The reader may recall (see chapter 3.02) that the York Hospital had been providing accommodation for Aboriginal patients, who were segregated from non-Aboriginal patients and placed on the hospital's verandahs. However, by 1950, these verandahs were in such a 'deplorable condition' that Aboriginal women who gave birth at the hospital were housed together with non-Aboriginal women for the postnatal resting period, also referred to as *confinement*. Pigeons had moved in under the roof and their droppings, being a health hazard, had caused the matron to relocate Aboriginal mothers to the maternity ward. The maternity ward was housed in a separate building to the main hospital where the verandas were located. White Australian mothers were reportedly not pleased with this arrangement and Councillor Christina Foreman took on the task to agitate for a separate maternity ward for Aboriginal women. It is not clear whether Foreman acted out of conviction or whether she did so at the request of a section of York's settler-Australian population, being the only female representative within the otherwise exclusively male municipal council, but it was likely a bit of both. Foreman did not question that Aboriginal women should have access to a maternity facility; however, she promoted that access to this medical service occur in a segregated environment. Foreman's sympathetic paternalistic form of racism was seemingly a strategy of appeasement, congruent with her earlier agitation for segregated toilets.[50]

When the maternity ward issue was first discussed at a council meeting in early July, Mayor Noonan also argued that Aboriginal mothers could not be placed back on the verandahs in their current condition. However, his line of argument was even less inclusive than Foreman's, in that he claimed those Aboriginal mothers with conditional citizenship rights 'were placed on the same footing as a white person'[51] and, therefore, could not be subjected to lesser conditions. Noonan's comment suggests that he was willing to accept that deserving Aboriginal people with conditional citizenship rights should receive the same treatment conditions as white Australians but this did not imply complete and indiscriminative integration. Councillor (and Manager of the *York Chronicle*) Henry Gordon Wake, on the other hand, did not make a secret of his approval of the idea of Aboriginal mothers being housed under 'deplorable conditions' and reportedly stated that 'much was being said about meeting the natives on equal terms, but he considered that as the natives did not live the same manner as most white persons this should be taken into account in cases of confinement'.[52] At the same council meeting, it was decided that Western Australia's Premier Ross McLarty be asked to make an official visit to York, as previously discussed in relation to the reserve (see chapter 6.03). Among the other matters already mentioned, council wished to raise the maternity ward 'issue' with the premier.[53]

When Premier McLarty visited York on 13 July 1950, he also inspected the hospital. Reportedly, the 'necessity of having a separate midwifery ward for native women was being stressed, it being stated that there was a definite antipathy shown by white women at being placed in the same ward'.[54] McLarty advised that there was currently no money for a new hospital in York but that he would address the requirement for a segregated maternity ward with the responsible department.[55] In late August, McLarty wrote to the council stating that Aboriginal women would likely continue using the maternity ward and suggested that they house Aboriginal mothers in one of the single rooms on the ward. He also committed £3,000 to various renovation works at the hospital. Foreman bemoaned that this proposal would leave no single rooms for white women, who would also have to share facilities with Aboriginal women. Foreman continued that 'white women knowing the conditions under which most of the natives in the area were living would not be very happy about it. The maternity ward, when first erected, had not been built for use by the natives'.[56] Mayor Noonan complained that the government was shelving its responsibilities in relation to Aboriginal people. Strongly resisting the notion of social inclusion, the council then decided to ascertain whether it was possible to send Aboriginal mothers back onto the verandahs once they had been renovated.[57] This proposition was not mentioned again in the following news articles concerning the matter. The Public Works Department clearly had doubts as to whether it would be able to make the old hospital building pigeon proof.[58] However, as we will discuss later, there is anecdotal evidence that Aboriginal women were being confined on the hospital veranda until the early 1960s.

Since early 1950, James Isaac Mann, MLA, Avon Valley, was the new local member of Parliament representing York, following the restructuring of Western Australian electorates. Mann was based in Beverley, which is located a short thirty-three-kilometre distance away from York and he had been the local member for the electorate of Beverley from 1930, until the inception of the Avon Valley electorate.[59] Mann had arranged Premier McLarty's visit and facilitated communication with government departments in relation to the hotly discussed maternity ward debate. In late September, Mann advised the council that the Department of Health had decided that no major additions would be made to the current hospital and that Aboriginal mothers may be housed in a private room, as suggested by McLarty. Eventually, York would receive a new hospital in which in 'any new buildings, all sections would be provided for'.[60] Mann prophesied that, in the foreseeable future, York's maternity ward would probably be utilised by the majority of women within the electorate, as other hospitals were closing or would otherwise not be available. Therefore, he warned that giving up one room to Aboriginal mothers could be detrimental to the adequate care of white mothers. Mann further stated that he felt that the accusation that 'country residents were "putting the boots" into the natives because of their complaints in recent months' was unfair. 'Unfortunately, city people did not know the conditions',[61] he said, and he sarcastically suggested sending Aboriginal women to Perth's private maternity hospitals instead, to see if city dwellers appreciated it. Mann was well aware that privately run hospitals in the country had a right to refuse admission and he should have known that Aboriginal people had been admitted to Perth metropolitan public hospitals, at least for the duration of his lifetime. Therefore, his rhetoric was baseless populism. During the ensuing discussion in council, it was suggested to erect a temporary timber construction for Aboriginal women.[62]

Mann was open in his racist and anti-assimilationist attitude. Only weeks earlier, he had ranted in Parliament about the alleged inability of Aboriginal people to integrate, which he based on racialist determinants:

they can be little more than hewers of wood and drawers of water as long as the world lasts. They are not like the American negroes. It is recognised that the Australian aboriginal is of an exceedingly poor class, and when there is in his composition a strain of white blood, he develops a cunning of a dingo. I know the people of this type well; they are to be found in my electorate in numbers. ... The member of Boulder need have no great ideas about the equality of mankind, because I am convinced there can be no equality between black and white. These people over the years have lived a nomadic life—a life of their own entirely—and it is impossible for them to adapt themselves to our ways of life. That cannot possibly be done in one generation or in 50 generations, and it is of little use talking of building houses and expecting them to live in them.[63]

With some merit, the *Workers Star* commented that 'Mann's nonsense smacks of Hitler race theories'.[64] Mann certainly appeared to be eager to support York's segregationist ambitions and, over the next few years, he would frequently take on a representative role in the resistance to integration. Members of York's local authorities have rarely been recorded to be as openly and ideologically racist as Mann expressed himself to be in State Parliament.

On 31 October, a deputation from the York Municipal Council consisting of Mann, Noonan and Foreman waited on the Minister for Health, Annie Florence Gillies Cardell-Oliver, and personally requested that a separate maternity ward for Aboriginal women be established. The same arguments discussed above were raised, and that Aboriginal people in general were becoming more 'hospital-minded', with concluding remarks made in reference to the official assimilation policy:

Until the standard of living of native people was lifted to something like parity with the living conditions and habits of the white population, it was considered that a line should be drawn, particularly in the matter of maternity cases.[65]

Minister Cardell-Oliver promised she would consider the deputation's request. Her support for the proposal was potentially influenced by the fact that the then seventy-four-year-old minister had a somewhat personal connection to York, having lived in town from 1912 to 1914, when she also gave birth to one of her children at the hospital.[66] The deputation had suggested having a 'native labour ward', created between the staircase and the general women's ward in the main hospital. The location was a walk-through pantry, with no windows or ventilation and not enough space for medical staff to work. Being on the upper floor, the food lift was also located in this storage room. The Commissioner and the Under Secretary of the Public Health Department declined the proposal and outlined, in no uncertain terms, that a separate ward was against the policy of assimilation and that the plan provided could only have been sketched by a lay person with no idea of how a hospital works.[67] It was suggested that one of the private rooms be utilised in the existing maternity section, while reasoning that such 'a policy might be mutually preferred by both classes of the community as a temporary measure pending assimilation'.[68] In relation to this matter, the Under Secretary of the Public Health Department had approached Commissioner Middleton in July, who had recommended separate accommodation because, reportedly, Aboriginal people disliked association with whites as much as whites with Aboriginal people.[69] Given that Aboriginal mothers were faced with constant hostility from settler-Australian mothers during their time of recovery, Middleton's comment should not come as a surprise.

On 14 November, Cardell-Oliver communicated to council via Mann that the deputations' suggestion to have Aboriginal women housed in the old part of the hospital was not practical and that Aboriginal mothers would have to be housed within the maternity ward. Her letter to Mann was very much sanitised and did not contain any of the criticism voiced by the Under Secretary and the Commissioner of Health. Cardell-Oliver suggested that one of the private rooms be made available with the provision of an additional bath and lavatory set aside for Aboriginal mothers. As diplomatically as could be, she refuted the deputations' bogus argument about the lack of space in the ward.

Minister Cardell-Oliver and Commissioner Henzell of the Health Department had inspected the York Hospital following the deputation's visit and concluded that the 'town and district had one of the best midwifery hospitals in the state and that the accommodation available was considerably greater than was necessary for the number of births per annum'.[70] Cardwell-Oliver reasoned that if one single bedroom was to be provided for Aboriginal mothers, this left white women with one bedroom for four, one bedroom for two and one single bedroom. Over the previous four years, there had been sixty-nine births per annum, which equated to four beds as a minimum requirement; therefore, York had four maternity beds more than the minimum requirement and could afford to give one to Aboriginal women. Councillor Foreman moved that the council should accept the proposal as it was the only option at present that allowed provisions 'for natives without them being placed in the same room as white women'; the council accepted.[71]

The public debate had come to rest with the council's acceptance of the minister's proposal. Seemingly, at no point were the ethics of segregation questioned by any active participant of the discussion, either from the local authority or state government. Though the Commissioner and the Undersecretary for Public Health raised concerns in relation to assimilation, they were happy to accommodate the provision of a separate room for Aboriginal mothers. Otherwise, questions were raised and recommendations and decisions were made about 'how' and not 'if' to implement segregation. However, there was one outside commentator who dared to speak up against this segregationist frenzy in York. In a letter to the editor of the *West Australian*, Madeleine Cope, President of the Native Rights and Welfare League, voiced her disgust about the deputation from York, which had been reported in the same daily publication. Cope called out the deputation's paradoxical, prejudiced views, which insisted that Aboriginal women only be allowed to be housed with white women once their living conditions were lifted to something like parity with those of whites. She likened this idea to parents not letting their child into the water until it could swim. Cope assured:

[t]he good people of York need have no fear that they will be contaminated, by being in the same ward with coloured mothers. Everyone is given a bath and clean clothes on entering hospital, and if suffering from any transmissible disease, would certainly be isolated (be she black or white). The whole thing is a vicious circle.[72]

Cope's activist stance is refreshing to read among the numerous bigoted comments and arguments voiced by members of York's municipal council and the member of Parliament. Reading between the lines of her letter, however, one cannot escape Cope's well-meaning yet patronising generalised assumptions about Aboriginal people in York. Cope appears to have bought into the claim that the issue was entirely centred around lifestyle behaviours. Aboriginal people in York lived in a variety of circumstances—some may have lived in poorly maintained hygienic conditions but others would not. The demand for segregation in the maternity ward did not distinguish between the levels of hygiene of individuals nor any other behavioural attributes deemed desirable or undesirable. It distinguished between black and white, Aboriginal and non-Aboriginal. Therefore, the argument for segregation was racist at its core.

The deputation to Minister Cardell-Oliver also triggered a discussion among three women's organisations who publicly voiced their opinions in relation to segregation in hospitals, with two organisations arguing against segregation. This was followed by further letters to the editor, with two out of three commentators being in defence of Aboriginal patients.[73] The Labor Women's Organisation wrote directly to Minister Cardell-Oliver declaring that the request for a segregated maternity ward was against the principle of raising the status of 'our native women' as laid down in the United Nations Charter.[74] That the York maternity ward issue was picked up in public discourse in Perth and turned seemingly in favour of general inclusiveness may be regarded as the silver lining of this whole sad affair. Those sections of society who were white Australians at heart were not going to give up their privileges without a fight and the headlines that were created are evidence of the struggle to retain the status quo.

While the public debate ceased with the council's acceptance of Minister Cardell-Oliver's proposal, the hospital administration and patients were not pacified as yet. A year later, on 22 November 1951, the recently appointed matron of the York Hospital, Christine Chipper, who had also just immigrated to Australia, wrote to the Public Health Department complaining that Aboriginal women had to use the same facilities as 'patients' (non-Aboriginal was implied as the norm) in the currently fully booked maternity ward. Chipper went on:

> As you know I am English, & before I could admit the natives, I had to bathe them, they both live in tents, & were indescribably filthy. I did not relise the feeling that does exist & had to use more than tact to pacify the private patients. I consulted with the medical officer to pacify the patients, I found it most difficult to nurse both without strife.[75]

The matron was seemingly overwhelmed by the reality of settler-Australian country life—that is, if we take her comment about being English to mean that she did not know how to handle the situation of white Australian antagonism towards the presence of Aboriginal mothers because this was new terrain to her. Chipper was obviously unhappy having to bathe patients before admitting them and did not seem to question the reasons for their living conditions, but her letter suggests that she was otherwise more concerned with making her work doable without 'strife'. She had looked up the hospital's records and referred to correspondence from the previous year, when separate amenities were promised. Chipper was informed that a separate toilet and bathroom would not be built at this juncture.[76]

Not satisfied with the reply form the Public Health Department, the secretary of the York Hospital Welfare Committee, Ms C.K. Whitfield, wrote to the Minister for Health on 12 December 1951. Due to an anticipated high number of maternity cases over the next month, Whitfield asked to have Aboriginal maternity cases shifted into the general ward in the main building, as non-Aboriginal patients and the public were not happy with the current 'aggravating position'. This proposal was apparently suggested by the matron. Cardell-Oliver confirmed that building the promised separate amenities had to be postponed due to the Commonwealth Government's anti-inflation policy, which had just come into effect a couple of months earlier and reduced the funds available to state governments, who had to curtail non-essential spending. However, the minister refused Whitfield's proposal to shift Aboriginal women into the general ward as it was considered medically unsound and it also contravened regulations governing the use of hospital beds.[77]

Whitfield had seemingly anticipated the likelihood that her request would be declined, so she had sent a copy of her letter to J.I. Mann, MLA, asking to add his 'weight to our fight for separate quarters for natives using the Maternity Ward, and in the meantime that the natives be admitted only to the general ward'.[78] In January 1952, Mann wrote to Premier McLarty who sought advice from Minister Cardell-Oliver who, in turn, explained the situation. In her reply, she also noted that, in the York District, the total Aboriginal population was 137 persons 'of all grades and ages. The problem, therefore, does not appear to be acute, though it has developed local feeling'.[79] Mann did not give up and saw McLarty in person in March. Not only did Mann ask for a separate toilet and bathroom, he also repeated the request for a segregated maternity ward. Eventually, McLarty agreed to make funds available for the former but made it clear that the latter would not eventuate, considering the then current financial position.[80]

Again, segregation itself was not questioned on public record; costs were the deciding factor. Lack of suitable tenders and available funds caused further delays, which also affected general, much-needed renovations at the York Hospital that were promised in 1950. A tender for the required works was eventually accepted in December 1952, after inclement weather on 6 October had caused further damage to the hospital, including the maternity ward ('caved in asbestos'); this was followed by a deputation to Minister Cardell-Oliver in November by the York Hospital Welfare Committee. From the records, it is not clear whether the separate toilet and bathroom were constructed with the general renovations that had to be completed by the end of June 1953 but, given that all complaints on the record about Aboriginal women sharing space and amenities with white Australians had ceased by early

1953, it seems likely that the work was completed. When a plan for the next major renovations was drafted in June 1959, there was no trace of any specially assigned spaces for Aboriginal patients that were named as such. However, adjoining the female ward in the main building were two new partitions with one bed each located on the extended verandah. It is not unlikely that these partitions were intended for Aboriginal patients but the Public Works Department, who drafted the plan, was either not aware of this intention or chose not to name these partitions as quarters for Aboriginal women, as this would not have been deemed appropriate in light of the official assimilation policy.[81]

Anecdotal evidence suggests that segregation remained in the York Hospital beyond the 1950s. Marion Kickett, for example, reported that she was born on the verandah of the York Hospital in 1962.[82] In 1963, York was planned to receive a brand-new hospital at a different location. When the first draft plan was up for discussion in early 1961, Matron Shirley opined that a four-bed ward and two single rooms would be adequate, adding that since she had been at York, there had been only one 'native midwifery case'.[83] York's local authorities were also consulted. The plans were then to be amended to add a further two-bed room in the maternity ward. The purpose of this additional room was not explicitly stated; however, it seems rather likely that its intention was to accommodate Aboriginal mothers. When the new hospital was opened in April 1963, it provided only five midwifery beds. How these were allocated, segregated or not, was no longer recorded on the hospital file. Officially, it seems segregation was henceforth no longer deemed appropriate.[84]

The foregoing episode is interesting as it does not involve the Department of Native Affairs, except for one comment voiced by Commissioner Middleton. It illuminates that the adoption of the policy of assimilation had not really penetrated all government departments. Segregation, at least partial segregation, was still by and large an accepted reality up to the early 1960s, which might have been accommodated in totality had it been financially permissible. Following this sojourn into the field of community agitation for ongoing segregation, we will now further discuss town housing and the Aboriginal housing policy, starting, once again, in mid-1950.

6.06 V: Town housing schemes—1. Antecedents

As we have discussed further above, during the patrol in May 1950, the municipal council was advised about a proposed housing scheme whereby Aboriginal people were supposed to buy their own blocks of land in anticipation that pisé (rammed earth or mud wall) houses would be erected thereon by the department. Whether it was for aesthetic, sanitary or humanitarian considerations—or a mix of all three, possibly with the same order of ascribed importance as listed above—the council appeared to be keen. Shortly after the Katanning conference, Town Clerk Baker wrote euphorically to the department and asked when the building scheme would commence. He expressed the hope that it be immediately and inquired how Aboriginal people could be assisted to start saving. Commissioner Middleton replied that the process would be very slow because there was only one mobile works unit in the area. In July, departmental officers conducted a special patrol in the region with a view to setting up savings trust funds. On the occasion of the officers' visit, they also met the council's health inspector, D.F. O'Leary, who inquired about the scheme.[85] As there was still no progress by October, the council asked when the scheme would finally commence. On 9 October, Middleton replied that the department was currently unable to do anything as it was waiting for Cabinet and the Treasury to approve works. Unknown to York's municipal council, the idea of homes being erected by the department's mobile works unit had been shelved as it had become apparent that the unit was ill-equipped to complete such a housing scheme without extra-departmental assistance. Council then decided to approach Premier McLarty directly, as it was felt that he had shown an interest in matters concerning Aboriginal people's living conditions when visiting York in July.[86]

After receiving council's letter, Premier McLarty asked the Minister for Native Affairs, Doney, for comment. One major concern raised by Doney was how public opinion would react if an Aboriginal housing scheme was to commence while public housing demands for settler-Australians had not yet been met. Because of this apparent issue, Doney suggested that the government may consent to the construction of one or two houses for Aboriginal people 'as a token of our intention to proceed with the larger programme when conditions permit'.[87] McLarty advised on 27 November that he was agreeable to the erection of six to eight houses under the condition that they be for 'better class natives' who are able to obtain the basic wage or above and, in combination with child endowment payments, should therefore be able to pay rent. Premier McLarty meant six to eight houses for the whole South West Land Division; the northern part of the state was not even considered for this early proposal.[88] Coincidentally, a few days before York's town clerk sent a letter to McLarty, Madeleine Cope wrote to McLarty, urging him to take action on the implementation of the proposed housing program as reported on the ABC (Australian Broadcasting Corporation) a few months earlier. Cope was introduced earlier (see chapter 6.05), as she had also been vocal against segregation in York's maternity ward. Cope appealed to McLarty's responsibility, claiming that the public was concerned and expected action, and she urged that the 'time-worn excuse of no material, no labour' not be used this time, while arguing that both materials and labour were being found for many less urgent causes.[89] It seems not unlikely that Cope's letter assisted to some degree in McLarty's decision-making process.

McLarty was also provided with a departmental report that stated that nearly 100 per cent of Aboriginal people in the southern part of the state lived in poor housing conditions and that such conditions would 'strengthen the barriers against assimilation'.[90] The report writer drew this conclusion from his following personal observations as patrol officer:

> In most cases, native families, invariably including a large number of children, live in small single roomed battered tin and bag humpies. These hovels are not wheatherproof; rain pours in from the roofs and sides; wind whistles relentlessly through the cracks, past men, women and children huddled around open fires; dampness rises from the cold floors which are the earth. Lots of animals enjoy better housing. …

> Because these hovels are not wheatherproof, any furniture, clothing and household utensils the people purchase whilst

endeavouring to give expression to self respect, is soon ruined. In time the most resolute realize the utter futility of trying to keep up a decent standard under these conditions and slip into a slovenly way of living.

From these home conditions children are sent to school to sit and play with white children. Strangely enough, the majority of these children and their clothes are clean. This gives an example of the pride these people have in their children. However, this does not alter the fact that the children and adults living under these conditions are easy prey to disease which could be introduced to and effect the whole community. ... Also, because of these living conditions, the people are shunned and the children segregate themselves.[91]

Whether Aboriginal camp-dwellers where 'shunned' solely because of their living conditions remains debatable as the report writer fails to identify racism as a root cause for the poor living conditions altogether. Given that 'assimilation' was official Western Australian state policy, emphasising in the report that the current living conditions of most Aboriginal people in the South West Land Division were hindering the progress of this policy, carried a certain amount of political leverage to induce the premier to act. The focus on material disadvantage is hardly surprising as this could be addressed, in theory, relatively straightforward through the implementation of a housing program. Accordingly, potential outcomes may be gained within the term of a government and could be listed as achievements by such government.

The report recommended that the Public Works Department or State Housing Commission take over the construction side of things. It was also recommended that the houses be subsidised because, despite public opinion that Aboriginal people were earning well, field work experience suggested otherwise due to the seasonal fluctuations of earnable income. Whatever swayed McLarty to approve this severely limited housing scheme, on 6 December, Middleton instructed the central and southern district officers to look for suitable applicants in their respective districts.[92]

In mid-November 1950, Western Australia's State Health Council, which was established the previous year to assist in health-related policy and decision-making, submitted a resolution to the State Housing Commission of Western Australia. This resolution strongly recommended 'the establishment of a suitable housing scheme for half-caste natives similar to the State Housing Scheme now in operation for the white population'.[93] The housing scheme for settler-Australians was established in 1944 under a Commonwealth–state agreement. By March 1948, just under 1,500 homes had been built in total in Western Australia, and some 800 homes were still under construction. In 1950, the number of houses completed by the commission had risen to 1,500 annually and was expected to double over the next few years. The homes were built for low-income families and ex-military service men. In January 1951, an additional 1,050 homes for railway workers were promised within the year, and were given priority attention as railway workers reportedly left the industry due to housing shortages. This period witnessed severe building material shortages. The State Housing Commission had state-wide control over the supply and sale of certain building materials and it issued building permits in considering the supply issues. As discussed above (see chapter 4.02), the state government had not previously approved of any building works for Aboriginal people that could have interfered with the post-war state housing scheme for settler-Australians. In addition to a natural increase, Western Australia was experiencing its largest population growth since the 1890s gold rush due to post-war immigration of 'new Australians', hailing largely from southern and eastern Europe. As a result of this sudden population growth, the supply of homes built by the State Housing Commission lagged behind demand for many years.[94] The lack of housing for white Australians meant that Aboriginal housing concerns would remain peripheral for some years to come.

In January 1951, the State Housing Commission advised the Minister for Health that in consultation with the Commissioner of Native Affairs, it had been agreed that when houses were available, a limited number would be provided for purchase by specially selected Aboriginal families on 'reasonable terms' under the provisions of the *State Housing Act 1950*, subject to three conditions. First, applicants had to be selected and recommended by the Department of Native Affairs. Second, the department would have to carry out periodical inspections, and third, the payment of instalments had to be guaranteed by the state government.[95] The third condition required Cabinet's approval and, thus, in late April 1951, Commissioner Middleton asked Premier McLarty to consider the proposal by the State Housing Commission. Middleton advised that an early start on the project was unlikely but he wished to have the principle of the proposal accepted. He added that, at the time, there were only twelve to fifteen suitable tenants in the South West Land Division and he would ensure that selection would be stringent.[96]

The acting premier and leader of the Country Party at the time, Arthur Frederick Watts, replied on 1 May 1951 that Cabinet had not approved of the State Housing Commission's proposal. He suggested that the Department of Native Affairs should seek funding to erect small and inexpensive dwellings in suitable country locations similar to the Transition Camp at Donnelly River Mill, which was a camp for mainland European immigrants.[97] When advising the State Housing Commission of Cabinet's decision, Middleton commented that this was a serious set-back for the 'better type half-castes' in the South West Land Division and he inquired whether Aboriginal people with exemption certificates could be treated as white applicants for whom the third condition did not apply.[98] The State Housing Commission replied, advising that it would consider taking five Aboriginal families onto its ordinary waitlist who would not be required to have exemptions but they would also not receive preferential treatment. These were five families from Geraldton and Doodlakine who had been mentioned to the commission earlier that year. The commission further advised that it would assess the living conditions of the applicant families at the time of their applications and if they were found unsatisfactory, these families would be 'discarded' from the waitlist. By November, the State Housing Commission had agreed to erect up to six modest homes for Aboriginal families under a separate scheme at a cost of £1,000 each, which could be paid off over a period of years.[99]

During a patrol in March 1951, members of York's municipal council 'expressed pleasure' when being informed about the housing scheme and hoped that York would be one of the selected centres for

205

the scheme. Two families in the York District had been identified by departmental Officer B.A. McLarty as potential candidates for the housing scheme. The road board's secretary, Haley, who was also agent of the Commonwealth Employment Services, promised to assist by securing employment with the basic wage for the male head of one of the two families so this man would be eligible under the State Housing Commission scheme as stipulated by Premier Ross McLarty. Departmental Acting District Officer Bruce Alan McLarty commented in his report that it was the first time he had dealt with the road board without a note of disharmony.[100]

Besides its many uncertainties, the limited housing scheme had one major flaw, as already noted in March by departmental Officer McLarty. The scheme referred to the so-called 'better class' of Aboriginal applicants, whose living habits were deemed to be comparable to those of settler-Australians, notwithstanding that many settler-Australians did not live up to this 'standard'. However, those who classified as 'better class' were reportedly often already renting or buying their homes and did not need departmental assistance. While the Department of Native Affairs' leadership recognised the provision of housing for Aboriginal people as a welfare measure to improve livelihoods, the state government and the State Housing Commission seemed to hold onto the belief that housing for Aboriginal people was a privilege that should only be afforded to those who could be considered already assimilated and would thus not pose a financial or political risk. By June 1949, the Aboriginal population in the South West Land Division was believed to be approximately 3,170 persons, and would have slightly increased by mid-1951. According to departmental observations, the majority of this population was in need of housing but many would not have classified as 'better class' and, therefore, did not stand a chance to be accepted for this early housing scheme.[101]

With a view to building more than a handful of homes made with ordinary building materials that were short in supply anyway, renewed interest in pisé houses grew when the Department of Native Affairs was approached by the Commonwealth Experimental Building Station in February 1951. The federal government was experimenting with pisé houses for Aboriginal people in the Northern Territory and was then also looking westward. In a press statement, Commissioner Middleton commented that Western Australia had already considered pisé houses but had to abandon the idea as it was faced with resistance from many road boards whose cooperation would have been essential. However, he noted that suitable clays to build mud bricks had been discovered in the Darling Ranges and Eastern Wheatbelt areas. Nevertheless, Middleton signalled continued interest in a potential pisé housing scheme and so did the print press, who continued reporting about pisé houses sporadically over the next year. In November 1951, Middleton encouraged all field officers in all regions to experiment with earth wall constructions, as it was practically impossible for the department to obtain conventional building material. Eventually, by mid-1952, the idea to have pisé houses constructed in the South West Land Division under a building scheme was not further pursued but in a circular letter to district offices and institutions, it was suggested that missions may wish to consider the erection of such buildings. The reason for this decision is not noted in the records available to this author but it would likely have had something to do with previous experiences with local authorities' attitudes, combined with the hope that the State Housing Commission would soon be able to provide a significant number of conventional homes.[102]

6.07 V: Town housing schemes—2. Conventional housing scheme

At that same time, Middleton was still trying to have the limited State Housing Commission building scheme implemented and also argued for an increase of the number of houses permitted to be built. In February 1952, Middleton asked Doney to place the housing matter before Cabinet to empower and direct a housing authority to implement a comprehensive housing scheme. Notably, Middleton reasoned that housing was required for Aboriginal families who were willing to conform, to a certain degree, to the department's assimilation policy: 'particularly those whose children are attending State Schools and generally, during daylight hours, live after the manner of whites and not aboriginals'.[103]

Reportedly, departmental officers were frequently the targets of dissatisfaction expressed by Aboriginal people who had applied for the scheme. In late July 1952, Commissioner Middleton urged Minister Doney to address the matter with the Minister for Housing, noting that Aboriginal people were complaining that 'all they ever get is promises—and who can deny that there is truth in their assertions?'[104]

Coincidentally, Doney had already raised the matter days earlier when he pleaded to the Minister for Housing to have at least two cottages erected without undue delay. Doney cited continued pressure from all parts of the state but particularly from associations in the metropolitan area. On 12 August 1952, the Minister for Housing advised that provisions had been made in this year's housing program for the erection of two pre-cut timber-framed homes at York for the housing of two families, both of whom owned land in York and had been recommended by the Commissioner of Native Affairs. Furthermore, these homes would be erected under the provisions of the *State Housing Act*, which meant the new residents would be subject to the same obligations, responsibilities and penalties for non-compliance as settler-Australians. The Minister for Native Affairs, Doney, made the news public on 21 August.[105]

That York was selected as site for the first homes to be erected was not accidental. On one hand, there were already a couple of Aboriginal families who had purchased their own blocks where they had, for the time being, erected their own camps. It was not yet common across the region for Aboriginal people to own their own blocks. On the other hand, as York had two local authorities, this had ensured that local matters concerning Aboriginal people in the York District were carried into the public realm almost continuously for over a decade, given that both authorities had been rather vocal about almost everything concerning Aboriginal people in their respective areas. Thus, the ongoing complaints by both local authorities would have swayed the Department of Native Affairs to recommend to the State Housing Commission to commence its housing program in York. Earlier in 1952, a rather typical chain of events had unfolded that doubtless 'assisted' in keeping York at the forefront of the department's attention. It started in March, when three Aboriginal men were convicted for depositing nightsoil around their camps, which was contrary to the *Health Act*. A fiery complaint letter was written to the Department of Native Affairs requesting that action be taken to remedy the position as council was extremely dissatisfied with the state of affairs. Two of the three convicted men living in the Cowan Road area owned their own blocks and all three men lived in camps with their families. At the time, Sergeant Dowsett had already relinquished his protector position, there was no new local protector to attend court for the hearing on behalf of the accused and the department was unable to send a representative. The last point led to the *York Chronicle* posing the rhetorical question as to whether the department's interest in Aboriginal people was waning. This comment would likely have further fuelled the siege-mentality of some sections of York's settler-Australian community, who might have been feeling increasingly 'left alone' to deal with the Aboriginal presence in town.[106]

District Officer McLarty replied to council's complaint letter. He pointed out, as District Officer Andersen had done in relation to the reserve in late 1950, that this was a matter for the local health authority and the department could not do anything other than provide sound advice to the Aboriginal persons concerned and warn them about the possible consequences of breaching *Health Act* regulations. Referring to council's letter, McLarty insinuated that the council not only took offence at the nightsoil issue but was generally displeased with the poor living and housing conditions and suggested that the council may offer some practical solutions to ameliorate the situation, other than repeating 'the vague exhortation' that *something* needed to be done.[107] McLarty advised the council that money was tight, that the department's own attempts at providing housing had failed, that McLarty had five to six hundred families in his district requiring housing and that the State Housing Commission had 'offered to consider applications from six (repeat SIX) natives for the construction of workers' dwellings'.[108] He continued that one of the families in the Cowan Road area had already applied and another family was in the process of doing so. When McLarty's letter was discussed, Mayor Noonan referred to the premier's visit of 1950, claiming that the department had apparently forgotten what it had promised at the time about the erection of pisé houses.

Noonan suggested, referring to McLarty's letter, that it would appear that the department had no idea at all how to meet the situation and that all they wanted to do was 'pass the buck'.[109] Other councillors brought up the recent court hearing and, given that no departmental officer attended, they concluded that it was 'still a case of remote control from a city office with nothing being done'.[110]

The council decided to send a copy of McLarty's letter to the premier, as well as to J.I. Mann, MLA, and to various members of the Legislative Council with a request that the matter be taken up by the Minister for Native Affairs. The town clerk was also tasked to write to the department advising that he was happy to discuss the matter further, on the sites in question, with any officer.[111] The Minister for Native Affairs replied, repeating what McLarty had already written about the current housing scheme. Reportedly, the letter was not further discussed, suggesting that the council had hoped for more. However, in the same meeting, an unnamed councillor inquired with the health inspector whether the Aboriginal people currently living in camps could be ordered out of town. The health inspector clarified that he could condemn the buildings but that the families in question would be able to remain in town if they so desired.[112] This statement is rather interesting, as York was still a declared prohibited area and none of the Aboriginal people in question held conditional citizenship or exemption certificates in 1952. The health inspector's comment further hints at the suggestions made earlier that the prohibited area was informally no longer being enforced. Alternatively, the health inspector may have purely referred to his own powers, being unable to order Aboriginal people out of town under the *Health Act*, and was perhaps not aware of the prohibited area declaration.[113]

Be that as it may, the apparent nightsoil issue and the resident status of Aboriginal town dwellers were not further publicly discussed at this juncture, and the council would soon discover the State Housing Commission's building proposals. The above suggestion that York's local authorities, with their often obnoxious ways of presenting arguments to suit white Australian community needs, were likely instrumental in the selection of York for the inauguration of the housing scheme was also believed by outside commentators. However, in this case, the local authorities' intentions were not ascribed hypocritical motivations. For example, in an article in the weekly newspaper, *Northam News*, the town of York was commended for taking positive action in 'convincing' the State Housing Commission to build a certain number of homes for Aboriginal people.[114] When in October, Commissioner Middleton publicly commented on the two homes to be built in York, he recognised that the current building scheme was still only tokenistic and he openly urged the State Housing Commission to implement a considerably larger housing program. Middleton argued that because Aboriginal people made up five per cent of Western Australia's population, they should receive five per cent of the houses allocated by the State Housing Commission. With an annual building rate of 1,500 homes, this would have amounted to seventy-five houses per year, which would still not have addressed actual demand, as Aboriginal people lived in severely disproportional poverty, compared to settler-Australians. Middleton himself indirectly acknowledged that even five per cent would have been inadequate, stating in the same article that 1,000 Aboriginal families south of Northampton were in need of accommodation.[115]

In the meantime, the two families in York were waiting for their houses to be built, while a third family had also voiced interest in the current housing scheme. By April 1953, construction had still not commenced and during a patrol, the two families expressed their disappointment to a departmental officer about the lag between paying their deposits and the commencement of building. Simultaneously, the new Minister for Native Affairs, William 'Bill' Hegney, inquired about the housing situation, and Middleton advised that a contractor had been secured for the two houses in York but that building was yet to commence, as the builders were busy elsewhere.[116]

On 28 May, both the *York Chronicle* and the *West Australian* reported on the most recent meeting of the York Municipal Council. The *West Australian*'s headline was 'crafted' in time-tested hysterical tabloid style, and read: 'Natives Encroach on a Townsite'[117], comparing Aboriginal people with the threat of an enemy intruding into one's territory. The *York Chronicle*'s headline was, again, somewhat more moderate, and read: 'Native Camps Again in Evidence in Town'[118], but the inferred message was the same. It was reported that several Aboriginal people had left 'their' reserve on the upper Beverley Road and had been setting up camp in several localities in town. Both papers stated that a departmental officer was expected to visit York the following week and that this situation would be addressed with him; however, only the *York Chronicle* specifically reported that the town clerk's anticipated discussion with the departmental officer would hopefully result in 'having the natives returned to the reserve'.[119]

The publishing of these news articles was somewhat unexpected. For almost a year, there had been no reports in the local newspaper with any complaints about Aboriginal housing and camps in York (there were, however, short articles about alcohol-related 'offending' and conditional citizenship). Departmental patrol reports during this period also did not suggest any great fluctuation of Aboriginal residents within the town and district. It may have been the case that some families were visiting temporarily between patrols and, therefore, remained undetected, but they would not have stayed for long. Further, those Aboriginal families who lived in camps within the municipality in mid-1953 did so either on their own blocks or camped with permission on other people's private land. The only extraordinary story reported in the news at the time was a weather event that offers a possible but not overly convincing explanation for council's sudden hysteria. There had been significant rain in May 1953 (the wettest May in thirty-two years) and many paddocks were reportedly water logged. Later, in June, a minor flooding event was also recorded. Perhaps some reserve dwellers evacuated the reserve temporarily, given that it was located directly on the Avon River, which may have, in turn, caused some ignorant councillors to claim that white Australians were inconvenienced by the increased presence of Aboriginal people residing within the town's boundaries as weather refugees.[120] However, there is no further evidence to support this hypothesis other than the weather reports, and this 'camp issue' was also not raised again, which makes it even more peculiar. Anecdotal evidence indicates that the Kickett family, at least, never had to leave the reserve due to flooding as the area on the reserve where the family lived was slightly elevated and thus not affected by flooding.[121] It appears more likely that council was not aware that an additional two or three Aboriginal families were now in town, two of whom also hoped to apply for State Housing Commission rentals or workers' dwellings.

Noteworthy, though, is that in early April 1953, the local management of the *York Chronicle*—which was then owned by Country Newspapers Pty Ltd, based in Perth—changed hands from former councillor Henry Gordon Wake to councillor Clifton John Ashbolt, also known as Jack Ashbolt. C.J. Ashbolt (not to be confused with grocery store owner and councillor Fred Ashbolt —for example, see chapter 3.10) had been at this particular council meeting and perhaps it was he who had fed the story to the *West Australian* and—even more likely— who was responsible for the populist tone of the *York Chronicle* article.[122] Ashbolt had been involved with this newspaper, its predecessor and the now incorporated *York Leader* from approximately 1919 until retiring from the *York Chronicle* in 1955, when he would take up the position of York's town clerk. He had been councillor for three separate periods since 1924 and, as discussed above (see chapter 2.04), he had already, in 1938, agitated against the presence of Aboriginal people in the York District. Much later, in March 1974, it was reported that Ashbolt had retired from corresponding for the ABC and the *West Australian*, which suggests that he had likely been feeding information to the *West Australian* for quite some time. That he had some involvement with the matter does not, therefore, appear farfetched.[123]

Whatever the cause of these two simultaneously published news articles, Minister Hegney had written to Middleton a few days earlier, inquiring again about progress with the housing scheme, and he urged that at least a few homes be built as soon as possible.[124] The news articles may have accelerated the response to his request, as construction of the two York homes soon commenced and was completed in October 1953. However, the prospect that these two Aboriginal families would soon live in homes on par with those of settler-Australians was not necessarily welcomed by some of York's white community, as reported by District Officer McLarty:

> When the houses were under construction the selected applicants complained to me that it was a regular Sunday afternoon excursion for people to drive out and inspect the

buildings remarking loudly in the hearing of the natives that the houses were 'too good for niggers' and that they would come back in a few months' time 'to see how many floor boards had been used for firewood'.[125]

The reference to floorboards being used for firewood appears to have originated in a few incidents from across Western Australia, which private landlords had complained about during the 1940s. As these occurrences were also mentioned in newspapers, the stories may have become word-of-mouth *truths* that neatly fitted into the highly prejudiced worldview of many members of the settler-Australian community.[126]

The keys to the first two standard State Housing Commission homes (workers' dwellings) in Western Australia that were built specifically for Aboriginal people were handed over to the new occupants by District Officer B.A. McLarty on 22 October 1953. The two Perth-based newspaper outlets, the *West Australian* and the *Daily News*, both reported this event favourably. The *York Chronicle* printed the most comprehensive article—all three articles appear to have been based on the same source, perhaps a departmental press release—however, it finished with cynicism and derision:[127]

The experiment is one for which the Native Affairs Dept. is to be commended and the future will tell whether it will be successful and assist in the assimilation of native population amongst the whites.[128]

The notion of 'experiment' suggested to the reader that Aboriginal people were yet to prove themselves 'worthy' of living in houses in town. Contrary to the *York Chronicle*'s pessimism, the *West Australian*'s headline enthusiastically promoted the idea of assimilation, reading: 'Keys To Unlock Modern Homes For Old Families'. One way of reading this headline is that 'old families'—as in 'original Australians'—received the keys to unlock modern homes and, therefore, were able to enter modernity, leaving their 'old' and, by implication, outdated Aboriginal lifestyles behind. This headline seems to be a thoughtfully crafted piece of assimilation propaganda; however, it is not suggested here that the Aboriginal families who moved into these homes shared the same enthusiasm for ideological assimilation. Most likely, they simply wanted material improvements to live more comfortable lives. These lifestyle improvements came at a cost, as the two families had suddenly new expenditures, with fortnightly instalments of £5 13s 11d and £5 13s 2d, respectively, which significantly affected the families' budgets.[129]

Commenting on the situation in his area, District Officer McLarty noted in 1955 that it was obvious that new financial commitments for most Aboriginal families housed in State Housing Commission homes stretched their resources to the limit. The majority of bread winners earned not more than the basic wage and this, with a large family, could do little more than cover the basic needs of food, clothing and rent. It provided no margin for sickness, or the purchases of furniture.[130] In relation to sickness, the earlier discussed Natives Medical Fund ceased to exist when the *Native Welfare Act 1954* replaced the *Native Administration Act 1947* in 1955 and the employment permit system was abolished. Thenceforth, medical expenses had to be covered by the affected individuals themselves, which meant further expenditures from a small household income if their employers had previously obtained permits.[131] In any event, given that rural employment was largely on a 'casual' basis, most Aboriginal people who had now these regular financial commitments had no access to paid sick days to cover ongoing costs if they were too unwell to work.

6.08 V: Town housing schemes—3. Intermediate housing program

While the two homes were still under construction, an 'intermediate' housing program for Aboriginal people had been decided on and York was once again to be the testing field. Officially, it was claimed that these substandard homes were intended as a first step to accustom Aboriginal families, who were deemed not ready yet for standard State Housing Commission homes, to living in houses in towns—though, in fact, lower costs seem to have been the underlying reason for this offshoot housing scheme. For the financial year of 1953–1954, twenty-five purpose-built homes were approved, of which twenty were to be erected in the South West Land Division. Initially, in June 1953, departmental officers were instructed to screen for applicants that presented with the highest needs. However, a month later, F.W.G. Andersen, who was now Deputy Commissioner, reported that he had opted to screen for the 'most-deserving' families, who would receive first preference. This meant that, once again, selection was based on assessed *worthiness*, rather than deciding eligibility purely on a needs basis, as housing remained a privilege that had to be earned.[132]

While ideological reasons for this decision may also have been at play, from a departmental perspective, selecting the 'most-deserving' families had, in this instance, chiefly pragmatic reasons. That is because the Department of Native Affairs was anxious to select applicants that were deemed likely to be success stories, as it was otherwise feared that the State Housing Commission would not continue the housing program in the following years. Departmental officers had to assess applicants for the likelihood of 'rent recovery or business risk', 'aptitude to maintain decent living standards in a home' and means 'to provide some furniture in a new home'.[133] Only Aboriginal people 'in-law' were to be considered, which excluded families with exemptions and conditional citizenship, as well as individual adults found to have a quarter Aboriginal ancestry (*quadroons*) or less under the racialist blood quantum categorisation.[134]

The State Housing Commission designed a house that was accepted under the *Commonwealth State Housing Act* as accommodation for settler-Australians or Aboriginal people. It was believed to comply with all building standards but was particularly intended to suit the accommodation of large families. The following particulars refer to the improved model with small changes to the York prototype:

These houses are approximately 10 squares in area and of timber frame construction clad with weatherboard and asbestos. The roof is of galvanised iron and there is a considerable area of louvred windows. The kitchen-living room is 225 sq. ft. in area—has a stainless steel sink and drainer and an insul heat stove with canopy. There are two spacious sleepout rooms for the children and a separate sleepout room for adults. A front verandah and back porch are provided for, together with a wash room with copper, troughs and bath.[135]

This intermediate housing scheme was to provide both rental and purchase homes, either on State Housing Commission-owned or on privately owned blocks, as per the earlier initiated scheme that only provided purchase homes on a loan basis. Until 1959, ninety-seven such homes were built state-wide.[136] An Aboriginal family who owned two blocks at the corner of Cardwell and Cowan Roads, opposite the former traditional camping ground on Lot 159, was going to have the prototype house (Type 79) built on one of these blocks. This family had voiced interest in the various proposed housing schemes from early on and had land to their disposition, each of which appeared to be deciding factors for initial selection. Initially, the family opted for a rental arrangement but then decided to obtain a purchase home. For either housing scheme, block owners had to transfer ownership of their blocks to the State Housing Commission. This particular family had to transfer one block, on which the house was going to be built, but they could keep the other block where they kept their camp until the house was finished. Other families remained camping on the same blocks on which the houses were being built.[137]

By July 1954, the intermediate prototype home was completed. This house had been erected on built-up earth, which was necessary as the block was located on the slope of a hill. When a departmental officer visited the family on 15 July and inspected the new house, which was apparently ready for occupation, he found that the house was flooded in the living room and in both sleep outs. Due to heavy rain, water had run down the slope through the back door of the house. Two days later, the departmental officer returned and instructed the family to dig out drains around the house and they were then able to drain the water from the building. The family indicated that they would move into the home over the next few days; however, the floors would still have been wet.[138] Departmental officer McLarty commented a year later that it could not be denied that the house was a 'poor old job'.[139] The ground-level concrete floors were damaged during the flooding. When built, the concrete had a glazed surfaced, which was now destroyed and, consequently, the floors were impossible to keep clean. During McLarty's visit, he spoke with the woman who was head of the household and was outspoken about this 'modern' home's quality:

> She feels that she has been sold a pup by the Housing Commission and it is no consolation to her to know that her house was the experiment on which future improvements were based, nor that what she has now is better than the old humpy. Her comment was: 'I don't mind going back to the humpy if I have to'.[140]

McLarty commented that although he was of the opinion that the house was better than the camp, it was doubtful that the difference between the two was really worth the extra expense. According to his calculations, the house would have cost the family approximately £4,500 by the time it was paid off while the actual costs for construction were only £1,800.[141]

In October 1955, McLarty had just returned from a patrol tour through the Central District (the upper half of the South West Land Division) and provided a summary of widespread complaints concerning the Type 79 homes. He reported that leaking roofs were almost universal and, in one case, ineffective plumbing caused a health hazard. McLarty continued:

> Complaints about non-lining of the exterior rooms were made in every case. Lining was omitted in an effort to reduce cost of construction, but as the effect is to render the rooms almost unliveable, the expenditure of £200 on sealing these rooms is essential. It cannot be argued that health regulations prohibit the sealing of these low roofed rooms, because the type 79 houses being built for rental by white people in Bassendean have this amenity.[142]

With examples like the one above, it is no wonder that Aboriginal people had doubts about white Australian sincerity in relation to assimilation's promises of socioeconomic integration and equality.

6.09 1954: Final public acts of community resistance towards Aboriginal housing in town

We shall now return to 1954. This year would culminate in the York Municipal Council's final efforts of active resistance towards Aboriginal housing in York during the 1950s, which was carried into the public sphere through the *York Chronicle*. However, the first part of this year was also rather eventful. In March, the council complained about three humpy-style camps located on Bland Road in the north-western section of the municipality, and forwarded a report by the local health inspector. During the council meeting, when the report was discussed, it was decided that the buildings should be condemned if the occupants were not to be provided with better accommodation. Writing to the department, the town clerk, Douglas Charles Field, wished it to be known that while it was the council's desire to 'help these people', Aboriginal people were expected to comply with the local by-laws, which they currently did not. As their latrines were reportedly of the same materials as their camps, these latrines were not flyproof, which was a further breach of local by-laws. The report referred to 'slum type' buildings—the first time that such terminology had been used by York's local government authority.[143] Slums had been part of Western Australian public discourse for quite some time but slum conditions were usually ascribed to the metropolitan areas of Perth and Fremantle and were not seriously considered country town issues.[144] While town reserve living conditions almost everywhere across Western Australia would have been classified as slum-type or shanty town housing, they were not usually referred to as such. This was likely because 'slums' were only mentioned if identified as located within settler-Australian living spaces, and reserves tended to be just outside.

Ideally, the 'slum' narrative could have assisted in accelerating the provision of housing for these Aboriginal camp dwellers with whatever assistance the council might have been able to offer (which was apparently none). However, the report by York's health inspector appeared rather to emphasise the alleged detriment that the white townsfolk suffered due to the camps' presence. The council's motivation to write the letter was most likely related to its claim that the presence of the Aboriginal camps was devaluating neighbouring properties. There was no word about this in the news article but, sure enough, York's town clerk D.C. Field listed this as a reason in his letter to the department. According to Field, owners of these properties would not have been able to sell their properties even at a reduced rate. The council's letter concluded that, 'Irrespective of colour or creed, those natives are the owners of the land, and as such should be made to comply with the By-Laws of the town'.[145] Town Clerk Field seemed to insist on the responsibilities relating to equality under the law, while disregarding issues of inequity that affected a large proportion of Aboriginal people.

In a similar situation to the one that occurred a year earlier in the Cowan Road and Hope Street area (see previous chapter), one of the residents in Bland Road had already applied for assistance under the *State Housing Act* and the other two families intended to apply under the same scheme, which was supported by the Department of Native Affairs. Whether the council was advised accordingly is not known to this author, as a subsequent correspondence file has seemingly not survived and the matter was not further reported in the *York Chronicle*.[146] It is noteworthy, though, that two of the three camps had been recently erected by two families on several jointly owned lots that had been sold to them by the municipal council nine months earlier. The land had been for sale by tender and the two families proposed £25 for a portion of it. The council then decided to accept their offer under the condition that the whole land be purchase for £30.[147] Both families were already known to the council and had been living in camps in the York District for many years. Therefore, it should not have come as a surprise that they were not able to erect standard homes from the very moment that they purchased the land.

That the camps on Bland Road were not further discussed at this stage may have been because, within a couple of weeks, the public turned its focus to yet another site. This next site was in Grey Street, located much closer to the town centre. The State Housing Commission had erected a few standard workers' dwellings on Grey Street, one of which was allocated to an Aboriginal family who had moved in by 22 March 1954. White Australian residents in the area and some councillors expressed their opposition to the family living in this home. It was stated that residents did not really have anything against the family occupying the house but they anticipated that 'frequent gatherings'[148] of Aboriginal friends and family would now occur as a result of the family's presence—to which they voiced their opposition. Councillor N.L. Harring introduced the matter to the council meeting on behalf of the opposing residents, who apparently agreed that Aboriginal people should be provided with housing but asked that they be 'given their own section of the town'.[149] Councillor Laurie Theofler Davies commented that he did not think it was right that houses in the closely populated sections of town should be granted to Aboriginal people. Davies and councillors F. Ashbolt, C.J. Ashbolt and the mayor, A.F. Noonan, all questioned why the council was not consulted as to the location's suitability and it was agreed that this omission would be raised with State Housing Commission. Noonan conceded that during a visit by the Minister for Housing a few months earlier, he had recommended this particular family for the provision of housing but he thought that a house for them would be erected elsewhere and not in Grey Street. The only reported voice of reason during this council meeting was that of councillor George Frederick Chipper, who spoke in favour of this Aboriginal family and pointed out that there had been no complaints at the previous house that the family had occupied. He further noted that the family was very clean and the husband was engaged in permanent employment.[150]

A month passed and, at the council meeting on 19 April, a petition from seven residents of Grey Street was received, as reported by the *York Chronicle*:

> The petition protested against the letting by the State Housing Commission of a house in Grey Street to persons of aboriginal blood. They asked the Council to take immediate action to have such a procedure stopped.[151]

In support of the petitioning Grey Street residents, the council decided to forward their petition to the State Housing Commission. At the same council meeting, a letter from the State Housing Commission was read, in which the commission explained its current housing program for intermediate-type homes. For the first time, the State Housing Commission mentioned that the intermediate-type home was part of a three-stage plan, rather than two-stage plan. The first stage would involve a 'modest-type' house. The second or intermediate stage would provide a 'better-type' house, and would be followed by the third stage, delivering a conventional 'workers' dwelling'.[152] Plans for the intermediate-type home were supplied to the council. Importantly, the letter sought appeasement and the council was advised that it would be consulted henceforth in relation to suitable families and building locations. Two particular blocks were suggested and the council was asked for comment in relation to their suitability. It was requested that the council appoint a committee to assist the State Housing Commission in 'a friendly way in raising the standard of the families' way of living'.[153] The letter also made the point that segregation was definitely not desired. The council decided to discuss the matter at a later meeting to allow for an inspection of the two proposed blocks to be made.[154]

In early May, the State Housing Commission advised York's municipal council that the petition had been received but did not further comment on it at this point in time. The answer would be made in a public statement that lambasted the petitioners' attitude. Western Australia's Minister for Housing, H.E. Graham, commented on the petition from Grey Street on 29 May, as reported in the *Sunday Times*. Graham reportedly stated that he was disappointed and disgusted at the attitude of people who displayed bias against 'our colored cousins' and he thought that the petition was a 'terrific example of man's inhumanity to man'.[155] In his public comment, he did not wish to identify the affected Aboriginal family, or the country town, to save the family from further embarrassment. However, the *York Chronicle* reprinted the article almost verbatim and commented at the end on York's petition, which would have left no doubt for the local reader that Graham was talking about Grey Street in York. Graham listed several positive attributes about the family and their conduct and noted that the 'wife' was very distressed by the attitude of those behind the petition. Graham declared that he was determined to implement the current housing program irrespective of prejudice. He made sure that his message was understood as intended, without any room for misinterpretation:

> This family will definitely stay in the house. We have refused to give even a moment's consideration to moving them. Instead of people being hostile they should be proud of the fact that a native, despite natural obstacles, could raise himself to such a high standard.[156]

While slamming the petitioners' and the council who endorsed the petition, Graham's finishing sentence nevertheless comments that the family raised themselves to a high standard despite 'natural obstacles'. The word 'natural' lends itself to an inference of biologically determined disadvantage. Nineteenth-century social Darwinist theory echoes through this comment. In the past, this type of racism had served as an excuse to accept the assumed pending extinction of Aboriginal peoples. Now, it served to emphasise assimilation's declared benevolence in that this policy allegedly managed to produce success stories despite deficits ascribed based on racist determinist assumptions.[157] Conveniently, the notion of 'natural obstacles' could also be used to explain and excuse delays with the housing program and assimilation in general by shifting responsibility onto Aboriginal people rather than white Australia. So, while some politicians and government administrators held sympathetic views towards Aboriginal people and did not shy away from defending these views in public, the general consensus prevailed that becoming part of the settler-Australian community was a privilege that had to be earned, rather than a birthright.

Following Minister Graham's public commentary aimed at York, matters relating to Aboriginal housing were not discussed in York's municipal council meetings for a few months. For example, completion and occupation of the intermediate prototype home on Cowan Road in July had not attracted any local media attention, most likely because it was not particularly close to the town centre, and the block on which the house was built had already been in the possession of Aboriginal families for a number of years. However, renewed opposition to Aboriginal housing erupted again in late November 1954. Once again, a Perth metropolitan daily newspaper reported first on the matter, which suggests that whoever fed the information to the newspaper felt that York's current affairs should be brought to the attention of the larger metropolitan public to galvanise support. A special meeting of the York Municipal Council was held on 29 November because Town Clerk Field had learned earlier on this day about further houses for Aboriginal people that were planned to be built in Grey Street. A contractor for the State Housing Commission had told him that three intermediate-type homes would be built on land purchased by the commission.[158]

The mayor and eight councillors attended the meeting, of which C.J. Ashbolt, L.T. Davies, P.M.A. Glass and A.F. Noonan were the most outspoken participants, as reported in the *York Chronicle*. Their grievances were the same as on earlier occasions. They feared that these homes would become meeting places, which they claimed occurred whenever several Aboriginal families lived close together. A recent example at Cowan Road was cited where allegedly upwards of ninety Aboriginal people had 'congregated' over the weekend. The alleged adverse effect on property values was also raised. The biggest issue seemed to be, however, that the council had not been consulted and was being 'overridden'. Referring to earlier in the year, Glass reportedly said that he thought the housing minister might be annoyed by the local protest resulting in the petition. Consequently, Glass suggested that the minister might have intended to aggravate the position by not giving the council any say in the matter, and he demanded that strong 'opposition should be made against these high-handed methods'.[159] Unsurprisingly, the country–city dichotomy was also brought to the forefront when Davies remarked that he had yet to see where Aboriginal people were being assimilated in the residential suburbs of the city. In conclusion, J.I. Mann, MLA, was asked to arrange a deputation to the premier.[160]

Scheduled for two days later, the deputation had to make do with the Minister for Housing, H.E. Graham. Mann headed the deputation, supported by two members of the Legislative Council, Leslie Charles Diver and Jack McIntosh Thomason, as well as four representatives of the York Municipal Council (Noonan, C.J. Ashbolt, Davies and Field) and two members of the Pingelly Road Board. The deputation presented the concerns discussed in the special meeting and added a further point. There was apparently general dissatisfaction with the intermediate-type 'natives' home'.[161] Beside claims of neighbourhood property depreciation, the deputation argued that erecting an intermediate-type home close to the standard workers' dwelling, which was occupied by a young Aboriginal family, would be to this young family's detriment. This family, whom the deputation expressed concern about, was the very same family who had been on the receiving end of Grey Street residents' and councillors' agitation earlier this year. Now, in a disingenuous attempt to prevent the erection of intermediate-type homes, the deputation claimed it wished to protect the family. Following the deputation's formal protest, Minister Graham reportedly reprimanded the party for their collective attitude in no uncertain terms. He stated that it was the policy and intention of the state government to do something worthwhile for Aboriginal people who had been in the past 'more or less treated like dogs'.[162] Graham argued that the majority of the white community had shown no sympathy for such an idea, and needed elementary training to improve their approach to Aboriginal people 'so that they would be considered as human beings and not animals'.[163] Graham criticised the general lack of action by white Australians that usually followed hollow declarations about proposed improvement to Aboriginal living conditions. Further, Graham stated that the general attitude of whites was that 'the native must be put somewhere out of sight'.[164] While segregation was not desired anyway, this would also encourage the establishment of 'dark-town' sections.[165]

In relation to the claim that the country had to carry the burden of assimilation, Graham told the deputation that housing projects were already up and running in three metropolitan suburbs (East Victoria Park, Carlisle and Bassendean). There, too, local white Australians had been reluctant to accept the new residents, but he asserted that their presence had not been detrimental to the districts. Graham pointed out that the condition of the houses occupied by Aboriginal people was good, unlike some houses occupied by white Australians. Graham then appealed to the members of the deputation that it was essential to show tolerance and that the longstanding prejudice against Aboriginal people must be broken down. To appease the deputation's heated temper, he also assured them that it was not the intention of the government to place Aboriginal houses indiscriminately and that 'only the better class of natives would be selected'.[166] Thus, the social inclusion of Aboriginal people remained conditional and was propagated as such for reasons of acceptance among local authorities. After finishing his speech, Minister Graham clarified that, in the case of York, there must have been a misunderstanding, as only one of the three State Housing Commission homes would be an intermediate-type home for an Aboriginal family and he ensured that this type of house would not be flouting any of the municipal building by-laws. In the end, he stated that he would have another look at the situation in York and would advise in due course.[167]

Graham did send a letter to the municipal council a few days later when he confirmed the decision that one intermediate-type home would be built for an Aboriginal family on Grey Street, close to the intersection with Ford Street. Graham reiterated that the housing program was definitely in accordance with state government policy and he wished to make it clear that the utmost care would be exercised by the State Housing Commission in making homes on town sites only available to those families considered suitable. This council meeting appears to have been when the council finally conceded *defeat* in relation to the provision of housing for Aboriginal people in town—for the time being, at least. Reportedly, councillors realised that there was nothing they could do and that they had run into a 'brick wall'.[168] Although council accepted state government policy, it merely tolerated the Aboriginal presence in town, which becomes very clear in the following quote:

> It was still their unanimous opinion that it was most unfair to residents in that area. The fact was also mentioned that the house when erected will be just across the street from Faversham House where between 30 and 40 war veterans were living.[169]

The remark about Faversham House once more highlights the council's adverse feelings towards Aboriginal people. The underlying message is that settler-Australian men who fought for (white) Australia in wars should not have to live across from an Aboriginal family, considering their sacrifice for the country. Consequently, this put council in an embarrassing and shameful position as it was powerless to prevent this from occurring. Even when it had been established that the intermediate-type homes did not satisfy York's building by-laws, it was ascertained that council could not do anything about it, as it did not have the right to veto buildings erected by state government agencies. While refusing to come to terms with its powerlessness in this matter, the council decided that Minister Graham must be alerted to his failure to make good on the assurance given to the deputation that council by-laws would not be flouted.[170] Departmental Officer J. Harman commented that he had been advised that the council's action in the whole affair was not supported by all council members. Harman did not suggest who or how many members had not supported council's hysteria but it is probable that Councillor G.F. Chipper was among them, as he had also opposed the petition earlier this year.[171]

Widespread acceptance of Aboriginal people within York's settler-Australian community and civic life was seemingly still a far cry from becoming a reality, but December 1954 arguably marked the end of active resistance by the municipal council towards Aboriginal housing in town. For now, a certain degree of official tolerance of the fact that Aboriginal people would be living across town had been achieved. Neither the departmental records available to this author nor municipal council meetings, as reported in the *York Chronicle*, mentioned any further action taken by the municipal council in relation to Aboriginal housing throughout the remainder of the 1950s and 1960s (from 1960, the *York Chronicle* was incorporated into the *Northam Advertiser*). The only noteworthy discussion held in council in relation to housing throughout the rest of the 1950s occurred in April 1959, when several councillors objected to Aboriginal people living in a pensioners' flat in town; however, this discussion did not result in any action being taken by the council.[172]

While it appears that the council had accepted that its continuous agitation against Aboriginal housing would not gain the aspired-to outcomes, it should also be noted that after 1954, progress with the provision of further housing in town began to stall. In February 1957, there were only four Aboriginal families occupying state rental homes in York. Five further families rented other homes and the remaining families and individuals either camped or had their residences at their places of employment, spread across the York District. The department determined that, at the time, there were no further families suitable for the housing scheme. For the time being, new Aboriginal housing was being provided in other districts. The department had to be careful with who they recommended for supported housing, as, by mid-1956 in York, two families had been evicted and one family had signed over their child endowment monies in a last bid to retain their home due to increasing rental arrears. The evictions also occurred due to rental arrears, which were reportedly caused by several factors, for example, fluctuating incomes, loss in the family, difficulties with adjusting to a new lifestyle, fallouts between families—more so, because of visiting family members—and family obligations.[173] District Officer McLarty indicated that he would only recommend a family for the Aboriginal state housing project if the bread winner was permanently employed, which excluded those families who needed it most. The three houses in question had been built in the east ward, where the families had bought their lands, and, by chance, they happened to be located very close to each other. One family was reported to be not overtly concerned when served with a repossession notice and McLarty commented that it was in the general interest of the housing scheme 'to break up this artificial native "settlement" at York'.[174] The department and the State Housing Commission were now determined to prevent any such groupings for further housing provisions in town, York and elsewhere.

The State Housing Commission worked on business principles; it was not a purely welfare-oriented agency. Its policy was tailored towards equality in principle but failed to account for issues of inequity in relation to Aboriginal tenants, in particular, those who were leaving the camps behind for the first time in their lives but were largely still living a very similar lifestyle for socioeconomic and cultural reasons, as well as out of necessity.[175] The Department of Native Welfare (the change of name occurred in mid-1955 when the *Native Welfare Act 1954* took effect) was not oblivious to how uncooperative local authorities, who lacked sympathy and political will to assist with the implementation of a just, functioning and sustainable Aboriginal housing project, were partially responsible for the failure of the housing scheme. The department was obviously unable to require from York's local authorities a sympathetic view, but it knew of other districts where the local authorities acted in a much more welcoming manner, citing Bruce Rock and Quairading as examples.[176]

In the next section, we will discuss the first opportunity for Aboriginal people to publicly socialise in the York town, which commenced in mid-1954.

6.10 The Coolbaroo dances in York

On 20 May 1954, the *York Chronicle* reported that approximately 200 Aboriginal people from York and adjacent districts had, for the first time locally, 'enjoyed a properly organised dance' at the Masonic Hall in town 'and danced to the strains of an orchestra from the city'.[177] The dance was organised by the Perth-based Coolbaroo League and was held on Saturday 15 May. It was further noted that the success that had been achieved should encourage the Coolbaroo League to continue the dance in York. The tone of this article was generally positive and lacked any nuances of a threat narrative—otherwise so common in the discourse of the period—which was somewhat surprising in the context of the *York Chronicle*'s often negative writing style in relation to Aboriginal people, which only changed for the better when new management took over in mid-1955. Aboriginal people were referred to as 'aborigines' rather than the then commonly used term, 'natives'. Using the term 'aborigines' indicated a certain degree of respect towards Aboriginal ancestry, whereas the term 'native' denied particular Aboriginal lineage and was intentionally vague as discussed earlier (see chapter 2.03). As it turned out, this article was a partially verbatim, and partially rewritten, copy of a news article that appeared two days earlier in the *West Australian* and that could have been a last-minute editing job, which may explain the positive reporting style.[178] As we will see, in later articles published over the following months, the *York Chronicle* reverted to its usual style, which suggests that this first article was not based on correspondence from C.J. Ashbolt.

The Coolbaroo League was established in 1946 in Perth by a small group of Aboriginal people. They organised regular dances in East Perth exclusively for Aboriginal people, with the exception of non-Aboriginal spouses or invitations from League members. Coolbaroo is a Yamatji (Murchison region) word for magpie. The bird's black and white colours alluded to the mixed ancestry of many Aboriginal people in the South West Land Division, but also to living in both worlds: *black* and *white*— or in between. However, Coolbaroo also referred to the co-existence of *black* and *white* and sought to assert that *black* and *white* were equal. The Coolbaroo League was a unique institution that provided Aboriginal people a source of entertainment in a culturally safe environment, which they were otherwise not able to enjoy. At its inception, there were only a couple of similar organisations Australia-wide. The dances were attended by all age groups and attracted people from the metropolitan area, as well as from country towns. While the dances provided light-hearted entertainment and a vehicle for socialisation, the Coolbaroo League was also politically active in the form of passive resistance to the racist status quo. Its very inception took authorities some time to become accustomed to and the dances in Perth were initially subject to increased police surveillance and harassment.[179]

In 1947, the League formed its own youth organisation: the Coolbaroo York Club. Despite its name suggesting that it was based in York, the youth organisation met in Perth in the rooms of a settler-Australian youth club located in Holman House on 46 Stirling Street. Holman House was associated with Western Australia's Labor party and it also housed Labor's official organ the *Westralian Worker*.[180] In the mid-1950s, the Coolbaroo League had its own newspaper-style periodical, the *Westralian Aborigine*, which had, at its peak, approximately 650 subscriptions. Although Commissioner Middleton and his predecessor, McBeath, attempted to align the League with their culturally dismissive and destructive interpretation of assimilation, the Coolbaroo League, and its newspaper, remained independent throughout the League's existence. It advocated for its own interpretation of assimilation, which focussed on improved living conditions and the abolishment of racist legislation, while insisting on retaining Aboriginal identity within the settler-Australian majority society. After a short break during parts of 1948 and 1949, the Coolbaroo League and its dances existed in Perth until 1960 and the dances were held in several changing locations in East Perth and Perth City. Between 1950 and 1955, the dances were held on Friday nights at the Braille Hall, corner of Newcastle and Stirling Streets. The authorities appeared to have ignored the fact that, technically, this hall was located just within the prohibited area because Newcastle Street had been the northern demarcation line since an amendment in 1948. In 1954, the Coolbaroo League started organising monthly dances in a few country towns to which the organisers, including a small band, travelled each time from Perth.[181] Coinciding with the first dance held in York, the town's prohibited area had been formally cancelled only two days earlier. Whether the event's timing was correlated to the cancellation is not evident from the records.[182]

In April 1954, the *Westralian Aborigine* advertised the upcoming first Coolbaroo dance at York. It was reported that a 'bright programme including lucky spot prize, dances and novelties' had been arranged, that a three-piece orchestra would provide music and that supper would be available as well.[183] The admission charges were to be three shillings and six pence for adults and one shilling for children. In comparison, the periodical *Westralian Aborigine* cost six shillings. It was also explicitly stated that no liquor or intoxicated people were allowed at any Coolbaroo League functions.[184] The no-alcohol condition had been in place since the League's inception. It was meant to ensure peaceful events without unnecessary disturbances through excessive alcohol consumption and the few intoxicated 'trouble makers' who attempted to attend the dances were turned away at the entrance.[185] Perhaps more importantly, the no-alcohol provision was also to ensure that authorities had no justifiable grounds to shut down or prevent these functions given that the consumption (or technically rather 'possession') of alcohol was a criminal offence for all non-exempted Aboriginal people who came under the *Native Administration Act 1947*. Nevertheless, even those individuals who were denied entry due to intoxication were inadvertently jeopardising the functions' continuity with each police attendance that their behaviour attracted. In early 1955, the settler-Australian journalist Boronia 'Bonnie' Giles noted in her weekly column in the *Daily News* the difficulties that the Coolbaroo League faced. She commented under her pen name, Mary Felber:

> They have to be very strict about behaviour because people will seize on the slightest excuse to say that natives are badly behaved and, of course, sometimes, some are. So they have to be very careful about low-type whites and keep them away from their dance. They have to be hard on their own people when some noble citizen has given them too much wine. They have to have the best-conducted of dances, and I think they do.[186]

Following the positive press report on York's first dance in May 1954, several news reports in the following months focussed on the alleged poor behaviours of a handful of attendees inside and outside the Masonic Hall. In July, two local Aboriginal men were both sentenced by justices of the peace P.M.A. Glass and S.P. Harvey to twenty-one days of imprisonment each for having been drunk on Joaquina Street in the vicinity of the dance. The *Daily News* titled the article 'A Warning for the Spoiling Minority'.[187] Glass reportedly issued a warning during sentencing that future 'offenders' would also be severely dealt with. Glass then changed his tone to praise the dances:

> The dances arranged by the Coolbaroo League were, he said, providing a much appreciated amenity for the native population. The functions were very well conducted and the actions of a very small minority would not be allowed to interfere with the pleasure of the majority.[188]

Glass' seemingly sympathetic words reveal that the Aboriginal presence in town remained conditional. How would it otherwise have been possible that two so-called 'offenders' could question with their presence the continuity of social functions attended by 200–300 people? Surely, two drunk white Australian persons making a scene outside a community dance would not have caused Glass to ensure the public that these two persons would not be allowed to interfere with the dance's attendees, whose conduct had been deemed satisfactory. The general assumption would have been that the conduct of the majority of settler-Australian attendees was indeed satisfactory; however, due to prejudiced assumptions about Aboriginal people, Glass evidently felt compelled to state explicitly that there was no reason to complain about most attendees.[189]

In August, an Aboriginal man from Northam was sentenced to twenty-one days' imprisonment for having been apparently disorderly at the dance in the same month. Then, in September, three Aboriginal persons from Northam—one woman and two men—were each sentenced to terms of imprisonment. The woman received three months with hard labour for disorderly conduct and assaulting another attendee at the dance, whereas the men each received three months and seven days with hard labour for drunkenness and assaulting Constable Charles Buckley. While details about this incident were not described in the news article or the court's charge book, it should be noted that Buckley had arrived in York earlier in 1954 and would be prosecuting the majority of cases against Aboriginal people leading to imprisonment during this year. He appeared to have moved on by early 1955. Although it was reported that the dances were 'well-conducted affairs,' the emphasis in all articles was placed on Aboriginal 'offenders' and law enforcement, which made the Coolbaroo dances, by default, an institution that required policing. This kind of reporting reinforced the well-trodden threat narrative in relation to Aboriginal people appearing in the print media.[190] To be tolerated, Aboriginal people were expected to live up to a highly virtuous ideal that exceeded white Australian behavioural norms, and failure to live up to these expectations resulted in persecution through settler-Australian law.

While the settler-Australian press presented the Coolbaroo dances from a law-enforcement perspective, the *Westralian Aborigine* reported about personal stories and social trends concerning the actual dances. For example, the reader would learn that the Coolbaroo League was one of the first organisations in Western Australia to introduce 'novelty dances' in July 1954 in Perth, Narrogin and York—these were the 'Roo-Roo-Kangaroo' and the 'Creep'. It was reported that the dancing legend Frank Mippy not only attended all dances at Narrogin but also travelled to York and Perth. Coolbaroo League committee member Bertha Issacs was featured as being in charge of catering and having brewed her thousandth cup of tea for the winter season in 1954 at the Coolbaroo September dance in York. Bertha had gained the title of 'Tea Queen' with a reputation as one of Western Australia's leading tea brewers. The *Westralian Aborigine* wrote that it was said of her at the York dance that '[a]nyone can make tea, but no one can make it like Bertha'.[191]

In December of that year, it was reported that a seemingly increasing number of Aboriginal people were buying cars, which was evidenced by the number of cars parked up at the most recent Coolbaroo dance in York. Nearly thirty cars of various styles, makes and models were sighted near the Masonic Hall. With a subtle nuance of pride, it was reported that several 'of the latest model cars including three Holdens were seen as well as many "hot-rods"'. These stories showed the human and social character of the dances, which were at odds with the typical *drunk & disorderly* stories featured in the white Australian press. Similar local settler-Australian functions were usually depicted in the *York Chronicle* in great detail, a practice that was not afforded to the Coolbaroo dances. Given that the *Westralian Aborigine* was circulated and sold mainly among Aboriginal people, it is unlikely that many settler-Australians ever came across this type of positive community news reporting.[192] The *Daily News* reported in December about a Christmas event in York that had attracted 400 Aboriginal people and was organised by the Coolbaroo League under the name 'Christmas With The Natives', where Father Christmas handed out presents to the children. While reported in a generally positive light, the article lacked any personal nuances and warmth of the kind that only the *Westralian Aborigine* was willing to convey.[193]

As to the *York Chronicle*'s attitude, in January 1955, there was one notable exception in relation to the tone of reporting about Coolbaroo events. This exception likely occurred for the simple reason that the article involved the mayor and a councillor. The Coolbaroo League was going to hold a beauty contest in Perth in February 1955, with participants from Narrogin, York, Mullewa and Perth. On 22 January, the Coolbaroo York section was planning to have its preliminary judging of the competition.[194] Miss Coolbaroo events had been held from the early days of the Coolbaroo League and bathing suits competitions were added in the 1950s, as they were common in Western societies at the time. However, it was noted that the competitions held by the Coolbaroo League lacked the seriousness of contemporary white Australian events and winners were often determined by the need to boost their self-confidence, for example, rather than according to a strict merit system. As Anna Haebich put it succinctly, it was a competition based on social experience rather than 'dog-eat-dog' competitiveness.[195] The *York Chronicle* reported that upwards of 350 Aboriginal people from York, Northam, Goomalling, Quairading and other adjacent districts crowded into the Masonic Hall to witness the selection of the young woman who would represent these districts:

> There were five competitors and they appeared in bathing costumes and were judged for appearance, carriage, deportment. etc. The Judges were the Mayor of York (Mr. A. F. Noonan), Cr. P M A. Glass and two members of the metropolitan Native Welfare Committee. The decision rested with Miss Stack, of Northam and she was the recipient of a sash which was presented to her by Mr. Noonan. The function was organised by the Coolbarroo League and dancing was enjoyed by those present.[196]

Whether Noonan, Glass and the two members of the metropolitan Native Welfare Committee (which was made up of sympathetic white Australians) made their decisions in the spirit of Coolbaroo tradition has not been preserved in the records. It is also not known to this author whether Noonan and Glass were invited or whether they had imposed themselves, more or less, as local dignitaries. They may have been invited as a matter of strategy, with a view to gaining backing and support from members of the municipal council by involving them. Whatever the reasons were for Noonan's and Glass's involvement in the competition, their presence would have created a somewhat awkward atmosphere, given that they had each been sentencing Aboriginal people in the York Court, often for 'offences' under racist legislation that specifically targeted Aboriginal people. Noonan had been sending Aboriginal people to gaol in York since 1939 and Glass had been on the bench of the York Police Court since 1947. Glass was, at the time, in 1955, overtaking Noonan in the role of the most regularly sitting justice of the peace.[197] As discussed in the previous chapter, both Noonan and Glass had also spoken out against Aboriginal housing in certain sections of town, which has been openly reported in the print media.

Also noteworthy was Noonan's position on the Natives (Citizenship Rights) Board. As discussed above (see chapter 5.06), Noonan and a magistrate decided on conditional citizenship applications for applicants residing in the municipality of York, while there was a separate board for residents in the road board district; both boards merged in 1957. Between the citizenship boards' inceptions, in October 1952 and January 1955, only two certificates of conditional citizenship were granted in York, namely, to an elderly couple in September 1954. Then, suddenly, from March 1955, conditional citizenship certificates were granted frequently. Between March 1955 and December 1956, twenty-six certificates were granted.[198]

Noonan may even have encouraged certain individuals to apply after the Coolbaroo League had been active in York for three-quarters of a year and he had taken part as a judge in the beauty competition. If this was not the case, then his partaking may have led at least some individuals to believe that they might have a better chance now than earlier. Also coinciding with these events was the passing of the Native Welfare Bill on 30 December 1954. The new Act had been in the making for over two years and was heatedly discussed in the Western Australian Parliament and reported in the daily newspapers. For example, the department had attempted to provide all Aboriginal people of mixed ancestry in the South West Land Division with full citizenship rights by birth, which had been vehemently opposed by a majority of parliamentarians. However, the new Act had a substantial number of draconian provisions deleted, including those relating to prohibited areas and the enforcement of curfews.[199] This may have signalled to local authority members on Aboriginal citizenship rights boards, such as Noonan and William Henry Robinson (representing the York Road Board), that times were changing. On the other hand, a number of Aboriginal people in York were perhaps postponing applications from 1952 onwards in the hope that their citizenship rights by birth would finally be recognised, as patrol officers would have likely discussed with some individuals that this was what the department was trying to achieve with the amendment of the Act. Thus, when the amendment did not bring about the anticipated change, people may have increasingly resumed applying to overcome the legislative restrictions imposed on Aboriginal people 'in-law'. Another reason for the sudden uptake may have been the housing situation. Given that the departmental housing program was progressing relatively slowly, being granted conditional citizenship enabled Aboriginal people in the 1950s to become eligible for placement on the general state housing waiting list.[200]

One to three months would usually elapse from the date that an Aboriginal person lodged an application in court until the hearing before the board.[201] Therefore, the onset of this 'wave' of conditional citizenship approvals somewhat coincided with Noonan and Glass' involvement in the Coolbaroo beauty competition. It may have been sheer coincidence; however, it appears possible that the Coolbaroo dances in York, in some way or another, influenced the uptake of conditional citizenship by providing a point of contact between the local authorities and Aboriginal people, which may have simultaneously assisted in diminishing 'white' fear of the Aboriginal 'other'—at least to some degree.

The news report about the beauty competition marked an end to local reporting about the Coolbaroo dances in York. It appears that some dances had to be cancelled as the League struggled to organise transport at times but dances were held more or less frequently, at least until and during 1957, as advertised in the *Westralian Aborigine*, if not beyond. The regular dances in York continued to be held in the Masonic Hall; however, for a bigger 'ball' type event in October 1956, the York Town Hall was secured, which had to be approved in a council meeting. The Coolbaroo dances were only mentioned in two more news article in the *York Chronicle*. In December 1955, it was suggested during a council meeting that patrons of the Coolbaroo dances were responsible for leaving a mess on the grounds of the neighbouring infant health clinic. The result of the discussion was an agreement that a fence be erected dividing both properties. In the following February, it was reported that three Aboriginal persons appeared in court, one for being under the influence of alcohol at the Coolbaroo dance and two young men for being disorderly on Hope Street after the dance. Besides this, the Coolbaroo dances had apparently ceased to be newsworthy.[202] On one hand, the absence of further news reports suggests that the Coolbaroo dances were no longer perceived as a threat by the majority of the white community—or, at least, this was the assumption of the editor of the *York Chronicle*. On the other hand, this absence also suggests that Aboriginal social life in York was only a topic of interest for settler-Australian readers when it provided sensationalist content, otherwise it was simply ignored.

While the Coolbaroo dances in York no longer featured much in the settler-Australian press, unfortunately, the Coolbaroo League had reason to report a negative experience in York in the *Westralian Aborigine*. In early 1956, members of the Coolbaroo League from Perth, who had travelled to York for a Coolbaroo dance, had reportedly been refused dine-in service in a café in York. When further Coolbaroo members arrived with two settler-Australians as part of their group and sat down at a table in the same café, the other members of their party, who had arrived earlier, informed them about their experience and that the newly arrived members were unlikely be served. Consequently, the café proprietor was questioned, and intimated that he would serve Aboriginal people who were in company of white people. Otherwise, he could not afford to allow table service for Aboriginal people as this was apparently bad for his business because 'white people objected to seeing natives in the shop' and if he allowed one Aboriginal person to dine-in, he would have to allow every Aboriginal person to. However, he was happy to serve takeaway (cold drinks).[203] The party then ventured to the café across the road, where they were informed that they would be permitted to dine in, although the proprietor preferred Aboriginal customers to opt for takeaway as he had to refuse service to a number of Aboriginal people 'because they were dirty'.[204] This experience occurred only one month after Coolbaroo League members were at the receiving end of an unwarranted string of racist, verbal abuse by the proprietor of a hotel in Katanning, who changed his attitude when he learned that patrons to whom he had rented his rooms via telephone were Aboriginal. Such news reports, as printed in the *Westralian Aborigine*, provide a rare insight into the lived experiences of Aboriginal people in York during these contentious times. Given that the Coolbaroo League members appeared rather surprised about the café proprietor's attitude in York, it may be inferred that the situation in Perth was slightly better than in the country.

The Coolbaroo dances remained the only public social space in York during the 1950s where Aboriginal people could enjoy themselves freely without having to fear being subjected to racist prejudice in some shape or form. Perhaps encouraged by the early dances in York, the Quakers-based Society of Friends approached the municipal council in late October 1954 and inquired whether council was willing to provide land for the erection of recreational facilities for Aboriginal people in York's east ward, where the first three State Housing Commission homes were located. Members of the society were willing to sacrifice their Christmas holidays to complete the works. Council advised that it did not own any land in close proximity to the homes (which seems odd, as Lots 151 to 159 remained municipal endowment lands, but these may have been leased at the time). Several councillors then pointed out that such amenities might be of use on the 'native reserve', which would have had the perceived benefit of being 'out of sight and out of mind'.[205] Even if the Society of Friends had been successful in securing land, there would likely have been some well-meaning but patronising oversight conducted through this friendly society. Therefore, for Aboriginal people to enjoy unbiased and independent socialising in York town during the 1950s, there really was nothing like the Coolbaroo League dances.

6.11 The York Chronicle and the remainder of the 1950s

As briefly mentioned earlier (see chapter 6.09), after 1954, the *York Chronicle* only reported once more on Aboriginal housing as discussed in a council meeting. In April 1959, several councillors objected to Aboriginal people living in a pensioners' flat in town. Councillor Laurie Theofler Davies had introduced the matter to council, stating that he held the belief that one of the new flats for old-age pensioners had been occupied by Aboriginal people. He expressed that he thought it was not right to allow Aboriginal people into the flats as these had been built for a specific purpose. He also suggested that council raise strong objections and that if allowed to continue to occur, this would set a detrimental precedent ('very bad principle')[206]. Councillor Marwick generally agreed with Davies' objections but pointed out that the Aboriginal people in question were, in fact, old-age pensioners with conditional citizenship rights and he doubted that council had any jurisdiction about the matter. Councillor S.J. Prunster's comments suggested that he did not wish to take sides but was looking for a practical solution. Only Councillor Frank George Hunt spoke up on behalf of the Aboriginal pensioners: 'I understand that the flat is being quite respectably kept. They will be good people if they are left alone by others'.[207]

Hunt did not only support the idea that Aboriginal pensioners would be living in these flats, he also pointed to an issue that is usually muted in the public records. Hunt seemed to suggest that certain behaviours, in particular, vis-à-vis settler-Australians, were reactive in nature, adding the conditional clause 'if they are left alone'. Therefore, Hunt's comment inferred that settler-Australians had to change their attitudes and behaviours, too, for Aboriginal people to be able to integrate into settler-Australian community. The council concluded that, given the authorities were satisfied, there was nothing the council could do about it. Tolerance, as it seemed, held still a very fragile status by the end of the 1950s. The newspaper article about this council meeting came to the attention of Native Welfare Commissioner Middleton, who ascertained that four old-age pensioner flats had been built in York, of which one was let to an Aboriginal couple. Middleton was advised that the State Housing Commission apparently did 'not discriminate against coloured tenants when it considers the coloured applicants have suitable standards'.[208]

In relation to these various council meetings over the years that have been discussed here, it should be always remembered that they were published in the local newspaper and it does not seem unlikely that some Aboriginal individuals picked up the paper every now and then and read what the official representatives of the settler-Australian community had to say about Aboriginal people. At this point in time, the literacy rate of Aboriginal adults was generally not very high but there would have always been at least a few literate individuals who could have read those articles and then spread the word if they had so desired. The reader may recall (see chapters 3.04 and 3.06) the two women writing letters to the department in the 1940s in relation to curfews and the prohibition on attending the picture show. In particular, in relation to this council meeting in April 1959, one can conclude that Aboriginal people were still not considered 'part and parcel' of the settler-Australian community; they were merely tolerated. This was arguably for two reasons. First, none of the opposing council members appeared to be overly concerned about offending Aboriginal town residents by their bigoted, publicly voiced opinions, and second, the majority of council members apparently also did not believe that the tone of their discussion would meet with objections from the settler-Australian community. It should be noted that councillor Davies had complained only a month earlier that the *York Chronicle* was reporting 'everything' he said at the council meetings, which suggests that he was somewhat sensitive to community reactions that his various comments—not only in relation to Aboriginal people—might have triggered.[209] However, this evidentially did not stop him from openly sharing his segregationist views a month later.

While December 1954 had seemingly marked the end of council-based active agitation against Aboriginal housing across town—and the instance with the pensioners' flats in 1959 was the only other occasion that matters concerning Aboriginal people were publicly discussed at council meetings during the reminder of the 1950s—this does not mean that Aboriginal people vanished from public discourse, as expressed in the *York Chronicle*. Besides the news articles about the Coolbaroo dances, the *York Chronicle* sporadically published the granting of conditional citizenship rights until December 1956. From 1957, this practice was discontinued. In this particular year, only one certificate was granted in York, which may have influenced the decision to cease reporting on such occurrences, although more certificates were granted in York in the following three years. The most common type of news reports relating to Aboriginal people remained those concerning alcohol-related convictions in the York Police Court.[210] One court case from 1956, which was reported in depth, highlights the prevailing settler-Australian concerns about alcohol. The headlines were the largest on the front page of that issue, stating that a man received a fine of £20 for supplying liquor. The subheading claimed that it was about a 'case, which many York residents have been waiting for the outcome'.[211] All that had happened was that an Aboriginal man, not exempt from the *Native Welfare Act 1954*, had purchased and consumed a glass of beer at the York Agricultural Society's show on 15 September. The non-Aboriginal person who served the beer was being persecuted: This was the premise of the entire court case, which came to a conclusion three months later. Police Sergeant Arthur Edward Beard's evidence in court is worth quoting here, as it demonstrates how the author of the news article and assumingly also the readers took an interest in the case:

> In his evidence, Sgt. Beard, said that he in company with constable A. F. Jenkins, were in the vicinity of the main bar on the showgrounds, when he noticed Garlett approach the bar and speak to the accused. The accused then filled a glass with beer from a Jug. Sgt. Beard arrived on the scene just as the native had drained the glass. After smelling the glass Sgt. Beard asked the accused, why he had served Garlett. Blake replied, that the native had mislead him and told him, that he didn't come under the native act. Sgt. Beard quoted that Garlett was very well dressed on this day. He reported the incident to Mr. H. N. Haley, the holder of the temporary licence. Constable A. F. Jenkins corroborated the evidence by Sgt. Beard, and said that he had taken the native who was obviously affected by Liquor back to the police station and laid a charge of having received liquor against him.[212]

This Aboriginal man was one of 150–200 estimated Aboriginal patrons that day, and he was the only Aboriginal person to be charged with any offences that day in York.[213] The news article also revealed the system organised by the proprietors of the show to prevent Aboriginal people who could legally buy alcohol from sharing it. To purchase drinks or engage with any of the sideshow attractions, patrons had to buy 'tickets' as a form of show currency. Settler-Australian patrons could buy as many as they wished at once. Aboriginal patrons were restricted to purchasing one ticket at each sale.[214]

Fewer than two weeks after the show, several Aboriginal people appeared in the York Police Court for supplying and receiving alcohol. The person who supplied alcohol had conditional citizenship rights, obtained only three months earlier. Sergeant Wilcox addressed the sentencing justices of the peace, S.P. Harvey and P.M.A. Glass, requesting that they impose harsher penalties for receiving alcohol because the usual fine of £5 was apparently not a deterrent. The justices of the peace listened—and two persons received one month's imprisonment with hard labour just for obtaining alcohol. As indicated earlier, imprisonment had been imposed over and over again for alcohol-related offences targeting Aboriginal people, although, in recent years, the newspaper had usually only printed the outcomes and perhaps some background information leading up to the charges made. However, this article spoke to the public. Sergeant Wilcox seemed to be representing the opinion of many other settler-Australians and this article was most likely meant to serve as an indirect warning to Aboriginal people that, henceforth, penalties would be harsher for 'receiving' alcohol.[215]

One further court case is worth mentioning as it shows to what lengths police would go in their obsession with Aboriginal people consuming alcohol. On 8 January 1958, an Aboriginal woman in her early twenties was convicted under the *Native Welfare Act 1954* for receiving alcohol, for which she was sentenced to one month of imprisonment. Under section 65 of the *Police Act 1952*, she was further sentenced to three months of cumulative imprisonment for 'having insufficient or no means of support and deemed to be an idle and disorderly'.[216] On the previous day, this Aboriginal woman had consumed alcohol together with two young Italian men, who had apparently limited knowledge of the English language. The *York Chronicle* reported the court hearing. Referring to one of the Italian men:

Constable Jenkins said that he and Constable Howell saw the accused and another New Australian talking to two natives on a vacant block. They later went towards the river along Macartney street. The constables followed and crept along the ground over prickly bush and came up on the group with a flashlight.[217]

They then found the Aboriginal woman, the two Italian men and a bottle of wine. One of the two men ran away and the other was arrested. However, he had his charge for supplying alcohol dismissed as he was able to convince the sentencing justices of the peace, A.F. Noonan and S.P. Harvey, that he had no idea about the laws governing Aboriginal people. Police were instructed to visit the camp of the 'New Australians' and to educate everyone on the laws pertaining to Aboriginal people. One may wonder whether the police officers felt a sense of pride and satisfaction that their efforts were rewarded when the Aboriginal woman was gaoled for more than a quarter of a year for being Aboriginal and for being, apparently, homeless and without income.[218]

When, in late 1958, an amendment bill of the *Natives (Citizenship Rights) Act 1951* was discussed in Parliament, public discourse in York and surrounding districts picked up on the pro and contra debates surrounding the bill. Mock penal discussions between Junior Farmers of York, Northam and Beverley were won with points by those teams who had argued that negative outcomes would outweigh the benefits of Aboriginal people receiving citizenship rights by birth. As citizenship status and alcohol consumption were often named within the same breath of air, it does not seem surprising that such mock penal discussions turned against the granting of unconditional citizenship.[219] After all, Aboriginal people's presence in the *York Chronicle* during the second part of the 1950s was, to a large extent, made up of reports about court appearances in relation to alcohol. After the 1958 amendment of the *Native (Citizenship Rights) Act*, it took more than a decade for all Aboriginal people in Western Australia to be legally considered citizens, on equal terms with settler-Australians by 1972. That it did not occur earlier was arguably, to a great extent, a reflection of prevailing community attitudes in York and elsewhere across white Western

Australia, given that the members of Parliament who had been successfully blocking the abolition of conditional citizenship mostly represented the wishes of their electorates—at least the most vocal ones.[220] At this point, it is interesting to raise the question of influence. Did the *York Chronicle* largely influence its readers' opinions with its style of writing?—or was the style of reporting in the *York Chronicle* merely a reflection of openly voiced community attitudes in York at the time in an attempt to sell the product according to demand? It would likely have been a mix of both; however, the decision-making and style of writing did appear to fluctuate with changing editors and local managers. After York-born C.J. Ashbolt left the *Chronicle* in June 1955 to take on town clerk duties, the newspaper had several local managers until it ceased publication at the end of 1959.

With a very few exceptions that can be counted on one hand, Aboriginal people who appeared in court, or were otherwise deemed newsworthy, were generally identified as 'natives' in all the news pieces in the *York Chronicle* during the period covered here so far. In December 1956, for the first time, the *York Chronicle* reported the alcohol-related convictions of two Aboriginal men without explicitly stating that these men were 'natives.'[221] This news piece remained a one-off occurrence until November 1957. Thenceforth, most news articles reporting on Aboriginal people in the *York Chronicle* did not state that the individuals concerned were Aboriginal or 'native'.[222] One exception was the court case in January 1958 that we have just discussed. In general, at the time, convictions under the *Native Welfare Act 1954* decreased and were replaced by convictions under the *Police Act 1952*, which made it easier not to comment on a convicted person's Aboriginality. Locals would have known anyway.[223] From October 1957 until late June 1959, a certain G. Kent was the local manager of the *York Chronicle*, and it would have been a conscious decision made by Kent not to remark on an individuals' Aboriginality. As progressive as this may seem, this practice did not prevent Kent from printing a job advertisement for pig farmer and press officer of the Farmers' Union, D.W. Hill, in April 1959, which read:

Tractor Driver

3 WEEKS

£3 per day

No natives

Apply D W Hill.[224]

This example suggests that monetary considerations and loyalty to the white farming community determined the pace of progress towards social inclusion. After all, local country newspapers depended heavily on local business advertisements.

In September and December 1959, the *York Chronicle* also reported on the deaths of two Aboriginal persons without stating their Aboriginality. In relation to the second death, the *York Chronicle* wrote about the 'passing of an old and respected citizen of Quairading and York Districts'.[225] Both articles were proper obituaries. The only other time that the *York Chronicle* had published an obituary without making reference to the deceased person's Aboriginality was in September 1953, when a young Aboriginal woman who was reportedly well liked in town had suddenly passed away. Otherwise, Aboriginal people had not been afforded such final words of acknowledgement, that were qualitatively equal with those for whites, prior to 1959. Generally speaking, the social life of Aboriginal individuals was not featured at all, with very few exceptions spread over the past three decades.[226] It is not clear what the motivation was behind ceasing to state a person's Aboriginality. At first sight, it appears to have been a laudable change, as it removed the connotations of racist hysteria from such news articles. On second consideration, though, one may wonder whether the motivation was based on more than inclusive intentions. If the motivation was strictly assimilationist, not making any reference to a person's Aboriginality may have had the long-term aim of eradicating Aboriginality from the public realm altogether. Even if the underlying motivation was not strictly assimilationist, this practice could have resulted in the same outcome. Perhaps not for court appearances but for obituaries, it should surely have been appropriate to indicate the deceased's Aboriginality. However, this exemplifies the status of being

Aboriginal or 'native' in the South West Land Division at the time. Rather than suggesting connotations of an extant culture, identifying a person as 'native' brought up images of socioeconomic disadvantage, devoid of a living culture. Within the logic of this view, not stating a person's Aboriginality was, perhaps, intended to be a somewhat friendly, albeit ill-conceived, invitation to join white Australian society.

After the *York Chronicle* had ceased publication by the end of 1959, it was incorporated into the *Northam Advertiser*, which had a local agent reporting on matters in York. With this change, York news became secondary and peripheral within the context of this bi-weekly local newspaper. The *Northam Advertiser* had never stopped singling out Aboriginal individuals as 'natives' in its news pieces and, thus, the news reports about York also reverted to the general reporting style of pre-October 1957. This style of writing in the *Northam Advertiser* continued well into the mid-1960s.[227]

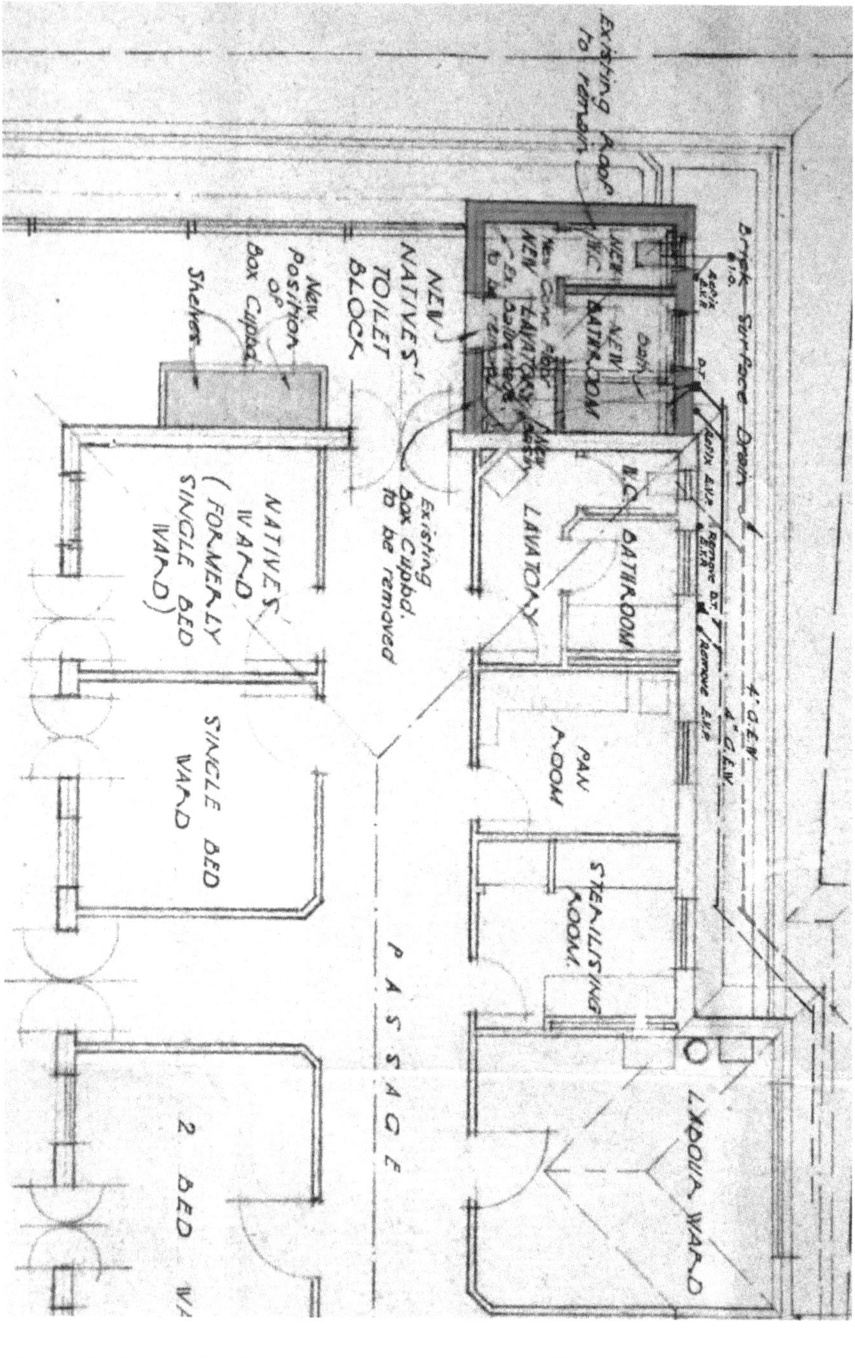

Figure 15: Revised plan for a segregated maternity ward (1951) - Department of Public Health, item 1948/0700, SROWA

WESTRALIAN aborigine

COOLBAROO LEAGUE   MAY - JUNE, 1954

ent Body Seeks For Aborigines

Some Colour On Sporting

Union of Australian University Students is pressing for six Commonwealth scholarships to aborigines each year.

SIGNS that some old colour being overcome on the sportin from the south of the State.

In both Borden and Ongeru ball teams have opened their ra

)s are
/ersity
in all
ses at
s.

For
natives
show
ballers
from
clubs.

Cit

hips a
granted
if the
re un-
educa-

Whit
in the
must H
before
ball cit

ed by
seven

At I
Stan
Rebel
and Me
admitt
In Ong
his nei
admitt

N

iips be
mmon-
n with
ar for
ertiary

Len
cently
ship ri

ese six
taken
to the
· Com-
ps.

sidera-
ents of
ps so
e from
to be
ıall be
cloth-
vances,

Na

D

P

where
a free
hostel.

Gaiety at York

The Coolbaroo League's first dance at York on May 15 was a drawcard for a big crowd.

A good orchestra provided a packed programme of modern and old time dancing.

From now on dances will be held at the Masonic Hall, York, once a month. The next dance will be held on June 26.

THE YARREN FAMILY RECENTLY moved into one of the newly-erected homes in York. It is built on similar lines to those to be constructed by the State Housing Commission soon. Since the death of Mrs. Yarren in February the task of housekeeping has fallen to members of the family. Rachael (left), Owen and Mr. Len Yarren (right) are pictured carrying out the necessary odd jobs about the home.

COC
d an c
praise
of the
Court

Spea
which
was co
disorde
having
J.Ps. D
the Cc
doing a
people

imittee
repre-
'overn-
ty and

iltation
versity
cholar-
ılished.

on the
ed on

Police Charge Native

A CHARGE against a native—brought during a firearms amnesty—of having held a firearm without a licence and not being a person exempt under

Figure 16: News article about a family in one of the two houses built under the Aboriginal State Housing Commission scheme - Westralian Aborigine May-June 1954, SLWA (Permission to use photograph courtesy Geraldine Metcalf)

249

Chapter 7. 1960s

7.01 Reserve Housing

The reader may recall that, in 1954, the York Municipal Council was advised of a three-stage Aboriginal housing scheme (see chapter 6.09). As discussed, the prototype home of the second or 'intermediate' stage had been built in York in 1954, and was followed by another second house of the same type in 1955. The third stage comprised standard State Housing Commission homes, of which several were built for Aboriginal families in York. However, at the time of the announcement of the scheme, the Department of Native Welfare had no concrete plans for the first-stage homes that were to be built on reserves. In mid-1955, the Minister for Housing, Herb Graham, approached Premier Albert Hawke in relation to housing for those Aboriginal people who were expected not to be able to assimilate. He acknowledged that the State Housing Commission had been providing housing for only a few 'hand-picked' families and that the kind of people he was thinking of were not suitable for such housing, which he expressed in no uncertain terms:

> There would appear to be no means by which semi-primitive coloured people of general low standard and entirely unaccustomed to living as do white people could be provided with reasonable shelter.[1]

This very finite view insisted on the alleged incapability of certain segments of Aboriginal communities to integrate within settler-Australian life. Those who did not try to be accepted into a largely paternalistic—if not often antagonistic—society were deemed incapable of integrating. The expectation was still that Aboriginal people had to try their hardest to integrate into white Australian society and failure to do so identified them as 'incapable'. Aboriginal people still had to prove their worthiness to be accepted. Some individuals and families might have been incapable of integrating at the time to live according to a white Australian ideal; however, an inclusive society would aim to address issues of inequity to increase capabilities and not to write-off disadvantage as an inhibitive criterion against joining mainstream society. There would also have been Aboriginal people who consciously resisted assimilation policy. Some may have witnessed what families had to endure who did sign up for town housing, as observed by Central District Officer McLarty in relation to York.[2] McLarty appeared to be chiefly concerned with potentially negative reactions from Aboriginal people who might experience white Australians' overtly paternalistic attitudes; however, he did not necessarily disagree with such paternalistic attitudes, as suggested by the below quotation:

> I suspect that many well-meaning people lost no opportunity of reminding the natives how lucky they were and exhorting them to live up to their opportunity. This is no doubt true, but constant repetition of it could cause resentment.[3]

The Western Australian State Treasury advised that some monies could be made available for suitable structures to be erected on reserves by the State Housing Commission, which would then be handed over to the Department of Native Welfare. However, Commissioner Middleton initially argued that the proposal was counterproductive to assimilation. In the country, where reserves could be obtained, the effect of providing cabin-type structures would be to abolish the plan for the better housing of Aboriginal people. Middleton outlined two concurrent reasons for his objection. First, with available cheap reserve housing, the white public would more strenuously oppose the provision of houses for 'better type natives' within the residential boundaries of their towns, and second, because Aboriginal people themselves would be satisfied to continue living in substandard conditions on Aboriginal reserves. This, Middleton argued, would further entrench segregated communities rather than work towards phasing them out. Middleton went on to outline a minimum standard that reserve homes should have:

> No building that does not provide separate bedrooms for the children according to sex, segregation of children from the adults, adequate living, cooking, ablution and laundry accommodation, with proper sanitation and hygiene facilities can be considered to be satisfactory to human beings anywhere. Consequently a building of not less than three bedrooms, living room, kitchen-dining room, bathroom, laundry and lavatory is required for the average family, irrespective of their social state. It must be remembered that the children of the humpy attend our schools with our children and are expected to maintain the same standard of personal hygiene. A better class humpy is not the answer to the problem.[4]

A 'better class humpy' it was going to be. An officer of the Department of Native Welfare at Geraldton, Sydney R. Adams, had developed a cheap-to-build basic home at the request of his senior officer (and Middleton's successor to be), Frank Ellis Gare, who sought to ameliorate the poor housing situation in the Central West region. A prototype was completed in January 1957 on an Aboriginal reserve in Geraldton, with assistance from some local businesses. This type of building would be later referred to as a Geraldton-type house.[5] Over the following six months, different types were developed. Type 1 had one room and a verandah, and was intended for singles. Type 2 had two rooms and a verandah, and was intended for couples. Type 3 had three rooms and a verandah, and was intended for families. These 'steel prefabricated structures were built on concrete floors, faced with zincanneal sheeting and corrugated iron roof'.[6] Type 4 was similar to Type 3 but had an inbuilt toilet and bath, and was generally intended for locations outside of reserves. All types had an insulated wood stove for cooking in one of the rooms. The camping reserve homes were initially not to be connected to the electricity network and did not have running water inside the house, as the department was providing communal ablution blocks and conveniences. The department was keen to erect

Geraldton-type homes across the state as the costs were lower than State Housing Commission homes. However, progress was slow, once again, because of insufficient finances (or lacking the political will to make such finances available). The department had anticipated erecting sixty Geraldton-type homes during the financial year 1958–1959, but treasury only approved six, which had to be built outside of gazetted Aboriginal reserves. Only in December 1959 was the reserve housing program approved by Premier David Brand, with estimated costs of £10,000 to be covered by the Consolidated Revenue Fund. The first reserves to receive Geraldton-type homes outside of Geraldton and Mullewa were located at Beverley, Narrogin, Gnowangerup, Katanning and Pingelly. All up, the first allotment comprised eighteen 'Geraldton Type 3' houses.[7]

By January 1963, fifty-six houses of various types had been built across Western Australia. This included thirty-nine 'primary transitional' Geraldton-type houses on reserves, eight Type 4 houses or similar structures on special housing reserves in towns that did not fall under the *Native Welfare Act 1905–1960*, as well as nine Type 5 houses, which had been developed in the meantime and were erected on ordinary town blocks. These 'standard transitional' Type 5 houses replaced the 'intermediate' Type 79A houses from the 1950s and, while these supposedly fulfilled local by-law criteria, they often did not meet the aesthetic expectations of non-Aboriginal town dwellers in the same way as the earlier model. Initially, rents charged were between five shillings and thirty shillings per week, depending on the type of home, with Type 3 homes being rented out for £0 7s 6d per week. By mid-1964, the total number of houses provided had risen to 333 on camping/town reserves and 126 standard transitional houses in towns. Middleton estimated that a further 1,130 homes were required to meet the then current demands.[8]

In an official statement for an ABC talkback radio program, which questioned why reserve houses were generally not equipped with running water and showers, then Minister for Native Welfare, Edgar Henry Mead Lewis, justified, in April 1965, the ongoing need for the transitional housing program and why reserve dwellers had to use communal facilities:

The transitional houses on reserves are very often the first improvement on a humpy available to the natives and they have to be educated to the use of these houses. It is for this reason that they have communal facilities at this stage of their social progress. From these reserves they graduate to the transitional houses in town and then later to conventional housing.[9]

However, Lewis forgot to mention that the very existence of the three-stage housing program was largely based on considerations of cost, and that the alleged need of the identified Aboriginal families to graduate through different stages of social development had been tailored around lack of finances. Despite this apparent need for reserve housing, in December 1966, it was reported that by mid-year, the department had erected 465 houses on reserves and would not build many more, claiming that it had 'virtually provided for all reserve dwellers'.[10] Additionally, 223 self-contained secondary transitional houses had been erected on township sites, plus twenty-nine conventional homes. A further 120 Aboriginal families were living in State Housing Commission homes. At this stage, the department openly stated that it aimed to abolish reserves as soon as it could provide non-segregated housing for the occupants.[11] Census data from 1966 indicate that approximately 7,800 Aboriginal people lived in the South West Land Division. Accounting for the number of homes provided by the department and the State Housing Commission, while considering that Aboriginal families were often rather large, it still appears unlikely that the balance of housing needs was satisfied by private rentals and accommodation provided by employers. This suggests that a rather large proportion of semi-transient Aboriginal people were disregarded as not needing housing.[12]

The reserve at York had been earmarked for primary transitional housing allocations by November 1960. Initially, it was suggested to build two Type 3 houses and one Type 2 house. The latter was meant to be occupied by an elderly couple living on the reserve. In relation to the Type 3 homes, a comment made by a departmental officer suggests that the department's welfare ambitions remained conditional and that assistance to improve Aboriginal families' quality of life still had to be earned in the departmental officer's view: 'Two families are more or less permanently employed and thoroughly deserve Type III houses'.[13] The Type 2 house was never built but the other two homes were completed by August 1961 for a total cost of £1,366 2s. One of the two families must have moved elsewhere, as the elderly couple was allocated one of the Type 3 family houses, as was also reported in the *Northam Advertiser*.[14]

In October 1962, a further two Type 3 houses were commissioned together with the toilets and ablution block, as discussed earlier (see chapter 6.04). Thirteen months later, they were ready for occupation; however, this time around, the new houses were not deemed newsworthy.[15] Because of overcrowding, there were plans for another two houses to be erected in the 1966–1967 financial year, but this did not eventuate given that, by the end of 1966, the department had changed its policy and decided to cease building homes on reserves with a view to phasing out reserves completely, as discussed above (within this chapter). J.J. Elliot, the departmental district officer overseeing York at the time, was able to justify that there was no longer a need for the additional two houses, as 'investigations during the last quarter show that the native folk responsible for the overcrowding quickly gain rural accommodation when pressed on the issue'.[16] This comment might have implied that those individuals that were 'bullied' from the reserve now contributed to overcrowding in private rentals or state housing homes if they had been unable to secure their own accommodation. For the Department of Native Welfare, the time-worn strategy of 'dispersal' seemed still to be a justifiable means to an end.

Soon after the first two reserve houses had been completed, a health issue with these houses became apparent. Member of the Legislative Council of Western Australia, Charles Roy Abbey, became involved when writing a letter to the Minister for Native Welfare, C.C. Perkins, about the lack of facilities on the York Reserve, discussed earlier (see chapter 6.04). On this occasion, Abbey also noted that 'because of the low, flat roof of the Geraldton-type houses a considerable amount of condensation occurs in winter causing some detriment to the health of the occupants'.[17] This kind of issue had apparently not occurred in Geraldton and Mullewa, where the prototype homes had first been built, due to the somewhat warmer climate. However, departmental staff acknowledged that because 'of the extremely cold winters and frosts in the Southern part of the State there is quite heavy condensation and consequent dripping from the ceilings of these cottages in the winter months', and the lining of these ceilings was identified to be a necessity.[18] There were no funds available at the end of 1961 and the only reserve where the ceilings were going to be lined was in York, because the local 'Native Welfare Committee' had offered to do the work. Materials were sent out costing £27 3s before the department realised that it would have to spend approximately £1,800 to provide ceilings in all fifty-nine Geraldton-type houses in the central and southern districts. It was decided so see whether the improvements in York would fix the condensation issue and, if they did, consideration would be given to securing further funding. In York, the lining of ceilings was completed during a 'busy-bee' weekend in March 1962, organised by the local Native Welfare Committee.[19] Similar to when the Aboriginal family on Cowan Road moved into their freshly built and flooded Type 79 house in 1954 (see chapter 6.08), one may wonder what the reserve dwellers thought of their brand-new 'health hazard homes' that were supposed to improve their quality of life and be a progressive first step towards *assimilation* into Western society—a society that kept insisting on its claim of modern superiority.

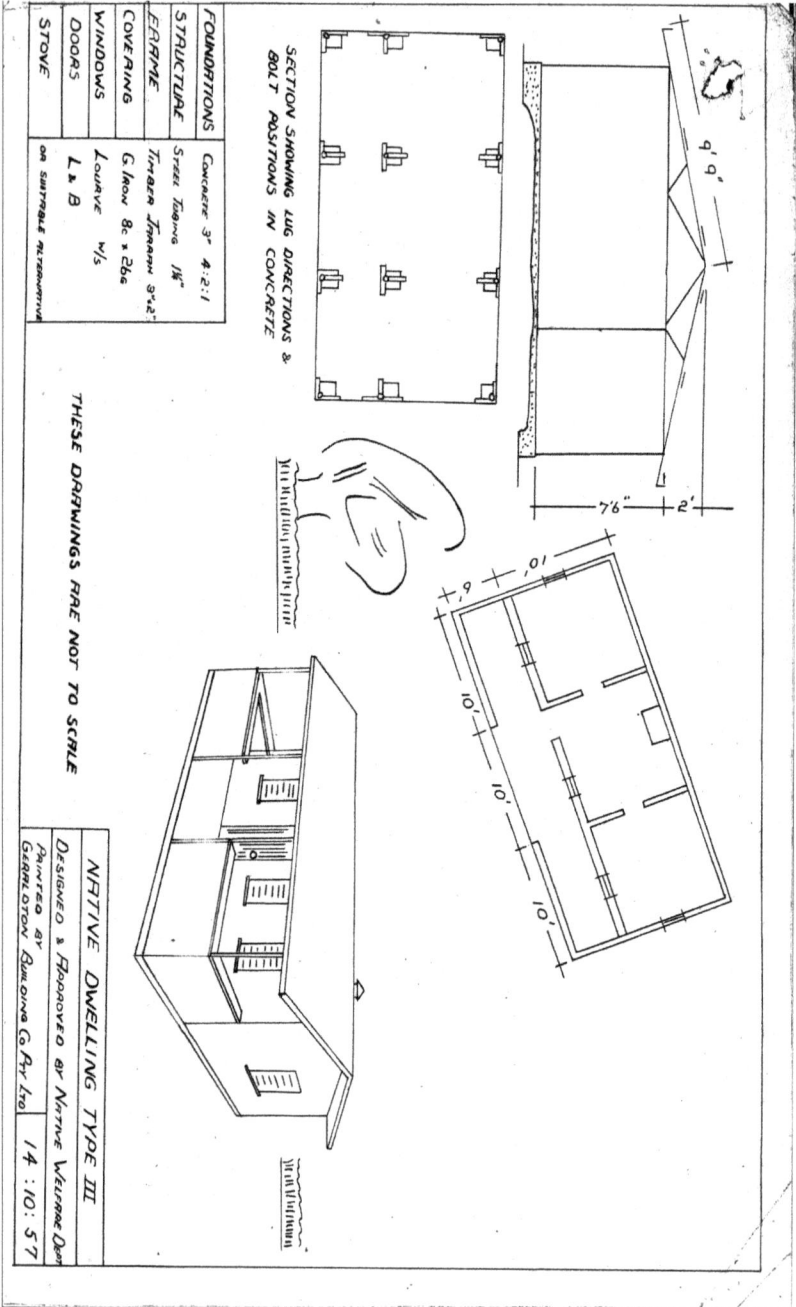

Figure 17: Plan of Geraldton Type III house as built on the York Reserve - Department of Native Welfare, item 1960/0415, SROWA

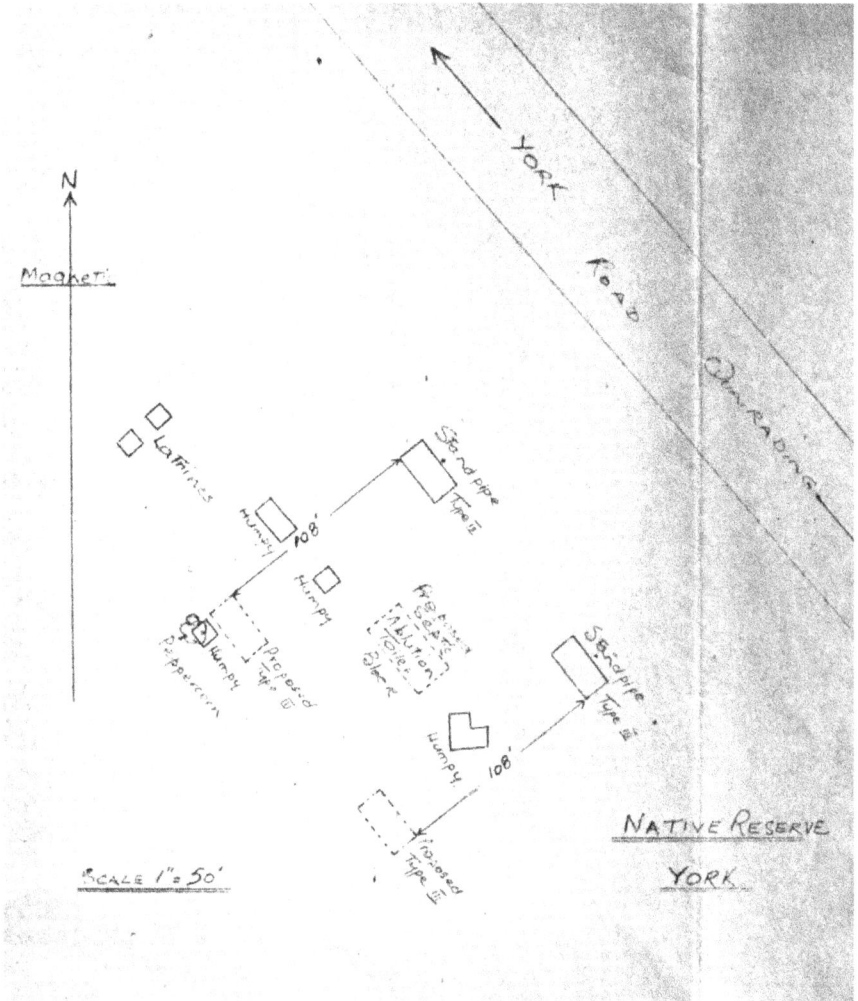

Figure 18: Plan of York Reserve depicting two completed houses, two proposed houses and amenities, as well as still existing camps (ca. 1962) – Department of Community Welfare, item A1821, SROWA

Figure 19: Janice Kickett holding Donna Narkle with Monty the dog next to Type III house on the York Reserve with camp in background (courtesy Marion Kickett)

Figure 20: Janice Kickett in front of Type III house on the York Reserve (courtesy Marion Kickett)

7.02 Native Welfare Committee

During the early 1960s, some active community support for Aboriginal people was developing in York with a focus on the reserve. Settler-Australian townsfolk might have remained somewhat uneasy with Aboriginal people living in town but reserve dwellers increasingly attracted the attention of well-meaning settler-Australians who sought to ameliorate their living conditions. Improving the reserve conditions rather than seeking to find alternative accommodation in town among settler-Australians, and thus upholding segregation, may have also been the underlying motivation of some committee members. Renewed community interest in Aboriginal people started publicly with the announcement of a new 'protector of natives'.[20] As it was reported in the *Northam Advertiser*, in May 1960, Envoy L. Wells of the Salvation Army was appointed local protector in York. There had been no local protectors in York since Sergeant Dowsett relinquished his protector position ten years earlier.

Dowsett's successor, Sergeant A.E. Beard, continued taking on some duties that were typically carried out by local protectors but he refused to be appointed to the position.[21] Wells' main focus was on assisting with employment but he was also tasked with handing out weekly rations to destitute Aboriginal families and individuals.[22] It seems likely that Wells was soon relocated by his church to another centre because, after a few months, he was no longer mentioned in the local newspaper and, by January 1961, a new local protector had been appointed. The new protector was the Methodist Reverend Prestage Lucas Sullivan, who recommended at a Methodist quarterly meeting on 3 January that, being a church, they should 'show friendliness and interest in local natives'.[23]

Simultaneously, in August 1960, at a Country Party meeting in York, it was decided that *something* should be done for the reserve children as the living conditions were deemed unfit for children by attendees of the meeting; however, no details were laid out.[24] Then, in June 1961, at the local Country Women's Association (CWA) meeting, a similar discussion took place about what role the CWA could play in helping Aboriginal people 'on the reserves around York to adjust to better living conditions, and in providing some amenities'.[25] It was decided to approach the department for guidance, and at the following CWA meeting, Reverend Sullivan attended to drum up support for establishing a 'native welfare council' (both terms, *committee* and *council*, were often used interchangeably, though the department encouraged calling the local organisations *committees*).[26] Sullivan had earlier voiced the intention to request a meeting of united organisations in town, with the aim of electing a 'native welfare council' to assist in 'local native affairs'.[27] A public meeting was to be held on Monday 21 August at the CWA rooms in an attempt to combine efforts. It was reported that:

> [i]nterest has been forthcoming from several quarters of the district and it is hoped to have these combined in one organisation. The Adult Committee of the Youth Club at its recent meeting, pledged support for a program organised by Mrs. L Negus; the CWA has discussed the matter in their meetings; the department is erecting houses on the York Reserve; and the churches continue their interest in this work, together with the Police department and local governing bodies.[28]

York's Native Welfare Committee was formed following this meeting, which was attended by about twenty-five 'York citizens', as well as two departmental officers who explained how native welfare committees and councils worked. For York, the current needs were narrowed down to assisting with furnishing the new reserve dwellings and helping to find employment. The *Northam Advertiser* reported that those elected to the committee were the following persons:

> Chairman, Mr. F Ashbolt; secretary-treasurer: Rev P L Sullivan; Committee Rev Timms, Messrs E Beckwith, D Jamieson, W Motherway, Misses Wendy Hill and B Jamieson, and Mesdames Timms, D Mills, F Morrell and D Negus.[29]

Native welfare committees were loosely formed local interest groups that aimed for the improvement of Aboriginal people's lives within the committees' respective districts. The first such local committee was formed in December 1946 in the Great Southern town of Narrogin. Increased community interest may have correlated with the advent of conditional citizenship, as the granting of the first certificate in the Narrogin court occurred in June 1946 for a man from Cuballing.[30] However, most native welfare committees were formed after the state-wide WA Native Welfare Council (Inc.) had been established in early 1952. An earlier Native Welfare Council was formed in 1939, which advocated for the improvement of Aboriginal livelihoods. It was formed by mission, church and civic groups; however, this body appears to have ceased operation in the mid-1940s before Middleton arrived in Western Australia.

The new Native Welfare Council was Commissioner Middleton's brainchild and its stipulated aim was to create a civic base to promote and assist with the assimilation of Aboriginal people as per state policy. The WA Native Welfare Council (Inc.) was independent from any state or federal agency but departmental records suggest that Middleton wielded influence nevertheless.[31] Local committees would then often do the field work promoted by the Native Welfare Council but they were mostly autonomous and not necessarily affiliated with the council. The onset of the 1960s witnessed further upspringing of native welfare committees in the South West Land Division. For example, in York's neighbouring towns of Northam and Beverley, native welfare committees were formed in November 1959 and in May 1961, respectively.[32]

Departmental officers often attended inaugural meetings to provide guidance and direction at the request of the committees, and a close relationship with the department was generally encouraged. In a way, the native welfare committees of the 1960s replaced the local protector system by acting as a local conduit between the department and Aboriginal people—usually reserve dwellers. In any event, protectors had been abolished with the assent of the completely overhauled *Native Welfare Act 1963*. Native welfare committees could assist with making improvements on reserves; assist with employment; hold film nights; organise sports clubs and light entertainment; set up kindergartens; disseminate departmental information materials (for example, assimilation propaganda); and run workshops in sewing, cooking and other practical fields. Importantly, committees were promoting Aboriginal social acceptance and advancement in their respective localities. The department recommended that committees focus on short-term achievable outcomes rather than too grand plans. While most committee members would have been motivated by the wish to help Aboriginal people, the department was well aware that overzealous 'do-gooders' could trigger resentment by Aboriginal people if white Australians attempted to lecture reserve dwellers on every aspect of their lives without seeking their points of view. As the 1960s progressed, the department advised native welfare committees that Aboriginal people should be strongly encouraged to actively participate and become effective officers of the organisation. 'If they were merely onlookers', it was argued in an instruction manual for native welfare committees, 'no useful purpose will be achieved and, in fact, only harm can result'.[33]

York's Native Welfare Committee was likely responsible for getting Abbey, MLC, involved, as it had offered to do the necessary work to mitigate the health risk associated with the ceilings of the two Geraldton-type houses on the reserve. When the busy bee was organised in March 1962, the committee also undertook to paint the houses with paint supplied by the department in six shades of green, blue and grey.[34] In October 1961, Daisy Negus, who was also the president of York's branch of the CWA, reported that she and a certain Ms Pavlovich were running a dress-making class for Aboriginal girls and women at the York Youth Club. Around the same time, York's Methodist Ladies Guild decided to donate 'yellow Indian head cloth' to Aboriginal homes for curtains, following a suggestion by Reverend Sullivan.[35] These are just a few examples from the available records of settler-Australian community members making an effort towards increasing inclusiveness.

The reader may recall that (see chapter 7.01), in 1955, Commissioner Middleton had reservations about providing reserve housing, arguing that it might undermine 'assimilation', as Aboriginal people could be shifted to reserves instead of being provided with town housing. Six years later, his concerns proved to be somewhat warranted in the case of York. During a municipal council meeting, it was discussed that complaints had been received about two Aboriginal families camping on Osnaburg Road. Councillor F. Ashbolt moved that the matter be passed on to the Native Welfare Committee and it was pointed out that, on the reserve, only two houses were available for Aboriginal people. Council then approached the Minister for Native Welfare requesting to have further housing erected on the reserve with a view to shifting the families camping on Osnaburg Road to the reserve. The minister agreed to give the matter consideration in the next financial year and, as already discussed (see chapter 7.01), two more houses were completed in 1963. However, the two families living on Osnaburg Road were still there in October 1963, and they were ordered to improve their camps, but no further word was spoken about shifting the camps.[36] What is evident though, is that segregation was still an accepted option for some townsfolk and the Native Welfare Committee was viewed by some people as a vehicle to 'assist' Aboriginal people to potentially find accommodation on the reserve outside of town instead of assisting with promoting and securing town housing.

Reverend Sullivan appears to have been the driving force behind the committee in the first few months; however, he was transferred to Dowerin in January 1962 and was replaced by Reverend Alan J. Rankine, who was transferred to York from a mission in Arnhem Land. A few months prior to his transfer, Sullivan was granted a weekly honorarium of £1 to cover the expenses for his welfare work on the recommendation of the acting district welfare officer—who appreciated Sullivan's work, as the officer was apparently unable to travel from Kellerberrin to York as much as was deemed desirable. Rankine filled Sullivan's secretary position within the Native Welfare Committee, initially continued Sullivan's work and would eventually also receive an honorarium for his reportedly extensive contribution. Having been a plumber by trade, he also proposed to lay water to both of the (then only two) reserve houses and the department agreed to supply the materials. By June 1962, this work had been completed and it appears that the committee ceased to function around the same time.[37] On 28 February, the *Northam Advertiser* reported the first 'annual' meeting of York's Native Welfare Committee, which suggests that the committee had initially planned to stay active for a while. A representative from the

South West Mission based in Northam was also present and talked about the work conducted in Northam. The news piece commented:

[The] Native Welfare Council in York has only been functioning a short time, and already are bringing to public notice the conditions on the York Reserve. With more support from a larger cross-section of the community, the work of the Council could be expended, and the excellent example of the Northam Council may be followed.[38]

The next ordinary meeting was set for 18 April but the local newspaper did not write a single further word about York's Native Welfare Committee and, following approval for the plumbing works to be carried out, the committee was also not mentioned again in the departmental file concerning the York Reserve. At this 'annual' meeting in February, it was reported that the Aboriginal people who lived in the two cottages were 'looking after them very well, and both have gardens and lawns, and all the water for these has to be carried in buckets from the stand tap'.[39] Given that water was then laid to the homes by Reverend Rankine, and ceilings were also installed, the committee may have decided that there was not much more need for their assistance, or the Aboriginal reserve dwellers may have indicated that they did not require any further help. Simultaneously, the committee may have formed the belief that other Aboriginal people in York did not require or appreciate the committee's work either. The committee certainly appears to have delivered short-term achievable outcomes, as suggested by the Department of Native Welfare—results that the state failed to provide in a timely manner.

While the committee in York was not mentioned again in the *Northam Advertiser*, Northam's Native Welfare Committee continued to be frequently discussed throughout the 1960s into the 1970s. Given that the *Northam Advertiser* had in its title written that it incorporated the *York Chronicle* and, therefore, claimed to represent York matters, it appears reasonable to conclude that activities of York's Native Welfare Committee would have likely been reported in the local news. One marked difference between Northam and York was that, until the late-

1960s, all Aboriginal housing provided by the state was located on the Northam Reserve. Northam did not have purpose-built houses in town during the 1950s as York did and, therefore, the conditions on the local reserve were more crowded than was the case in York, and more change was called for.[40] The exact fate of York's Native Welfare Committee is not known to this author but it likely dissolved either in the second half of 1962 or early 1963, because it was still mentioned in the department's annual report for the year ending on 30 June 1963 but was no longer in the following year's report.[41] Reverend Rankine remained in York until the end of 1965. News articles suggest that he had developed a keen interest in more traditionally inclined Aboriginal peoples and their culture and art when working in Arnhem Land. While Rankine may have been culturally more interested in northern Australia, departmental records indicate that he nevertheless remained engaged in assisting Aboriginal people in York, as he was one of only a dozen protectors state-wide who were recommended for a special ministerial letter of recommendation for their outstanding service shortly before protectors were practically phased out in 1964.[42]

Throughout the remainder of the 1960s, there were also no further reports in the *Northam Advertiser* about any activities of other groups based in York who may have provided support, engaged in social activities or advocated for Aboriginal people. This does not necessarily mean that there were none; however, their activities were not deemed newsworthy, either because they kept a modest profile or because York's local news reporter held a negative bias towards Aboriginal news devoid of sensationalist content. That there was some interest in Aboriginal matters is, for example, evidenced through the minute books of York's Methodist Ladies Guild. In August 1967, it was noted that the 'Ladies Guild were invited to hear Mr. Watson at a S.C.F. [Save the Children Fund] members meeting at the school on the "Aborigines & home management"'.[43] This suggests that Aboriginal affairs were certainly part of the ongoing discourse of certain sections of York's settler-Australian population.

7.03 National policy of assimilation

Newly arising community interest in York, including the formation of the Native Welfare Committee, had occurred around a time when the push for integration or absorption of Aboriginal people into predominantly Anglo–white Australian society gained a new nation-wide impetus through the federal *policy of assimilation*, which was agreed in January 1961 by ministers with Aboriginal portfolios from all states and territories, as well as federal representatives. Consistent with Western Australia's own assimilation policy, the new national policy stated that all Aboriginal people were:

> expected eventually to attain the same manner of living as other Australians and to live as members of a single Australian community enjoying the same responsibilities, observing the same customs and influenced by the same beliefs, hopes and loyalties as other Australians.[44]

To achieve socioeconomic equality, conditional to the above-cited demand for cultural homogeneity, it was stated that it was necessary to implement special temporary measures, which included advances in the fields of housing, employment, education, health, welfare supervision and other areas. As it was, Western Australia was already implementing a range of proposed methods, albeit with limited financial resources that were inadequate to fully put theory into practice. At this stage, though, the new national policy served only as a guiding principle but did not provide for Commonwealth finances. This new national policy may have confirmed Western Australian policy and accelerated pre-existing practices, but it arguably also created renewed awareness within the non-Aboriginal population. Western Australia's state policy of assimilation had been heatedly debated in the press since its inception in 1948 (as discussed further above) but now it was also a Commonwealth matter, which may have encouraged more people to rethink their attitudes towards Aboriginal people or to become more active if already positively inclined. Therefore, it does not appear accidental that York's Native Welfare Committee formed a short time after the national policy of assimilation had been formulated.[45]

7.04 Electricity and other improvements on the reserve

By the time that all four houses on the York Reserve had been completed in November 1963, they were still without electricity and, therefore, without proper lighting during the hours of darkness. Electricity was initially not planned to be provided for reserve houses. Until 1964, it had been departmental policy to restrict the provision of electricity for the use of overhead area lighting only, if reserves were connected to the electricity network at all. York's reserve was not.[46] Most settler-Australian townsfolk had been living with electricity for about half a century. The first electric light at York was switched on in June 1903 at Dinsdale's Mill and, five years later, a private company was commissioned to roll out electricity to consumers and businesses.[47] When the intermediate-type and standard State Housing Commission homes were erected in the 1950s in York, they were all connected to electricity.[48]

In April 1964, the then Minister for Native Welfare, E.H.M. Lewis, announced in an internal memo that reserve dwellings, for which rental was paid, should be fitted with one light point wherever electricity had been connected to the reserve. Two months later, he went public and announced that transitional houses on all reserves were to receive lighting as soon as possible. Under the headline 'Mark of a New Deal', Perth's *Daily News* reported that an 'ordinary household electric light bulb is the symbol of the state government's new approach to the education of Aborigines'.[49] For reserve children to be able to do their homework, electric light was to be provided, to place Aboriginal children on an 'equal footing with the children from white families'.[50] That Lewis presented this line of argument was certainly not coincidental because he held the ministerial portfolios for both 'native welfare' and also education from 1962 until 1971.[51]

As we have witnessed earlier (for example see chapter 6.04), to the consecutive departments dealing with Aboriginal affairs, the meaning of phrases like 'as soon as possible' often lacked any sense of urgency.

It took approximately three years for electricity to be connected to the York Reserve's homes.[52] The slow progress was down to state-wide delays. First, there was the question whether to provide power points to reserve houses and it was proposed that all reserve homes should be fitted with one power point for each house and a light in each room, which would be operated with a coin slot-meter attached to each dwelling. Then, there was discussion about the voltage to be provided. It was decided that dwellings would be connected with only 32 volts of electricity, which could not be used to run any appliances but worked for lighting. Communal facilities, however, would be connected with 250 volts of electricity. The reasons for this decision were initially based on costs but then turned to safety concerns—at least on paper. As the reserve dwellings were constructed with iron cladding, it was considered dangerous to supply electricity to these buildings at 250 volts.

The assumed social status of reserve dwellers was also weighted into the department's risk assessment. Not providing 250 volts to the dwellings was deemed a protective measure to save reserve dwellers from their own alleged incapabilities. In July 1965, the policy for the provision of electricity to reserves across Western Australia had been finalised, fifteen months after Minister Lewis announced that electricity would be provided as soon as possible. Although the idea of coin-operated meters was scrapped, time switches were to be provided for all lighting in dwellings and communal areas. As the department had decided it would carry the running costs, it limited the time that electricity would be provided. Whether intended or not, it thus continued to infantilise Aboriginal people living on reserves by controlling their behaviours through the time-restricted provision of electricity.[53]

Moving forward to April 1966, works still had not begun. The State Housing Commission had initially been asked to carry out installations but turned out not to be qualified and the Public Works Department took on the job. Reportedly, discussions between all three departments took place over the best part of a year. Then, the Department of Native Welfare accepted a tender in July 1966 for the work to be carried out for $1,148 by W.F. & H.M. Grafton of Northam (the Australian dollar had been introduced only a few months earlier[54]). The bill was paid on 25 May 1967, which suggests that electricity started to flow on the York

Reserve around that time, coinciding with the *1967 Referendum* (which will be briefly discussed further below in chapter 7.07).[55] Other improvements on the reserves were initially desired in the early 1960s, but were deemed too costly. These improvements included, for example, the installation of fly-wires and coin-operated telephones.[56] When the Western Australian branch of the United Nations Association of Australia publicly criticised the state of the reserves, the department admitted that it intentionally kept reserve facilities to a bare minimum to discourage Aboriginal people from staying on reserves permanently, as it was not desirable that 'they became permanent segregated townships'.[57]

However, prior to the installation of electricity, one arguably important improvement was made. Hot water systems were installed at the ablution block in York and all other reserves in the Central District during the financial year 1965–1966. Prior to that, the showers erected in 1963 only operated with cold water. The wood-fuelled system was built by the Central District's mobile works unit, which was operated by a 'husband and wife' team of the Church of England's South West Mission, based on the Northam Reserve.[58]

From late 1964, Reverend Bertram P. Wrightson and Mrs Wrightson ran this unit and also visited York regularly for 'welfare work' on the reserve and in town, once or twice per fortnight. When the couple was transferred to Kellerberrin after May 1967, there was no replacement and this kind of mission work appears to have ceased. Reverend Wrightson criticised the department in his final quarterly report for insufficient engagement by departmental officers, as the missionaries had only limited abilities to address the overwhelming welfare needs in their district. However, Wrightson also appeared to be disappointed with the limited gains they had made in their spiritual ambitions. The Wrightson's work was sometimes concurrent and sometimes combined with that of Northam's Native Welfare Committee, but only the missionaries ventured to York for welfare-related work.[59]

7.05 Drinking rights

During the 1960s, state and federal assimilation policies combined provided an ideological momentum for the Department of Native Welfare, in tandem with civic interest groups, to push for the incremental abolishment of one of the last restrictive pieces of legislation affecting Aboriginal people in Western Australia. This was about having the right to access and consume alcohol in the same manner as every other Western Australian resident and visitor alike. As mentioned earlier (see chapters 5.03 and 6.11), large segments of white Western Australian society suffered from an ingrained angst in relation to Aboriginal people and alcohol and simultaneously refused to acknowledge that, when occurring, alcohol-related antisocial behaviour was often the result of trauma caused by some 130 years of occupation, oppression and repression. Instead of addressing the root causes and aiming to heal the wounds that had been causing trauma, settler-Australian society was looking for short-term solutions and mostly fought the symptoms of the trauma. Therefore, the Western Australian State Government agencies and local authorities sought to control Aboriginal people's behaviour in relation to alcohol through the enforcement of harsh and racist prohibition legislation that exclusively targeted Aboriginal people. Further, many settler-Australians would always find an argument, at any given point in time, as to why Aboriginal people were not yet ready to be permitted legal access to alcohol. Historian Russel McGregor argued that, for Aboriginal people, the gaining of drinking rights was more than just having legal access to alcohol, it was also a matter of social inclusion, particularly for men:

> In Australia in the 1950s and 1960s most alcohol was consumed by men in public bars in ritual affirmations of the national ideal of mateship. Aboriginal exclusion from these rituals symbolically excluded them from the community of the (male) nation, and Aboriginal people were acutely aware of the implied insult. Their demand for drinking rights was not so much a demand for access to alcoholic beverages ... as a

demand to 'breast the bar' in demonstration of their equality
with other Australians.[60]

Despite widespread prejudices, non-Aboriginal civic support in the lead
up to the change of this type of inhibitive legislation was not unheard
of. The WA Native Welfare Council (Inc.) had been advocating for
drinking rights since 1956, pointing at statistics it had obtained that
showed that ninety per cent of Aboriginal persons in Fremantle Prison
(Western Australia's main prison at the time[61]), were incarcerated due
to illegal access to alcohol. In the print media, debates took place about
whether to grant drinking rights and citizenship rights, for a few years
before the change took place.[62] 1 July 1964 was to be the date that
Aboriginal people in the South West Land Division were no longer
subject to alcohol restrictions. On that day, a proclamation under the
recently amended *Licensing Act 1963* came into effect, which removed
Aboriginal people of the South West Land Division from the otherwise
extant prohibition. The Aboriginal population in the South West Land
Division was considered more socially advanced than populations in
other regions of the state. The department had also conducted an
educational campaign prior to 1 July in regard to the 'responsibilities of
citizenship'. Simultaneously, the completely overhauled *Native Welfare
Act 1963* came into effect, which no longer had any references to
alcohol.[63]

The Minister for Native Welfare, E.H.M. Lewis, and H.W. Gayfer,
MLA Avon, attended a weekly meeting of the York Rotary Club in early
April 1964, campaigning for support of the upcoming change in
legislation. Lewis ensured the present Rotarians that Aboriginal people
would be educated on their newly gained rights and responsibilities but
he also pointed out that many existing problems relating to Aboriginal
people and alcohol were due to the legislation that was about to be
amended, which had resulted in 'furtive methods' being practiced by
Aboriginal people in the past to obtain alcohol. Inferring prevalent
double standards in public discourse, Lewis appealed that the white
population set an example, with the object of guiding Aboriginal people
'in how to drink in moderation and in how to conduct themselves while
so drinking'.[64]

Lewis obviously anticipated resistance from sections of the settler-Australian community. An incident that occurred a month earlier in a hotel in York may have been related to the issue of accepting Aboriginal people in the white Australian hotel landscape. The *Northam Advertiser* reported that on Tuesday 10 March 1964, police were called to a local hotel where a man had been 'causing trouble'.[65] It is not clear whether hotel staff had asked the man to leave before police attended or whether only the police requested that he leave the premises but, on police arrival, he reportedly assaulted Relieving Sergeant R.H. Varney and then ran off. The man was later arrested at his home in the northern part of town. This first news article did not mention that the man was Aboriginal, two follow-on articles did. All three news articles did not report anything about what kind of 'trouble' this man had caused and it did not state anything about being intoxicated. It is quite possible that this man was behaving inappropriately for reasons unrelated to drinking rights and being Aboriginal. The news article is not clear. However, the silence regarding the reasons for the police being called and eventually assaulted is suspicious. This Aboriginal man had obtained conditional citizenship in 1960 in Kellerberrin and, before that, he had held an exemption certificate since 1955. Therefore, legally, he had every right to be on the hotel premises. It does not appear unlikely that this man's presence at the hotel had been challenged because he was Aboriginal, to which he might have taken offence and reacted adversely. The cause may have been the publican or a patron. In the end, the man was charged with four offences, namely, refusing to leave a licensed premises, resisting arrest, assaulting a public officer and escaping from custody. He was granted bail but was unable to obtain £10 personal bail undertaking for each charge, and stayed in gaol until being sentenced a month later. He pleaded 'not guilty' to all charges but was found guilty and sentenced to a total term of four months' imprisonment and fines by two local justices of the peace, R.M. Pemberton and W.A. Fricker.[66] A major weakness of the archival materials available is that they are mostly silent on the daily mocking, racist slurs and disrespectful, belittling and condescending behaviours to which Aboriginal people of all ages were often subjected. The inferred suggestion that the foregoing incident may have had a racist antecedent is based on the fact that in many country hotels, a 'colour bar' existed, whereby Aboriginal people were either not served altogether, were only sold takeaway alcohol, or were served in segregated areas. While not lawful, this informal colour bar reportedly remained well into the 1970s in some localities.[67]

The South West Land Division, including York, was bracing itself for 1 July 1964. In retrospective, the *Bulletin* summed up the contentions held by some sections of the settler-Australian population who had been anticipating that universal drinking rights would bring 'rape, mayhem, street battles and the collapse of rural life'.[68] The *Northam Advertiser*'s headline 'July 1 Quiet at York' and the following article confirm that similar sentiments had been held in York:

> The significance of July 1 was that it was the occasion in York District when all coloured people were granted permission to use full hotel facilities.
>
> Contrary to some opinion, there was no trouble at all, in fact, after the day's trading had ended, hotelkeepers reported that they had entertained none but the usual customers. The importance of the new deal for these original Australians has no doubt been appreciated by them and full care has been taken by the Native Welfare Department to ensure that they completely understand the benefits it entitles them to, as well as the penalties for transgression.
>
> General opinion in this town now holds that the problem is one that has been largely magnified in discussion and that breaches will be rarely encountered.[69]

Whether 'general opinion' in York really changed within the scope of two days is questionable. However, neither on numerous departmental records available to this author nor in the local newspaper were any instances recorded when local publicans refused to serve Aboriginal people in York after 1 July 1964. If refusals did occur in York, these were seemingly not reported. Either way, from mid-1965, the department encouraged Aboriginal people to lodge complaints with the police should they not be served in a hotel, following an episode at

Ongerup in the Great Southern region that gathered much publicity at the time.[70]

While the general alcohol prohibition was lifted in the South West Land Division by 1 July 1964, this did not apply to Aboriginal reserves. Under section 24 of the Native Welfare Regulations, which was a subordinate legislation to the *Native Welfare Act 1954/1963*, an Aboriginal person taking alcohol onto a reserve or being drunk on a reserve was liable for prosecution. Penalties varied from fines to terms of imprisonment of between three and twelve months. These regulations were also changed in 1964. Thenceforth, the penalties were reduced to fines or a maximum of twenty-one days of imprisonment.[71]

Only months before the change took effect in July 1964, an Aboriginal man with conditional citizenship rights was sentenced to three months' imprisonment with hard labour by justices of the peace P.M.A. Glass and A. Edmonds Hill for being drunk on the York Reserve. This was the same man who we have encountered earlier (see chapter 5.07) and who had been sentenced to eleven terms of imprisonment between 1957 and 1962 for alcohol-related 'offences.' In historical hindsight it looks very much as if this man had been made an example of in relation to excessive alcohol consumption and white Australian behavioural expectations. Then, in September 1964, after the change in the regulations had taken effect, this man was sentenced to the maximum penalty of twenty-one days' imprisonment for being drunk on a reserve, as well as three months' concurrent imprisonment for being declared a habitual drunk.[72]

One may ask the question whether this man had been behaving in a threatening manner towards reserve residents and the police merely used alcohol-related charges to protect reserve residents. While this man may have displayed problematic behaviours towards other Aboriginal people, it appears unlikely that these convictions under section 24 of the regulations were intended for the safety of other Aboriginal individuals. First, the sentences handed down were excessive. One night in lock up to sober up would have served the purpose of removing an unwelcome guest. Second, in September 1964, on the same occasion, there was another Aboriginal man charged by police. However, this man was convicted for being disorderly on a native reserve and for wilful damage by destroying louvre parts to the value of £1, for which he was sentenced to terms of imprisonment of one month and three months, respectively.[73] This indicates that the first man was likely 'only' drunk as police clearly could have charged him with disorderly behaviour if this had been the case. Last, police had a standing order to patrol the reserve regularly, which occurred usually on weekends. George Kickett, who grew up on the reserve during the 1950s and 1960s, commented that alcohol-infused violence did occur on the reserve occasionally and that police were sometimes called by a neighbour who would hear a commotion going on. However, this was an exception, not a rule, and Kickett considered the reserve generally to be a safe place. There are other instances on record from this period when different Aboriginal people were charged for disorderly offending on the reserve. Therefore, we may conclude from these three points that the sentencing to terms of imprisonment solely for being under the influence of alcohol on the reserve was a vicious form of population control against the backdrop of the assimilation policy and expectations of how Aboriginal people should behave within their ascribed submissive role.[74]

In mid-1966, there were a few instances of civic advocacy for the removal of the alcohol prohibition on reserves. First, Justice of the Peace J.N. Berger of Katanning raised the potential dilemma he might face on the bench if police were to charge an Aboriginal person who legally became drunk in town and then went peacefully home to the local reserve. If there were other Aboriginal people causing a 'fracas' on the reserve, Berger went on, the 'peaceful drunk' may be caught up in the ensuing tumult during police attendance, without having committed any wrongdoing. The acting Minister for Native Welfare replied to Berger that removing the alcohol restrictions on reserves would not conform with the department's long-term policy. Because reserves were not designed to be the permanent home of the occupants, it was hoped that the alcohol restrictions would encourage Aboriginal people to secure permanent housing in towns. It was feared that if reserves became too congenial then their existence would be perpetuated. The minister also commented that a police officer charging a sleeping Aboriginal person would be very 'officious' but, if this did occur, it was suggested that

277

Berger, being a justice of the peace, had the power to be lenient towards the peaceful drunk.[75]

Within the same month, the Great Southern town Gnowangerup's Native Welfare Committee and the shire council sent separate letters advocating for the removal of alcohol restrictions on reserves. Their reasoning was slightly different to that of Berger. Essentially, both envisioned that legal consumption of alcohol on reserves would lessen the presence of alcohol-consuming Aboriginal people in town. Therefore, potentially problematic behaviour due to excessive alcohol consumption would mostly be out of sight and out of mind. Minister Lewis replied that he was also not satisfied with the current position; however, he would need to make a very careful investigation into the whole question, as he needed to be satisfied that any steps to lift the restrictions would not lead to some unforeseen and undesirable results.[76] Then in August 1966, the Western Australian Division of the Liberal Party, who was, at the time, in government, forwarded a resolution, which had arisen at its annual conference:

> That following the granting of full citizenship rights to natives and in particular drinking rights in the South West Land Division, the Government be requested to permit natives the dignity of consuming liquor on the Reserve which is their place of residence.[77]

The Liberal Party received the same answer as the civic bodies at Gnowangerup. On first sight, this resolution appears to be of laudable intent. However, the way it is worded may also suggest that the authors of this resolution imagined Aboriginal people in general as reserve residents and not necessarily as town residents. At the usual slow pace of change in relation to policy matters concerning Aboriginal people in Western Australia, Minister Lewis's 'careful investigation' took another four years to result in change being implemented. Only by June 1970 had section 24 been removed from the Native Welfare Regulations and alcohol and drunkenness on reserves were no longer deemed punishable breaches.[78]

7.06 York housing provisions—the remainder of the 1960s and Narrogin's calling

As discussed earlier (see chapter 6.09), 1954 witnessed the last recorded acts of 'active' resistance to Aboriginal housing in York. This included a petition of residents agitating against an Aboriginal family being housed in their neighbourhood and a deputation of local government officials and members of Parliament being sent to the Minister for Housing when the municipal council learned of further housing being built in a part of town that council members deemed unsuitable. In both cases, the instigators of the protests were chided for their attitude and informed that their agitation was inappropriate and would bear no fruit. While this type of public resistance to Aboriginal housing in York does not seem to have been repeated after 1954, the general attitude in town was not necessarily one of unconditional social inclusiveness thenceforth. Indeed, there were further acts of passive resistance and complaints voiced by the shire council from 1965 into the 1970s. Triggers for the renewed opposition were at least twofold. First, only by the mid-1960s was there a renewed focus on Aboriginal housing to be provided in the townsite of York, in particular, transitional-type houses. And second, the shire council became somewhat stirred up in response to an agitating circular letter from Narrogin.

The department had sent plans of the newly designed Type 64 transitional homes (TN 3 401 to TN 3 403) to the municipal council of Narrogin, which resulted in this council carrying a number of resolutions at its meeting on 19 January 1965. These resolutions were to be 'circularised to all councils controlling towns of any size'[79] in the South West Land Division. Narrogin Council was complaining that the Department of Native Affairs had promised better transitional houses than the Geraldton Type 5 house, whereas it found that the new Type 64 homes were still substandard and would depreciate surrounding properties. It was also stated that Narrogin Council thought it unfair for country towns to carry the burden of absorbing Aboriginal transitional dwellings and that country towns should not be expected to have further transitional dwellings erected until such time that these types of homes had been proportionally constructed, on equal terms, in the metropolitan areas and large country towns. Furthermore, the town blocks required for transitional houses to be erected should only be recommended by the local authorities if a better type of home than Type 64 was to be provided. The last point was important as it had been departmental policy to obtain approval from local authorities for any townsites on which Aboriginal transitional/intermediate houses were to be built since the mid-1950s protests in relation to town housing.[80]

The Narrogin resolutions were promptly placed on York's municipal council meeting agenda later in January. Reportedly a discussion ensued and the mayor, P.M.A. Glass, noted that, in previous years, the issue with substandard houses had been a matter for contention. The town clerk, C.J. Ashbolt, supported the Narrogin circular and commented that the type of house 'required' by Narrogin Council would be at least a better version than those constructed on the local reserve. However, other opinions than these two were not reported in the local newspaper and the York Municipal Council's official stance on this matter remains somewhat unclear. It did not send a letter to the department in support of the Narrogin circular, as some other local authorities had done (Collie, Manjimup, Moora, Goomalling, Brookton and Koorda). Narrogin claimed that twenty-seven towns were supportive of its resolutions. Apparent inaction by York's council probably occurred because York had gone through a stage of active resistance to transitional housing in the mid-1950s when it was told, in no uncertain terms, to get used to the idea of transitional houses in town. Additionally, York's municipal council and the former road board district (already a shire since 1961) were just about to be merged into the Shire of York on 15 March and, therefore, councillors were probably preoccupied with administrative tasks in relation to this amalgamation process.[81]

While York's local authority seemingly did not make any public statements on the housing matter, Northam's municipal council expressed in late March its support for the resolutions as reported in the *Northam Advertiser*. This suggests that any motions carried by York's local authority would also have been reported, given that interest in the matter was clearly present. Ironically, when Northam pledged support, Narrogin had already somewhat backpedalled and agreed for some transitional homes to be erected in town under the condition that they be placed 'only in a State Rental Homes area and not adjacent to State purchase homes or privately owned land or buildings, provided they are clad on the outside with weatherboard dado and asbestos above'.[82]

In late May 1965, Minister Lewis went on a tour visiting sixteen country towns across the South West Land Division that had been earmarked for a total of fifty-six transitional homes. On his return, he claimed that he had convinced all visited localities of the transitional housing scheme.[83] Crucial for his success was that he had ensured the local authorities that transitional houses were to be built on the outskirts of town, and that families who proved satisfactory would later be moved into standard State Housing Commission homes. For the best part of 1965, transitional houses in country towns of the South West Land Division were a frequently discussed topic in various newspapers and on ABC news. In November, Minister Lewis publicly announced that he was considering reversing the existing policy of seeking consent from local authorities, as there were still some authorities, including two metropolitan ones, that kept refusing to allocate blocks for transitional homes.[84]

Consent was sought to develop 'harmonious' relationships with local authorities and neighbourhoods but it had never been a mandated requirement. While the department knew that its Aboriginal housing policy was more likely to succeed if it was not superimposed, local authorities were also aware that they could not act in an openly segregationist manner, as they had done in the past. For example, Narrogin Council had placed the emphasis of its complaints on the alleged depreciation of neighbourhoods due to substandard homes. However, as it had brought up the cliched country–city dichotomy, it appears rather likely that the depreciation argument was either a pretext to disguise complaints about being expected to accommodate further Aboriginal families in town—or that this was of at least equal importance to Narrogin Council. Given that Narrogin and other town and shire councils, including that of York, would have been well aware that agitating solely against an increase of Aboriginal housing in towns would not have brought any anticipated results in light of federal and state assimilation policies and associated opinions expressed in the press, complaining about the threat of financial losses resulting from the transitional houses' lower building standard may have seemed a politically safer option.

While local authorities in the mid-1960s appeared to have been less inclined to openly state that Aboriginal people were not welcome in, or suited for, certain areas in town, the *Northam Advertiser* did not make a secret of its apprehensive opinion. In December 1965, it published an article about a transitional house (Type 79A) in York that had been condemned. The article's style of writing carried connotations of vicious satisfaction when reporting about this failed housing 'experiment'. The author appears to have sided with supporters of the Narrogin resolutions and the agitators of the mid-1950s protests, and they clearly imagined that Aboriginal transitional housing belonged to the outskirts of town:

> Despite the appeals of ratepayers and electors several years ago, natives were housed in new homes in the central portion of the town of York.
>
> That this experiment in integration has been a failure, is proved by the low tender that has recently been accepted for the demolition and removal of a house in Grey St. Dirty, ill-kept, with stained and filthy walls, the house was condemned as being unfit for human habitation and this was agreed to at one stage by a Minister for Native Welfare, after it had housed native families for only a few years.[85]

For the reminder of the 1960s, this was the last news article in the *Northam Advertiser* that openly questioned the physical integration of Aboriginal people into York's townscape. However, for this period, there were not many news reports concerning Aboriginal people in York to begin with, whereas Aboriginal matters concerning Northam had ongoing coverage.[86]

In February 1966, the Department of Native Welfare approached the York Shire Council, seeking its opinion in relation to proposed transitional houses in residential areas of the town, as it had done a year earlier in Narrogin. Councillors requested some time to consider and to secure the views of rate payers. The department then provided plans of the Type 64 houses for council's perusal. At the March council meeting, a sub-committee was formed to investigate the proposal and to consult with the Member for Avon Harry Walter 'Mick' Gayfer, MLA, before replying to the department. The sub-committee consisted of councillors W.H. Robinson, C. Reynolds and C.H. Lee. Robinson, who had been chairman of the York Road Board for twenty-six years before amalgamation, was a peculiar choice for this sub-committee.[87] The reader may recall that (see chapter 4.06), back in October 1950, Robinson had become verbally abusive towards Departmental Officer McLarty when McLarty tried to discuss the integration of Aboriginal people and the underlying assimilation policy. The reason for this outburst was reportedly that Robinson deeply resented the very idea of Aboriginal people living within white spaces. Then, in 1953, a departmental officer attempted to mediate between Robinson and an Aboriginal contract employee, who claimed that Robinson was underpaying him. The officer reported that Robinson was known in York for 'sharp practice' and that the Aboriginal person seemed to have rightfully claimed to have been cheated. This officer also reported being subjected to verbal abuse by Robinson.[88] We mentioned above (see chapter 6.04) that Robinson attended a road boards conference in 1957, where he suggested that Aboriginal people take up small farm properties. Robinson's idea was to close down the York Reserve by shifting Aboriginal people further out onto country blocks, as opposed to letting them move into town. The foregoing examples suggest that having a vocal Robinson on this sub-committee in relation to transitional houses in residential areas could have resulted in a rather biased assessment. Of course, it is not impossible that Robinson underwent a change of heart over the following years and developed a more positive and inclusive attitude towards Aboriginal people. However, it is unlikely that it would have been a complete change in perspective—it may have been, instead, a shift towards indifference, as suggested by the committee's lack of action.

By mid-June 1966, the department lodged a renewed request seeking council's opinion as the sub-committee had seemingly failed to investigate the matter. If anything, this may further suggest that

Robinson was not overly enthusiastic about Aboriginal housing in town. A new sub-committee was formed consisting of councillors Robinson, N.C. Reynolds and S.C. Irvin. This time, the sub-committee swiftly approached Gayfer, who asked the department about the future housing plans for York, as the committee was to report back to the shire council the following week. Minister Lewis advised Gayfer that two further Type 3 houses were planned on the York Reserve for the 1966–1967 financial year (which, as we have learned earlier, were never built), in addition to the existing four houses. Lewis also advised that there were currently 'no standard transitional (Type 64) houses planned but that approval for sites for this type was being sought in anticipation of the time when the department could confidentially promote the reserve natives'.[89] The *Northam Advertiser* did not report any subsequent council discussion about the outcome of the investigation, which may serve as an indicator that the council was not particularly concerned at this point, given that the department had no concrete plans as yet. In fact, there are no records about new transitional housing in York town for the reminder of the 1960s.

Gayfer's comment suggests that the families on the York Reserve were not socially advanced enough or 'ready' to move into town as the department was allegedly not yet able to 'confidentially promote' such a move. This does not say anything about the reserve dwellers' own wishes. It may have been a conscious choice at the time to remain on the reserve for various reasons. According to the Wrightson missionaries' census, taken in mid-1965, York had a permanent Aboriginal population of just under 100 persons. 30 persons were living on the reserve and 66 were living 'off-reserve'.[90] Moving from a communal social environment of thirty people situated on a ten-acre block with river access onto a more or less isolated dwelling built for a nuclear family, surrounded by non-Aboriginal town folk who might have been prejudiced against an Aboriginal presence, may not have been that appealing for everyone concerned after all.

The department reported in October 1966 that the number of transitional houses was declining in the current financial year. Despite Minister Lewis having threatened a few times that he would disregard local authorities' wishes if they did not cooperate, the department was still sticking to the policy of seeking approval from local government bodies. However, it was reported that a number of local authorities were refusing permission for the department to erect transitional homes in their jurisdictions, which meant that the standard transitional housing program (step two out of three) was '*tailing off.*' The decline of the transitional housing program occurred when, reportedly for the first time, finances had been made available for all requested housing propositions (thirty-six in the entire state). The department indicated that there would be less of an issue with local authorities if more money was available to build standard State Housing Commission homes instead of transitional houses. Whether York was one of those local authorities who refused to give permission in 1966 is not evident from the records. Though a number of such localities had standard transitional houses erected on reserves, instead of being erected on the outskirts of towns, this was not the case in York.[91] Increased finances for housing would eventually become available through the Commonwealth, following a successful referendum that sought to remove racist and inhibitive sections of the Australian Constitution.

7.07 The 1967 Referendum

On 27 May 1967, a federal referendum was held that was to determine whether to change two sections of the Australian Constitution that related to Aboriginal people. The referendum asked whether section 51, clause xxvi, and section 127 should be removed. Section 51, clause xxvi prevented the federal government from making special laws in relation to Aboriginal people and section 127 dictated that Aboriginal people were not to be officially counted in national censuses. The referendum was the result of a decade of campaigning, which originated in the eastern states, driven by the Federal Council for the Advancement of Aborigines and Torres Strait Islanders (FCAATSI). The referendum and its preceding campaign were timely situated within the broader social justice movements that occurred in Western societies during the 1960s. During this period, 'the "big" questions about the value of humanity became important'.[92] Simplified, the referendum campaigners asked people to 'Vote Yes for Aborigines' by removing racist clauses from

Australia's Constitution. The referendum was unable to change racist state legislation and was, in many ways, arguably more of symbolic and affirmative importance than able to bring about instant practical changes—but not entirely.[93]

The 1960s activism was built on a period of increasing awareness in relation to Aboriginal matters. During the early 1950s, the United Nations' Universal Human Rights Charter had entered Australian public discourse, in particular, in relation to Australia's position in the world. The situation of Aboriginal people was increasingly discussed and viewed in a global context as Australia received international criticism for the treatment of its Aboriginal peoples. International pressure intensified in the 1960s, while domestically, awareness increasingly turned to activism.[94] Therefore, concerns for Aboriginal matters among settler-Australian society would have had compassionate origins on one side of the spectrum and self-serving incentives for image protection on the other. Although Western Australia was on the geographic and political periphery of the Australian continent, political awareness and activism also induced change in the west. For example, in relation to activism, organisations like the WA Native Welfare Council (Inc.) frequently advocated for legislative and policy changes in favour of freedom and equality for Aboriginal people. Citizen interest groups such as native welfare committees based their 'helping hand' approaches on increased awareness. Slowly, paternalism started to make way for emancipating activism. For example, in June 1963, the WA Native Welfare Council (Inc.) changed its name to the Aboriginal Advancement Council of WA in line with other states. This change of name was announced by stating that Aboriginal people did not like either terms—'Aborigines' or 'natives'—but that 'they' would prefer the former over the latter. This example is symbolic of a growing change of attitude towards Aboriginal affairs. Instead of deciding what was best for 'their' own good, an increasing number of settler-Australians were willing to listen to Aboriginal perspectives.[95]

Ideas questioning the status quo and resulting social movements tend to grow in cities, whereas rural areas are often attributed with fostering conservatism and reaction.[96] We have encountered this apparent country–city dichotomy already several times in this book when the ideas of progressive voices asking for change that came from the city were declared incompatible with the situation in the country. Aboriginal rights activists were faced with this issue in the eastern states when going on *freedom rides* to rural areas promoting Aboriginal rights and social advancement.[97] However, there was no such comparably strong movement in Western Australia. One remarkable feature of the 1967 referendum was the absence of an official 'No' campaign but there were passive options to demonstrate a 'No' stance. In the months leading up to the referendum, the *Northam Advertiser* did not report at all about the topic of the referendum. It appears that the paper refused to acknowledge what it was about, which may have served as a silent 'No' position. The *Northam Advertiser* only mentioned the referendum two days before it, when publishing the locations of polling stations, still without a single word to detail what the referendum was about. It also reported that members of Northam's branch of the Labor Party would hand out 'yes how to vote cards', still without stating what voting 'Yes' would mean.[98] Labor may have promoted the 'Yes' vote for the purposes of the other referendum question—to increase the number of members in the House of Representatives. It was printed only as a side note that responsibility for any comment on the federal referendum in this issue would be accepted by K.H. Thompson of Fitzgerald Street in Northam—only there was no comment. To be fair, the *Northam Advertiser* and the *York Chronicle* (before 1960) did not consistently report 'big' politics, but the referendum in 1944 was certainly discussed.[99] The difference between the two referenda in 1944 and in 1967 was that the former's outcome potentially directly affected settler-Australians as it sought to implement certain post-war measures on a five-year plan, while the latter could be conveniently ignored, having no apparent effect on settler-Australians' lives.

On 27 May, York town residents cast their vote at the York Court House. Given that Aboriginal people in Western Australia had been able to vote in federal and state elections since 1962, they were now able to vote in the referendum as well. An overwhelming 90.77 per cent of Australians voted 'Yes for Aborigines', as urged by FCAATSI's slogan. Western Australia had the highest percentage of 'No' votes at 19.05 per cent and four of the five highest nation-wide 'No' voting electorates were also in this state. York's electorate of Moore ranked fifth with 'No' votes at 20.82 per cent, just after Perth with 20.85 per cent. Even worse, twenty-four per cent of Moore's electoral subdivision of York voted 'No', with 87.3 per cent participation of enrolled electors. This subdivision stretched east in a relatively narrow strip from York over Quairading and Narembeen to Mount Walker, and back via Bruce Rock. While, nationally, Western Australia ranked below the eastern states in terms of the 'Yes' vote, the overall results were still extraordinary, as there had been no other referendum before with a stronger vote of endorsement. The naysayers remained a minority—although, twenty-four people out of a crowd of 100 who show up at the ballot still represent an unpleasantly large minority.[100]

In relation to Australia's assimilation policy, the referendum may be interpreted as a public endorsement of the physical integration of Aboriginal people. By implication, those people who would vote for constitutional change should therefore be expected to accept Aboriginal people as physically integrated within settler-Australian spaces—at least in theory. Anecdotal evidence suggests that the referendum did induce positive change in the ways that many of York's settler-Australian town folk thought about and behaved towards Aboriginal people. These changes may not have occurred instantly but over a number of years. Regardless, it has been suggested that many people who voted 'Yes' now felt increasingly compelled to put this affirmative vote also into practice. For example, George Kickett remembered that he and the other school-age children who lived on the reserve were not allowed to sit down when taking the school bus prior to the 1967 referendum. However, soon after the referendum, they were allowed to sit down.[101] Not being allowed to sit down would not have been an explicit policy on public record but would simply have been the bus driver's rule. Troubles with school bus services had been recorded earlier, and the reader may recall (see chapter 3.10) J. Fairhead's claim in 1946 that the school bus was unable to collect Aboriginal children as it had allegedly reached capacity.

York was serviced by several school buses going in all directions. As the bus services were contracted out, there were different service providers with their own rules and prejudices. For example, in 1950, the school bus servicing Gilgering picked up the children from a camp each day; however, as reported in 1952, the bus driving past the reserve refused to stop for the only school-aged child living on the reserve at the time, and a family member had to cycle the nine-year-old child to school every morning.[102] A family living on Talbot Road complained in the same year that the school bus did not stop to collect the family's three children 'despite the fact that it stops for a family of white children about three-quarters of a mile closer to town'.[103] A departmental officer who spoke with the school's headmaster, Mr Moore, ascertained that the bus driver was not obliged to stop for children who did not live more than three miles out of town but could if they wished to do so. Moore was reportedly also reluctant to raise the matter with the driver as he was continually being troubled by the school bus issue. This was somewhat surprising to the departmental officer, as Moore had otherwise presented himself as someone who had a keen interest in the well-being and scholarly success of York's Aboriginal children.[104]

Given that the reserve was also located fewer than three miles from the town centre, the bus driver was not obliged to stop for the child from the reserve—as opposed to the children from Gilgering—because the latter locality was approximately ten miles from York. In September 1954, a departmental officer reported that no complaints had been received in relation to York's school bus service and that it appeared that this service was adequately catering for Aboriginal children in the district outside the two-mile limit.[105] While the minimum distance for the compulsory collection of school children had been shortened by one mile, this did still not guarantee that the reserve children were being picked up, as the reserve was sometimes said to be two miles out of town, and sometimes a bit less than two miles. There are not many notes on record about the school bus service and the few that exist only refer to the outright refusal to transport children. Occurrences like the daily degradation and emotional abuse of children not being allowed to sit down because they were Aboriginal did not make it into the public records. Such occurrences seemingly did not matter as long as the service to transport children to school was provided. However, it should also be noted that the same type of detailed patrol reports accessible for the 1950s are not available for the 1960s.

The above example about the school bus service indicates a progressive change towards social inclusion over a period of at least twenty years, with the 1967 referendum providing the impetus for equal treatment of all students on the bus. Only the accounts of Aboriginal people who experienced this communal change of attitude can truly reflect their lived experience. Amendments to legislation or the Constitution can only provide a level playing field. It is not claimed here that racism in York vanished with the 1967 referendum. Anecdotal evidence certainly reports ongoing racist vilification thereafter. Aboriginal reserve dwellers were considered at the lowest level of the 'pecking order' in town. For example, Marion Kickett reported having been subjected to racism throughout her school life into the 1970s:

> No child would drink from the fountain after me nor would they use the same toilet I had used. I heard the song 'nigger nigger pull your trigger bang, bang bang' every day as well as the terms 'black boong', 'Abos' and 'Boon-a-rig-in-e' rather than 'Aborigine'.[106]

While racism was still prevalent, the general attitude of the settler-Australian community was apparently growing more inclusive, reflecting a broader change in society. This shift in general attitude may not have been able to eliminate racist vilification in town, but it would have assisted in shifting the racist voices from the position of accepted mainstream behaviour towards the realm of what was deemed non-acceptable behaviours.

One important material outcome of the referendum was that the federal government was now able to make special legislation for Aboriginal people. In practice, this meant that targeted funding for Aboriginal people could be made available, which was done first through the creation of the Office of Aboriginal Affairs in 1967, and later, in 1972, through the creation of the Department of Aboriginal Affairs. The Office of Aboriginal Affairs was only created following mounting pressure from the states as the federal government was initially content with inaction, wishing to leave Aboriginal policy, and thus responsibility, entirely in state hands.[107] Following persistent lobbying by the Aboriginal Advancement Council of Western Australia (successor of the WA Native Welfare Council [Inc.]), Premier David Brand approached Prime Minister Harold Holt in April 1967, asking for special funding assistance for Western Australia's Aboriginal housing program. Holt replied after six months advising that there would be no Commonwealth assistance for this purpose.[108] Two months later, Holt infamously disappeared while swimming in the ocean and was presumed dead. As the referendum's anniversary approached, under the new Prime Minister John G. Gorton, the Commonwealth was investigating the provision of monetary assistance from various Commonwealth departments to assist with, for example, housing, education and health. An ad hoc sum for the upcoming 1968–1969 budget was provided for housing, which was increased in the following years to more or less match state expenditures. Thus, Western Australia's budget for Aboriginal housing rose from $849,729 in the 1967–1968 financial year without Commonwealth assistance, to $2,029,000 in the 1970–1971 financial year with Commonwealth assistance.[109]

In this period, the number of conventional homes erected specifically for Aboriginal people under the three-stage-program increased from thirty-four houses to 329. This increase would have partly been a result of the condition tied to the Commonwealth monies, which stipulated that no more than twenty per cent of these funds could be spent on transitional housing.[110] At this stage, all Aboriginal people were also able to apply for State Housing Commission homes through the mainstream channels; however, the State Housing Commission claimed not to discriminate and, therefore, did not keep statistics on Aboriginal people occupying houses.[111] Standard transitional homes managed by the Department of Native Welfare increased from 225 to 293, while primary transitional homes on reserves were reduced from 455 to 414. Once again, it must be pointed out that these figures apply to the entire State of Western Australia, which had an estimated Aboriginal population of 29,000 at the time. Thus, while the new Commonwealth subsidies were certainly a welcome addition to the state budget, and can be interpreted as a direct outcome of the 1967 referendum, these funds remained severely inadequate to provide for the housing needs of

Western Australia's Aboriginal population. Nevertheless, without this additional Commonwealth funding, the Department of Native Welfare might not have been able to rehouse all remaining reserve dwellers by 1974, nor to close off the York Reserve for good.[112]

Chapter 8. 1970–1974

8.01 Council vs town housing

The 1967 referendum may have fostered an increased acceptance of Aboriginal people within York's settler-Australian community; however, the shire council's interpretation of acceptance was far from unconditional when it came to housing provisions in town. Reading between the lines of many records quoted herein, over the past two decades, the socioeconomic status of Aboriginal people and their perceived willingness to assimilate appeared to have become an increasingly important factor for settler-Australians when evaluating acceptability for social inclusion—purely race-based prejudices aside. However, 'race' remained the overarching common denominator by which Aboriginal people were classified. This suggests that some agitators against an Aboriginal presence in town may have still held entrenched racist beliefs but had simply become 'smarter', using non-racial arguments that inferred unsuitability for social inclusion, being well aware that outright racist demands for segregation were no longer socially acceptable and officially considered against government policy. This leads us to the last complaints voiced by the York Shire Council about Aboriginal housing in York within the timeline under review here. In this case, it appears that acceptance of Aboriginal people in town was, once again, at least partially conditional on the perception of economic benefits or on the detriments to the town believed to be caused by the Aboriginal presence.

We shall first briefly look at York's housing situation at the turn of the decade. In October 1969, the council discussed an ongoing 'housing crisis' in York and decided to approach Gayfer, MLA, to send a deputation to the Minister for Housing to ask for practical assistance in solving the issue.[1] Two months later, the council learned that the State Housing Commission had purchased two blocks in Grey and Pelham Streets without council consultation; the council was offended but decided not to take any action because much-needed houses were going to be built. These two blocks were for general State Housing Commission homes and not necessarily for Aboriginal people.[2]

In February 1970, the *Northam Advertiser* reported a 'housing boom' in York and that, in the past eighteen months, fourteen new homes had been built at an unprecedented pace not seen since the late 1940s post-World War II housing scheme.[3] Between 1944 and June 1971, the State Housing Commission had built sixty-six houses in York. The newspaper also reported a minor boom in real estate in York, mainly on the western side of the Avon River. Reportedly, interest in old, slightly run-down houses with a small parcel of land had increased, and many such properties were bought up by people who had chosen York for their retirement and were willing to put time and money into renovating the old homes. The practice of subdividing larger blocks began to emerge at this time. Former paddocks were transformed into 'choice residential areas' and 'surveyed blocks in picked positions' were becoming an apparent rarity. This coincided with speculations in relation to potential mining activity in the wider area, which went on for a few months, as it was hoped that York would be chosen as headquarters for mining businesses and associated services. However, such mining enterprises did not eventuate.[4] From an economic and developmental perspective, the foregoing paragraph may help to explain the council's attitude in relation to further anticipated Aboriginal housing in town during the early 1970s.

In July 1969, the Department of Native Welfare surveyed possible housing requirements for the next five years. York was estimated to require up to seven homes for this period, with two homes to be built in the first two years, and then one house in each of the following three years. Other towns in the departmental Central District had higher estimates. For example, Kellerberrin was estimated to require fourteen homes for the same period, Merredin seventeen homes and Quairading sixteen homes. The department was then on the lookout for suitable land on which to build conventional State Housing Commission homes under the Aboriginal housing scheme, but finding suitable land was not going to be easy. At first, the department considered a property on 66 Grey Street in November 1969 but funds were dwindling in early 1970 and it appears that no such purchase was made. Then, in April, a number of lots on Bland Street were offered to the department. These had been purchased from the council in 1954 by two Aboriginal families, as briefly outlined above (see chapter 6.09), who were still the owners of the blocks. The departmental housing officer, C.H. Maskiell, deemed this land unsuitable because it was located in a market garden area adjoining more undeveloped land. At the final stage of the three-stage housing program, the department appeared to be serious about integrating Aboriginal homes into the suburban townscape, as opposed to erecting homes on the outskirts.[5] In May, the Evangelical Presbyterian Mission (USA) Inc., based in Brookton, approached the department and offered a block of land for sale on Lot 172 Avon Terrace (asking price, $500), within walking distance of York's shopping area. The mission had initially planned to operate in York full-time but had abandoned the idea as, according to the mission, many Aboriginal people had moved away from York. The department eventually purchased this block of land in April 1971.[6]

By mid-June 1970, it had come to the town clerk's attention that an officer of the department had been trying to secure two sites in York for Aboriginal housing purposes and Town Clerk B.W. Lyons, in his periodical report, bemoaned that the council had not been approached yet regarding the department's housing plans.[7] Lyons wrote to the department complaining about the lack of consultation and he requested that building plans be provided as the council wished to be informed about all developments proposed within its shire. The letter was received but accidentally filed and forgotten, with the result that Lyons never heard back from the department. The two blocks in question were situated at Lots 15 and 16 Maud Street (a portion of York Town Lot 370), which were eventually purchased, around March 1971, by the department from Geoffrey Roy Inkpen but remained undeveloped. Thus, Lyons did not learn about the department's land acquisition until the following year; up until then, he may have held the belief that his protest letter had swayed the department not to purchase the blocks.[8]

In May 1972, the Crown Law Department Conveyance Section contacted Lyons to obtain the rating for these blocks to complete the transfer to the Department of Native Welfare. This was the moment that Lyons learned about the purchase and he instantly wrote to the department, apparently somewhat agitated, complaining that the council had never received a reply to his letter of 1970; he requested that the transfer be withheld until the council had found an opportunity to discuss the matter at its June meeting. Commissioner F.E. Gare replied, advising of the 'clerical error' and that, although these properties had been purchased by the department, this was done for potential future developments. Gare added that the transaction could not be reversed but noted that there were no concrete plans for any houses to be erected at present. On 16 June, Lyons replied to Gare, stating that the council was 'extremely annoyed' that the land purchase had occurred because of a filing error and he demanded that the department make every effort to have these blocks replaced with ones approved by the council. Lyons continued that the council's main issue was that the two blocks were adjoining and he reiterated that all future housing plans must be submitted to council for authorisation.[9]

On the same day, Lyons also wrote a letter to the Minister for Community Welfare, William Frank Hupeden Willesee. He attached a copy of his letter to Gare and expressed further, previously unmentioned, concerns:

> Council is very concerned, that it is forced into a position whereby it must adopt this attitude to protect the interests of this old and historic town of York.

> Without any consultation whatsoever with Council, the department has instigated action to purchase two adjoining building blocks in one of the choicest building site areas of the town.

> Apart from this being completely contrary to the stated departmental policy of keeping native town housing in single

units well apart from each other, this action cuts right across Council's desires and plans for this locality.

Council's attitude on this subject in general is still as was explained to you during your visit to York some time ago; namely that a high level common sense and co-operation must be applied by all parties to successfully assimilate better class native people into the white community.[10]

Lyons continued that it was felt that Willesee had been of the same opinion as the council during his visit and he requested that action be taken to reverse the purchase of these two blocks.

Several points become apparent in Lyons' letter. First, the integration of Aboriginal people remained conditional, in that council was only willing to accept a 'better class' of Aboriginal people within the white community—but even these supposedly 'better' Aboriginal families were not trusted to live side by side without causing disturbances. Second, reference to real estate value is made, in that the blocks on Maud Street were apparently situated in 'one of the choicest building sites areas' of York. As was argued in 1954 (see chapter 6.09), the Aboriginal presence was feared to have a significant negative impact on property prices. Maud Street is a small suburban road with approximately ten blocks directly fronting the street, and Lot 15 primarily faced onto Dinsdale Street. A complaint would, not unlikely, have been received by council from a resident in the Maud Street neighbourhood. The exact 'desires and plans' intended for this locality at the time are not known to this author; however, if there were any beyond personal interests of residents it may be pointed out that recreational reserve land was situated just across the road from Lot 15 on Dinsdale Street. Until the mid-1950s, the land had been used as a golf course and, by the mid-1970s, the York Pony Club would establish its grounds on this reserve. The site was large and it appears unlikely that a neighbour would have had the capacity to affect its usability. Whatever these desires and plans might have been in 1972, two houses inhabited by Aboriginal people were apparently deemed a threat to them.[11]

In the first paragraph, Lyons makes reference to protecting the interests of this 'old and historic' town of York. One might think that these attributes were unnecessary for Lyons' argument as any real or perceived concerns regarding Aboriginal housing would have been very similar in old and newer towns. However, at the time, York was starting to promote itself as a tourist destination. The Residency Museum would shortly be opened as Western Australia's first municipal museum and the York Shire Council was working together with other government bodies to secure funding for further tourism-based projects.[12] Therefore, potentially having two more Aboriginal families residing in walking distance to York's town centre seems to have caused panic among the council; otherwise, the comment about York being such an old and historic town would have been superfluous. Alternatively, Lyons may have inferred that because of its historic status, York deserved not to have further Aboriginal houses in town, in the same way as was argued in the early 1950s, when complaints were made that a house for an Aboriginal family was to be located opposite the veterans' residence, Faversham House (see chapter 6.09).

If we remember former mayor and councillor Charles Foreman's argument of 1933 (see chapter 2.01), which, while focussed on the benefits to business, pointed out that York was an early settlement and that it would be 'nice' to have some Aboriginal people 'about the place', we can see that acceptance of an Aboriginal presence had remained conditional throughout the early to mid-twentieth century. Endorsement was linked either to business interests or to expectations of conduct. Often one was weighed up against the other, but both were always tied to Aboriginality. Seemingly, the assimilation policy had not achieved its objectives. Although Aboriginal people were increasingly physically integrated into white Australian mainstream society, their Aboriginality remained the characteristic that distinguished them, and every family had to prove their worthiness to be accepted into settler-Australian society. Ideally, assimilation policy should not have been put into practice in the 'choicest building site areas of the town', according to Lyons, who would have acted on behalf of the council. However, it does not seem to have occurred to the council to request that one of the two lots on Maud Street should be supplemented so one house could be erected on Maud Street and another elsewhere.

Lyons' choice to undermine Commissioner Gare by writing simultaneously to Minister Willesee did not result in the desired outcome, because Willesee asked Gare for advice, and to compile a draft reply to Lyons. This appears to have been a common practice that is not unsurprising, as Ministers, who often have no real involvement with their ministerial portfolios prior to appointment, rely on the information provided by knowledgeable bureaucrats. Commissioner Gare advised Willesee of the background story in relation to the council's complaint and suggested that council's main concern appeared to be based on real estate values.[13] Gare further noted that it was not departmental practice to seek local government approval for conventional houses, as this practice was limited to transitional housing only. Furthermore, Gare conceded that the council may have had a sound reason for requesting a substitution of the Maud Street blocks but he recommended that a physical inspection be made to ensure that no discrimination was taking place. However, all further action, Gare concluded, would be henceforth the responsibility of the State Housing Commission, who was taking over all Aboriginal housing responsibilities as of 1 July 1972.[14] On this date, the Department of Native Welfare ceased to be operational. It handed over its welfare functions to the newly established Department of Community Welfare and control of Aboriginal housing to the aforementioned State Housing Commission; all other functions that could not be captured by existing government departments were handed over to the new Aboriginal Affairs Planning Authority. As to Lyons' demands, Minister Willesee advised him using Gare's recommendations.[15]

Whether council continued arguing about the Maud Street blocks with the State Housing Commission is not known to this author. However, the land appears to have remained undeveloped for some time. Again, the reason for this is not evident. The State Housing Commission may have bowed to pressure from council but it may also have been the case that there was no identifiable need for two more houses for Aboriginal people in York at the time. There had definitely been a need for housing only a year earlier, as we will see in the next and final section. After five years, the blocks were then transferred to the Shire of York in July 1977, who promptly sought approval in the following month to sell both. Once developed, the two lots now formed one private property, which fronted Dinsdale Street and faced the grounds of the York Pony Club. Except for a brief comment in June 1970, when the *Northam Advertiser* reported that a departmental officer was looking for suitable land, Aboriginal housing in York was not further discussed in the local newspaper until the end of 1974.[16]

8.02 The York Reserve—out of sight, out of mind

We will now be returning to the York Reserve for the final episode in this book. By 1969, it had become clear that town reserves in the South West Land Division would be closed in the foreseeable future. Surveys were conducted to identify which families were most suitable to be allocated town housing when it became available. By 1971, several families and pensioner couples on the York reserve had been rehoused. For example, most members of the Kickett family, who had been the longest permanent residents of the York Reserve, were allocated a house in town in preparation for the reserve's closure.[17]

However, the department was not yet ready to close the reserve completely and would utilise the vacancies to rehouse some families 'temporarily', for example, from the Perth metropolitan area. Shifting families from Perth to York appears to have been a typical political band-aid solution. At the time, Western Australia experienced a 'collapse of the rural industry' which meant, effectively, that many Aboriginal people who had made a living from farm work no longer had work available and many families decided to move to the Perth metropolitan area in the hope of a better life. However, rural Aboriginal people wishing to relocate to the Perth metropolitan area found this to be close to impossible, as moving to the city was strongly discouraged by the department due to a lack of employment and housing. This rural-to-urban migration pattern could also be witnessed in the non-Aboriginal population—but in terms of housing needs, Aboriginal people fared worse and often ended up in humpy-style camp housing or shanties on Perth's outskirts, as the responsible government departments failed to keep up with rising housing demand. Those Aboriginal people who stayed in country towns were increasingly unemployed or severely underemployed as a result of the modernisation of farming practices and the simultaneous deskilling of the Aboriginal labour force. Because the department was well aware of the situation, one could be justified in accusing it of using the York Reserve as a 'dumping ground' for Perth's overflow population.[18]

In his autobiographical book, *Fringe Dweller*, Robert Bropho vividly described his brief time living on the York Reserve when he, his wife and their ten children were moved from his sister's overcrowded house in a Perth suburb to York in early 1971. According to Bropho, he had approached the department in urgent need of housing and then 'accepted' an offer to go to York—for a lack of better options—even though this generation of the Bropho family originated in the Perth metropolitan area. Bropho made particular reference to an old-age pensioner who had been admitted to hospital for gastroenteritis.[19] According to a departmental report in a reserve file, the pensioner encountered by Bropho had contracted a rare type of bacillus dysentery, which is potentially fatal if contracted by children under twelve years. The pensioner was placed in isolation at York Hospital and all children from the reserve were excused from school and confined to the reserve.[20]

On 23 March, two departmental officers and local doctor Phillip Cray conducted a health inspection on the reserve because of this case of dysentery. Toilets and facilities on the reserve were found to be in good condition and Cray made positive remarks about their cleanliness. They inspected all houses, which they found to be generally clean, and all residents and their children were also 'reasonably clean and tidily dressed'.[21] However, Cray made two specific complaints—namely, that houses number three and four were grossly overcrowded and that the ground in front of one of the houses was waterlogged. Cray stated that the house in which the Bropho family had been placed contained the worst case of overcrowding he had ever seen. Citing recommendations by 'World Health Authorities', Cray stated that the family would require sleeping quarters with a total air capacity of 4,000 cubic feet, but the two rooms in which they slept had only a total air capacity of 1,420 cubic feet.[22] In laypersons' terms this means that there were too many people with too little oxygen to breathe. According to departmental Officer C.H. Maskiell, Doctor Cray demanded that the Bropho family be rehoused immediately. The doctor was advised that the placement was only temporary but Cray insisted that the Bropho 'family had to be rehoused and stated that he would take steps to ensure that they were removed from the reserve'.[23] House four was occupied by the ill pensioner and his wife, as well as his daughter, son-in-law and their four small children. According to the daughter, her own small family, who had come from Perth, had only meant to stay for two weeks until new accommodation in Perth was available; however, the two weeks had turned into three months without sight of change. Cray also insisted that this family be rehoused immediately, in particular, because it was living in the house of the dysentery patient. Maskiell finished his report by commenting that the placement of these two families on the York Reserve brought no credit to the department, but favoured the 'old adage "out of sight out of mind"'.[24] In an internal memo, the superintendent for the departmental Central District, J.E. Newland, addressed an unnamed 'native welfare' social work officer: 'I believe you have this matter in hand regarding the large family in small dwelling (namely Bropho family). Could you please advise if any solution to the matter is apparent?'[25]

There is no clear evidence that what happened next was the direct outcome of Doctor Cray's demands for immediate rehousing, or Newland's resulting inquiry about a 'solution'; however, the timing of the events that unfolded surely suggests a close correlation. As reported in *Fringe Dweller*, Robert Bropho and his wife were taken to court for allegedly neglecting their children and seven of their ten children were committed into departmental care for two years and forcefully removed to the New Norcia Mission, north of Perth. This occurred in April and was done under the *Child Welfare Act 1970*.[26] Heartbroken, the Brophos vacated house three on the York reserve 'voluntarily' the day after the court hearing and returned with their remaining three children to Perth. Robert Bropho strongly suggested that the department conspired with the magistrate to have his children removed without he and wife being given a chance to speak out in their defence. According to Bropho, word of mouth had reached him that the magistrate himself was reportedly a 'nigger-hater'.[27] Bropho also wrote about a 'white' homemaker, who had worked with his wife in Perth, and a 'black' welfare officer in Kellerberrin. Both women were required to give evidence in the court case. The welfare officer reportedly confided to Bropho prior to the hearing that she would lose her job if she did not testify against his family. According to Bropho, this 'native welfare' worker gave evidence that she had witnessed one of the Bropho children playing on the ground with a fly on his cheek, and that his mother was 'too lazy to brush it away'.[28] At the same time, one of the Bropho's sons was in hospital with gastroenteritis. This might have sufficed for the Department of Native Welfare as 'evidence' supporting the claim of neglect.[29]

Whatever was said in court, the evidence given by the white homemaker from Perth was most likely also not without prejudice. The departmental Homemaker Service had been established in 1968 with a view to teaching Aboriginal families how to run a settler-Australian household, when transitioning from reserve and fringe dwelling to conventional housing. Initially, homemakers were only white women, who reportedly had high expectations of how a household should be run and would have condemned ways of running a household that did not meet their own ideals. Bodies such as the Aboriginal Consultative Committee demanded early on that the Homemaker Service should be staffed by Aboriginal women because of the alleged negative biases held by many white homemakers, as well as the experience of intrusion felt by Aboriginal families, many of whom thought that they were quite capable of managing themselves without assistance. By mid-1970, approximately fifty per cent of homemakers were Aboriginal women but the department was unwilling to consider a completely Aboriginal staffed Homemaker Service at the time.[30]

The second family who had stayed with the sick pensioner in house four was then moved into vacated house three and, thus, Doctor Cray's demands for immediate action to rehouse both families were fulfilled without the department having to provide any extra housing. It appears that the cause of action taken by the department to seek forceful removal of the Bropho children originated locally, at the native welfare sub-district office in Kellerberrin—or at least without the knowledge of the commissioner. Between 21 April and 9 July, Acting Commissioner Bruce McLarty and Commissioner Gare, in their respective periods as commissioner, made three inquiries asking about the progress of rehousing the two families. Only on 26 July did the superintendent for the Central District, J.E. Newland, reply to the queries citing an interim report from the district officer at Kellerberrin.[31] The report discussed at length the situation of the remaining families in houses three and four and, only at the very end, did it briefly mention that the Brophos had vacated house three in April following the committal of the seven children. The information was noted by Gare, who provided no further comment, and, with that, the episode ended, as documented on the reserve file.[32]

While the documents do not provide clear evidence that the committal of the Bropho children occurred as a direct reaction to Doctor Cray's demands, it does seem not unlikely. The impetus for the department's action appears to have been Doctor Cray's threat to escalate matters if the Brophos were not rehoused. One cannot deny that a family with ten children is rather large and finding appropriate housing would not easily have been provided by transitional homes. It seems further likely that the department did not have any houses in the Central Division that would have satisfied the family's needs. As discussed in the previous chapter (7.01), at this time, three vacant blocks had been purchased in York for potential future housing, without there yet being any concrete plans for erecting homes. In any event, rehousing the Bropho family within York would have not been desirable for the department because of limited employment opportunities. Robert Bropho himself stated that, except for one 'back-breaking job' on a chaff cutter, for which he was getting too old, he had struggled to obtain employment in or around town.[33] The situation elsewhere in the Central District would have been very similar. Thus, in fear of being scolded by higher authorities, the removal of children from their parents would probably have seemed the easiest course of action for the 'native welfare' officer who made the decision.

This episode should also be seen in the context of assimilation and integration policy. If Doctor Cray had raised the matter with higher authorities and the department had had to admit that it was unable to rehouse the entire Bropho family in adequate accommodation, the department and the state government may have been faced with embarrassing questions in Parliament or challenged by civic social justice groups. At the lower level, the departmental officer responsible for having the family taken to court may have feared their career to be in jeopardy by this administrative issue with potential political consequences. That this was very likely a real concern at the time is evidenced through the department's record keeping. As Robert Bropho reported in *Fringe Dweller*, his family had been evicted from the Aboriginal housing project, Allawah Grove, in Perth, which forced his family to move back into metropolitan makeshift bush camps.[34] The eviction occurred in February 1969 when Allawah Grove was closed down, which is also documented on departmental records. Only a few months earlier, the Bropho family had moved into a house at Allawah Grove that had just been vacated. In this instance, they were deemed to be squatting.[35] Prior to this, in 1965, Robert Bropho's family had been evicted from Allawah Grove as regular tenants and also initially ended up putting up camps in the bush nearby. This eviction triggered a media interest that continued to reignite for three months, and included Minister Lewis having to answer questions in Parliament, to civic associations, as well as to the print and broadcast media.[36] The lack of Aboriginal housing in the Perth metropolitan area in general, along with settler-Australian views on having Aboriginal people living in their neighbourhoods, was being discussed in public discourse; however, the plight of the families evicted from Allawah Grove had provided the catalyst for the debate. The department had collected numerous newspaper articles, press statements and minutes of a deputation to the minister on the matter. In the *West Australian* newspaper, Lewis had openly floated the idea of referring the Bropho children to the Child Welfare Department for consideration of removal if the family was unable to secure housing and thus deemed to be neglecting their children.[37] Needless to say, housing in the metropolitan area was also conditional and focussed on so-called 'deserving' families. Severe limitations to the provision of adequate housing were mainly dictated by the State Housing Commission, the rental market and local metropolitan authorities vetoing the acquisition of land for Aboriginal housing.[38] Just as in 1965, the plight of the Bropho family (as well as further families) in relation to the pending closure of Allawah Grove in 1968/1969, attracted considerable media interest. Because of insufficient housing options in Perth, the department attempted to relocate families to the country. Most families resisted this initial attempt or returned to Perth quickly after a brief period. A rumour spread among the affected families that their children would be taken away if they refused to relocate to the country, which the department vehemently denied but it was reiterated that if parents were unable to secure accommodation, committal of their children was certainly a possibility. The whole affair, including the department's publicised struggles with successfully rehousing Robert Bropho's family, was viewed as an embarrassment to the Department of Native Welfare as commented by Commissioner Gare.[39]

Come 1971, the public relations disasters of 1965 and 1968/1969 would not have been forgotten by the department's Central District staff, as well as Commissioner Gare, who had been in office on both occasions. Minister Lewis left office on 3 March 1971 and was replaced by Labor's W.F.H. Willesee. It appears reasonable to assume that departmental staff were cautious not to leave a negative first impression on Willesee because of a housing issue spilling into the media.[40] Thus, the separation of the Bropho family in April 1971 in York, and the associated trauma this caused, was likely to have been political at its core.

8.03 The York Reserve—the final years

By the end of 1971, most former reserve residents had vacated the reserve and had been provided with accommodation elsewhere. However, the reserve continued to be used as an intermittent solution for dire housing needs. As late as January 1973, a new resident care taker was appointed. Care taker duties on the York Reserve had been made official from January 1964, following the completion of houses three and four in November 1963. Before the switch to Australian dollars, the caretaker at York received £2 per month. The policy of paying reserve dweller caretakers was introduced in 1961 and caretakers' pay depended on the number of reserve residents. The money was either paid or deducted from the rent at the discretion of 'native welfare' field staff.[41] Marion Kickett's mother, Pearl Kickett, held this position from 1964 until moving from the reserve in early 1971, and she gained a positive reputation for the continuously clean state of the toilets, which was acknowledged by 'native welfare' and by health workers alike. Her legacy was evident during the inspection by Doctor Cray in March 1971.[42]

The new caretaker, in January 1973, would not have held the position for long, as the York Reserve was clearly marked for closure. In February 1973, all remaining funds for the financial year allocated to the York Reserve, except for standing charges, were channelled to Northam to cover the costs of painting and renovation works on the Northam Reserve. That these excess monies were only $50 indicates that the department was unwilling to make any further significant investments into the reserve at York.[43] By February 1974, the reserve was used to house two families intermittently, until their State Housing Commission homes had been renovated, and another family moved into one of the houses 'illegally' but was then officially approved to stay. The person who had been appointed caretaker the previous year had left. A truck had demolished the power line on the reserve and $150 were granted for repairs and to check that the water supply was still in good order. At the same time, demolition of three of the four houses was anticipated once the two families had returned to their State Housing Commission homes to prevent squatters from occupying these houses. The Minister for Community Welfare was determined to close down the York Reserve at the earliest opportunity.[44]

By July 1974, all houses had been vacated and the Department of Community Welfare had arranged the dismantling of the houses and facilities through various tenders, the successful parties of which would scavenge for useful items in return for their work. Mr K. Gerwein of Northam purchased the first three houses at no cost and then agreed to pay to take the fourth. Other bits and pieces were demolished or 'rehomed' by the Eastern Districts Trading Company of York (various items), the Shire of Goomalling (urinal and cistern), the Shire of

Dowerin (four cisterns) and V.R. Fowler of Wongan Hills (four steel poles).[45] Water, which had been flowing for thirty-eight years, was disconnected in the same month. In November, clearing works were approved to remove the septic and drainage system and to clear all rubbish, including car bodies.[46]

On 20 December 1974, Shire Clerk B.W. Lyons wrote to the Department of Lands and Surveys, claiming that Aboriginal people had been erecting camp constructions since the houses had been removed, and he requested that the purpose of this reserve be changed to 'public use' so the shire council would be able to evict the persons allegedly camping on the reserve. In August 1975, Social Work Supervisor J.G. Brennan advised that, although he had not seen any camps on the reserve, it may have been used as a road stop, and he recommended transferral of the land to the Undersecretary of Lands for redistribution. Following some debate, by September 1977, the land was transferred, not to the Shire of York but to the Aboriginal Lands Trust with the power to lease. However, before this occurred, more than a quarter of the reserve's land, equating to 1.1380 hectares facing the Avon River, had been assigned to Cold Harbour Lot 27, leaving reserve 8567 on Cold Harbour Lot 25 with 3.0293 hectares. The new lot comprised the area that lies below the high-water mark, prone to flooding during winter. The reserve was originally gazetted for access to water before it was turned into a reserve for Aboriginal people. In Western Australia, land on river banks between the low and high-water mark must usually be designated Crown Lands, as dictated by section 16 (3) of the *Land Act 1971*. Exceptional circumstances allowing for the riverfront land to be part of the reserve ceased when the reserve was no longer used as a home by Aboriginal people and land use was reassessed and changed for the first time since 1936, which caused Lot 27 to be shelved by default. However, this also meant that families with a claim to the land were suddenly bereft of a substantial part of their former home grounds.[47]

When the Aboriginal Lands Trust applied to have the reserve transferred in mid-1975, this was on the recommendation of the federal Department of Aboriginal Affairs, who proposed that the land be kept for potential future light industrial developments by an Aboriginal enterprise and, before this had eventuated, the land could serve as camping ground for transient Aboriginal people under the provision that shire regulations did not preclude this. York Shire Council was approached on the matter. Unsurprisingly, the council requested that it be notified about any future Aboriginal enterprises planned on the reserve.[48]

Epilogue

In this book, we examined segregation and assimilation policies and practices in interaction with settler-Australian community attitudes in York, Western Australia. We followed a timeline of half a century between 1923 and 1974, which aligned with the official existence of the York Native Reserve. The reserve represents state-sanctioned segregation as a space entirely allocated to Aboriginal people, outside settler-Australian society. As long as it existed, the integration of Aboriginal people into mainstream society in York could never be fully achieved. The majority of events discussed here took place in the 1940s and 1950s. The former decade witnessed the peak of public demand for segregation and its implementation through state government agencies, while the latter witnessed the struggle of those agencies to turn the tide towards a more inclusive society. The early resistance to the implementation of the assimilation policy was not surprising given that the same state government agencies had heeded the calls for segregationist policies to be implemented until the official change of direction. The difficulty of achieving the social inclusion of Aboriginal people in York was apparent in the remaining period until 1974, during which local and external factors played their parts. This book should be regarded as a case study, because what occurred in York happened in similar ways in other towns in the South West Land Division. The book finishes in 1974 because this was the year the reserve was closed down, not because social inclusion had been achieved in York. The author is unable to comment on whether this may have occurred since.

What appears certain is that there are still many historic open wounds that require healing. Sometimes, they become visible only by chance. For example, in the mid-2010s Marion Kickett inquired about having a headstone placed belatedly on her baby sister's grave in the York Cemetery—her sister had passed away in 1965. She was advised that this was not possible as her sister was not the only person in this standard-sized grave. Together with Marion's sister, three Aboriginal infants who had been lost to her extended family in 1948, 1951 and 1964, were also buried. However, the total body count in this single grave is apparently thirteen, as, over time, three adult non-Aboriginal 'paupers' and several non-Aboriginal still-born babies were buried there as well.[1] It is difficult to trace who would have made these arrangements but, as this was an ongoing practice, various members of the York Cemetery's administration (comprising local government members) would likely have been involved in allocating the burial site. Though the financial position of the families of most of these buried persons is not known to this author, it is probable that they did not have the financial means for a standard funeral for their loved ones. This may have legally enabled the York Cemeteries Board to bury a number of people in the same 'open ground' grave site under provisions for 'poor' people, because contemporary legislation and local cemetery by-laws lacked clear definitions regarding such so-called 'open ground' burial practices. However, section 39 of the *Cemeteries Act 1897* (and subsequent amendments) clearly states that such 'poor' burials had to be conducted in the respective religious sections of the cemeteries that were relevant to the deceased, if their religious denominations were known. The burial records are clear that they were known, at least for the four Aboriginal cases mentioned above, and they were not all of the same faith.[2]

While Aboriginal and non-Aboriginal poor people were, in this case, subject to the same treatment, we should remember that, at the time, Aboriginal people were—with some exceptions— generally subject to poverty. Thus, the 'poor' treatment of the dead as a result of the lack of finances was often inseparable from being Aboriginal. Worse yet, even if Aboriginal people were able to pay for a standard funeral, a dignified farewell for family and friends to attend was not guaranteed as the burial practices of the undertaker also had to be taken into account. For example, when a twelve-year-old child of the Kickett family died in 1938, it was noted on record that the undertaker often buried Aboriginal deceased persons at York at inconvenient (early and late) hours or without sufficient notice, resulting in relatives being unable to attend funerals and that this undertaker also sometimes took the bodies to Northam for burial. At the time, Sergeant Clifford was instructed to address these complaints with the undertaker in question with a view to ensuring that Aboriginal relatives of a deceased person would be able to attend the funeral and be notified in a timely manner.[3]

The undertaker in question was Harry Stanley Brooks of Northam, who often held the government contracts for York during the 1930s and 1940s (conducting low-cost funerals for destitute persons and 'natives'). Undertakers often complained about such government contracts, as they allegedly barely covered costs and some undertakers only agreed to them in an attempt to secure fully paid funerals along the way. Hence, it is not difficult to imagine that the undertaker would have tried to maximise his income by cutting corners and costs, disregarding the needs of grieving family members. However, it should be noted that the complaints about the undertaker in York were not tied only to contract burials. Brooks appears to have done some job-sharing with York's undertaker, James Lauder Wansbrough, though Wansbrough is not mentioned in a negative light in the records available to this author.[4] Wansbrough's successor, S.P. Harvey, who held the business from early 1948 until his death in 1963, is also not mentioned in negative terms in relation to burials, though he held for a number of years the government contracts for York and some neighbouring towns. Harvey's successor, Geoff Inkpen (local representative for Purslow Northam) is not mentioned at all in the departmental records.[5] Nevertheless, past negative experiences with undertakers in York would have further assisted in diminishing any incentive to obtain sufficient funds for a fully priced burial in a private grave, even if the wider family might have had the financial capacity to collectively gather such funds. It can take a very long time to reinstate broken trust and this notion certainly does not only apply to funerals; it also pertains to the relationships between Aboriginal people and settler-Australians, and between Aboriginal people and government authorities of all tiers.

A few words on history writing in general: History is selective. An author can only work with what has been selected for publishing in a newspaper, or placed on government record, or shared in oral accounts. Then, the author makes their own selections and needs to analyse and interpret the records to hand. By this token, for example, a two-year gap of silence on the records does not necessarily equate to two years of peaceful non-eventfulness in real life. It may just indicate that nothing extraordinary was recorded that challenged the status quo, because if the status quo was exercised without issues, no complaints and subsequent reports eventuated. This means that most records fail to capture the unchallenged daily racism of the periods under review. 'Sudden' silence can also indicate a change of record keeping. For example, many departmental records of the 1950s concerning York have been preserved, but there are far fewer from the 1960s. This may have been done intentionally or by chance. For example, in the early 1960s, a sub-office at Kellerberrin was established and, with it, records may have been administered somewhat differently than anticipated by head office or could have been lost or destroyed. For the same period, there is extensive material available from the Southern District Office based in Narrogin and comparatively less so from the Central District Offices. Record keeping in the 1960s changed by focussing increasingly on efficiency, which included culling records that were deemed to have no historic value. Ways of recording information also changed over time and appear to have become more welfare minded, while the thorough patrol reports of the 1950s disappeared at the end of the decade (at least the patrol report file format did).[6]

Somewhat related to the qualitative and quantitative practices of recording and preserving information is the consideration that field staff were not necessarily as open minded and progressive as policy may have assumed, and as Commissioner Middleton, and later Commissioner Gare, had presented themselves. Officers further down the 'food-chain' often voiced more damning and bigoted views in their internal reports than official policy would have endorsed. The records are also selective in terms of gender, which reflects the sexist Western society during the period under review. A married woman's name is often not mentioned in records, and she is purely referred to by adding 'Mrs' to the husband's full name (for example, 'Mrs John Smith'), regardless of whether or not she was Aboriginal. Thus, female identities are often omitted from the narrative that emerges through studying such state records and newspaper articles. This gap in information extends to women's 'maiden' or birth-family names, and the association of certain families with York and other places. However, it should be pointed out that women, rather than men, were outspoken in a constructive manner about the inhumane restrictions they faced in York, as exemplified by the letters written by Aboriginal women in the records. Indeed, these written examples may serve as evidence that women have had much more important roles in history than mainstream accounts have led us to believe through the almost exclusive portrayal of male historic protagonists.

Although this book's theme is located within the field of Aboriginal history, in line with works using a similar approach, it informs more about settler-Australian society than it does about Aboriginal people. With a few exceptions (for example, the letters written by Aboriginal women to the department, statements in court proceedings or the Coolbaroo dances), stories of the Aboriginal people of York are not captured in this book. This omission may be symptomatic of the largely passive role of Aboriginal people in York and other rural areas in relation to the implementation of government policy and settler-Australian community attitudes. Moreover, this omission is arguably a reflection of settler Australian indifference towards Aboriginal points of view. After all, the truth-telling exercise aims at setting the record straight about the *wrongs* committed by the settler society that are positioned uncomfortably vis a vis a proud settler Australian heritage-based history.

It is not unlikely that most Aboriginal people simply wanted to live their lives and tried to get by as best as they could within an often-hostile environment. The only reason that this book was written is because settler-Australians took issue with the Aboriginal presence within 'white spaces'. As suggested by the research material available to this author, resistance to the status quo largely did not occur by actively trying to change the oppressive system but rather by passively attempting to navigate it. This book has been unable to portray the experience of Aboriginal people who had to live within this system of control and repression and questions in this regard remain to be

315

answered elsewhere. How did it feel to be degraded as 'second-class' humans, having severe restrictions imposed on one's life and being persecuted for taking the liberty to engage in behaviours that were perfectly acceptable and legal in settler-Australian society? How did it feel to face every day racism in town? How did it feel knowing that the state could simply take one's children away and there was nothing one could do about it? How did it feel having to justify oneself constantly in front of departmental officers? In later years, how did it feel having to prove one's social advancement to become eligible for housing in a non-segregated environment? How did it feel applying for conditional citizenship in one's own country with the view of being liberated from governmental and racist social control, to be eligible for aged or disability pensions and maternity allowances, to be able to vote, to consume alcohol and to be allowed on hotel premises? Aboriginal stories are best told by Aboriginal people and there is a growing array of literature and other media outputs available that are authored or told by Aboriginal people from York, or with strong connections to York and Balardong country. This book was written with the aim of being complementary to such personal, primary accounts.

At the time of writing, the reserve land is in process of being transferred from the state government-administered Aboriginal Land Trust to the Ballardong Aboriginal Corporation. Since the closure of the reserve, the land has had many claimants who have had different visions as to the future use of the former reserve, which has resulted in the land not being able to be utilised by Aboriginal custodians for over forty years. With the pending land transfer, it appears that this is about to change for the benefit of the Balardong Aboriginal community.[7] Although the built environment and the people who live on Country may change over time, the land remains the same and retains all its history. It may be worth visiting the York Regency Museum, which has on permanent display panels about the stories of two Aboriginal families in York—one living on the reserve and one living in town. One may also visit the York Court House and sit down for a moment in one of the small cells that were only intended for lock-up purposes and not for serving a sentence of up to three months (during the period under review). Records indicate that, over the decades, many Aboriginal people spent weeks on end in these small cells, essentially just for being Aboriginal. One may stop on the roadside of the former York Reserve (on Quairading Road, coming from town, just before the train crossing, facing the Avon River) and take in the view of this one block of land that was left for Aboriginal people to inhabit in the York District—a district that forms a substantial part of Balardong country.

Lot 159, which was discussed at the beginning of this book (see chapter 1.01) and where Aboriginal people camped until 1924, has remained municipal land and now forms part of Candice Bateman Park, situated between Newcastle, Cowan and Cardwell Streets. The park was named in memory of a fifteen-year-old Aboriginal girl from York, who tragically died in a train accident in 2001. Her brother, Chance Bateman, an Australian Football League personality, was instrumental in the establishment of the memorial park. The Bateman family has longstanding family roots in the York District, and while this personal tragedy is not necessarily associated with Aboriginality, it seems otherwise fitting that a memorial for an Aboriginal person has been erected on this particular block of land, as it provides for a symbolic link back into continuous Aboriginal land use.[8]

References

Sources that are annotated with SLWA were obtained from the State Library of Western Australia: https://slwa.wa.gov.au/.

Sources that are annotated with SROWA were obtained from the State Records Office of Western Australia: https://archive.sro.wa.gov.au/.

Records from Western Australian state departmental files have been sourced from both the State Records Office of Western Australia and the State Library of Western Australia. The former holds all state government records; however, 'open access' files of a vast number of these records are also publicly accessible via microfiche at the State Library.

At the time of writing, all Western Australian legislation and Government Gazettes quoted herein can be freely accessed via the Parliamentary Council's website: https://www.legislation.wa.gov.au/.

At the time of writing, all Western Australian parliamentary debates (Hansard) can be freely accessed via the website of the Western Australian Parliament: https://www.parliament.wa.gov.au/.

At the time of writing, all newspaper articles until and including 1954 quoted herein can be freely accessed online via Trove, provided by the National Library of Australia: https://trove.nla.gov.au/.

York Chronicle and *Northam Advertiser* newspaper articles from 1955 to 1974 were sourced from microfilm at the State Library of Western Australia. *Westralian Aborigine* newspaper articles were sourced from the State Library of Western Australia, the National Library of Australia and the National Archives of Australia (Perth). Most other newspaper articles published after 1954 were sourced from clippings in departmental records.

Introduction

[1] Shire of York, "History", York Visitor Centre, accessed 29 October 2019, http://visit.york.wa.gov.au.

[2] South West Aboriginal Land & Sea Council, "About the Balardong Region", Kaartdijin Noongar, accessed 29 October 2019, https://www.noongarculture.org.au/Balardong/; Sylvia Hallam, *Aborigines of the York Area* (York: The York Society, 1998), vii.

[3] Anna Haebich, *For their own Good: Aborigines and Government in the South West of Western Australia, 1900-1940* (Nedlands: University of Western Australia Press, 1992), p. 9.

[4] Haebich, *For their own Good,* p. 70-89.

[5] Bain Attwood and Andrew Markus, *The 1967 Referendum – Race, Power and the Australian Constitution* (Canberra, ACT: Aboriginal Studies Press, 2007), p. 10-14.

[6] Anna Haebich, *Spinning the Dream – Assimilation in Australia 1950-1970,* (North Fremantle: Fremantle Press, 2008), p. 10-11.

[7] *Avon Gazette and York Times*, "The Town of York", 22 December 1924, p. 5, Trove; "Railway Maps of Western Australia", Picryl.com, accessed 13 August 2023.

[8] York Town Council, "Nominal rolls of Chairman, Mayors, Councillors and Town Clerks and extracts from Council minute books. The town of York was absorbed by the Shire of York in 1965", call number PR14522/YOR/3 - 0/s, SLWA; Trove, National Library of Australia, https://trove.nla.gov.au/, - there will be numerous references throughout this book confirming this.

[9] Government of Western Australia, Parliamentary Counsel's Office, Western Australian State Legislation, https://www.legislation.wa.gov.au/.

Chapter 1. 1920s

[1] Department of Native Welfare, Reserve for Natives – York, Reserve 8567, 10ac, series 2030, consignment 993, item 1933/0341, f. 1, SROWA; *Eastern Chronicle*, "Municipal Council", 28 March 1924, p. 2, Trove; *Avon Gazette and York Times*, "An Old Resident Passes – The Late Mr. W T Craig", 19 April 1929, p. 2, Trove.

[2] Native Welfare, item 1933/0341, f. 1.

[3] Ibid.

[4] *Inquirer,* "Report of the Guardian of Aborigines, York", 16 March 1853, p. 3, Trove.

[5] *Perth Gazette and Independent Journal of Politics and News*, "Domestic Sayings and Doings", 30 Nov 1855, p. 3, Trove.

[6] Survey Office of Western Australia, York 14 - Plan of new Suburban Lots in York Townsite by F. T. Gregory - Also Lots by G.H. Roe [scale: 10 chains to an inch], series 235, consignment 3868, item 423, SROWA.

[7] *Inquirer and Commercial News*, "Advertising", 27 March 1867, p. 2, Trove; "Edith Cowan Centenary: No Fit Place for a Woman – Personal Life", Parliament of Western Australia, accessed 16 July 2022, https://www.parliament.wa.gov.au.

[8] *Inquirer and Commercial News*, "Legislative Council", 10 October 1860, p. 3, Trove; Western Australia, *Aborigines Protection Act 1886* (No. 25 of 1886).

[9] *Inquirer and Commercial News*, "The Natives of Western Australia",
15 July 1868, p. 3, Trove.

[10] *Eastern Districts Chronicle*, "Miscellaneous Memoranda", 18 March 1884, p. 3, Trove.

[11] *Western Mail*, "York News", 12 May 1888, p. 17, Trove.

[12] Bryan Rochelle, *Report of the Ethnographic Site Identification Noongar Cultural Heritage Survey, Shire of York, June 2021*, Snappy Gum Heritage Services Pty Ltd for Shire of York, https://www.york.wa.gov.au.

[13] Native Welfare, item 1933/0341, f. 3.

[14] Survey Office of Western Australia, York 14 - Plan of new Suburban Lots in York Townsite by F.T. Gregory - Also Lots by G.H. Roe, series 235, consignment 3868, item 421, SROWA (online source). – These kinds of plans were often used over a period of many years and were progressively updated.

[15] Department of Lands and Surveys, Reserves for Certain Purposes – York – 2342, 2343, series 211, consignment 1755, item 1893/01247, vol. 1.

[16] Ibid.

[17] *Avon Gazette and York Times*, "Correspondence", 5 October 1923, p. 2, Trove.

[18] Native Welfare, item 1933/0341, f. 3-5.

[19] Ibid., f. 6.

[20] *Eastern District Chronicle*, "Municipal", 24 October 1924, p. 3, Trove; *Government Gazette of Western Australia*, No. 46 (Perth, WA: Government Printer of Western Australia, 1924), p. 1558, 1560; Department of Lands and Surveys, York Sheet 1 [Tally No. 505352], series 2168, consignment 5698, item 1750, f. 12, 26, 72, SROWA.

[21] Native Welfare, item 1933/0341, f. 8.

[22] Ibid.

[23] *Government Gazette of Western Australia*, No. 41 (Perth, WA: Government Printer of Western Australia, 1924), p. 1332; *Government Gazette of Western Australia*, No. 5 (Perth, WA: Government Printer of Western Australia, 1903), p. 178-180.

[24] Department of Land Administration, S.S. Survey for Cold Harbour Estate (York), series 211, consignment 541, 1902/08471, f. 26, SROWA.

[25] Department of Land Administration, item 1902/08471.

[26] *Government Gazette*,(1924), p. 1332.

[27] Government of Western Australia, *Aborigines Act 1911* (No. 42 of 1911).

[28] Anna Haebich, *For their own Good: Aborigines and Government in the South West of Western Australia, 1900-1940* (Nedlands: University of Western Australia Press, 1992), p. 127.

[29] Haebich, *For their own Good,* p. 189-190.

[30] Ibid., p. 380-381.

[31] *York Chronicle*, "Municipal Council", 20 May 1927, p. 2, Trove.

[32] Ibid.

[33] Aborigines Department, *Report of the Chief Protector of Aborigines for the Year Ending 30th June, 1928* (Perth, WA: Government Printer of Western Australia, 1929), 13; Aborigines Department, *Report of the Chief Protector of Aborigines for the Year Ending 30th June, 1929* (Perth, WA: Government Printer of Western Australia, 1930), 11, https://aiatsis.gov.au.

Chapter 2. 1930s

[1] *York Chronicle*, "Native Ration Station at York", 15 July 1932, p. 3, Trove.

[2] Haebich, *For their own Good,* p. 166.

[3] Ibid..

[4] Department of Native Affairs, Native Matters – York – General File, series 2030, consignment 993, item 1938/1037, f. 2-3, SROWA.

[5] Ibid.

[6] Ibid.

[7] Native Affairs, item 1938/1037, f. 2-3.

[8] Marion Kickett, "Examination of How a Culturally-Appropriate Definition of Resilience Affects the Physical and Mental Health of Aboriginal People" (PhD diss., University of Western Australia, 2011), p. 17.

[9] Ibid.

[10] Haebich, *For their own Good,* p. 265.

[11] Aborigines Department, *Annual Report of the Chief Protector of Aborigines: Western Australia, Year Ended 30th June 1928,* (Perth: Government Printer, 1929), p. 12-13; Aborigines Department, *Annual Report of the Chief Protector of Aborigines: Western Australia, Year Ended 30th June 1929,* (Perth, WA: Government Printer of Western Australia, 1930), p. 10-11; https://aiatsis.gov.au.

[12] Haebich, *For their own Good,* p. 284-289.

[13] Department of Native Affairs, Quairading – Establishing of a Mission at, series 2030, consignment 993, item 1930/0037, f. 26, SROWA.

[14] Department of Native Affairs, item 1930/0037, f. 60.

[15] Department of Native Affairs, Royal Commission on the Treatment of Aborigines – vol 2 (main file in action), series 2030, consignment 993, item 1933/0333, no folio – pdf page 182, SROWA.

[16] Henry Reynolds, *Truth Telling: History, Sovereignty and the Uluru Statement*, (Sydney: NewSouth Publishing, 2021), p. 101-104.

[17] Department of Native Affairs, Census of Aboriginals and Half-Castes, series 2030, consignment 993, item 1928/0304, various pages, SLWA.

[18] *York Chronicle*, "Municipal Council", 6 December 1935, p. 3, Trove.

[19] Department of Lands and Surveys, York Sheet 3 [Tally No. 505354], series 2168, consignment 5698, item 1752, SROWA. - This map situates Lots 16 and 17 north of reserve 212; however, here in this text it has been cited how Council reported it.

[20] Native Welfare, item 1933/0341, f. 13.

[21] Ibid., f. 14; *York Leader and Quairading and Dangin Herald*, "Municipal Council", 7 February 1936, p. 3, Trove.

[22] Native Welfare, item 1933/0341, f. 15-17.

[23] Haebich, *For their own Good,* p. 131-133.

[24] Ibid., p. 235.

[25] Native Welfare, item 1933/0341, f. 21.

[26] Ibid., f. 20.

[27] Ibid., f. 21.

[28] Ibid., f. 22-29.

[29] Ibid., f. 25-26.

[30] Ibid., f. 25-26.

[31] Ibid., f. 22-30.

[32] *West Australian*, "The Half-Caste Problem – No 1", 23 July 1936, p. 16, Trove; *West Australian*, "The Half-Caste Problem – No 2", 24 July 1936, p. 26, Trove; *West Australian*, "The Half-Caste Problem – No 3", 25 July 1936, p. 21, Trove, "The Half-Caste Problem – No 4", 27 July 1936, p. 16, Trove.

[33] Royal Commission Appointed to Investigate, Report and Advise Upon Matters in Relation to the Condition and Treatment of Aborigines and Moseley, Henry Doyle, *Report of the Royal Commissioner appointed to investigate, report, and advise upon matters in relation to the condition and treatment of Aborigines* (Perth, WA: Government Printer of Western Australia, 1935), http://nla.gov.au/nla.obj-52802043; Western Australia, *Hansard Parliamentary Debates, Sixteenth Parliament – First Session*, vol. 97-98, Legislative Council (22 September 1936), p. 710-722, (29 September 1936), p. 821-833, (29 September 1936), p. 878-889, (1 October 1936), p. 932-935,

(10 December 1936), p. 2600-2606, Legislative Assembly (10 December 1936), p. 2614-2625.

[34] *West Australian*, "Estimates for 1936-1937", 9 September 1936, p. 18, Trove; *West Australian*, "Vigilans Et Audax – The State Budget", 9 September 1936, p. 16, Trove; *Mirror*, "An Upset Budget", 12 September 1936, p. 14, Trove.

[35] Native Welfare, item 1933/0341, f. 34; *West Australian*, "State Basic Wage – Court Fixes Rates", 11 June 1936, p. 20, Trove.

[36] Native Welfare, item 1933/0341, f. 32.

[37] Ibid., f. 38-39.

[38] Government of Western Australia, *Aborigines Act 1905* (No. 14 of 1905); Government of Western Australia, *Aborigines Act 1911* (No. 42 of 1911); Government of Western Australia, *Native Administration Act 1936* (No. 43 of 1936); Government of Western Australia, *Native Welfare Act 1954* (No. 64 of 1954).

[39] Royal Commission on the Condition of the Natives, *Report* (Perth, WA: Government Printer of Western Australia, 1905), p. 28, https://www.parliament.wa.gov.au.

[40] York Clerk of Courts, Charge Book, series 408, consignment 3794, items 1 and 2, SROWA; *Aborigines Act 1905*; *Aborigines Act 1911*; *Native Administration Act 1936*; *Native Welfare Act 1954*; Government of Western Australia, *Native Welfare Act 1963* (No. 79 of 1963).

[41] Patrick Wolfe, *Traces of History: Elementary Structures of Race* (London – New York: Verso, 2016), p. 38-39; Western Australia, *Aboriginal Native Offenders - Amendment Act 1874* (Vict. 38, no. 8 of 1874); John McCorquodale, "The Legal Classification of Race in Australia", *Aboriginal History* vol. 10, no 1-2 (1986): p. 11, https://www.jstor.org/stable/24054589; Christine B Hickman, "The Devil and the One Drop Rule – Racial Categories, African Americans, and the U.S. Census", *Michigan Law Review* vol 95, no. 5 (1997): 1178-1179, https://repository.law.umich.edu/mlr/vol95/iss5/2.

[42] *West Australian*, "Letters to the Editor: Position of Natives", 31 May 1950, p. 13, Trove; Wolfe, *Traces of History,* p. 80-83.

[43] Haebich, *For their own Good,* p. 48.

[44] Ibid., p. 48-49.

[45] Marilyn Lake and Henry Reynolds, *Drawing the Global Colour Line – White Men's Countries and the Question of Racial Equality* (Carlton, Vic: Melbourne University Press, 2008), p. 247-248.

[46] Government of Western Australia, *Aborigines Act 1905* (No. 14 of 1905).

[47] Western Australia, *Hansard Parliamentary Debates, Thirteenth Parliament – Sixth Session,* vol. 83, Legislative Council (3 December 1929), p. 1903-1904.

[48] Haebich, *For their own Good,* p. 157; Pat Jacobs, *Mister Neville* (Fremantle, WA: Fremantle Arts Centre Press, 1990).

[49] Russel McGregor, *Indifferent Inclusion: Aboriginal People and The Australian Nation* (Canberra: Aboriginal Studies Press, 2011), 11.

[50] McGregor, *Indifferent Inclusion,* 58; Anna Haebich, *Broken Circles – Fragmenting Indigenous Families 1800 - 2000* (Fremantle: Fremantle Press, 2000), 279.

[51] Western Australia, *Native Administration Act 1936.*

[52] Ibid.

[53] *West Australian,* "The 1936 Session", 14 December 1936, p. 18, Trove.

[54] Native Welfare, item 1933/0341, f. 52.

[55] *York Chronicle,* "Municipal Council", 18 November 1938, p. 2, Trove.

[56] Ibid.

[57] Native Welfare, item 1933/0341, f. 54.

[58] Ibid.

[59] *York Chronicle,* "Swimming", 11 November 1938, p. 3, Trove.

[60] Native Welfare, item 1933/0341, f. 54.

[61] Pat Jacobs, *Mister Neville.*

[62] Haebich, *For their own Good,* p. 159; Aboriginal History WA, "Family History", Department of Local Government, Sports and Cultural Industries, accessed 14 May 2024, https://www.dlgsc.wa.gov.au.

[63] Haebich, *Broken Circles*, 216, 280-286; Department of Native Affairs, Certificate of Citizenship, Legislation Re, series 2030, consignment 993, item 1944/0463, f. 69, SROWA; Department of Native Affairs, Sister Kate's Home – For Quarter-Caste Children, series 2030, consignment 993, item 1949/0077, f. 1, SROWA.

[64] Department of Native Affairs, Education – Irregular attendance of native children at schools – General correspondence re, series 2030, consignment 993, item 1949/0490, f. 8, SROWA; Department of Native Affairs, Royal Commission on the Treatment of Aborigines – vol 1, series 2030, consignment 993, item 1933/0333, no folio – pdf pages 79-81, SROWA.

[65] Native Welfare, item 1933/0341, f. 59; *York Chronicle,* "York Road Board", 14 April 1939, p. 3, Trove.

[66] Native Welfare, item 1933/0341, f. 63.

[67] Ibid.

[68] Ibid., f. 65.

[69] Ibid.

[70] Ibid., f. 66.

[71] Ibid.

[72] *York Chronicle,* "York Road Board", 16 June 1939, p. 3, Trove.

[73] *York Leader and Quairading and Dangin Herald*, "Municipal Council", 9 June 1939, p. 3, Trove.

[74] Ibid.

[75] Native Welfare, item 1933/0341, f. 67; *York Leader and Quairading and Dangin Herald*, "New Town Clerk Appointed", 28 April 1939, p. 2, Trove.

[76] Native Welfare, item 1933/0341, f. 67.

[77] Ibid., f. 69.

[78] Ibid.

[79] Ibid., f. 70.

[80] Ibid.

[81] *York Chronicle*, "Municipal Council", 29 September 1939, p. 2, Trove.

[82] Ibid.

[83] Ibid.

[84] Department of Native Affairs, Native Matters – York – General File, series 2030, consignment 993, item 1938/1037, f. 1, SROWA; *Government Gazette of Western Australia*, No. 56 (Perth, WA: Government Printer of Western Australia, 1964), p. 2526.

Chapter 3. 1940s

[1] *West Australian*, "The Native's Friend – Mr. A O Neville Farewelled", 21 March 1940, p. 18, Trove; *Northern Times*, "Native Affairs – New Commissioner", 17 October 1940, p. 3, Trove; Pat Jacobs, *Mister Neville* (Fremantle, WA: Fremantle Arts Centre Press, 1990), p. 268, 271.

[2] *York Chronicle*, "York Road Board", 12 July 1940, p. 3, Trove.

[3] Ibid.

[4] Native Affairs, item 1938/1037, f. 4.

[5] Ibid., f. 6.

[6] Ibid.

[7] Ibid.

[8] Haebich, *For their own Good*, p. 171.

[9] Ibid., p. 313; Department of Native Affairs, Prohibited Areas – General Correspondence, series2030 cons993 item 1940/1244, f. 46.

[10] Department of Native Affairs, Placing Natives on Abandoned Farms in Quairading District - Establishment of Eastern Wheatbelt Settlement, series2030 cons993 item 1936/0316.

[11] Native Welfare, item 1933/0341, f. 137, 151; Native Affairs, item 1938/1037, f. 6, 12, 66-67, 82, 107.

[12] Native Affairs, item 1938/1037, f. 10; Haebich, *For their own Good*, p. 36.

[13] Haebich, *For their own Good*, p. 349.

[14] Native Affairs, item 1938/1037, f. 10-11.

[15] Native Welfare, item 1933/0341, f. 73; *York Chronicle*, "York Road Board", 13 December 1940, p. 1, Trove.

[16] Ibid.

[17] Native Welfare, item 1933/0341, f. 74-84.

[18] Ibid., f. 79.

[19] Native Affairs, item 1930/0037, f. 162-163; *York Chronicle*, "Quairading District Hospital – Annual Meeting", 26 July 1940, p. 4, Trove.

[20] Aborigines Department, Half-Caste Women in Great Southern Districts – Confinement of – Complaint re Lack of Hospital Facilities, series 2030, consignment 993, item 1936/0221, f. 42-44, SROWA.

[21] Department of Native Affairs, York – Medical Treatment of Natives, series 2030 cons993 item 1941/0155, f. 31, SLWA.

[22] Native Affairs, item 1941/0155, f. 32.

[23] Ibid., f. 3.

[24] Haebich, *For their own Good,* p. 345.

[25] Native Affairs, item 1938/1037, f. 25-27.

[26] Department of Native Affairs, Annual Report - Reports by Police Officers (Regulation 79), series 2030, consignment 993, item 1943/0558, f. 36, SLWA.

[27] Native Affairs, item 1941/0155, f. 5.

[28] Native Welfare, item 1933/0341, f. 137; Native Affairs, item 1938/1037, f. 61.

[29] Native Affairs, item 1941/0155, f. 25.

[30] Native Welfare, item 1933/0341, f. 85.

[31] Ibid.

[32] Native Welfare, item 1933/0341, f. 86.

[33] *York Leader and Quairading and Dangin Herald*, "Municipal Council", 7 February 1941, p. 3, Trove; *York Chronicle*, "Municipal Council", 7 February 1941, p. 3, Trove.

[34] *York Chronicle*, "Road Board", 14 February 1941, p. 1, Trove.

[35] Native Welfare, item 1933/0341, f. 89.

[36] Ibid., f. 87, 90.

[37] *West Australian*, "Seasonal Conditions – Water Difficulties Increases", 15 February 1941, p. 5, Trove.

[38] Native Welfare, item 1933/0341, f. 87, 90.

[39] Ibid., f. 94.

[40] Native Welfare, item 1933/0341, f. 112.

[41] Ibid., f. 113, 120.

[42] Native Affairs, item 1938/1037, f. 21-24.

[43] Ibid., f. 13-14.

[44] Ibid.

[45] Ibid., f. 15-18.

[46] Ibid., f. 19-20.

[47] *Eastern Districts Chronicle*, "York Municipal Council – Ordinary Meeting May 18", 29 May 1909, p. 3, Trove; *York Chronicle*, "A Mayoral Record – Elected Five Years in Succession", 25 November 1932, p. 2, Trove.

[48] *Western Mail*, "York Facts", 24 September 1931, p. 40, Trove.

[49] Haebich, *For their own Good,* p. 236.

[50] *Native Welfare Act 1954.*

[51] Native Affairs, item 1938/1037, f. 28.

[52] Ibid., f. 29.

[53] Ibid.

[54] Ibid.

[55] Government of Western Australia, *Native Administration Act 1941* (No. 4 of 1941).

[56] Department of Native Affairs, Census of Aboriginals and Half-Castes, series 2030, consignment 993, item 1928/0304, p. 176, SLWA; Department of Native Affairs, Regulation 171 (Population Returns) 1941/1942, series 2030, consignment 993, item 1943/0340, f. 36, SLWA; Department of Native Affairs, Annual Reports – Circular 171 to Police Officers – Population Returns 1943/1944, series 2030, consignment 993, item 1945/0356, f. 64, SROWA; Department of Native Affairs, C N A Annual Report 1946/1947 – Circular 171 to Police Officers – Population Returns, series 2030, consignment 993, item 1947/0398, SLWA; Department of Native Affairs, C N A Annual Report - 1950/1951 – Population Returns, series 2030, consignment 993, item 1951/0322, f. 68, SROWA; Department of Native Affairs, C N A Annual Report – Population Returns, series 2030, consignment 993, item 1952/0342, f. 54, SROWA; Department of Native Welfare, Census and Population Returns of Natives in Western Australia, series 2030, consignment 1733, item 1963/0115, f. 18, SROWA.

[57] Government of Western Australia, *Land Act 1933* (No 37 of 1933).

[58] *York Chronicle*, "Municipal Council", 5 March 1943, p. 3, Trove.

[59] *York Chronicle*, "Municipal Council", 9 April 1943, p. 3, Trove [It is reported that inspections occurred on 24/02 and 28/02, however, it appears likely that this date was printed in error and that the inspections occurred on 24/03 and 28/03 instead given that the inspections were discussed on 6 April at the Council meeting and that a decision to take action was made in early March].

[60] *York Chronicle*, "Presentation to Cr. C Foreman", 27 November 1952, p. 1, Trove; York Town Council, "Nominal rolls of Chairman, Mayors, Councillors and Town Clerks and extracts from Council minute books. The town of York was absorbed by the Shire of York in 1965", call number PR14522/YOR/3 - 0/s, SLWA; *Northam Advertiser*, "Death of Mrs. C Foreman", 21 May 1970, p. 9, SLWA.

[61] *York Chronicle*, "Municipal Council", 19 March 1943, p. 3, Trove.

[62] *York Chronicle*, "Municipal Council", 18 February 1944, p. 3, Trove.

[63] Ibid.

[64] *Government Gazette of Western Australia*, No. 9 (Perth, WA: Acting Government Printer of Western Australia, 1906), p. 246; *York Chronicle*, "Obituary – Mr. Samuel Charles Rich", 13 June 1941, p. 2, Trove.

[65] *York Chronicle*, "Social & Personal", 11 July 1941, p. 2, Trove; *York Chronicle*, "Municipal Council", 20 March 1942, p. 3, Trove; *York Leader and Quairading and Dangin Herald*, "Municipal Council", 20 March 1942, p. 3, Trove.

[66] Native Affairs, item 1938/1037, f. 36.

[67] *York Chronicle*, "Municipal Council", 25 August 1944, p. 3, Trove.

[68] *Mirror*, "Knife Flashes in York Melee", 13 November 1948, p. 7, Trove.

[69] *York Chronicle*, "Municipal Council", 22 September 1944, p. 3, Trove.

[70] Ibid.

[71] *York Chronicle*, "Municipality of York – Notice of Sale", 30 August 1951, p. 5, Trove; *York Chronicle*, "Obituary", 3 September 1953, p. 7, Trove.

[72] Native Affairs, item 1938/1037, f. 100-103.

[73] *York Chronicle*, "Municipal Council", 6 October 1944, p. 3, Trove.

[74] *York Leader and Quairading and Dangin Herald*, "Municipal Council", 9 March 1945, p. 4, Trove.

[75] *York Leader and Quairading and Dangin Herald*, "Municipal Council", 9 November 1945, p. 3, Trove.

[76] *York Chronicle*, "York Council Meeting", 27 June 1947, p. 3, Trove.

[77] *York Chronicle*, "Municipal Matters", 11 July 1947, p. 5, Trove.

[78] *York Chronicle*, "York Municipal Council", 10 October 1943, p. 5, Trove.

[79] Native Affairs, item 1938/1037, f. 38.

[80] *York Chronicle*, "Municipal Council – The Native Question", 18 February 1944, p. 3, Trove.

[81] Register - Prisoners, York Gaol, series 1664, consignment 1442, item 1, SROWA; York Clerk of Courts, Charge Books – Police Court, series 408, consignment 3794, item 1, p. 37109, SROWA.

[82] *York Chronicle*, "Municipal Council – The Native Question", 18 February 1944, p. 3, Trove.

[83] Ibid.

[84] Ibid.

[85] Ibid.

[86] *York Leader and Quairading and Dangin Herald*, "The Native Question", 25 February 1944, p. 2, Trove.

[87] Ibid.

[88] Wendy Birman, "Baker, Clarence Patrick (Paddy) (1898 – 1986)", Australian Dictionary of Biography, accessed 4 December 2022, https://adb.anu.edu.au;

York Chronicle, "Baker's Talkies to End After 25 years", 14 June 1956, p. 1, SLWA; *York Chronicle*, "Advertisement – Bakers Pictures", 30 July 1959, p. 11, SLWA.

[89] Native Affairs, item 1938/1037, f. 36-43.

[90] Native Affairs, item 1938/1037, f. 36-43.

[91] Ibid., f. 39-40.

[92] Ibid., f. 39-44.

[93] Native Affairs, item 1938/1037, f. 47.

[94] Ibid., f. 71.

[95] Ibid., f. 73.

[96] York Clerk of Courts, Charge Books – Police Court, series 408, consignment 3794, item 1, SROWA.

[97] *York Chronicle*, "Native Problem – Further Discussion at Council Meeting", 13 June 1947, p. 1, Trove.

[98] *York Chronicle*, "Native Affairs discussed", 17 October 1947, p. 3, Trove.

[99] George Kickett, "The Native Reserve York, WA", oral history interview by Roland See, 1 October 2019, audio, 01:07:23, author holds original audio file.

[100] *Government Gazette of Western Australia*, No. 23 (Perth, WA: Government Printer of Western Australia, 1948), p. 1268; Author's research based on Western Australian Government Gazettes, Police Gazettes, and departmental records.

[101] Saul Yarran, "Saul Yarran", in *Us Fellas*, edited by Colleen Glass and Archie Weller, pp 130-146 (Perth: Artlook Books, 1987), p. 136; *Government Gazette of Western Australia*, No. 31 (Perth, WA: Government Printer of Western Australia, 1951), p. 808.

[102] *York Chronicle*, "Municipal Council", 21 January 1944, p. 3, Trove.

[103] Native Affairs, item 1938/1037, f. 36.

[104] *York Chronicle*, "Municipal Council", 31 March 1944, p. 3, Trove.

[105] Native Affairs, item 1938/1037, f. 123-126 – The acting Inspector reports of "Ascot Park", however, this is most likely a typing error as there is no Ascot Park in York and Avon Park is a popular park close to town centre; Ascot is a location in Perth.

[106] *York Leader and Quairading and Dangin Herald*, "Municipal Council", 28 September 1945, p. 3, Trove.

[107] Native Affairs, item 1938/1037, f. 123-126.

[108] *York Chronicle*, "York Municipal Council", 15 August 1947, p. 7, Trove; *York Chronicle*, "Erection of Public Conveniences to be Proceeded with", 15 December 1949, p. 1, Trove; *York Chronicle*, "Municipal Matters", 23 August 1951, p. 5, Trove.

[109] Native Welfare, item 1933/0341, f. 131b, 133a-135a.

[110] "Biographical Register of Members of the Parliament of Western Australia", Parliament of Western Australia – Website, accessed 29 October, 2022.

[111] Native Welfare, item 1933/0341, f. 133b.

[112] Ibid.

[113] Fady Aoun, "Whitewashing Australia's History of Stigmatising Trade Marks and Commercial Imagery", *Melbourne University Law Review*, vol 42, no. 3 (2019), 692, https://law.unimelb.edu.au.

[114] York Clerk of Courts, Magistrate's Evidence Books – Police Court, series 414, consignment 3797, item 3, f. 111-117, SROWA.

[115] *York Leader and Quairading and Dangin Herald*, "Unlawful Assault – Three Natives Charges", 16 March 1945, p. 5, Trove; York Clerk of Courts, item 3, f. 111-117. *West Australian,* "German Mass Murders", 27 November 1944, p. 5, Trove; Register - Prisoners, York Gaol, series 1664, consignment 1442, item 1, SROWA.

[116] Native Welfare, item 1933/0341, f. 133b.

[117] *York Chronicle*, "York Road Board", 16 March 1945, p. 2, Trove.

[118] Native Affairs, item 1938/1037, f. 54.

[119] Ibid.

[120] Native Affairs, item 1938/1037, f. 53.

[121] *West Australian*, "Basic Wage – Quarterly Declaration", 27 October 1944, p. 4, Trove.

[122] Department of Native Affairs, Unemployed Natives – Utilization of services during War Period, series 2030, consignment 993, item 1942/0004, f. 6-7, SROWA.

[123] Department of Native Affairs, item 1942/0004, f. 9-10.

[124] Ibid., f. 64, 66.

[125] Ibid., f. 53-57.

[126] Department of Native Affairs, Evacuation and Military Control of Natives in Coastal Areas south of Northampton, series 2030, consignment 993, item 1943/0592, f. 1, 39-46, 62-71, SROWA; Department of the Army – Central Office, Protected and controlled area (Natives and Coastal), series MP508/1, item 4/702/1116, National Archives of Australia.

[127] Department of Native Affairs, item 1943/0592, f. 18.

[128] Ibid., f. 61, 16.

[129] Ibid., f. 18-19.

[130] *York Leader and Quairading and Dangin Herald*, "Municipal Council", 13 July 1945, p. 3, Trove.

[131] Native Affairs, item 1938/1037, f. 56-57.

[132] Ibid., f. 57.

[133] Ibid., f. 61.

[134] *Mount Barker and Denmark Record*, "Local & General – Child Endowment", 19 May 1941, p. 2, Trove; *Geraldton Guardian and Express*, "Letter to the Editor - Child Endowment – Position of Natives", 19 July 1941, p. 2, Trove; Find &

Connect, "Western Australian Glossary Term – Child Endowment", accessed 13 November 2023, https://www.findandconnect.gov.au.

[135] *Irwin Index*, "Child Endowment – Benefit for Aboriginals", 18 March, 1944, p. 4, Trove; Department of Native Affairs, item 1942/0004, f. 52.

[136] *Daily News*, "Native Endowment Spending Supervised",2 October 1945, p. 5, Trove.

[137] Native Affairs, item 1938/1037, f. 55.

[138] *Daily News*, "Child Endowment Scheme Criticised", 23 September 1944, p. 9, Trove.

[139] *Daily News*, "Aborigines Save More Money than Whites", 27 September 1944, p. 10, Trove.

[140] *Narrogin Observer*, "The Aborigines – To the Editor", 5 August 1944, p. 3, Trove.

[141] *Daily News*, "Endowment Up 2/6, Pension 5/6", 8 March 1945, p. 15, Trove.

[142] Department of Native Affairs, Inspector & Patrol Officer - Central - Patrol Reports, series 2030, consignment 993, item 1950/0800, pdf p. 86-87, SROWA.

[143] Native Welfare, item 1933/0341, f. 142.

[144] Native Affairs, item 1938/1037, f. 58-60.

[145] Ibid.; Register - Prisoners, York Gaol, series 1664, consignment 1442, item 1, SROWA.

[146] Native Affairs, item 1938/1037, f. 61.

[147] Ibid.

[148] Ibid.

[149] Ibid.

[150] Native Affairs, item 1938/1037, f. 64.

[151] York Clerk of Courts, Magistrate's Evidence Books – Police Court, series 414, consignment 3797, item 4, f 78-81, SROWA.

[152] Ibid.

[153] York Clerk of Courts, Index – Charges – Police Court – 1910 to 1971, series 409, consignment 3795, item 1, SROWA.

[154] Ken Colbung, "On Being an Aboriginal – A Personal Statement", in *Aborigines of the West – Their Past and their Present – Revised Edition*, edited by Ronald M Berndt and Catherine H Berndt (Perth: UWA Press, 1980), p. 101.

[155] Department of Native Welfare, *Annual Report of the Commissioner of Native Welfare for the year ended on 30 June 1955*, (Perth, WA: Government Printer of Western Australia, 1955), p. 43.

[156] Native Affairs, item 1938/1037, f. 75-77.

[157] Ibid.

[158] *West Australian*, "Coloured Children – Need for Education – Position in York District", 28 August 1946, p. 11, Trove.

[159] Department of Native Affairs, Exclusion of Half-Caste and Native Children from State Schools, series 2030, consignment 993, item 1933/0231, SROWA; *Wagin Argus and Arthur, Dumbleyung, Lake Grace Express*, "Half-Caste Problem", 24 November 1938, p. 5, Trove.

[160] *Government Gazette of Western Australia*, No. 22 (Perth, WA: Government Printer of Western Australia, 1920), p. 681; Department of Native Affairs, item 1933/0231, f. 1-35.

[161] Department of Native Affairs, item 1933/0231, f. 105; *West Australian*, "Range of Education – Statistics for 1937 – 1938", 24 November 1938, p. 22, Trove.

[162] Personal e-mail correspondence with Dr Marion Kickett, September 2023; Tracey Kickett, "Resistance: A process of survival for Balardong people" (Hon. diss., University of Sydney, 2000), p. 92; *Avon Gazette and York Times*, "An Old Resident Passes – The Late Mr. W T Craig", 19 April 1929, p. 2, Trove; Department of Native Affairs, Central District - Patrol Officer Reports, series 2030, consignment 993, item 1951/0695, f. 59-67; *York Chronicle*, "Death of Louisa Craig", 1 October 1959, p. 1, SLWA.

[163] Department of Native Affairs, item 1933/0231, f. 125-125, 137, 149-150.

[164] Department of Native Affairs, Exclusion of Half-cast children and native children from State Schools, series 2030, consignment 993, item 1943/0222, f. 16, SROWA.

[165] Department of Native Affairs, Education of Natives – Establishment of Schools in Native Settlements staffed by fully qualified Education Department Officers, s2030, consignment 993, item 1942/0745, f. 15, SROWA; Department of Native Affairs, *Annual Report of the Commissioner of Native Affairs for the Year ended 30th June 1942*, (Perth, WA: Government Printer of Western Australia), p. 16-18, SLWA; Department of Native Affairs, *Annual Report of the Commissioner of Native Affairs for the Year ended 30th June 1943*, (Perth, WA: Government Printer of Western Australia), p. 16-18, SLWA.

[166] *Government Gazette of Western Australia*, No. 34 (Perth, WA: Government Printer of Western Australia, 1944), p. 19 (631).

[167] Ibid.

[168] Department of Native Affairs, Irregular attendance of Native Children, series 2030, consignment 993, item 1949/0490, f. 7-12, SROWA.

[169] Ibid., f. 12.

[170] Ibid., f. 7-12; Department of Native Affairs, Education of Natives - Policy - General correspondence, series 2030, consignment 993, item 1949/0921, f. 94-95, 97, SROWA.

[171] Department of Native Welfare, Reserve for Natives – York, Reserve 8567, 10ac, series 2030, consignment 993, item 1933/0341, f. 148-150, SROWA; Department of Native Affairs, *Annual Report of the Commissioner of Native*

Affairs for the year ended on 30 June 1942, (Perth, WA: Government Printer of Western Australia), p. 16-18.

172 Native Welfare, item 1933/0341, f. 148-150.

173 Ibid.

174 Native Welfare, item 1933/0341, f. 148-150.

175 Department of Native Affairs, C N A Annual Report 1946/1947 – Circular 171 to Police Officers – Population Returns, series 2030, consignment 993, item 1947/0398, no folio, SLWA; Department of Native Affairs, C N A Annual Report - 1950/1951 – Population Returns, series 2030, consignment 993, item 1951/0322, f. 68, SROWA.

176 *York Chronicle*, "Municipal Council", 24 May 1946, p. 3, Trove.

177 Native Affairs, item 1938/1037, f. 78, 122.

178 *West Australian*, "Aborigines' Status – Citizenship Rights – Provision Already Exists", 18 February 1946, p. 10, Trove.

179 Native Affairs, item 1938/1037, f. 82.

180 Ibid.

181 Ibid., f. 83.

182 Ibid., f. 83.

183 York Clerk of Courts, Charge Books – Police Court, series 408, consignment 3794, item 1, SROWA.

184 *York Leader and Quairading and Dangin Herald*, "York Sports – Most Successful Meeting",7 June 1946, p. 3, Trove.

185 *York Leader and Quairading and Dangin Herald*,7 June 1946.

186 *York Chronicle*, "York Sports", 7 June 1946, p. 3, Trove.

187 Native Affairs, item 1938/1037, f. 83.

188 Ibid., f. 90.

189 Ibid., f. 86-89.

190 Ibid.

191 Ibid.

192 Ibid.; York Clerk of Courts, Charge Books – Police Court, Series 408, consignment 3794-1.

193 *York Leader and Quairading and Dangin Herald*, "Municipal Council", 28 June 1946, p. 3, Trove.

194 *York Chronicle*, "Municipal election", 19 July 1946, p. 2, Trove.

195 Department of Community Welfare, Property - York Reserve 8567 - Buildings and Land, series 1099 consignment 2532, item A1821, SROWA.

196 Native Affairs, item 1938/1037, f. 90.

197 Ibid., f. 91.

198 Ibid.; *Geraldton Guardian and Express*, "The Native Problem – Murchison Requests Statement by Minister", 27 July 1946, p. 4, Trove.

[199] *York Chronicle*, "Municipal Council", 14 June, 1946, p. 3, Trove; *Government Gazette of Western Australia*, No. 19 (Perth, WA: Government Printer of Western Australia, 1940), p. 663.

[200] *York Chronicle*, 14 June, 1946; Shire of York, *Local Heritage Survey 2019 – Heritage Places*, 2019, p. 73, https://www.york.wa.gov.au; York Clerk of Courts, Charge Books – Police Court, series 408, consignment 3794, item 1, SROWA.

[201] *York Chronicle*, "Municipal Council", 16 August 1946, p. 3, Trove.

[202] Ibid..

[203] Western Australia, *Hansard Parliamentary Debates, Eighteenth Parliament – Third Session*, vol. 117, Legislative Council (14 August 1946), p. 264-265; "Biographical Register of Members of the Parliament of Western Australia", Parliament of Western Australia – Website, accessed 19 November, 2022; *West Australian*, "Our Coloured Folk", 19 April 1930, p. 10, Trove; Graham Seal, *Inventing Anzac – The Digger and National Mythology* (St Lucia: University of Queensland Press, 2004), p. 86.

[204] *Hansard*, Legislative Council (14 August 1946), p. 264-265.

[205] Native Affairs, item 1938/1037, f. 96-97; Department of Native Welfare, *Annual Report of the Commissioner of Native Welfare for the year ended on 30 June 1959,* (Perth, WA: Government Printer of Western Australia, 1960), p. 8, https://aiatsis.gov.au/.

[206] Native Affairs, item 1938/1037, f. 98.

[207] Ibid.

[208] Native Welfare, item 1933/0341, f. 148-150.

[209] Ibid.

[210] Native Affairs, item 1938/1037, f. 101.

[211] Ibid.; Native Welfare, item 1933/0341, f. 148-150.

[212] Native Welfare, item 1933/0341, f. 148-150; Native Affairs, item 1938/1037, f. 99; *York Leader and Quairading and Dangin Herald*, "Municipal Council", 30 August 1946, p. 6, Trove.

[213] Native Welfare, item 1933/0341, f. 148-149.

[214] Personal email correspondence with Dr Marion Kickett, September 2023; Department of Native Affairs, Annual Report, Reports by Police Officers (Regulation 79), series 2030 cons993 item 1943/0558, f. 36.

[215] *West Australian*, "Health of Natives – Statutory Medical Fund", 20 December 1939, p. 19, Trove; *Gnowangerup Star*, "Native Affairs", 12 September 1953, p. 1, Trove; *Daily News*, "WA turns a new leaf in native affairs", 20 May 1955, p. 2, Trove.

[216] Department of Native Affairs, District Office – Central – Patrol Reports, series 2030, consignment 993, item 1949/0189, f. 107-109, SLWA; Department of Native Affairs, Inspector & Patrol Officer - Central - Patrol Reports, series 2030, consignment 993, item 1950/0800, f. 51-53, SLWA; Department of Native

Affairs, Central District - Patrol Officer Reports, series 2030, consignment 993, item 1951/0695, f. 59-67; *Beverley Times*, "Valuable Farm Properties sold at York", 11 March 1960, p. 4, Trove; "Louisa Margaret *Duperouzel* Craig", Findagrave.com, accessed 30 November 2022.

[217] Native Welfare, item 1933/0341, f. 149-150.

[218] Native Affairs, item 1938/1037, f. 107.

[219] Ibid., f. 104.

[220] Ibid., f. 106.

[221] Ibid., f. 107; York Clerk of Courts, Charge Books – Police Court, series 408, consignment 3794, item 1, SROWA.

[222] Government of Western Australia, *Justices Act 1936* (No. 11 of 1936).

[223] Ibid.; Western Australia, *Hansard Parliamentary Debates, Twentieth Parliament – Second Session*, vol. 129, Legislative Council (20 November 1951), p. 767.

[224] *York Leader and Quairading and Dangin Herald*, "York By-Election – Mr. A Noonan's Candidature", 6 November 1942, p. 5, Trove.

[225] *York Leader and Quairading and Dangin Herald*, "Municipal Council", 27 December 1946, p. 5, Trove.

[226] Department of Native Affairs, York - Prohibited Area, series 2030, consignment 993, item 1947/0270, f. 1, SROWA.

[227] *York Leader and Quairading and Dangin Herald*, "Municipal Council", 31 January, 1947, p. 5, Trove.

[228] Native Affairs, item 1947/0270, f. 3, 6.

[229] *York Leader and Quairading and Dangin Herald*, "Municipal Council",28 February, 1947, p. 4, Trove.

[230] Ibid.

[231] Native Affairs, item 1947/0270, f. 2-9.

[232] Ibid., f. 13.

[233] Ibid.; "Biographical Register of Members of the Parliament of Western Australia", Parliament of Western Australia – Website, accessed 6 October, 2023.

[234] Native Affairs, item 1938/1037, f. 109-111; Native Affairs, item 1947/0270, f. 10.

[235] Native Affairs, item 1947/0270, f. 14-16.

[236] Government of Western Australia, *Native Administration Act 1936* (No. 43 of 1936).

[237] Department of Native Affairs, Prohibited Area - General Correspondence, series 2030, consignment 993, item 1940/1244, f. 17, SROWA.

[238] Department of Native Affairs, City of Perth - Prohibited Area, series 2030, consignment 993, item 1927/0038, SROWA; Western Australia, *Native Administration Act 1936*.

[239] Native Affairs, item 1927/0038.

[240] Crown Law Department, City of Perth – Prohibited are for abo. Natives – Advice re boundaries of, series 2664, consignment 1042, item 1947/1719, SROWA; For the mentioned convictions one may peruse Trove; Native Affairs, item 1940/1244, f. 10.

[241] Native Affairs, item 1940/1244, f.11-12.

[242] Department of Native Affairs, Alvan House (Mt Lawley) Prohibited Area, series 2030, consignment 933, item 1950/0758, f. 8, SROWA.

[243] Native Affairs, item 1940/1244, f. 11-12; *Government Gazette of Western Australia*, No. 14 (Perth, WA: Government Printer of Western Australia, 1950), p. 2731; Anna Haebich, *For their own Good: Aborigines and Government in the South West of Western Australia, 1900-1940* (Nedlands: University of Western Australia Press, 1992), p. 313.

[244] Government of Western Australia, *Native Administration Act 1941* (No. 4 of 1941); York Clerk of Courts, Charge Books – Police Court, series 408, consignment 3794, item 1, SROWA.

[245] Native Affairs, item 1947/0270, f. 20.

[246] *York Chronicle*, "Native Problem – Further Discussion at Council Meeting", 13 June, 1947, p. 1, Trove.

[247] Ibid.; *York Chronicle*, "Cr Noonan Mayor", 4 April 1947, p. 1, Trove.

[248] Native Affairs, item 1947/0270, f. 22.

[249] *York Chronicle*, "The Native Problem. Creates Discussion", 16 May, 1947, p. 1, Trove.

[250] Native Affairs, item 1938/1037, f. 112-117.

[251] *York Chronicle*, 16 May, 1947.

[252] Department of Native Affairs, Housing General, series 2030, consignment 993, item 1947/0991, f. 7, SROWA.

[253] *York Chronicle*, 16 May, 1947.

[254] This author checked all WA Government Gazettes that listed the issuing of conditional citizenship. However, one person who was issued with an Exemption certificate in Northam in 1944 lived in York at the time.

[255] *York Chronicle*, 16 May, 1947.

[256] Ibid.

[257] Department of Native Affairs, Annual Reports – Circular 171 to Police Officers – Population Returns 1943/1944, series 2030, consignment 993, item 1945/0356, f. 64, SROWA; Department of Native Affairs, Annual Reports 1946/1947 – Circular 171 to Police Officers – Population Returns, series 2030, consignment 993, item 1947/0398, no folio, SROWA.

[258] *York Chronicle*, 16 May, 1947.

[259] *Westralian Worker*, "Farm Workers' Award", 10 January 1947, p. 2, Trove; *Western Australian Industrial Gazette*, AWARD – A.W.U. (Farm Workers), No,

6 of 1946, vol. 26, p. 205; *Western Australian Industrial Gazette,* AWARD – A.W.U. (Farm Workers), No, 422 of 1964, vol. 44, p. 857; https://www.wairc.wa.gov.au.

[260] *York Chronicle,* 16 May, 1947, Trove.

[261] *York Chronicle,* 16 May, 1947.

[262] Ibid.

[263] Native Affairs, item 1938/1037, f. 112-116; G. C. Bolton and Tresna Shorter, "McDonald, Sir Robert Ross (1888–1964)", Australian Dictionary of Biography, accessed 8 December 2022, https://adb.anu.edu.au/.

[264] *York Chronicle,* "Native Affairs Discussed – Visit of Minister and departmental Officers", 17 October, 1947, p. 3, Trove.

[265] *York Chronicle,* "York Municipal Council" & "Advertising", 14 November, 1947, p. 6, http://nla.gov.au/nla.news-page28000182.

[266] Department of Local Government, Sport and Cultural Industries, Aboriginal History Research Services, "Family History", accessed 20 August 2022, https://www.dlgsc.wa.gov.au/.

[267] Register - Prisoners, York Gaol, series 1664, consignment 1442, item 1, SROWA; *York Chronicle,* "Natives in Trouble", 27 January, 1949, p. 2, Trove; *West Australian,* "Native on two Charges",3 February, 1950, p. 5, Trove.

[268] *Government Gazette of Western Australia,* No. 41 (Perth, WA: Government Printer of Western Australia, 1948), p. 2098; *Northam Advertiser,* "Police Court", 15 July, 1944, p. 5, Trove.

[269] York Clerk of Courts, Charge Books – Police Court, series 408, consignment 3794, item 1, SROWA.

[270] Native Affairs, item 1938/1037, f. 121.

[271] Ibid.

[272] Ibid.

[273] York Clerk of Courts, Charge Books – Police Court, series 408, consignment 3794, item 1, SROWA.

[274] Native Affairs, item 1938/1037, f. 121.

[275] *Government Gazette of Western Australia,* Various issues (Perth, WA: Government Printer of Western Australia, 1946 – 1948), p. 1543 (1946), p. 431 (1947), p. 1722 (1947), p. 326 (1948), p. 1268 (1948), p. 1268 (1948), p. 2337 (1948), p. 51 (1949).

[276] McGregor, *Indifferent Inclusion,* 148.

[277] Department of Native Affairs, District Office. Central - Patrol Reports, series 2030, consignment 993, item 1952/0576, no folio, SROWA.

[278] McGregor, *Indifferent Inclusion,* 77; Anna Haebich, *Spinning the Dream – Assimilation in Australia 1950-1970,* (North Fremantle: Fremantle Press, 2008), 221; *West Australian,* "Citizen Rights for Natives", 24 February, 1950, p. 9, Trove; *West Australian,* "Assimilation of Natives", 23 May, 1950, p. 7, Trove.

[279] Department of Native Affairs, Prohibited Area - General Correspondence, series 2030, consignment 993, item 1940/1244, f. 46, SROWA.

[280] Department of Native Affairs, *Annual Report of the Commissioner of Native Affairs for the year ended on 30 June 1951*, (Perth, WA: Government Printer of Western Australia, 1953), p. 10.

[281] *Gnowangerup Star*, "Local Government", 26 May 1951, p. 2, Trove.

[282] Angela Lapham, "Stanley Middleton's response to assimilation policy in his fight for Aboriginal people's equality, 1948–62", *Aboriginal History*, vol. 40, no.1 (2016), p. 6; *Government Gazette of Western Australia*, No. 52 (Perth, WA: Government Printer of Western Australia, 1948), p. 2546.

[283] York Clerk of Courts, Charge Books – Police Court, series 408, consignment 3794, item 1, SROWA; *York Chronicle*, "Natives in Court", 13 January 1949, p. 5, Trove; Native Affairs, item 1938/1037, f. 120.

[284] George Kickett, "The Native Reserve York, WA", oral history interview by Roland See, 1 October 2019, audio, 01:07:23, author holds original audio file.

Chapter 4. Jan 1949 to June 1950

[1] Minister's Correspondence File - Native Affairs, series 3841, consignment 769, item 2, p. 20-21, SROWA.

[2] Anna Haebich, *Spinning the Dream – Assimilation in Australia 1950-1970*, (North Fremantle: Fremantle Press, 2008), 218-222; Department of Native Affairs, District Office – Central – Patrol Reports, series 2030, consignment 993, item 1949/0189, SLWA; Minister's Correspondence File - Native Affairs, series 3841, consignment769, item 3, p. 169-177, SROWA; Western Australia, *Hansard Parliamentary Debates, Nineteenth Parliament – Second Session*, vol. 121, Legislative Council (21 October 1948), p. 736-743.

[3] Department of Native Affairs, District Office – Central – Patrol Reports, series 2030, consignment 993, item 1949/0189, p. 103-109.

[4] Native Affairs, item 1938/1037, f. 121; Native Affairs, item 1949/0189, p. 103-109, SLWA; York Clerk of Courts, Charge Books – Police Court, series 408, consignment 3794, item 1, SROWA.

[5] Native Affairs, item 1949/0189, 108.

[6] Ibid., 133.

[7] Ibid., 108-109.

[8] Ibid.; *Western Australian Industrial Gazette*, vol. XXIX, Half-Year ended 30 June 1949 (Perth, WA: Government Printer of Western Australia, 1950), p 5, https://www.wairc.wa.gov.au.

[9] Native Affairs, item 1949/0189, 108; Government of Western Australia, *Health Act* Reprint 1949 (No. 43 of 1911); Native Affairs, item 1938/1037, f. 122, 124.

[10] Department of Native Affairs, Housing General, series 2030, consignment 993, item 1947/0991, f. 10-38, SROWA.

[11] Native Affairs, item 1947/0991, f. 10-38.

[12] Native Affairs, item 1938/1037, f. 130.

[13] Native Affairs, item 1938/1037, f. 128.

[14] Ibid., f. 135-138.

[15] Native Affairs, item 1938/1037, f. 101; Department of Community Welfare, Property - York Reserve 8567 - Buildings and Land, series 1099 consignment 2532, item A1821, f. 1-2, SROWA.

[16] Native Affairs, item 1949/0189, no folios, pages 131-132.

[17] Department of Native Affairs, Marriages, series 2030, consignment 993, item 1949/0066, f. 5, SROWA.

[18] Department of Native Affairs, Royal Commission on the Treatment of Aborigines – vol 1, series 2030, consignment 993, item 1933/0333, no folio – pdf page 10, SROWA.

[19] Native Affairs, item 1949/0189, 131-132; Department of Native Affairs, Marriages, series 2030, consignment 993, item 1949/0066, f. 5, SROWA.

[20] Department of Community Welfare, Property - York Reserve 8567 - Buildings and Land, series 1099 consignment 2532, item A1821, f. 1-2, SROWA.

[21] Ibid.

[22] Ibid.

[23] Native Affairs, item 1938/1037, f. 135; Native Welfare, item 1933/0341, f. 161-162.

[24] *York Chronicle*, "York Road Board", 25 August, 1949, p. 4, Trove.

[25] Government of Western Australia, *Dog Act 1903* (No. 74 of 1948, reprinted 1959).

[26] Native Affairs, item 1938/1037, f. 118a; *York Chronicle*, "Public Conveniences at York", 25 July 1947, p. 1, Trove.

[27] Native Affairs, item 1938/1037, f. 98b;

[28] *York Chronicle*, "Sanitation at Native Reserve", 17 November 1949, p. 1, Trove.

[29] Native Affairs, item 1949/0189, p. 100.

[30] Ibid., p. 77.

[31] Ibid., p. 87.

[32] Ibid., p. 77.

[33] "Biographical Register of Members of the Parliament of Western Australia", Parliament of Western Australia – Website, accessed 11 February, 2023.

[34] *York Chronicle*, "Natives Abuse Citizenship Rights", 5 January 1950, p. 1, Trove.

[35] Native Affairs, item 1949/0189, p. 24, 33.

[36] Department of Native Affairs, District Office – Central – Patrol Reports, series 2030, consignment 993, item 1950/0720, f. 9-1, SROWA.

[37] Native Affairs, item 1949/0189, p. 10-11, 87-89; Department of Native Affairs, Welfare Officer - Patrol Report, series 2030, consignment 993, item 1951/0797, f. 25-26; Department of Native Affairs, Central District - Patrol Officer Reports, series 2030, consignment 993, item 1951/0695, f. 56-59; *York Chronicle*, "York Road Board", 25 May 1950, p. 4, Trove.

[38] Native Affairs, item 1950/0720, f. 2.

[39] Native Affairs, item 1951/0797, f. 25-26.

[40] *West Australian*, "York Natives' Humpies", 8 April 1950, p. 6, Trove.

[41] Native Affairs, item 1938/1037, f. 104b.

[42] *York Chronicle*, "Municipal Matters", 16 March 1950, p. 3, Trove; *York Chronicle*, "Municipal Matters", 13 April 1950, p. 3, Trove.

[43] Native Affairs, item 1938/1037, f. 105b.

[44] *York Chronicle*, "Armchair Administrators", 27 April 1950, p. 1, Trove.

[45] Ibid.

[46] *West Australian*, "Concerns over Natives' Camps at York", 4 May 1950, p. 6, Trove.

[47] Ibid.

[48] Native Affairs, item 1938/1037, f. 106b.

[49] Department of Community Welfare, Property - York Reserve 8567 - Buildings and Land, series 1099 consignment 2532, item A1821, 4-5, SROWA.

[50] Ibid.

[51] *West Australian*, "Assimilation of Natives", 23 May 1950, p. 7, Trove.

[52] Ibid.

[53] *York Chronicle*, "York Road Board", 25 May 1950, p. 4, Trove.

[54] Ibid.

[55] Department of Native Affairs, Inspector & Patrol Officer - Central - Patrol Reports, series 2030, consignment 993, item 1950/0800, f. 27. - (McLarty named the chairman as "Donaldson;" however, this must have been a typing error as Robinson was chairman from the late 1930s into the 1960s).

[56] Native Affairs, item 1949/0189, p. 10, 86-87; Native Affairs, item 1950/0800, f. 51.

[57] Department of Community Welfare, Property - York Reserve 8567 - Buildings and Land, series 1099 consignment 2532, item A1821, f. 6-8, SROWA.

[58] Native Affairs, item 1949/0189, p. 10; Native Affairs, item 1950/0800, f. 20, 42.

[59] Department of Native Affairs, District Office – Central District – Patrol Reports, series 2030, consignment 993, item 1953/0124, f. 7.

[60] Native Affairs, item 1938/1037, f. 109b.

[61] Native Affairs, item 1949/0189, p. 10; *York Chronicle*, "Municipal Matters", 25 May 1950, p. 2, Trove.

[62] Native Affairs, item 1938/1037, f. 109b.

[63] Peter E. Gordon, "The Authoritarian Personality", Verso Books Blogs, 25 August 2020, https://www.versobooks.com.

[64] Native Affairs, item 1949/0189, p. 88.

[65] Native Affairs, item 1950/0800, f. 51-53.

[66] Community Welfare, item A1821, f. 6-8.

[67] Department of Native Welfare, Central District - Patrol Reports - Patrols Officer, series 2030, consignment 993, item 1956/0106, f. 20-21, SROWA; Native Affairs, item 1938/1037, f. 120-121, 100b-103b, 113b.

Chapter 5. Modes of exemption

[1] Haebich, *For their own Good,* p. 89; Government of Western Australia, *Native Welfare Act* (No. 79 of 1963).

[2] Department of Native Affairs, Certificate of Citizenship. Legislation Re, series 2030, consignment 993, item 1944/0463, f. 10, SROWA.

[3] Police Department of Western Australia, Re Policy of natives holding certificates of exemption being permitted to obtain liquor – vol. 1, series 76, consignment 430, item 1942/0420, SROWA; Native Affairs, item 1949/0189, f. 20; Government of Western Australia, *Licensing Act 1911* (No. 32 of 1911), reprint 22 April, 1964; Department of Native Welfare, Amendments to Legislation Dealing with Natives, series 2030, consignment 993, item 1965/0242, f. 10, SROWA.

[4] Government of Western Australia, *Electoral Act 1940* (No. 47 of 1940); Government of Western Australia, *Land Act 1933* (No. 37 of 1933); Government of Western Australia, *Dog Act 1948* (No. 74 of 1948), reprint 25 August, 1959; Government of Western Australia, *Shearers Accommodation Act 1912* (No. 43 of 1912); *Government Gazette of Western Australia*, No. 22 (Perth, WA: Government Printer of Western Australia, 1920), p. 681.

[5] Native Affairs, item 1944/0463, f. 25.

[6] *Government Gazette of Western Australia*, No. 54 (Perth, WA: Government Printer of Western Australia, 1945), p. 1079, - Gazette published cancellation of exemption no 121 which was issued in January 1940.

[7] Haebich, *For their own Good,* p. 163, 190, 352-353.

[8] Department of Native Welfare, *Annual Report of the Commissioner of Native Welfare for the Year ended 30th June 1960,* (Perth, WA: Government Printer of Western Australia, 1960), p. 43, https://nla.gov.au/nla.obj-2139167168/.

[9] Department of Native Welfare, Native Administration Act - Certificate of Exemption - General correspondence, series 2030, consignment 993, item 1958/0243, f. 70-72, SROWA.

[10] *Government Gazette of Western Australia*, No. 56 (Perth, WA: Government Printer of Western Australia, 1964), p. 2526; Government of Western Australia, *Native Welfare Act 1963* (No. 79 of 1963).

[11] Native Affairs, item 1944/0463, f. 7-25.

[12] Ibid.

[13] Russel McGregor, *Indifferent Inclusion: Aboriginal People and The Australian Nation* (Canberra: Aboriginal Studies Press, 2011), p. 112.

[14] Ibid.; Department of Native Affairs, *Annual Report of the Commissioner of Native Affairs for the year ended on 30 June 1949*, (Perth, WA: Government Printer of Western Australia, 1951), p. 6-7.

[15] McGregor, *Indifferent Inclusion*, xii, p. 103; *Daily News*, "Integration Steps Up", 8 November 1966, cutting in following state record SROWA: Department of Native Welfare, Native Housing Policy, series 2030, consignment 1724, item 1965/0042; Department of Native Welfare, Native Housing – Policy Matters, series 2030, consignment 1724, item 1968/0200, f. 196.

[16] Department of Native Affairs, Inspector & Patrol Officer - Central - Patrol Reports, series 2030, consignment 993, item 1950/0800; Department of Native Affairs, Central District Office - Patrol Officers Etc. - Patrol Reports, series 2030, consignment 993, item 1951/0695; Department of Native Affairs, District Office. Central - Patrol Reports, series 2030, consignment 993, item 1952/0576; - all SROWA.

[17] Native Affairs, item 1944/0463, f. 7-25.

[18] Department of Native Affairs, Citizenship Rights - Legal and departmental Rulings, series 2030, consignment 1733, item 1945/1263, f. 61-63, SROWA; Government of Western Australia, *Natives (Citizenship Rights) Act* (No. 23 of 1944).

[19] Western Australia, *Natives (Citizenship Rights) Act 1944* (No. 23 of 1944).

[20] Government of Western Australia, *Native Welfare Act 1954* (No. 64 of 1954); Native Affairs, item 1944/0463, f. 48, 53; Department of Native Welfare, *Annual Report of the Commissioner of Native Welfare for the Year ended 30th June 1971*, (Perth, WA: Government Printer of Western Australia), p. 8, https://nla.gov.au/tarkine/nla.obj-2139268876; Author's research on Exemptions and Citizenship Certificates.

[21] Native Affairs, item 1944/0463, f. 63; Author's research on Exemptions and Citizenship Certificates.

[22] Department of Native Welfare, Native Citizenship Rights, series 2030, consignment 1733, item 1964/0249, f. 204, SROWA; Government of Western Australia, *Natives (Citizenship Rights) Act 1950* (No. 44 of 1950); Government of

Western Australia, *Natives (Citizenship Rights) Act 1964* (No. 82 of 1964); Native Affairs, item 1944/0463, f. 48; Author's research on Exemptions and Citizenship Certificates.

[23] Department of Native Welfare, Publicity – Press Release Publications, series 2030, consignment 1724, item 4 1958/0029, f. 35, SROWA; *Westralian Aborigine*, "That Burning Question of Citizenship Rights", October 1954, p. 4, SLWA; Author's research on Exemptions and Citizenship Certificates; Haebich, *Spinning the Dream*, 273-274.

[24] Native Affairs, item 1944/0463, f. 56.

[25] *York Chronicle*, "Citizen Rights for Natives", 15 December, 1949, p. 1, Trove; *York Chronicle*, "Natives Abuse Citizenship Rights", 5 January, 1950, p. 1, Trove; *West Australian,* "Citizen Rights For Natives", 24 February, 1950, p. 9, Trove.

[26] York Clerk of Courts, Charge Books – Police Court, series 408, consignment 3794, item 1, SROWA.

[27] Author's research on Exemptions and Citizenship Certificates; York Clerk of Courts, Charge Books – Police Court, series 408, consignment 3794, item 1, SROWA.

[28] *Beverley Times*, "Native Affairs – Katanning Conference", 19 May 1950, p. 2, Trove; *York Chronicle*, "Conference on Native Affairs at Katanning", 8 June, 1950, p. 4, Trove.

[29] *Great Southern Herald*, "Conference of Native Affairs", 9 June, 1950, p. 3, Trove; Native Affairs, item 1944/0463, f. 78-85.

[30] Crown Law Department, Natives (Citizenship Rights) Act. Amendment Act 1950 – preparation of bill, series 2664, consignment 1042, item 1950/2899, no folios, SROWA; Native Affairs, item 1944/0463, f. 90-93.

[31] Western Australia, *Hansard Parliamentary Debates, Twentieth Parliament – Second Session*, vol. 129, Legislative Assembly (6 November 1951), p. 485-510, (8 November 1951), p. 547-573, Legislative Council (20 November 1951), p. 759-773, (21 November 1951), p. 834-855.

[32] Pat Jacobs, *Mister Neville* (Fremantle, WA: Fremantle Arts Centre Press, 1990), p. 296.

[33] "Biographical Register of Members of the Parliament of Western Australia", Parliament of Western Australia – Website, accessed 15 January, 2023.

[34] Native Affairs, item 1944/0463, f. 90-93; Legislative Assembly (6 November 1951), p. 485-510.

[35] Katherine Ellinghaus, "The Poison Chalice: Exemption Policies in Twentieth Century Australia and the Writing of 'History'", in *Black, White, and Exempt – Aboriginal and Torres Strait Islander Lives under Exemption*, edited by Lucinda Aberdeen and Jennifer Jones, pp. 24-41 (Canberra: Aboriginal Studies Press, 2021), p. 33-34.

[36] Native Affairs, item 1944/0463, f. 7-9.

[37] Western Australia, *Hansard Parliamentary Debates, Eighteenth Parliament – First Session*, vol. 113, Legislative Assembly (10 October 1944), p. 1019-1021; "Biographical Register of Members of the Parliament of Western Australia", Parliament of Western Australia – Website, accessed 15 January, 2023..

[38] Native Affairs, item 1944/0463, f. 56, 69, 71.

[39] Ibid., f. 56-57

[40] Author's research on Exemptions and Citizenship Certificates.

[41] Legislative Council (20 November 1951), p. 762.

[42] Author's research on Exemptions and Citizenship Certificates.

[43] Department of Native Welfare, *Annual Report of the Commissioner of Native Welfare for the Year ended 30th June 1960*, (Perth, WA: Government Printer of Western Australia, 1960), p. 43, https://nla.gov.au/nla.obj-2139167168/; Federal Australian Government, *Social Services Consolidation Act* (No. 26 of 1947), https://www.legislation.gov.au.

[44] Department of Native Welfare, Central District - Patrol Reports (Patrols Officer) series 2030, consignment 993, item 1956/0106, f. 159, SROWA.

[45] "Enrolment: Blood Quantum Calculator", Pascua Yaqui Tribe, accessed 15 January, 2023, https://www.pascuayaqui-nsn.gov; Author's research on Exemptions and Citizenship Certificates; *Government Gazette of Western Australia*, No. 75 (Perth, WA: Government Printer of Western Australia, 1951), p. 2182.

[46] Native Welfare, item 1956/0106, f. 159.

[47] Ibid.

[48] Government of Western Australia, *Natives (Citizenship Rights) Act 1944* (No. 23 of 1944); *Government Gazette of Western Australia*, No. 85 (Perth, WA: Government Printer of Western Australia, 1959), p. 2747; Author's research on Exemptions and Citizenship Certificates.

[49] Department of Native Affairs, Native (Citizenship Rights) Act - 1944 Legal and Departmental Rulings, series 2030, consignment 1733, item 1945/1263, f. 64, 78-81, SROWA; Native Affairs, item 1944/0463, f. 7-25; Department of Native Affairs, Citizenship, series 2030, consignment 933, item 1949/0074, no folio, SROWA.

[50] Native Affairs, item 1949/0074, no folio – speech by George Howard to Rotary Club Perth (1954); Haebich, *Spinning the Dream*, p 220.

[51] Author's research on Exemptions and Citizenship Certificates.

[52] *York Chronicle*, "Mr. Noonan's Career", 4 April 1947, p. 1, Trove.

[53] *York Chronicle*, "No Closed Business for York – Council Declares Policy", 5 April 1956, p. 1, SLWA; *Government Gazette of Western Australia*, No. 36 (Perth, WA: Government Printer of Western Australia, 1956), p. 1125.

[54] York Clerk of Courts, Applications for Citizenship, series 412, consignment 3800, item 1, SROWA.

[55] Department of Native Affairs, Natives (Citizenship) Act. Constitution of Natives (Citizenship Rights) Boards, series 2030, consignment 993, item 1952/0419, no folio, SROWA; *York Chronicle*, "Citizenship Rights For Natives – Board To Be Appointed", 14 August 1952, p. 3, Trove; Author's research on Exemptions and Citizenship Certificates.

[56] *York Chronicle*, "Councillors Clash On Bowling Matter", 17 January, 1957, p. 3, SLWA.

[57] *Government Gazette of Western Australia*, No. 52 (Perth, WA: Government Printer of Western Australia, 1957), p. 1832; *York Chronicle*, 1955 – 1959, author holds digitised copies from microfilm, SLWA.

[58] Federal Australian Government, *Maternity Allowance Act* (No. 8 of 1912), https://www.legislation.gov.au.

[59] Department of Native Affairs, District Office – Central – Patrol Reports, series 2030, consignment 993, item 1949/0189, no folio, SLWA.

[60] Federal Australian Government, *Maternity Allowance Act* (No. 4 of 1942); Federal Australian Government, *Maternity Allowance Act* (No. 12 of 1944).

[61] Department of Native Welfare, Central District - Patrol Reports (Patrols Officer) series 2030, consignment 993, item 1956/0106, f. 158, 152, SROWA; Department of Native Welfare, Copies of Lectures or Talks given by Departmental Officers, series 2030, consignment 1733, item 1966/1554, no folio, SROWA.

[62] *York Chronicle,* "Unlawfully on Native Reserve", 11 December, 1952, p. 1, Trove; Author's research on Exemptions and Citizenship Certificates; York Clerk of Courts, Charge Book, series 408, consignment 3794, items 1 and 2, SROWA.

[63] Charge Books, items 1 and 2; Native Affairs, item 1947/0270, f. 9.

[64] Department of Native Welfare, item 1956/0106, f. 35, 151; *Northam Advertiser*, "Old York Identity Passes On", 21 October 1960, p. 11, SLWA.

[65] Personal correspondence with Dr Marion Kickett, October 2023.

[66] Charge Books, items 1 and 2.

[67] *York Chronicle*, "Conference on Native Affairs at Katanning", 8 June, 1950, p. 4, Trove.

[68] Charge Books, items 1 and 2; Author's research on Exemptions and Citizenship Certificates.

[69] Author's research on Exemptions and Citizenship Certificates; York Court, Charge Book, items 1 and 2.

[70] Native Affairs, item 1944/0463, f. 94, 118.

Chapter 6. 1950s

[1] Native Affairs, item 1938/1037, f. 113.

[2] Native Affairs, item 1949/0189, p. 20; *York Chronicle*, "Disgraceful Scene at Forrest Oval", 14 May 1948, p. 1, Trove.

[3] *York Chronicle*, 14 May 1948.

[4] Native Affairs, item 1938/1037, f. 117-119; *York Chronicle*, "Colour Ban", 19 March 1948, p. 1, Trove; *York Chronicle*, "The Football Colour Ban", 23 April 1948, p. 6, Trove.

[5] Native Affairs, item 1949/0189, p. 20.

[6] Ibid.

[7] *York Chronicle*, "Conference of Native Affairs at Katanning", 8 June 1950, p. 4, Trove.

[8] Ibid.

[9] *York Chronicle*, "Visit of Premier to be Requested", 6 July 1950, p. 1, Trove.

[10] *West Australian*, "Native Dwellings Shock Premier", 14 July 1950, p. 6, Trove; *York Chronicle*, "First Hand Information – Native Reserve Visited", 20 July 1950, p. 1, Trove; *York Chronicle*, "Visit of Premier McLarty Should Have Good Results …", 20 July 1950, p. 1, Trove.

[11] *York Chronicle*, 20 July 1950, p. 1.

[12] Ibid.

[13] Department of Community Welfare, Property - York Reserve 8567 - Buildings and Land, series 1099 consignment 2532, item A1821, f. 10, SROWA.

[14] Ibid.

[15] Community Welfare, item A1821, f. 12.

[16] Bruce Alan McLarty was Premier Ross McLarty's first cousin once-removed according to data derived from Western Australia's Department of Justice – Births, Deaths and Marriages index, accessed 31 August 2024, https://www.wa.gov.au.

[17] Community Welfare, item A1821, f. 16.

[18] Ibid., f. 12; Native Affairs, item 1949/0189, p. 24, 33; Department of Native Affairs, District Office – Central – Patrol Reports, series 2030, consignment 993, item 1950/0720, f. 9-1, SROWA.

[19] George Kickett, "The Native Reserve York, WA", oral history interview by Roland See, 1 October 2019, audio, 01:07:23, author holds original audio file; "Bark Painting – Vivienne Narkle", Kinship Connections WA, 11 November 2012, accessed 24 September 2019, no longer online – author holds copy; Marion Kickett, "Examination of How a Culturally-Appropriate Definition of Resilience Affects the Physical and Mental Health of Aboriginal People" (PhD diss., University of Western Australia, 2011), p. 17.

[20] Community Welfare, item A1821, f. 17.

[21] Ibid., f. 18.

[22] Ibid.

[23] Community Welfare, item A1821, f. 18-19; *York Chronicle*, "Jubilee Celebrations – Road Board Members Slighted",19 October 1950, p. 5, Trove.

[24] Community Welfare, item A1821, f. 19.

[25] Ibid., f. 20-21.

[26] Ibid., f. 10.

[27] Ibid., f. 22.

[28] Ibid., f. 24.

[29] Ibid., f. 25.

[30] Ibid., f. 26.

[31] Community Welfare, item A1821, f. 26-28.

[32] Ibid., f. 29.

[33] Department of Native Affairs, *Annual Report of the Commissioner of Native Affairs for the year ended on 30 June 1949*, (Perth, WA: Government Printer of Western Australia, 1951), p. 28; Native Affairs, item 1950/0800, f. 27-29.

[34] Community Welfare, item A1821, f. 33-34.

[35] *York Chronicle*, "Facilities on Native Reserve", 14 December 1950, p. 2, Trove.

[36] Community Welfare, item A1821, f. 35-43.

[37] Department of Native Affairs, Central District - Patrol Officer Reports, series 2030, consignment 993, item 1951/0695, f. 67, SROWA.

[38] *York Chronicle*, "York Road Board", 20 December 1951, p. 5, Trove.

[39] Department of Native Affairs, District Office. Central - Patrol Reports, series 2030, consignment 993, item 1952/0576, p. 82, SROWA.

[40] Native Affairs, item 1952/0576, p. 73; Community Welfare, item A1821, f. 35-43.

[41] Department of Native Affairs, District Office - Central District - Patrol reports, series 2030, consignment 993, item 1953/0124, f. 22-23, SROWA.

[42] Ibid.

[43] *York Chronicle*, "Board Conference Discusses Lack of Native Facilities" 19 December 1957, p. 2, SLWA.

[44] Department of Native Welfare, Housing for natives – General Correspondence, series 2030, consignment 993, item 1956/0150, f. 106, SROWA.

[45]Community Welfare, item A1821, f. 50.

[46] Government of Western Australia, *Local Government Act 1960* (No. 84 of 1960); *Northam Advertiser*, "Preparing for Changeover", 31 May 1961, p. 4, SLWA.

[47] Community Welfare, item A1821, f. 51-63.

[48] Ibid., f. 65-84.

[49] Native Affairs, item 1951/0695, f. 8-12.

[50] *York Chronicle*, "Maternity Hospital - Provision of Accommodation for Native Women", 6 July 1950, p. 1; Public Health Department, York Hospital – Buildings and Grounds, series 268, consignment 1003, item 1948/0700, f. 96, 99, SROWA.

[51] *York Chronicle*, "Maternity Hospital - Provision of Accommodation for Native Women", 6 July 1950, p. 1; http://nla.gov.au/nla.news-page28002119.

[52] Ibid.

[53] *York Chronicle*, "Visit of Premier to Be Requested", 6 July 1950, p. 1, http://nla.gov.au/nla.news-page28002119; Public Health Department, item 1948/0700, f. 96, 99.

[54] *York Chronicle*, "Visit of Premier McLarty Should Have Good Results", 20 July 1950, p. 1, Trove.

[55] *West Australian*, "Native Dwellings Shock Premier", 14 July 1950, p. 6, Trove; *York Chronicle*, 20 July 1950, p. 1.

[56] *York Chronicle*, "Hospital Renovations", 31 August 1950, p. 1, Trove.

[57] Ibid.

[58] Public Health, item 1948/0700, f. 100.

[59] *York Chronicle*, "Avon Valley Electorate", 23 February 1950, p. 3, Trove.

[60] *York Chronicle*, "No Additions for the York Hospital", 28 September 1950, p. 1, Trove.

[61] Ibid.

[62] Ibid.

[63] Western Australia, *Hansard Parliamentary Debates, Twentieth Parliament – First Session*, vol. 126, Legislative Assembly (7 September 1950), p. 652.

[64] *Workers Star*, "People want fair deal for natives", 15 September 1950, p. 8, Trove.

[65] *West Australian*, "Natives at Hospital – Move for Separate Maternity Ward", 1 November 1950, p. 9, Trove.

[66] Ibid; "Biographical Register of Members of the Parliament of Western Australia", Parliament of Western Australia – Website, accessed 19 November, 2022.

[67] Medical Department, York Hospital – Accommodation for Natives, series 268, consignment 1003, item 1962/5080, f. 7-8, SROWA.

[68] Ibid.

[69] Public Health, item 1948/0700, f. 112.

[70] *West Australian*, "A Bed for Natives", 30 November 1950, p. 9, Trove; *York Chronicle*, "Natives at Maternity Hospital – Minister's Suggestion Accepted", 30 November 1950, p. 1, Trove; Public Health, item 1948/0700, f. 134-135.

[71] Ibid.

[72] *West Australian*, "Letters to the Editor – Natives in Hospital", 10 November 1950, p. 10, Trove.

[73] *Daily News*, "Women Differ on Question of Native Segregation", 4 November 1950, p. 4, Trove; *West Australian*, "Letters to the Editor – Natives in Hospital", 30 November 1950, p. 27, Trove.

[74] Medical Department, item 1962/5080, f. 9.

[75] Public Health, item 1948/0700, f. 177-118; *Western Mail*, "People", 21 October 1954, p. 20, Trove.

[76] Public Health, item 1948/0700, f. 180-182.

[77] Medical Department, item 1962/5080, f. 11-13.

[78] Ibid., f. 2-8.

[79] Ibid.

[80] Medical Department, item 1962/5080, f. 2-8.

[81] Public Health Department, York Hospital – Buildings and Grounds, series 268, consignment 1003, item 1952/5592, f. 7-59, SROWA; Public Health Department, York Hospital – Buildings and Grounds, series 268, consignment 1003, item 1956/5164, f. 140-149, SROWA.

[82] Marion Kickett, "A Story of Connection, Belonging and Resilience", in *My Country, My Life, My Words*, edited by Dr Marion Kickett and Tracey Kickett (Leschenault, WA: Leschenault Press, 2023), p. 74.

[83] Medical Department, York Hospital Buildings, series 455, consignment 1539, item 1962/5743, f. 34, SROWA.

[84] Medical Department, item 1962/5743, f. 29-30, 211.

[85] Native Affairs, item 1938/1037, f. 111b; Department of Native Affairs, Housing General, series 2030, consignment 993, item 1947/0991, f. 44, SROWA.

[86] Native Affairs, item 1947/0991, f. 72-73; *York Chronicle*, "Municipal Discussions", 12 October 1950, p. 3, Trove; *York Chronicle*, "Municipal Matters", 26 October 1950, p. 5, Trove.

[87] Native Affairs, item 1947/0991, f. 75.

[88] Ibid.

[89] Native Affairs, item 1947/0991, f. 64-66.

[90] Ibid., f. 60.

[91] Ibid., f. 60.

[92] Ibid., f. 56-60, 76-77.

[93] Ibid., f. 111.

[94] *West Australian,* "The State Housing Commission – Its Work and Policy Reviewed", 22 April 1948, p. 11, Trove; *Western Mail*, "Spotlight on Housing Progress", 27 July 1950, p. 26, Trove; *West Australian*, "1,050 Homes Required", 19 January 1951, p. 2, Trove;

[95] Native Affairs, item 1947/0991, f. 111.

[96] Ibid., f. 117.

[97] Ibid., f. 122.

[98] Native Affairs, item 1947/0991, f. 122; "Biographical Register of Members of the Parliament of Western Australia", Parliament of Western Australia – Website, accessed 8 March, 2023.

[99] Department of Native Affairs, Housing of Natives – General Correspondence, series 2030, consignment 933, item 1951/0679, f. 1, 27, SROWA; *Sunday Times*, "Approved Natives will get Houses", 4 November 1951, p. 5, Trove.

[100] Native Affairs, item 1950/0800, f. 51-53; *West Australian*, "Criticism of Lag in Building Needs", 31 August 1950, p. 3, Trove.

[101] Department of Native Affairs, Department of Native Affairs, *Annual Report of the Commissioner of Native Affairs for the year ended on 30 June 1949*, (Perth, WA: Government Printer of Western Australia, 1951), p. 28; Native Affairs, item 1950/0800, f. 53.

[102] Native Affairs, item 1947/0991, f. 97 cont., Native Affairs, item 1951/0679, p. 108-198.

[103] Native Affairs, item 1951/0679, f. 159.

[104] Ibid., f. 108.

[105] Native Affairs, item 1951/0679, f. 109; *Daily News*, "Houses to be Built for Natives", 20 August 1952, p. 7, Trove.

[106] *York Chronicle*, "Natives Prosecuted for Health Act Offences", 20 March 1952, p. 5, Trove.

[107] *York Chronicle*, "Conditions at Native Camps", 17 April 1952, p. 5, Trove.

[108] Ibid.

[109] Ibid.

[110] Ibid.

[111] Ibid.

[112] *York Chronicle*, "Municipal Council", 12 June 1952, p. 5, Trove.

[113] Author's research based on Western Australian Government Gazettes, Police Gazettes, and departmental records.

[114] *Northam News*, "York's New Approach to Native Problem", 17 December 1952, p. 6, Trove.

[115] *West Australian*, "S.H.C. to Build Rented native Homes", 30 October 1952, p. 5, Trove.

[116] Department of Native Affairs, District Office. Central - Patrol Reports, series 2030, consignment 993, item 1952/0576, p. 10-13, 134, SROWA; Department of Native Affairs, Housing of Natives – General Correspondence, series 2030, consignment 933, item 1951/0679, f. 135, SROWA.

[117] *West Australian*, "Native Camps Encroach on A Townsite", 28 May 1953, p. 10, Trove.

[118] *York Chronicle*, "Native Camps again in Evidence in Town", 28 May 1953, p. 3, Trove.

[119] *York Chronicle*, 28 May 1953, p. 3; *West Australian*, 28 May 1953, p. 10.

[120] *Daily News*, "Phone Calls Race Ahead", 24 June 1953, p. 2, Trove; *York Chronicle*, "York Rainfall", 28 May 1953, p. 1, Trove; Department of Native Affairs, Native Matters – York – General File, series 2030, consignment 993, item 1938/1037, f. 2-3, SROWA; Native Affairs, item 1951/0695, p. 10.
[121] Personal correspondence with Dr Marion Kickett, November 2023.
[122] State Library of Western Australia, *York Chronicle* Collection, Publishing Notes in Reel, 1955-1956, viewed January 2023.
[123] *Beverley Times*, "C J Ashworth Retires", 23 September 1966, p. 7, Trove ('Ashworth' is a typing error in the headline only); *Eastern Districts Chronicle*, "Federal Elections", 5 December 1919, p. 5, Trove; C. J. Ashbolt, "Verbatim Transcript", oral history interview by Jean Teasdale, 1975, SLWA; *Northam Advertiser*, "York Council Meets", 28 March 1974, p. 7, SLWA.
[124] Native Affairs, item 1951/0679, f. 136.
[125] Department of Native Affairs, District Office - Central District - Patrol reports, series 2030, consignment 993, item 1953/0124, f. 7-9, SROWA.
[126] Department of Native Affairs, Natives in Occupation of Houses – National Security, Landlord and Tenant Regulations Governing, series 2030, consignment 993, item 1943/1270, SROWA; *Geraldton Guardian and Express*, "The Native Problem – Murchison Requests Statement by Minister", 27 July 1946, p. 4, Trove.
[127] *Daily News*, "York Native Families get two Modern Homes", 23 October 1953, final edition, p. 13, Trove; *West Australian*, "Keys to Unlock Modern Homes for Old Families", 24 October 1953, p. 4, Trove.
[128] *York Chronicle*, "Native Families Take Over Modern Homes", 29 October 1953, p. 1, Trove.
[129] Native Affairs, item 1951/0679, f. 179.
[130] Native Affairs, item 1953/0124, f. 8.
[131] Government of Western Australia, *Native Welfare Act 1954* (No. 64 of 1954).
[132] Native Affairs, item 1951/0679, f. 147, 155
[133] Ibid., f. 141-140.
[134] Ibid.
[135] Department of Native Welfare, Housing for Natives – General Correspondence, series 2030, consignment 993, item 1955/0276, f. 121, SROWA.
[136] Department of Native Welfare, Copies of Lectures or Talks given by departmental Officers, series 2030, consignment 1733, item 1966/1554, p. 43, SROWA; *Sunday Times*, "25 Houses for Natives", 21 June 1953, p. 3, Trove; Department of Native Welfare, Housing for Natives – General Correspondence, series 2030, consignment 993, item 1958/0270, f. 188-189, SROWA
[137] Native Affairs, item 1951/0679, f. 161.
[138] Native Affairs, item 1952/0576, p. 6-11.

[139] Native Affairs, item 1953/0124, f. 23.

[140] Ibid.

[141] Native Affairs, item 1953/0124, f. 23.

[142] Ibid., f. 8.

[143] Native Affairs, item 1951/0679, f. 199-201.

[144] *Daily News*, "Perth Slum Probe to Start", 25 May 1938, p. 2, Trove; *Daily News*, "Opinion - Just How Bad are Our Slums?" 20 July 1950, p. 8, Trove; *Daily News*, "Coogee 'Slums' Shock Hardened Minister", 9 April 1951, p. 2, Trove; *Sunday Times*, "Worst Slum is Starting to Go", 6 December 1953, p. 7, Trove.

[145] Native Affairs, item 1951/0679, f. 199-201; *York Chronicle*, "Municipal Matters", 4 March 1954, p. 5, Trove.

[146] Native Affairs, item 1951/0679, f. 199-201.

[147] *York Chronicle*, "Still No Health Inspector", 30 July 1953, p. 7, Trove.

[148] *York Chronicle*, "Houses for Natives", 25 March 1954, p. 5, Trove.

[149] Ibid.

[150] Ibid.

[151] *York Chronicle*, "Municipal Council", 22 April 1954, p. 6, Trove.

[152] *York Chronicle*, "Housing for Natives", 22 April 1954, p. 1, Trove.

[153] Ibid.

[154] Ibid.

[155] *Sunday Times*, "Minister Disgusted by Protest against Home for Native", 30 May 1954, p. 5, Trove.

[156] *York Chronicle*, "Municipal Matters", 13 May 1954, p. 6, Trove; *York Chronicle*, "Houses for Natives", 3 June 1954, p. 1, Trove.

[157] Anna Haebich, *Broken Circles – Fragmenting Indigenous Families 1800 - 2000* (Fremantle: Fremantle Press, 2000), 132; Anna Haebich, *Spinning the Dream – Assimilation in Australia 1950-1970*, (North Fremantle: Fremantle Press, 2008), 144-146.

[158] *Daily News*, "York Protests at Native Homes Plan", 30 November 1954, p. 11, Trove.

[159] *York Chronicle*, "Erection of Houses for Natives in Grey Street Opposed", 2 December 1954, p. 1, Trove.

[160] Ibid.

[161] *West Australian*, "Natives will be Part of the Community", 3 December 1954, p. 8, Trove; *York Chronicle*, "Deputation to Minister on Native Housing", 9 December 1954, p. 1, Trove.

[162] *York Chronicle*, 9 December 1954, p. 1.

[163] Ibid.

[164] Ibid.

[165] Ibid.

[166] Ibid.

[167] *York Chronicle*, 9 December 1954, p. 1.

[168] *York Chronicle*, "Houses for Natives will be Built in Grey Street", 16 December 1954, p. 1, Trove.

[169] Ibid.

[170] Ibid.

[171] Department of Native Welfare, Central Districts – Patrol Reports (Patrol Officer), series 2030, consignment 993, item 1956/0106, f. 57, SROWA.

[172] *York Chronicle*, 1955 – 1959, author holds digitised copies from microfilm, SLWA.

[173] Native Welfare, item 1956/0106, f. 146.

[174] Native Affairs, item 1953/0124, f. 6-9, 40-48; Native Welfare, item 1956/0106, f. 109-113; Department of Native Welfare, Housing for natives – General Correspondence, series 2030, consignment 993, item 1956/0150, f. 207-209, SROWA.

[175] Aboriginal Affairs Planning Authority, Native Housing – Policy Matters, series 2030, consignment 993, item 1971/1116, f. 32-38, SROWA.

[176] Native Affairs, item 1953/0124, no folio (Central District Patrol Report No 1 of 58/59, July 1958).

[177] *York Chronicle*, "Aborigines Enjoy Dance", 20 May 1954, p. 1, Trove.

[178] *West Australian*, "League Holds Dance for York Natives", 18 May 1954, p. 13, Trove; *York Chronicle*, 20 May 1954, p. 1.

[179] Anna Haebich, *Spinning the Dream – Assimilation in Australia 1950-1970*, (North Fremantle: Fremantle Press, 2008), 283-299; *Daily News*, "Planning their own 'Utopia'", 20 December 1947, p. 14, Trove.

[180] *Daily News*, "Aboriginal Youths form own Club", 2 August 1947, p. 17, Trove; *Daily News*, "Mystic Rites in Youth Club", 3 August 1946, p. 8, Trove; "From Revolutionary to Realist", Shaping the Nation – John Curtin and Australia, accessed 25 April 2023, https://john.curtin.edu.au/.

[181] Department of Native Welfare, Coolbaroo Club – Conducted by Natives in Metropolitan Area, series 2030, consignment 993, item 1947/0146, f. 22, 139-140, 158, SLWA; Haebich, *Spinning the Dream*, 283-299; Department of Native Affairs, City of Perth - Prohibited Area, series 2030, consignment 993, item 1927/0038, f. 75, SROWA.

[182] Department of Native Affairs, York - Prohibited Area, series 2030, consignment 993, item 1947/0270, f. 28, SROWA.

[183] *Westralian Aborigine*, "Coolbaroo Work goes Further Afield", April 1954, SLWA.

[184] Ibid.

[185] Haebich, *Spinning the Dream*, 292.

[186] *Daily News* "Friday Night with the Coolbaroo League", 14 February 1955, p. 12, Trove.

[187] *Daily News*, "A Warning for the Spoiling Minority", 26 July 1954, p. 7, Trove.

[188] *York Chronicle*, "Natives Sentenced to 21 Days' Imprisonment", 29 July 1954, p. 1, Trove.

[189] *Daily News*, 26 July 1954, p. 7; *York Chronicle*, 29 July 1954, p. 1.

[190] *West Australian*, "Bad Behaviour Brings Gaol", 24 August 1954, p. 10, Trove; *York Chronicle*, "Natives Sent to Gaol", 23 September 1954, p. 1, Trove; York Clerk of Courts, Charge Book, series 408, consignment 3794, item 2, SROWA.

[191] *Westralian Aborigine*, "Try the New Dance", July 1954, SLWA; *Westralian Aborigine*, "His Dancing is a Legend", August 1954; *Westralian Aborigine*, "No other than Bertha", September 1954.

[192] *Westralian Aborigine*, "More Natives Buying Cars", December 1954.

[193] *Daily News*, "Santa for Narrogin", 17 December 1954, p. 11, Trove.

[194] *York Chronicle*, "Native Beauty Contest", 27 January 1955, p. 1, SLWA; *Westralian Aborigine*, "Mark these Dates on Your Calendar", December 1954, SLWA.

[195] Haebich, *Spinning the Dream*, 293-194.

[196] *York Chronicle*, "Native Beauty Contest", 27 January 1955, p. 1, SLWA.

[197] Register - Prisoners, York Gaol, series 1664, consignment 1442, item 1, SROWA; York Clerk of Courts, Charge Books – Police Court, series 408, consignment 3794, items 1 and 2, SROWA.

[198] Author's research on Exemptions and Citizenship Certificates. - In comparison, in the towns of Katanning and Narrogin there were approximately fifteen and twenty-one certificates issued, respectively, for the earlier period, while the trend continued after April 1955. In neighbouring Northam, however, there were only around three certificates issued during both periods combined. Hence, while this idle period in York in relation to the granting of conditional citizenship rights was not an outright exception, it was also not the rule.

[199] *West Australian*, "Native Bill called 'Premature and Unwise,'" 5 December 1953, p. 7, Trove; Government of Western Australia, *Native Welfare Act 1954* (No. 64 of 1954).

[200] Department of Native Welfare, Housing for Natives – General Correspondence, series 2030, consignment 993, item 1955/0276, f. 82, SROWA; *Government Gazette of Western Australia*, No. 85 (Perth, WA: Government Printer of Western Australia, 1953), p. 1696.

[201] Department of Native Affairs, Native (Citizenship Rights) Act - 1944 Legal and departmental Rulings, series 2030, consignment 1733, item 1945/1263, f. 34-38, SROWA.

[202] *Daily News*, "Says Mary Felber ... Can You Help?" 25 February 1955, p. 15, Trove; *York Chronicle*, "Municipal Matters", 22 December 1955, p. 3, SLWA; *York Chronicle*, "York Police Court", 02 February 1956, p. 1, SLWA; *York*

Chronicle, "S H C Houses: Minister's Aid to be Sought", 26 July 1956, p. 1, SLWA; *Westralian Aborigine*, "Coolbaroo Winter Season Dances", June-July 1957, SLWA.

[203] *Westralian Aborigine*, "League members snubbed by non-Australian", March-April 1956, p. 1, National Library of Australia.

[204] *Westralian Aborigine*, "League men treated to round of racist abuse", January-February 1956, p. 1, National Archives of Australia.

[205] *York Chronicle*, "Land Wanted for Native Recreation Centre", 4 November 1954, p. 1, Trove.

[206] *York Chronicle*, "Councillor Objects to Natives Living in Flats", 9 April 1959, p. 1, SLWA.

[207] Ibid.

[208] Department of Native Welfare, Housing for Natives – General Correspondence, series 2030, consignment 993, item 1958/0270, f. 117, SROWA.

[209] *York Chronicle*, "Local Newspaper Reports 'Everything' Says Cr Davies", 12 March 1959, p. 1, SLWA.

[210] *York Chronicle*, January 1955 to December 1959, SLWA.

[211] *York Chronicle*, "Supplying Liquor to Native Costs Man £20 Fine", 20 December 1956, p. 1, SLWA.

[212] Ibid.

[213] York Clerk of Courts, Charge Book, series 408, consignment 3794, item 2, SROWA.

[214] *York Chronicle*, "Supplying Liquor to Native Costs Man £20 Fine", 20 December 1956, p. 1, SLWA.

[215] *York Chronicle*, "Drink too Prevalent amongst Natives", 27 September 1956, p. 8, SLWA.

[216] York Clerk of Courts, Charge Book, series 408, consignment 3794, item 2, SROWA; Government of Western Australia, *Native Welfare Act 1954* (No. 64 of 1954); Government of Western Australia, *Police Act 1892-1952* Reprint 23 March 1953 (No. 27 of 1892).

[217] *York Chronicle*, "Liquor Charges in York Police Court", 9 January 1958, p. 1, SLWA.

[218] Ibid.

[219] *York Chronicle*, "Effects of Liquor", 16 October 1958, p. 2; *York Chronicle*, "York J. F. has Narrow Win", 18 December 1958, p. 4; *York Chronicle*, "Beverley News", 1 January 1959, p. 2, - all SLWA.

[220] Western Australia, *Hansard Parliamentary Debates, Twenty-Second Parliament – Third Session*, vol. 150, Legislative Council (22 October 1958), p. 1657-1682.

[221] *York Chronicle*, "York Police Court", 13 December 1956, p. 1, SLWA.

[222] *York Chronicle*, December 1956 to December 1959, SLWA.

[223] York Clerk of Courts, Charge Book, series 408, consignment 3794, item 2, SROWA.

[224] *York Chronicle*, "Situations Vacant", 16 April 1959, p. 15, SLWA.

[225] *York Chronicle*, "Cyril Yarran Dies", 3 September 1959, p. 1, SLWA; *York Chronicle*, "Death of Charlie Winmar", 31 December 1959, p. 1, SLWA.

[226] *York Chronicle*, "Obituary", 10 September 1953, p. 1, Trove.

[227] *Northam Advertiser*, 1960 to 1974, SLWA.

Chapter 7. 1960s

[1] Department of Native Welfare, Housing for Natives – General Correspondence, series 2030, consignment 993, item 1955/0276, f. 175, SROWA.

[2] Department of Native Affairs, District Office - Central District - Patrol reports, series 2030, consignment 993, item 1953/0124, f. 7-9, SROWA.

[3] Ibid., f. 8.

[4] Department of Native Welfare, item 1955/0276, f. 177-179.

[5] Department of Native Welfare, Housing for natives – General Correspondence, series 2030, consignment 993, item 1956/0150, f. 50-66, SROWA.

[6] Department of Native Welfare, Native Housing – Policy Matters, series 2030, consignment 1724, item 6 1961/0668, f. 194, SROWA.

[7] Department of Native Welfare, Housing for Natives – General Correspondence, series 2030, consignment 993, item 1958/0270, f. 16-28, SROWA; Department of Native Welfare, Housing and Camping Reserves – Housing. General Correspondence, series 2030, consignment 993, item, 1960/0415, f. 1-2, 24-27, 30, SROWA; Department of Native Welfare, Native Housing – Policy Matters, series 2030, consignment 1724, item 6 1961/0668, f. 193-194, SROWA.

[8] Department of Native Welfare, item 6 1961/0668, f. 8, 37-40, 61, SROWA; Department of Native Welfare, Native Housing Policy, series 2030, consignment 1724, item 1965/0042, f. 11-12, 110-111, SROWA.

[9] Department of Native Welfare, Housing - Camping & Housing Reserves – General, series 2030, consignment 1724, item 1965/0209, f. 1-2, SROWA.

[10] Department of Native Welfare, item 1965/0042, f. 120.

[11] Ibid.

[12] Department of Native Welfare, Census and Population Returns of Natives in Western Australia, series 2030, consignment 1733, item 1963/0115, f. 215, SROWA.

[13] Department of Native Welfare, Housing & Camping Reserves – Housing – General Correspondence, series 2030, consignment 993, item 1960/0415, f. 174-176, SROWA.

[14] *Northam Advertiser*, "Native Welfare Committee Formed", 25 August 1961, p. 8, SLWA; Department of Native Welfare, Special Housing Allocation 1960/1961, series 2030, consignment 993, item 1961/0185, f. 124, SROWA.

[15] Department of Community Welfare, Property - York Reserve 8567 - Buildings and Land, series 1099 consignment 2532, item A1821, f. 74, 84, SROWA; Department of Native Welfare, Native Housing Reserve – York, series 2030, consignment 1733, item 1952/0345, f. 9, SROWA.

[16] Department of Community Welfare, item A1821, f. 61.

[17] Ibid., f. 51.

[18] Department of Native Welfare, item 1961/0185, f. 157-159.

[19] Department of Native Welfare, item 1961/0185, f. 141, 161-162; Department of Community Welfare, item A1821, f. 68.

[20] *Northam Advertiser*, "Protector of Natives Appointed", 13 May 1960, p. 8, SLWA.

[21] Ibid.; Department of Native Affairs, District Office. Central - Patrol Reports, series 2030, consignment 993, item 1952/0576, p. 206, SROWA.

[22] *Northam Advertiser,* "Protector of Natives Appointed", 13 May 1960, p. 8, SLWA.

[23] Methodist Church York, Minutes of Quarterly Meetings, MN 172, Acc. 2811A/8, SLWA; Department of Native Welfare, Protectors of Natives – List of 1961 – General Correspondence, series 2030, consignment 993, item 1961/0007, f. 16, SROWA.

[24] *Northam Advertiser*, "Country Party Meeting at York", 27 August 1960, p. 11, SLWA.

[25] *Northam Advertiser*, "Art Discussion at York C.A.A", 7 June 1961, p. 8, SLWA.

[26] *Northam Advertiser*, "York C.W.A. has 'Treasure' Day", 12 July 1961, p. 4, SLWA.

[27] Methodist Church York, Minutes of Quarterly Meetings, MN 172, Acc. 2811A/8, SLWA.

[28] *Northam Advertiser*, "Native Welfare Council", 11 August 1961, p. 8, SLWA.

[29] *Northam Advertiser*, "Native Welfare Committee Formed", 25 August 1961, p. 8, SLWA.

[30] *Narrogin Observer*, "Native Welfare – Local Committee Formed", 14 December 1946, p. 8, Trove; Author's research based on Western Australian Government Gazettes, Police Gazettes, and departmental records.

[31] Department of Native Affairs, Native Welfare Council, series 2030, consignment 1733, item 1952/0271, f. 1-25, SROWA; Department of Native Welfare, Organisations, Associations & Societies, series 47, consignment 2817, item 25-01, f. 23-30, 64, SROWA; Australian Aborigines Amelioration

Association, "Native Welfare Council – New Body Formed", *The Ladder* vol. 1, no. 9 (March 1939), p. 13-14, NLA, https://nla.gov.au.

[32] Department of Native Welfare, Northam Native Welfare Committee, series 2030, consignment 993, item 1960/0117, f. 4, SROWA; Department of Native Welfare, *Annual Report of the Commissioner of Native Affairs for the year ended on 30 June 1959*, (Perth, WA: Government Printer of Western Australia, 1960), p. 6; Department of Native Welfare, Organisations Associations & Societies, series 47, consignment 2817, item 25.17, f. 43, SROWA.

[33] Department of Native Welfare, item 25.17, f. 54-60.

[34] *Northam Advertiser*, "York elects Native Welfare Officers", 28 February 1962, p. 5, SLWA; Department of Native Welfare, Housing – General Correspondence, series 2030, consignment 993, item 1961/0462, f. 4-6, SROWA.

[35] *Northam Advertiser,* "President reports to York CWA", 11 October 1961, p. 12, SLWA; Methodist Church York, Methodist Ladies Guild – Minute Book, MN 172, Acc. 8993A/4, SLWA.

[36] *Northam Advertiser*, "House Unfit to Live in",16 October 1963, p. 5, SLWA; *Northam Advertiser*, "Late Shopping for York", 15 December 1961, p. 8, SLWA; *Northam Advertiser*, "Illegal Burning Will Be Prosecuted", 17 November 1961, p. 9, SLWA; *Northam Advertiser*, "Inefficiency Alleged in York Council Work", 17 January 1962, p. 6, SLWA.

[37] Community Welfare, item A1821, f. 66-67, 73; *Northam Advertiser*, "York Social", 12 January 1962, p. 5, SLWA; Native Welfare, item 1961/0007, f. 129; Department of Native Welfare, Protectors of Natives, series 2030, consignment 993, item 1946/0002, f. 52, SROWA.

[38] *Northam Advertiser*, "York elects Native Welfare Officers", 28 February 1962, p. 5, SLWA.

[39] *Northam Advertiser*, "York elects Native Welfare Officers", 28 February 1962, p. 5, SLWA; Department of Community Welfare, item A1821.

[40] *Northam Advertiser*, "Native Welfare Dept. to Kow-Tow to Council", 9 March 1967, p. 1; *Northam Advertiser*, "Council Approves Native Housing", 6 April 1967, p. 7; *Northam Advertiser*, "Northam Native Reserve Conditions Slated", 4 July 1968, p. 1; *Northam Advertiser*, "Council Agrees to Restrict Native Housing", 13 March 1969, p. 1&4 – all SLWA.

[41] Department of Native Welfare, *Annual Report of the Commissioner of Native Welfare for the Year ended 30th June 1963*, (Perth, WA: Government Printer of Western Australia, 1963), p. 13, https://nla.gov.au; Department of Native Welfare, *Annual Report of the Commissioner of Native Welfare for the Year ended 30th June 1964*, (Perth, WA: Government Printer of Western Australia, 1964), p. 42, https://nla.gov.au.

[42] *Northam Advertiser*, "Departing", 19 November 1965, p. 12, SLWA; *Northam Advertiser*, "Entries Down at York Flower Show – Native Art", 11 May 1962, p.

7, SLWA; *Northam Advertiser*, "York Apex Entertained", 20 July 1962, p. 9, SLWA; Native Welfare, item 1964/0002, f. 6 & 23.

[43] *Northam Advertiser*, 1960 to 1970, SLWA; Methodist Church York, Methodist Ladies Guild – Minute Book, MN 172, Acc. 8993A/5, SLWA; *Northam Advertiser*, "S.C.F. Activity in York", 4 May 1967, p. 15, SLWA.

[44] Paul Hasluck, *The Policy of Assimilation*, Decisions of Commonwealth and State Ministers at the Native Welfare Conference, Canberra, January 26th and 27th 1961 (Canberra, ACT: Commonwealth Government Printer, 1961), https://aiatsis.gov.au; Department of Native Welfare, *Annual Report of the Commissioner of Native Welfare for the Year ended 30th June 1967*, (Perth, WA: Government Printer of Western Australia, 1967), p. 7, https://nla.gov.au.

[45] Hasluck, *The Policy of Assimilation.*

[46] Department of Native Welfare, Housing – Housing & Camping Reserves – General Correspondence, series 2030, consignment 993, item 1962/0080, f. 104-105, SROWA; Department of Native Welfare, Native Housing – Policy Matters, series 2030, consignment 1724, item 6 1961/0668, f. 43, SROWA.

[47] *Western Mail*, "York", 13 June 1903, p. 19, Trove; *Beverley Times*, "York Notes", 19 December 1908, p. 5, Trove.

[48] Department of Native Welfare, Housing for Natives – General Correspondence, series 2030, consignment 993, item 1956/0150, f. 41-42, SROWA.

[49] Native Welfare, item 1962/0080, f. 105, 116.

[50] Ibid., f. 116.

[51] "Biographical Register of Members of the Parliament of Western Australia", Parliament of Western Australia – Website, accessed 13 June, 2023.

[52] Department of Community Welfare, item A1821, f. 82.

[53] Department of Native Welfare, Native Housing Policy, series 2030, consignment 1724, item 1965/0042, f. 14-23, 118, SROWA; Department of Native Welfare, Housing - Camping & Housing Reserves – General, series 2030, consignment 1724, item 1965/0209, f. 17-18, SROWA.

[54] "Defining Moments - Decimal Currency", National Museum of Australia, accessed 24 November 2023, https://www.nma.gov.au.

[55] Department of Native Welfare, item 1965/0209, f. 73, 85-86; Department of Community Welfare, item A1821, f. 56, 82.

[56] Department of Native Welfare, item 1962/0080, f. 24-26, 56, 67;

[57] Department of Native Welfare, item 1965/0042, f. 58-60.

[58] Department of Native Welfare, *Annual Report of the Commissioner of Native Welfare for the Year ended 30th June 1966*, (Perth, WA: Government Printer of Western Australia, 1966), p. 38, https://nla.gov.au; Department of Native Welfare, Church of England – South West Mission, series 2030, consignment 993, item 1960/0993, f. 183, SROWA.

[59] *Northam Advertiser*, "Northam Missioner's Quarterly Report", 18 May 1967, p. 4, SLWA.

[60] Russel McGregor, *Indifferent Inclusion: Aboriginal People and The Australian Nation* (Canberra: Aboriginal Studies Press, 2011), 148.

[61] Gordon Stephenson and J. A. Hepburn, *Plan for the metropolitan region, Perth and Fremantle, Western Australia, 1955: a report prepared for the Government of Western Australia* (Perth: Government Printing Office, 1955), accessed 25 October 2023, http://nla.gov.au.

[62] Department of Native Affairs, Native Welfare Council, series 2030, consignment 1733, item 1952/0271, f. 101, SROWA; Department of Native Welfare, Native Citizenship Rights – General Correspondence, series 2030, consignment 993, item 1961/0854, (several news articles across file), SROWA.

[63] *Government Gazette of Western Australia*, No. 56 (Perth, WA: Government Printer of Western Australia, 1964), p. 2526; Government of Western Australia, *Native Welfare Act 1963* (No. 79 of 1963); Government of Western Australia, *Licensing Act 1963 (No.4)* (No. 87 of 1963); Department of Native Welfare, Publicity – Press Release Publications, series 2030, consignment 1724, 1958/0029, f. 35, SROWA.

[64] *Northam Advertiser*, "Minister Talks on Native Welfare", 15 April 1964, p. 8, SLWA.

[65] *Northam Advertiser*, "Man Knocks Police Sergeant Unconscious", 13 March 1964, p. 8, SLWA.

[66] *Northam Advertiser*, 13 March 1964, p. 8; *Northam Advertiser*, "Remanded to Perth", 26 March 1964, p. 6, SLWA; *Northam Advertiser*, "Gaol after Striking Police Man", 3 April 1964, p. 6, SLWA; Author's research based on Western Australian Government Gazettes, Police Gazettes, and departmental records.

[67] Department of Native Welfare, Amendment to Legislation Dealing with Natives, series 2030, consignment 993, item 1965/0242, f. 1-12, SROWA; Department of Native Welfare, Discrimination Laws for Aborigines in W.A. – Press cuttings & Correspondence re Abolishment, series 2030, consignment 1724, item 1968/0600, f. 55, SROWA.

[68] *Bulletin*, "Second Thoughts on the Demon Drink", vol. 93, no. 4784, 4 December 1971, p. 21, https://nla.gov.au.

[69] *Northam Advertiser*, "July 1 Quiet at York", 3 July 1964, p. 8, SLWA.

[70] Department of Native Welfare, item 1965/0242, f. 16.

[71] *Government Gazette of Western Australia*, No. 60 (Perth, WA: Government Printer of Western Australia, 1957), p. 2112; *Government Gazette of Western Australia*, No. 55 (Perth, WA: Government Printer of Western Australia, 1964), p. 2509;

[72] *Northam Advertiser*, "Native Gaoled", 23 October 1963, p. 4, SLWA; *Northam Advertiser* "Habitual Drunk", 4 September 1964, p. 10, SLWA.

[73] *Northam Advertiser*, "Native Gaoled", 23 October 1963, p. 4, SLWA; *Northam Advertiser* "Habitual Drunk", 4 September 1964, p. 10, SLWA.

[74] York Courthouse Complex, introductory video, 19:01, National Trust WA, 2006, accessed at York Courthouse Complex on 22 August 2019; George Kickett, "The Native Reserve York, WA", oral history interview by Roland See, 1 October 2019, audio, 01:07:23, author holds original audio file.

[75] Department of Native Welfare, item 1965/0242, f. 115-118.

[76] Ibid., f. 120-125.

[77] Ibid., f. 210-211.

[78] *Government Gazette of Western Australia*, No 61 (Perth, WA: Government Printer of Western Australia, 1970), p. 1881;

[79] *Northam Advertiser*, "Native Housing", 27 January 1965, p. 5, SLWA.

[80] Ibid.; Department of Native Welfare, item 1965/0042, f. 118.

[81] *Northam Advertiser*, "Native Housing", 27 January 1965, p. 5, SLWA; *Northam Advertiser*, "Financial Position at Amalgamation", 26 March 1965, p. 12, SLWA; Department of Native Welfare, Housing of Natives – Protests against Standard of Houses built in Townsites, series 2030, consignment 1733, item 1965/0088, f. 1-20, SROWA.

[82] Department of Native Welfare, item 1965/0088, f. 15; *Northam Advertiser*, "Native Housing Problem", 3 March 1965, p. 3, SLWA.

[83] Department of Native Welfare, Housing - Camping & Housing Reserves – General, series 2030, consignment 1724, item 1965/0209, f. 13-16, SROWA.

[84] Ibid.; Department of Native Welfare, item 1965/0088, f. 17-61.

[85] *Northam Advertiser*, "Demolition", 10 December 1965, p. 11, SLWA; Department of Native Welfare, Central District - Patrol Reports (Patrols Officer) series 2030, consignment 993, item 1956/0106, f. 150., SROWA.

[86] *Northam Advertiser, 1965 – 1970, SLWA – Author checked all issues.*

[87] *Northam Advertiser*, "Aborigine's Transitional Housing", 18 February 1966, p. 9, SLWA; *Northam Advertiser*, "Inquiry on Aboriginal Housing", 16 March 1966, p. 7, SLWA; *York Chronicle*, "Road Board Chairman – Mr. W H Robinson Appointed", 12 May 1939, p. 2, Trove.

[88] Department of Native Welfare, District Office – Central Patrol Reports, series 2030, consignment 993, item 1952/0576, no. 461 – 463, SROWA.

[89] *Northam Advertiser*, "Transitional Housing Scheme",17 June 1966, p. 12, SLWA; Department of Native Welfare, Native Housing Reserve – York, series 2030, consignment 1733, item 1952/0345, f. 9, SROWA.

[90] Department of Native Welfare, Church of England – South West Mission, series 2030, consignment 993, item 1960/0993, f. 210-211, SROWA.

[91] Department of Native Welfare, item 1965/0042, f. 110-117.

[92] Jennifer Clark, *Aborigines & Activism – Race, Aborigines & the Coming of the Sixties to Australia* (Crawley: University of Western Australia Press, 2008), 180-185.

[93] Ibid.

[94] Anna Haebich, *Spinning the Dream – Assimilation in Australia 1950-1970*, (North Fremantle: Fremantle Press, 2008), p. 207-209; *Daily News*, "Native Affairs Head Criticises Treatment", 6 November 1950, p. 2, Trove; *Farmers' Weekly*, "The Racial Issue", 20 November 1952, p. 3, Trove; *West Australian*, "Letters to the Editor", 19 March 1951, p. 5, Trove; *West Australian*, "Australia 'Shamed' on Native Policy", 26 July 1952, p. 10, Trove;

[95] Department of Native Affairs, Native Welfare Council, series 2030, consignment 1733, item 1952/0271, f. 2, SROWA.

[96] Walter J Nicholls, "The Urban Question Revisited", *International Journal of Urban and Regional Research*, vol. 32, no. 4 (December 2008), p. 844, DOI: 10.1111/j.1468-2427.2008.00820.x.

[97] Clark, *Aborigines & Activism,* p. 171.

[98] *Northam Advertiser*, "Referendum Polling Places", 25 May 1967, p. 1, SLWA; *Northam Advertiser*, "Northam A.L.P. Advises Against Debates", 25 May 1967, p. 2, SLWA; *Northam Advertiser*, "Referendums", 25 May 1967, p. 17, SLWA.

[99] *York Chronicle*, "The Referendum – Yes Campaign", 18 August 1944, p. 3, Trove.

[100] Bain Attwood and Andrew Markus, *The 1967 Referendum – Race, Power and the Australian Constitution*, second edition (Canberra, ACT: Aboriginal Studies Press, 2007) p. 58-59; *Northam Advertiser*, "Referendum Polling Places", 25 May 1967, p. 1, SLWA; Commonwealth of Australia, State of Western Australia – Statistical Returns, Referendum (Canberra, ACT: 1967, p. 11), Q324-99 STA, SLWA.

[101] George Kickett, "The Native Reserve York, WA", oral history interview by Roland See, 1 October 2019, audio, 01:07:23, author holds original audio file.

[102] *York Chronicle*, "Road Board Discussions", 16 November 1950, p. 4, Trove; *York Chronicle*, "Passing the Buck", 14 September 1950, p. 1, Trove; Department of Native Affairs, Central District - Patrol Officer Reports, series 2030, consignment 993, item 1951/0695, p. 7 of Patrol Report No. 4 of 1951/52, SROWA.

[103] Department of Native Affairs, District Office. Central - Patrol Reports, series 2030, consignment 993, item 1952/0576, p. 5. of Patrol Report No. 4 of 1952/53, SROWA.

[104] Ibid.

[105] Department of Native Affairs, item 1952/0576, f. 32-35.

[106] Marion Kickett, "Examination of How a Culturally-Appropriate Definition of Resilience Affects the Physical and Mental Health of Aboriginal People" (PhD

diss., University of Western Australia, 2011), p. 35-36; George Kickett, "The Native Reserve York, WA."

[107] "Post Referendum", *Smoke Signals*, vol. 6, no. 3 (1967), p. 28, - as quoted in Attwood and Markus, *The 1967 Referendum,* p. 146-147.

[108] Department of Native Welfare, Aboriginal Advancement Council of WA (Inc.) – Reports and General Correspondence, series 2030, consignment 1733, item 1966/1516, f. 1-4, 49, 62, SROWA.

[109] Department of Native Welfare, Native Housing – Policy Matters, series 2030, consignment 993, item 1968/0200, f. 13, 198, SROWA; "Harold Edward Holt CH", Visit Parliament - Art at Parliament - Stories and Histories, Parliament of Australia, accessed 6 July 2023, https://www.aph.gov.au/.

[110] Department of Native Welfare, item 1968/0200, f. 59.

[111] Department of Native Welfare, item 1965/0042, f. 69-73.

[112] Department of Native Welfare, *Annual Report of the Commissioner of Native Welfare for the Year ended 30th June 1972*, (Perth, WA: Government Printer of Western Australia, 1972), p. 7, 14, https://nla.gov.au.

Chapter 8. 1970–1974

[1] *Northam Advertiser*, "Council Takes Action to Avert Water Shortage", 30 October 1969, p. 10, SLWA.

[2] *Northam Advertiser*, "New Houses for York", 24 December 1969, p. 5, SLWA.

[3] *Northam Advertiser*, "Housing Boom in York", 12 February 1970, p. 12, SLWA.

[4] *Northam Advertiser*, "York Housing", 24 February 1972, p. 9, SLWA.

[5] Department of Native Welfare, Central Division – Conventional Housing Sites – Country Areas, series 2030, consignment 993, item 1969/0700, f. 26, 75-76, 114, 116, 124, 154-156, 168-169, SROWA.

[6] Department of Native Welfare, item 1969/0700, f. 174; Department of Native Welfare, Conventional Housing Sites – Central Division – Country Area, series 2030, consignment 1733, item, 1970/1291, f. 189, SROWA.

[7] *Northam Advertiser*, "Shire Clerk's Report", 18 June 1970, p. 9, SLWA.

[8] Department of Native Welfare, item 1969/0700, f. 193; Department of Native Welfare, Conventional Housing Sites - Central Division - Country Areas, series 2030, consignment 1724, item 30 1971/0873, f. 76, SROWA; Department of Native Welfare, Conventional Housing – Forward Planning – All Divisions, series 2030, consignment 1733, item 1971/0335, f. 7, SROWA; Department of Native Welfare, item, 1970/1291, f. 125, 182.

[9] Department of Native Welfare, item 30 1971/0873, f. 76-79.

[10] Department of Native Welfare, item 30 1971/0873, f. 80-82.

[11] Shire of York, *Local Heritage Survey 2019 – Heritage Places*, 2019, p. 271, https://www.york.wa.gov.au; *York Chronicle*, "York Golf Club Looks for New Links", 4 November 1954, p. 1, Trove; *Northam Advertiser*, "Pony Club Off to a Good Start", 2 April 1970, p. 5, SLWA – This author has been unable to establish when exactly the pony club moved onto the grounds on Dinsdale Street; however, the foregoing news article suggests that in 1970 it was still based at its former grounds on Forrest Oval.

[12] *Northam Advertiser*, "Rev. M. Ward President of the York Society", 4 May 1972, p. 6, SLWA.

[13] Department of Native Welfare, item 30 1971/0873, f. 83-86.

[14] Ibid.

[15] Department of Native Welfare, *Annual Report of the Commissioner of Native Welfare for the Year ended 30th June 1972*, (Perth, WA: Government Printer of Western Australia, 1972), p. 7, https://nla.gov.au/.

[16] *Northam Advertiser*, all issues 1970 to 1974, SLWA; Government of Western Australia, *Certificate of Title*, vol. 497, f. 58, Transfer A536578, Lots 102 and 103 (former Lots 15 and 16) on York Town Lot 370, Plan 725; *Government Gazette of Western Australia*, No. 47 (Perth, WA: Government Printer of Western Australia, 1977), p. 2657.

[17] Marion Kickett, "Examination of How a Culturally-Appropriate Definition of Resilience Affects the Physical and Mental Health of Aboriginal People" (PhD diss., University of Western Australia, 2011), p. 100; Department of Native Welfare, Housing Survey of Camping Reserve Population - All Divisions, series 2030, consignment 1733, item 1969/0520, f. 177, SROWA.

[18] Department of Native Welfare, Native Housing – Policy Matters, series 2030, consignment 993, item 1968/0200, f. 228, 231-232, 259, SROWA;

[19] Robert Bropho, *Fringe Dweller* (Sydney, NSW: Alternative Publishing Co-operative Limited, 1980), p. 46.

[20] Department of Community Welfare, item A1821, f. 95-96.

[21] Ibid.

[22] Ibid.

[23] Ibid.

[24] Ibid.

[25] Ibid.

[26] Bropho, *Fringe Dweller*, p. 46-47; York Clerk of Courts, Index – Charges (Police Court), series 409, consignment 3795, item 1, SROWA.

[27] Bropho, *Fringe Dweller*, p. 46-47.

[28] Bropho, *Fringe Dweller*, p. 46-47.

[29] Ibid.

[30] Department of Native Welfare, Central Division – Aboriginal Consultative Committee – Reports and Correspondence, series 2030, consignment 993, item

1968/0121, p. 78, SROWA; Department of Native Welfare, Administration - staff
- Field. Part time services Homemakers, series 47, consignment 1525, item 01-
05/9, f. 75-94, 121, SROWA.

[31] Department of Community Welfare, item A1821, f. 97-101.

[32] Ibid., f. 100-101.

[33] Bropho, *Fringe Dweller*, p. 46.

[34] Ibid., p. 38-40.

[35] Department of Native Welfare, Allawah Grove - General Correspondence,
series 2030, consignment 1733, item 1969/0038, f. 24-110, SROWA.

[36] Department of Native Welfare, Housing – General Correspondence, series
2030, consignment 993, item 1961/0462, f. 82-192, SROWA.

[37] Native Welfare, item 1961/0462, f. 82-192; *West Australian*, "Dept to Act on
Family", 22 June 1965, f. 97 in afore-mentioned file.

[38] Native Welfare, item 1961/0462, f. 82-192.

[39] Native Welfare, item 1969/0038, f. 24-110.

[40] "Biographical Register of Members of the Parliament of Western Australia",
Parliament of Western Australia – Website, accessed 28 October, 2023.

[41] Department of Community Welfare, item A1821, f. 102, 107; Department of
Native Welfare, Housing – Housing & Camping Reserves – General
Correspondence, series 2030, consignment 993, item 1962/0080, f. 118,
SROWA.

[42] Kickett, "Resilience", p. 16; Department of Community Welfare, item A1821,
f. 107.

[43] Department of Community Welfare, item A1821, f. 163.

[44] Ibid., f. 164-165.

[45] Ibid., f. 173-175.

[46] Ibid., f. 180-183.

[47] Government of Western Australia, *Land Act 1933* (Reprint 17 May 1973).

[48] Department of Community Welfare, item A1821, f. 186, 202-207; Aboriginal
Affairs Planning Authority, York Reserve 8567, series 1779, consignment 5296,
item 1975/0057, f. 6, 15, SROWA.

Epilogue

[1] Personal correspondence with Dr Marion Kickett, January to February 2024;
York Burial Records, accessed August 2019 at the York Regency Museum and
update information kindly provided by the York Society February 2024.

[2] Government of Western Australia, *Cemeteries Act 1897* (No. 23 of 1897);
Government of Western Australia, *Cemeteries Act 1897-1966* (Reprint 19th
October 1970); Government Gazette of Western Australia, No. 27 (Perth, WA:

Government Printer of Western Australia, 1935), p. 1131-1132 (as well as subsequent amendments of York's cemetery by-laws published in the following Government Gazettes: no. 35 of 1935, no. 44 of 1937, no. 27 of 1939, no. 3 of 1941, no. 7 of 1941, no. 35 of 1943, no. 51 of 1944, no. 97 of 1950, no. 72 of 1951, no. 95 of 1956, no. 88 pf 1960, no. 30 of 1965; Department of Public Health, Burial of Destitutes, series 268, consignment 2488, item 1958/0783, SROWA.

[3] Department of Native Affairs, Tommy Kickett and Family – Personal File, consignment 1351, item 1934/0016, f. 27, courtesy of Dr Marion Kickett.

[4] *Northam Advertiser*, "Advertising", 1 February 1936, p. 1, Trove; *West Australian*, "Debts All Met – Undertaker's Vicissitudes", 25 October 1945, p. 10, Trove (Brooks claimed in court that he only started working in his wife's undertaker business in 1942, whereas he had already advertised the business under his name in 1936); Department of Native Affairs, item 1934/0016, f. 27-29, 82 – In relation to job sharing: on file, Brooks was reimbursed for a burial in 1942 while the burial record indicates that the burial was conducted by Wansbrough; Wansbrough held the government contract in the previous year: Government Gazette of Western Australia, No. 7 (Perth, WA: Government Printer of Western Australia, 1941), p. 216; Department of Public Health, item 1958/0783.

[5] *York Chronicle*, "Advertising", 2 April 1948, p. 2, Trove; *York Chronicle*, "Advertising", 9 April 1948, p. 2, Trove; *Northam Advertiser*, "Death of Mr S.P. Harvey", 27 March 1963, p. 2, SLWA; *Northam Advertiser*, "Advertising", 21 June 1963, p. 8, SLWA.

[6] Lauren Marsh and Steve Kinnane, "Ghost Files – The Missing Files of the Department of Indigenous Affairs Archives", *Studies in Western Australian History*, vol 23 (2003), p. 111-127; Department of Native Welfare, Records - Disposal Procedure (Destruction Repository, Archives), series 2030, consignment 1733, item 1962/0094, SROWA.

[7] Personal correspondence with Dr Marion Kickett, May 2024; Aboriginal Affairs Planning Authority, item 1975/0057, f. 28-107; George Kickett, "The Native Reserve York, WA", oral history interview by Roland See, 1 October 2019, audio, 01:07:23, author holds original audio file.

[8] "Candice Bateman", Monument Australia, accessed 29 July 2023, https://monumentaustralia.org.au; Laura Lee, *Lorna's Story*, Museum Penal (York, WA: Regency Museum, 2006).

www.ingramcontent.com/pod-product-compliance
Lightning Source LLC
Chambersburg PA
CBHW051255020426

42333CB00026B/3222